A MORAL ENTERPRISE

Father Francis Canavan, S.J.

A MORAL ENTERPRISE

POLITICS, REASON, AND THE HUMAN GOOD

Essays in Honor of Francis Canavan

Edited by
KENNETH L. GRASSO *&* ROBERT P. HUNT

ISI BOOKS
WILMINGTON, DELAWARE
2002

Cover design by John M. Vella. Interior design by John M. Vella and Brooke Haas.

Cataloging-in-Publication Data:

A moral enterprise : politics, reason, and the human good / edited by Kenneth L. Grasso and Robert P. Hunt. —1st ed. —Wilmington, DE : ISI Books, 2002.

    p. ; cm.

    Includes bibliographical references and index.
    ISBN 1-882926-80-3
       1. Political science. 2. Common good. 3. Social sciences. I. Grasso, Kenneth L. II. Hunt, Robert P.

    JA71 .M67 2002   2001097055
    320—dc21   CIP

Published in the United States by:

    ISI Books
    Intercollegiate Studies Institute
    Post Office Box 4431
    Wilmington, DE 19807-0431
    www.isi.org

Manufactured in the United States of America

CONTENTS

ACKNOWLEDGMENTS

We would be remiss if we did not express our heartfelt gratitude to all those whose assistance helped make this volume possible. Thanks are in order to our contributors for agreeing to join with us in honoring Father Canavan. We also need to thank Michael Uhlmann for providing sage advice and assistance that was truly beyond the call of duty.

Special thanks go to Jeffrey O. Nelson, the publisher of ISI Books, without whose urging this volume wouldn't exist, and to Jeremy Beer, our editor at ISI, for his unfailing patience, wise advice, and editorial assistance. Working with Jeremy has truly been a pleasure.

Thanks must also be extended to two of Ken Grasso's former graduate assistants at Southwest Texas State University, Reymundo Chapa and Michael Boatner, for their work on the volume, as well as to Rebecca A. Liounis for her assistance with the preparation of the manuscript.

We also wish to express our gratitude to our institutions—Southwest Texas State University and Kean University of New Jersey—for their ongoing support and encouragement of our scholarship. Most of all, we wish to thank our families for their patience and encouragement.

INTRODUCTION

The Achievement of Francis Canavan

KENNETH L. GRASSO
ROBERT P. HUNT

A t its 1996 annual meeting, the Society of Catholic Social Scientists presented its annual "Pius XI Award for Contributions Toward the Building Up of a True Catholic Social Science" to Francis Canavan, S.J. Several years earlier, the Fellowship of Catholic Scholars had presented Canavan its Cardinal Wright Award. Father Canavan's political thought has been the subject of roundtable discussions and symposia at the American Political Science (1998) and Christendom College (2000). At the Christendom symposium, he was also honored for his many years of loyal and selfless dedication to his Church and for the important contribution that his work has made to contemporary American intellectual life. All of these accolades represent the well-deserved and long-overdue recognition of a man who in 1995 was described by Gerard V. Bradley (one of the contributors to the present volume) as "one of the great political theorists of the last thirty years."[1] The other contributors to the present volume—friends, colleagues, and former students of Father Canavan— concur with Bradley.

Born in 1917, Father Canavan received his primary and secondary education in the public schools of NewYork City and Long Island. (Canavan not only attended the same elementary school that had educated another future Jesuit, John Courtney Murray, some fifteen years earlier; he also graduated from Lawrence High School with Harry V. Jaffa and Joseph Cropsey, both of whom, like Canavan, went on to become prominent political theorists.) He received his B.S. and M.A. degrees from Fordham University in 1939 and 1947, and his Ph.L. from St. Louis University in 1944, where he began to immerse himself in the study of Thomistic philosophy. He earned his S.T.L. from Woodstock College in 1951 (at Woodstock he met his fellow alumnus of the "Jamaica Model School," John Courtney Murray, who subsequently became his mentor and a major influence on his work) and his Ph.D. from Duke University in 1957. He entered the Society of Jesus the same year he received his B.S. and was ordained in 1950.

Over the course of his career Canavan has taught at Regis High School (1944–1945), Canisius College (1945–1946), St. Peter's College (1950–1956), and Fordham University (1966–1988). From 1960 to 1966 he served as associate editor of the magazine *America*. Since 1988 he has been professor emeritus of political science at Fordham.

While at Fordham and at Duke, Canavan studied with two men who would have a great impact on his academic interests and development as a political theorist, Moorhouse I. X. Millar, S.J. and John H. Hallowell. It was Millar who first encouraged Canavan to read Edmund Burke, and it was Hallowell who guided Canavan in the writing of his doctoral dissertation on Burke's conception of political reason. One of the nation's leading political philosophers, Hallowell, an Episcopalian, wrote from an unapologetically Christian perspective and sought to articulate a theory of politics—and more particularly, of constitutional democracy—that was rooted in the Christian vision of man and society.

Much of Canavan's subsequent work, including his groundbreaking studies of Burke's political thought, has elaborated upon a central presupposition that he shared with Hallowell, namely, that "underlying every system of government there is some predominant conception of the nature of man and the meaning of human existence. More often than not, this idea of man is implicit rather than explicit. But if not always explicit, it is always fundamental."[2] In other words, every society defines itself by how it answers certain basic questions about human nature and the goods that make for human flourishing. The decision not to answer these questions at all is, paradoxically, just as much an answer as any other, and the practical consequences for any constitutional order are profound. In short, politics is an inescapably moral enterprise.

Canavan's doctoral dissertation on Burke, entitled *The Political Reason of Edmund Burke*, was published in 1960 by Duke University Press. It was followed by two subsequent volumes on Burke's thought: *Edmund Burke: Prescription and Providence* (Carolina Academic Press, 1987) and *The Political Economy of Edmund Burke* (Fordham University Press, 1995). No less an authority than Peter J. Stanlis (another contributor to the present volume) has remarked that Canavan's work has earned him "a very high permanent place of honor among Burke scholars, living or dead."[3] Each of Canavan's major works on Burke has attempted to get to the heart of what Canavan sees as central, inescapable questions: What is Burke's view of human nature and society? Upon what deeper metaphysical framework does Burke's view of human nature depend for sustenance? And how does all of this impact Burke's own prescriptions (and animadversions) in the arena of practical politics?

At the risk of oversimplifying matters, Canavan's writings on Burke might be said to focus on the restoration of Burke to his rightful place in the pantheon of Christian political thinkers. This restoration, Canavan believes, is particularly important in light of the effort of some scholars to portray Burke as a Humean skeptic or historicist precursor to Hegel. For example, some Burke scholars have portrayed Burke as a man skeptical not only of Enlightenment enthusiasms and abstract metaphysical systems but as a principled opponent of any effort to ground political life within a larger metaphysical framework. Others have interpreted Burke's defense of tradition, convention, and "prejudice" to mean that he was a follower of the historical *Zeitgeist* in whatever direction it might happen to be moving at the moment. Canavan has argued that each of these interpretations of Burke's thought is mistaken.

On the contrary, according to Canavan, "Burke did his political thinking within the framework of a 'realistic' metaphysics derived from the biblical and Christian doctrine of creation."[4] At the heart of Burke's thought is the vision of a divinely created and "teleologically" ordered universe, "composed of creatures with distinct natures serving natural ends, subject to natural laws, and all directed to the ultimate purpose of the Creator," and whose "intelligible order [was] accessible to human reason."[5] Or, as Canavan argues elsewhere,

> Burke believed in a common human nature created by God as the supreme norm of politics. But he knew that human nature realizes itself in history through conventional forms, customs, and traditions, which constitute what he called the second nature of a particular people. Convention can and often enough does distort our nature, but it is not opposed to it. . . . Convention, made as it should be to satisfy the needs of nature, is not its enemy, but its necessary clothing. The statesman must therefore frame his policies with a practical wisdom that understands his people, their history, their traditions, their inherited rights and liberties, and their present circumstances. To do otherwise is to court disaster.[6]

The focus of Canavan's work has been the recovery of the authentic Burke. At the same time, it is obvious that his interest in Burke is not purely historical in nature. He shares Alfred Cobban's view that "as a school of statesmanship," Burke's work possesses "permanent value."[7] Burke's writings, he contends, offer us "a richer and fuller way of understanding" political life "than one founded on the sovereign individual and his rights."[8] Burke's "profound and luminous mind" offers us "a way of thinking about politics . . . and its problems which makes it possible to approach them rationally, while avoiding both unprincipled expediency and doctrinaire idealism."[9] Thus, even though "Burke is not a major figure in the history of political philosophy" (and even though he is most certainly not a defender of constitutional democracy in the modern sense), his work nevertheless teaches many lessons that contemporary America needs badly to learn if it is to sustain its experiment in democratic self-government.[10]

If Burke's work has been Canavan's primary interest, it has hardly been his only one. His writings include an acclaimed study of the political theory of freedom of speech (which was named to *Choice*'s "Outstanding Academic Book List for 1985"), in which Canavan criticizes the approach to freedom of speech adopted by a number of leading civil libertarians. He has also written numerous essays exploring the problem of law, religious pluralism, and public morality in contemporary America, various aspects of contemporary Catholic social thought, the American Catholic scene, and the interaction between Catholicism and American culture. In many of these works, Canavan (like his mentor John Courtney Murray) attempts to outline a public philosophy for contemporary America rooted in a richer and sounder model of man and society than that which informs the liberal intellectual tradition.

This effort has prompted Canavan to examine the relationship between Catholicism, liberalism, and the Western constitutional tradition. Canavan's work rejects at least three readings of that relationship. First, he rejects the effort to effect a quasi-Hegelian synthesis of Catholicism and liberalism that brackets the Catholic tradition's spiritual and moral commitments in the name of a political *modus vivendi* with the liberal model of man and society. Second, he rejects the "neoconservative" argument that sees the liberal tradition of politics as little more than a political orientation in favor of limited government and a free economy which is separable from certain subjectivist variations of contemporary liberalism. Third, he rejects the "confessionalist" effort to restore the Church to its pre–Vatican II political commitments, an effort that makes the Catholic intellectual tradition an opponent not only of liberalism, but of human rights and religious freedom, however narrowly or broadly defined.

For more than thirty years, Canavan has argued—perhaps even more clearly and cogently than John Courtney Murray himself—for a different view of the relationship between Catholicism and liberalism. Twenty years before Alasdair MacIntyre asked liberal "anti-perfectionists" to tell us about their (undiscussed) *telos,* and thirty years before Michael Sandel warned of the dangers of the procedural republic, Canavan became one of the most incisive critics of liberal secularism and its narrow sectarian agenda. Rather than blurring the distinction between the Catholic and liberal intellectual traditions, Canavan has highlighted them. Unlike the "neoconservatives," he has argued that the contemporary "retheoretization" (Murray's term) of American (and Western) constitutionalism is a product not of a deformation of the liberal tradition of politics but rather is a flowering of that tradition's model of man and society. But unlike the "confessionalists," Canavan has affirmed the legitimacy, in principle, of what George Weigel has called "the Catholic human rights revolution" and its defense of constitutional democracy and religious freedom.[11]

Canavan's account of the genesis and development of the liberal intellectual tradition builds upon Hallowell's work. For Canavan, as for Hallowell, liberalism was never *just* a political movement. It was informed by a revolutionary and distinctively modern epistemology and metaphysics that emphasized the principle of the atomic, autonomous individual. Thus, subjectivism "is the essence of liberalism" and "the subjectivity of all values . . . is the direction in which the inner dynamism of liberal thought has moved from the beginning."[12] However much "we may applaud the historical achievements of liberalism"—its role in breaking "the power of absolute monarchs" and fostering the rise of "limited, constitutional government"—the liberal model of man and society, Canavan is convinced, embodies an irremediably flawed theory of politics and "is now a menace rather than a support of constitutional democracy."[13] "The corrosive acid of [liberalism's] individualism" threatens to dissolve the matrix of institutions, virtues, and convictions on which a free society depends for its vitality and viability. The "better theoretical foundation" that our public life "so badly needs," Canavan insists, must take its bearings from an anthropology that sees man "as a social being from whose nature flow relations to his family, neighbors, fellow workers, the community and the political order." These relations "are the foundation of both rights and obligations that are prior to and independent of consent."[14]

To put the matter simply, the Catholic intellectual tradition supplies this "better theoretical foundation" for constitutional democracy, human rights, and religious freedom. Unlike the "confessionalists," who either reject or minimize the social teachings of the Second Vatican Council, Canavan insists that the far-reaching developments in the Church's social magisterium over the past five decades have their roots in a new and deeper understanding of the ideas that lie at the heart of the Catholic intellectual tradition. For example, *Dignitatis Humanae*'s defense of religious freedom is rooted in a new understanding of the implications of one of Catholic social thought's foundational principles, namely, the principle of limited government. The modern popes have "made both the protection of the rights and the fulfillment of the obligations of the person the natural and God-given purposes of society. Both the rights and the obligations depend upon the teleology inherent in man's nature and supernatural destiny; the obligations are derived not from the rights but from the goods that are the goals of human nature."[15]

The Church's embrace of constitutional democracy cannot and must not be seen, however, as effecting some sort of rapprochement with liberalism. At the heart of the Church's principled defense of constitutional democracy lies a substantively different model of man and society than that which lies at the heart of liberalism. Rather than seeing "man as a sovereign will free to make of itself and the world as it pleases," Catholicism "envisions a person who is obliged to frame his life through free choices in accordance with a law built into our common human nature by the Creator, who is the first truth and supreme good, and by Christ's call to a higher, supernatural life."[16] Catholic social ontology envisions man not as a sovereign self but as a social being who "realizes and develops himself through communion with other persons" in a wide array of institutions and associations that have come to be called intermediary groups.[17] In sharp contrast with liberalism, the Catholic mind sees "human society as a community of communities . . . not as a collection of individuals who contracted with each other to set up a mutual-protection association called the state."[18]

Canavan does not argue that our American experiment in self-government must be a Catholic experiment. Rather, he argues that the American experiment depends upon resources that liberalism cannot now (and, arguably, never could) provide. The Catholic intellectual tradition, shorn of accomodationism or triumphalism, supplies some of those resources in its deeper and richer personal and social ontology, and it would be well for our fellow Americans to tap into that ontology in reconstituting a viable public philosophy.

The contributors to this *Festschrift* are unified not so much in their perspectives on the theoretical and practical issues raised in this essay, but rather in their thoroughgoing admiration for Father Canavan and his work. The contributors address a number of the issues raised in Canavan's work, and the varied subject matters addressed reflect both the breadth of Canavan's interests and his underlying commitment to a conception of political life that appreciates its inherently moral, yet limited, nature.

Peter Stanlis, F. P. Lock, and Joseph Pappin address both the meta-physical foundations for and the practical ramifications of Edmund Burke's political theory. Stanlis argues that Burke's appeals to tradition and moral prudence in Britain's dealings with the American colonies made Burke more perceptive than many of his contemporaries on the problems inher-ent in the idea of a British "empire." Lock argues that, rather than reject-ing the idea of natural or human rights, Burke's thought contains the outlines of an approach to these rights that can help us overcome the hyperindividualism and ahistorical rationalism that have characterized the predominant Western theories of human rights. And, building upon the arguments advanced by Canavan himself, Pappin contends that Burke's politics depend on a Christian metaphysical realism rather than on Humean skepticism or Hegelian historicism.

Burkean politics, Canavan argues, is grounded in an Aristotelian un-derstanding of practical reason and the virtue of prudence, for as Burke himself noted, "the rules and definitions of prudence can rarely be exact; never universal."[19] "[T]he decisions of prudence (contrary to the system of the insane reasoners)," therefore, "are determined on the more or the less, the earlier or the later, and on a balance of advantage and inconvenience, of good and evil."[20] In her contribution to the present volume, Germaine Paulo Walsh explores the Aristotelian distinction between theoretical and practical virtue—a distinction, one could argue, that underlies both Burke's prudentialist rejection of the Enlightenment's "insane reasoners" and Canavan's Thomistic criticism of the liberal intellectual tradition.

The essays by Gerald McCool, S.J., Joseph Koterski, S.J., and Keith Pavlischek focus on the development of the Catholic intellectual tradi-tion, its social teaching, and its capacity to provide a moral-realist de-fense of human rights, ordered liberty, and religious freedom. Father McCool traces the development of Catholic social teaching in the nine-teenth and twentieth centuries and the Church's movement toward the acceptance of democracy and religious liberty. Like Canavan, McCool argues that the social teachings of the Second Vatican Council represent a development rather than a distortion of the Church's view of man and society. Father Koterski, in a manner reminiscent of the great Catholic political theorist Yves Simon, argues for the naturalness of, and necessity for, political authority as a means of sustaining a society committed to ordered liberty. Pavlischek takes issue with Catholic political theorist Robert George's defense of religious liberty, arguing that George's "new natural law" theory is inconsistent with certain core features of Thomistic political thought. If religious liberty is to be defended, as Pavlischek believes it should be, it must be grounded in a more teleologically oriented view of man and society.

As has been noted, one of Canavan's central concerns has been the Catholic intellectual tradition's contribution to the development not only of a principled defense of religious freedom but of a sounder theory of church-state relations than that supplied from within the liberal intellectual tradition. He recognizes that to reject the liberal theory of religious liberty is not to reject religious liberty per se. And to reject the liberal view of church-state relations does not necessarily entail a defense of the confessional state. Drawing from Canavan's effort to highlight the distinctions between the Catholic and liberal traditions, Robert Hunt argues that the Catholic and liberal understandings of religious liberty have different underlying assumptions and practical ramifications. He contends in particular that Catholics ought not to embrace a liberal individualist reading of the religion clauses of the First Amendment of the U.S. Constitution. Thomas Spragens argues for a somewhat friendlier reading of the liberal tradition of politics, and seeks a genuinely liberal, pluralist solution to the problem of church-state relations that is shorn of the kind of political triumphalism found among some religionists and liberal secularists. Or, as Spragens puts it, "we need to shun those who seek to enlist us in supposedly new but in fact old, improper, and counterproductive crusades either to establish a 'Christian Commonwealth' or to '*ecrasez l'infame*'."

Gerard Bradley, George McKenna, and Kenneth Grasso focus more closely upon the practical strengths and weaknesses of the liberal model of man and society. Bradley takes up Canavan's question of whether the liberal defense of "neutrality" on divisive moral and social issues is, in fact, a political shell game. He contends that the vexing question of the moral and legal status of marriage in contemporary America cannot be resolved by liberal appeals to the "neutrality" principle. McKenna argues that the "common sense" liberalism of the New Deal has been supplanted by a more socially radical brand of liberalism that seeks to dissolve social norms and reshape the institutions of society. He asks whether the older brand of liberalism has the intellectual and political resources to cast out the newer brand. Grasso draws heavily on Canavan's (and Hallowell's) analysis of the collapse of the liberal intellectual tradition, and traces what he believes to be its inevitable degeneration into skepticism and nihilism and the practical consequences of that degeneration for an experiment in democratic self-government.

The effort to sustain the American experiment in self-government by restoring it to its proper foundations becomes the focus of the essays by Harry Jaffa, W. Norris Clarke, S.J., Hadley Arkes, and George Carey. Jaffa criticizes several prominent conservative thinkers for what he sees as their rejection of the natural law tradition of the American founding. He contrasts these conservatives with the statesmanship of Lincoln and the teachings of Pope John Paul II. Father Clarke, following Pierre Manent, argues that the sustenance of a healthy democracy may depend upon a religiously grounded public philosophy. He contends that the "underlying code of ethics" upon which democracy depends to support its sound functioning "must derive its authority to impose moral obligation on free human beings from some source higher than the human."

Catholic political philosopher Robert George has noted that for at least thirty years, Father Canavan has been the "most incisive and trenchant critic" of the sort of liberal judicial activism that, "far from preserving authentic pluralism, would advance the *sectarian* moral agenda of liberal secularism."[21] Consistent with Canavan's concerns, the essays by Arkes and Carey focus more narrowly upon the role of the judiciary in contributing to, or undermining, the American experiment in self-government. Arkes argues that, whatever its vices, judicial legal positivism (represented by figures such as Robert Bork and William Rehnquist) forces us to consider the proper moral foundations of law and often has a better appreciation of its practical limitations than does liberal activism. Carey contends that such activism has changed the very nature of our constitutional order from an experiment in republican self-government to one that depends on judicial ukase to realize its goals and purposes.

In his concluding essay, James Schall, S.J., pays tribute to the character of Father Canavan's mind through an examination of his book reviews and shorter, more journalistic pieces. These writings enable us to see a side of Canavan, his "wit and sharp opinion," that might otherwise be known only to those personally acquainted with him. It serves, therefore, as a fitting end to this *Festschrift*.

The contributors to this *Festschrift* make no effort to conceal their admiration for Canavan's work. His work exhibits a thorough command of the literature on the subjects it addresses, an extraordinary knack for getting to the heart of complicated theoretical issues (including the ability to make the sort of subtle distinctions necessary to come to grips with the matter at hand), and a talent for articulating complex subjects in a concise and jargon-free manner.

Canavan offers us a model of how a Catholic political thinker ought to engage his discipline and, more broadly, his culture. He has done so by combining a thorough command of contemporary scholarship in his chosen discipline with a deep knowledge of, and fidelity to, his own intellectual tradition. Precisely for this reason, he has engaged the best scholarship in contemporary political theory without becoming captive to that theory's intellectual categories. And he has shown the ability to assimilate what he believes to be the valid insights that have emerged in contemporary political theory while retaining the critical distance needed to evaluate that theory in the light of Catholic faith and the intellectual tradition that has developed under that faith's aegis.

"The Catholic mind," Canavan has remarked, "is by nature a synthesizing mind." As a consequence, "every thinking Catholic has the lifelong task of harmonizing his faith with the findings of human reason that are available to him in his time."[22] Canavan's work illustrates just how such a mind operates. His work neither uncritically embraces nor uncritically rejects contemporary culture and thought. Rather, it engages in an act of critical engagement with that culture from the perspective of Catholic faith, appropriating what he reasons is valid within that culture and rejecting what is not. In so doing, Canavan mirrors the efforts of the thinker who had perhaps the greatest impact on his own intellectual develop-

ment, St. Thomas Aquinas. At a time when far too many Catholics confuse engaging the world with abjectly capitulating to the reigning
Weltanschauung, and when the only alternative some persons offer against
capitulation is sectarian withdrawal from the world (of the type traditionally associated with certain forms of Protestantism), we are truly
fortunate to have Canavan's work available to remind us of how a truly
catholic mind should approach its surrounding culture.

In the decades prior to the Second Vatican Council, thinkers such as
Jacques Maritain, Yves Simon, and John Courtney Murray helped lay the
groundwork for the political theory presupposed by the Council's teaching. In the ecclesiastical silly season that followed Vatican II, many aspects
of the Catholic tradition's social and political thought all but disappeared
in favor of various intellectual fads, such as Marxian liberation theology.
The work of Maritain, Simon, and Murray seemed to disappear from
view as well, and little was done to build on the foundations they so ably
laid. During those dark post-conciliar days, Francis Canavan was one of
the very few thinkers who kept the authentic tradition of Catholic social
thought—and the intellectual project of developing a fuller and richer
defense of constitutional democracy, human rights, and religious freedom—alive. For this commitment to politics as an inescapably moral,
yet limited, enterprise grounded in a rich conception of reason and the
human good, we owe him an immense debt of gratitude.

Edmund Burke and British Views of the American Revolution: A Conflict over Rights of Sovereignty

PETER J. STANLIS

From 1763 to 1783, British views of the American Revolution varied widely. There was no monolithic conviction among Tories, Whigs, or radical eighteenth-century Commonwealthmen, nor among various segments of the British population at large. The central political principles at issue between Britain and her American colonies were perceived by only a few men, and even when such men agreed in basic political theory, and held the same conception of empire, they differed in regard to practical policy. Undoubtedly, the broad range of British views of the American Revolution reflected the usual differences men have about complex social, political, religious, and economic problems. But three significant viewpoints can be identified in what was probably the fundamental conflict over the nature of government between Britain and America—the question of British rights of sovereignty. These differences were manifested in practical politics in conflicts over such matters as taxation and representation, revenue and regulation, freedom and subordination.

Perhaps no one understood the central issue of legal and political sovereignty more clearly than Francis Bernard, royal governor of Massachusetts Bay from 1760 to 1769. In a letter from Boston, on 23 November 1765, he wrote:

The question [is] whether America shall or shall not be subject to the legislature of Great Britain. . . . All the political evils in America rise from the want of ascertaining the relation between Great Britain and the American colonies. Hence it is, that ideas of that relation are formed in Britain and America so very repugnant and contradictory to each other. In Britain the American governments are considered as corporations empowered to make bye-laws, existing only during the pleasure of Parliament, who hath never yet done anything to confirm their establishments, and hath at any time a power to dissolve them. In America they claim . . . to be perfect states, no otherwise dependent upon Great Britain than by having the same King, which, having complete legislatures within themselves, are no way subject to that of Great Britain, which in such instances as it has heretofore exercised a legislative power over them, has usurped it. In a difference so very wide, who shall determine? The Parliament of Great Britain? No, say the Americans . . . that would be to make them judges in their own cause. Who then? The King? He is bound by charters, or constitutions equal to charters, and cannot declare against his own grants. So . . . there is no superior tribunal to determine upon the rights and principles of the American colonies. . . .[1]

Historically, the "superior tribunal" that determined the rights of sovereignty over America was the War of Independence.

The issue of sovereign rights was precipitated by the Stamp Act, which the Grenville ministry passed in 1765, and by the Townshend Act of 1767, which followed its repeal. The Americans resisted both these acts and so forced a resolution of the question of sovereignty. British responses to American resistance assumed three possible courses of action: to grant the colonies outright independence; to compel colonial obedience to Parliament through force; or to conciliate the colonies by granting each colonial legislative assembly considerable legal sovereignty over its internal affairs, including the right of taxation, while maintaining British imperial sovereignty in external affairs.

British Declarations in Favor of American Independence

During 1774–5, Josiah Tucker, Dean of Gloucester, preached in favor of granting the American colonies immediate independence from Britain. After hostilities began, in a series of pamphlets, Tucker argued that it was impossible for Britain to conquer her colonies, that a protracted civil war would be an economic disaster for the mother country, and that, since the Americans refused to submit to the jurisdiction of Parliament, it was best "to separate totally from the Colonies." Tucker, a moderate Tory and severe critic of Locke's theory of a revocable social contract, in effect applied that thinker's theory by asserting that it was in Britain's economic self-interest to break her historical, contractual relationship with America. Later, in *Four Letters on Important National Subjects* (1783), Tucker expressed satisfaction that America was independent and lamented that Britain had not "totally cast them off" without war, as it would have "saved both them and us . . . blood and treasure." But at the time Tucker's views were dismissed by Samuel Johnson as a "wild proposal" and by Edmund Burke as "childish."

Other Britons privately shared those views. Horace Walpole, an ardent Whig, wrote to Horace Mann in 1770: "The tocsin seems to be sounded in America. That continent . . . is growing too mighty to be kept in subjection to half a dozen exhausted nations in Europe."[2] David Hume, a Tory, expressed a similar view to William Straham in 1771: "Our union with America . . . in the nature of things, cannot long subsist." In October 1775, Hume upstaged Jefferson with his own declaration of independence: "Let us, therefore, lay aside all anger, shake hands, and part friends. Or if we retain any anger, let it only be against ourselves for our past folly; and against that wicked madman, Pitt, who has reduced us to our present condition."[3] On 19 June 1775, James Boswell recorded a conversation with Hume: "He said, It was all over in America. We could not subdue the colonists. . . . He said we may do very well without America, and he was for withdrawing our troops altogether."[4] Hume's close friend Adam Smith, an independent Whig, advanced, in his *Wealth of Nations* (1776), economic, political, and psychological reasons why the Americans should be independent in all internal affairs, including the right of taxation, with or without an imperial union with Britain.[5] Hume and Smith may have expressed the views of Francis Hutcheson, professor of moral philosophy at Glasgow from 1730–1746, who advanced a theory that it was "unnatural" for self-sufficient colonies to remain in subjection to a mother country, and unwise, for economic and humanitarian reasons, for nations to maintain "grand unwieldy empires." In his *System of Moral Philosophy* (1755), Hutcheson utilized the "natural rights" theories of the classical republican Robert Molesworth, and argued that if a mother country passes "oppressive laws . . . with respect to . . . colonies so increased in numbers and strength that they are sufficient by themselves . . . they are not bound to continue in their subjection."[6]

Arguments for American independence based upon metaphysical "natural rights" were advanced by a heterogeneous group of Calvinist nonconformists, political revolutionaries, ideological radicals, and Commonwealthmen, such as Richard Price, Joseph Priestley, "Junius," John Cartwright, Brand Hollis, Tom Paine, Mary Wollstonecraft, and Catherine Macaulay. Their revolutionary theories derived from Milton, Algernon Sidney, Molesworth, and especially John Locke, and were championed by such politicians as Wilkes, Shelburne, and Pitt. Typical of this group was John Cartwright (1740–1824), who, in a series of letters in the London *Public Advertiser* in the spring of 1774, rejected the recognition by both Burke and Tucker that Britain enjoyed prescriptive legal sovereignty over America:

> Parliament hath not the rights of sovereignty over his majesty's American subjects. We have no need of profound learning . . . nor even of the history of the respective provinces and their different origins; neither do we want copies of grants, charters, or acts of parliament, in order to judge of the question before us. . . . Let us then hear no more of a right in our present-constituted parliament to govern the Americans, as being derived from any former exercise of this sovereignty, from the original dependency and protection of the emigrants and infant colonies, or from the tenour of grants and charters! The respective governments in America are no longer dependent colonies; they are independent nations.

On a simple appeal to inherent and unalienable abstract rights held to be original in every one, and with complete indifference to historical origins and chartered legal rights of British sovereignty, twenty-seven months before Jefferson's celebrated document was revised and adopted by the Continental Congress, Cartwright declared the American colonies independent. As Bernard Bailyn has shown in *The Ideological Origins of the American Revolution* (1967), in America between 1750 and 1776, Cartwright's type of ideological argument was expressed in over four hundred pamphlets.

Clearly, even before hostilities began in 1775, a variety of British Tories, Whigs, and radical Commonwealthmen, for reasons that were very different and even contradictory, favored independence for America. But their views were either privately held or dismissed as impractical by the dominant powers in the British government and by the public. As the war continued, however, and especially after Burgoyne's defeat at Saratoga late in 1777, many who had favored a policy of force or of conciliation became advocates of immediate American independence.

Public Opinion, King, and Ministry: A Policy of Force

During the 1770s, public opinion, King George III, and a substantial majority in Parliament backing the North ministry remained adamantly opposed to independence for the colonies. After important concessions failed to satisfy the Americans, they favored the use of military force to maintain British sovereignty over the colonies. In February 1775, after North's proposal for transferring the exercise of the right to tax to the colonial assemblies had been rejected, King George and his ministry believed the Americans left Britain no choice but to use force. On 18 February 1775, Horace Walpole, a severe critic of the North ministry, wrote to William Mason that a great majority in both Houses favored war, and that they believed the colonies would submit in three months. He told friends in France that the war was "fashionable" in England. In September 1775 *The Gentleman's Magazine* noted that, "no plan of reconciliation will ever be formed that will content the present ministry and the present Continental Congress." In December the same publication reported: "It is now the declared design of Government to employ the whole national force . . . to compel them to acknowledge the supremacy of the British legislature. . . ." In March 1776 it lamented the unreasonableness of the Americans, and noted that in Britain, "The temper and spirit of the nation are so much against concessions, that if it were the intention of administration, they could not carry the question."[7] Edward Gibbon, a staunch supporter of the North ministry, has testified that the policy of force remained popular in England until the second session of the 1781–82 Parliament:

> In the first session of the new parliament, administration stood their ground; their final overthrow was reserved for the second. The American war had once been the favourite of the country: the pride of England was irritated by the resistance of her colonies, and the executive power was driven by national clamour into the most vigorous and coercive measures. But the length of a fruitless contest, the loss of armies, the accumulation of debt and taxes, and the hostile confederacy of France, Spain, and Holland, indisposed the public to the American war, and the persons by whom it was conducted;

the representatives of the people followed, at a slow distance, the changes of their
opinion, and the ministers who refused to bend, were broken by the tempest.[8]

The original unanimity between public opinion, King, and ministry, that
a policy of force would soon defeat the American rebels, evaporated as the
war continued.

The policy of force rested upon the solid, legal foundation of constitutional law as propounded in William Blackstone's *Commentaries on the
Laws of England* (1765–69). Blackstone based constitutional law on "ethics, or natural law," which gave a moral foundation for the legal and
political sovereignty of all established governments. He argued that, "the
power and jurisdiction of parliament . . . is absolute." Ultimate power
must rest somewhere, and Parliament was the place entrusted by the
English constitution for that sovereignty. Blackstone denied that any "state
of nature," prior to the existence of organized society, provided a moral
basis for judging the legal and political uses of power in society, because
"man was formed for society," and only historically developed societies
provided the constitutional norms and means for judging practical legal
sovereignty. Blackstone specifically noted and rejected the "rights of man"
doctrines that derived from Locke's social contract theory, because he
believed that such doctrines dissolved society. They introduced anarchy
by making the very existence of government depend upon the arbitrary
will of each individual, or the collective will of numbers of individuals,
rather than the corporate reason and will of many generations of men
embodied in the constitution.

Practically all of the pamphlets written in defense of Parliament's
sovereign rights over the American colonies rested upon assumptions
similar to Blackstone's constitutional principles of government. Soame
Jenyns, in *The Objections to the Taxation of Our American Colonies,
briefly Considered* (1765), rejected the popular thesis that taxation without representation was tyranny, and argued that the Americans should be
satisfied with "virtual" representation. Jenyns concluded that Parliament
had a perfect "right" to tax America as it saw fit.

By far the most powerful and profound defense of Britain's unqualified "rights" of sovereignty over America was written by Samuel Johnson
(1709–1784), in four pamphlets: *The False Alarm* (1770); *Thoughts on . . .*

Transactions Respecting Falkland's Islands (1771); *The Patriot* (1774); and *Taxation No Tyranny* (1775). Johnson believed in limited constitutional monarchy as prescribed by England's common law. In *The False Alarm* he argued against Lockean "natural rights," which made the popular will and rights of electors supreme over constitutional authority and legal precedents. In his three other pamphlets, despite his very harsh opinion of the North ministry, Johnson defended the administration's American policy against such critics as Wilkes, "Junius," Mrs. Macaulay, and the Rockingham Whig opposition. Indeed, Johnson came close to being the official spokesman for the King and the North ministry.

Johnson's political theory presupposed that government is a matter of moral necessity for man, and not a voluntary relationship between rulers and subjects. Government evolves through history, and is not derived from any pre-civil "state of nature" or original social contract. Therefore it cannot be legally dissolved by disaffected citizens. These ideas applied to the bonds between Britain and America. Britain held undoubted dominion over her colonies by "prescriptive tenure"; she had "natural and lawful authority" because the colonies "were settled under English protection; were constituted by an English charter; and have been defended by English arms."[9] These empirical facts of history and law made the American colonies constituent parts of the British empire, with Parliament and King supreme in all rights of sovereignty throughout the whole. By accepting British protection, the Americans assumed British rule. Legislative powers had indeed been granted to the colonial assemblies by Britain, but as Johnson noted, these assemblies had "acted so long with unquestioned authority" that they had "forgotten whence that authority was originally derived."[10] To Johnson, the colonies owed their political existence to their royal charters, which bound them to Parliament as the source of all legal sovereignty. Like King George III, Johnson believed the colonies had conspired to become independent before Parliament had taxed them. By denying British sovereignty, the Americans now made it necessary to subdue them. The conflict was not over money or taxes, but over legal power, and the Americans were the aggressors: "They consider themselves as emancipated from obedience, and as being no longer the subjects of the British crown. They leave us no choice but of yielding or conquering, of resigning our dominion, or maintaining it by force."[11] The American revolutionaries appealed to abstract slogans about "rights" in order to justify exempting themselves from taxes under British sovereignty; but to Johnson such ideological appeals, based on a revocable social contract in a supposed state of nature, destroyed all historically developed constitutional governments and made even the existence of institutionally organized society impossible.

Johnson's social and political arguments, officially approved by the North ministry, were also popular with the British public. As Boswell noted, they were "congenial with the sentiments of numbers at that time." They were taken to reinforce the mercantile economic theory, held by great numbers of Englishmen, that colonies were founded and existed for the economic benefit of the mother country. Johnson's pamphlets on America provided a strong rationale for the British policy of force.

Edmund Burke's Policy of Conciliation
and the Transition from Colonial to Federal Empire

When we turn to Edmund Burke, we find that historians have generally limited their study of his speeches and writings on the conflict between Britain and her colonies to his best-known works: *A Short Account of a Late Short Administration* (1766); *Observations on 'The Present State of the Nation'* (1769); *Thoughts on the Cause of the Present Discontents* (1770); *Speech on American Taxation* (1774); *Speech on Conciliation with the Colonies* (1775); and *A Letter to the Sheriffs of Bristol* (1777). On the basis of his themes and arguments in these works, historians have concluded that his conception of legal and political sovereignty never went beyond what he called "the constitution of the British empire."[12] But it would be a serious error to assume that this conclusion adequately reflects his final views, since he later modified them in important respects.

For a greater understanding of Burke's final beliefs regarding the constitution of the British empire, it is necessary to study these works in conjunction with his less-known writings on American colonial affairs: *A Bill for Composing the Present Troubles in America* (16 November 1775); *Address to the King* and *Address to the British Colonists in North America* (1776); and *A Letter to the Marquis of Rockingham* (6 January 1777). A careful reading of these somewhat obscure pieces reveals some important changes in Burke's conception of the British empire and the nature of sovereignty within it—changes that foreshadow the latter-day concept of a British commonwealth of independent nations.

The beginning of the conflicts between Britain and her American colonies may well be said to have commenced on the Heights of Abraham in Quebec, when the Marquis de Montcalm surrendered French Canada to the British in September 1759. The politically keen-witted Montcalm prophesied that with this military victory, Britain would lose her American colonies. With the conquest of Canada in the French and Indian Wars (1754–1763)—the American counterpart of the European Seven Years' War—the realization of a worldwide colonial empire was given an enormous impetus in the minds of the British public and its government. Up to this time, the American colonists had necessarily looked to the mother country for protection against the Spaniards to the south and the French to the north; but with the removal of any military threat from the French, the Americans felt much less need to look to Britain for defense against external enemies, and they began to feel much more self-reliant.

This process was reflected in their demands for greater legislative power for their royally chartered and popularly elected colonial assemblies. Within a decade or so, all of the colonies had acquired a considerable degree of self-government. As Burke was to note in 1774, looking back on the origins of the crisis, America had acquired by 1763 "every characteristic mark of a free people in all her internal concerns. She had the image of the British constitution. She had the substance. She was taxed by her own representatives. She paid them all. She had in effect the sole disposal of her own internal government."[13] In the light of this vital development in colonial self-rule, the practical exercise of British sovereignty over America clearly required greater prudence and equity than ever before, and these qualities, Burke went on to argue, were found wanting in government policy.

For example, he pointed out that, in the very year that the Treaty of Paris officially gave Canada to Britain and removed any military danger to the colonies, a "huge increase of military establishment was resolved on" by the Grenville administration, to be financed through "revenue to be raised in America."[14] Burke believed that the conflict over sovereignty began when Parliament decided to establish a standing army in the colonies and to tax them to pay for it and for the recent war with France. Many Americans suspected that the standing army of 26,000 men and seventy ships of war was aimed at their chartered liberties. They also regarded the claim of Parliament to tax them as an attack upon their constitutional rights.[15] As the conflicts over these issues became more and more intense, the grand design of British imperialism pushed the colonies towards full independence.

To Burke, 1764 was the turning point in Britain's policy toward her American colonies, because in that year, for the first time, Parliament was not content to control America through commercial regulations, but instead sought to secure revenue through taxation. This fatal policy was briefly reversed under the Rockingham administration from July 1765 to July 1766. During that year the Rockingham Whigs combined the repeal of the Stamp Act, which gave the colonies particular freedom from taxation by Parliament, with passage of the Declaratory Act, which affirmed that "Parliament . . . had full power and authority . . . to bind the colonies . . . in all cases whatsoever." Burke noted that the Stamp Act was repealed "on principles, not of constitutional right, but on those of expediency, of equity, of lenity." The Declaratory Act was passed "not from any opinion they entertained of its future use in regular taxation," but because "the general reasonings which were employed against that power went directly to our whole legislative right; and one part of it could not be yielded to such arguments without a virtual surrender of all the rest."[16] Burke recognized that legal sovereignty could not be divided. But in 1769, when he wrote these words, he was prepared to sacrifice Britain's "right" of taxation in order to retain her legal sovereignty over America.

Two important themes run through all of Burke's writings and speeches on the conflicts between Britain and her American colonies: the violation of historical experience and the lack of moral prudence in the uses of political power by Parliament. In place of these two basic requirements for peace and equity, the King's ministers, Grenville and North, engaged in *a priori* ideological speculations about their abstract "right" to tax the colonies. In sharp contrast, Burke believed that the royal charters of each colony, the Navigation Acts of 1651, 1660, and 1663, and the Declaratory Act of 1766, were the "corner-stone of the policy of this country with regard to its colonies."[17] Until hostilities took a military turn, he paid little attention to the colonial charters. Instead, he reiterated the theme in the work he had published with his kinsman William Burke, *An Account of European Settlements in America* (1757), and stressed the need to maintain the long-established mercantile economic system by which Britain regulated the trade and commerce of the colonies. But even in this early work, he had warned against excessive control of the colonies and, although he admitted that Britain derived the greater advantage under mercantilism, he stated that the colonies also benefited from that economic arrangement. Until the early 1770s he argued that Parliament should consult and follow past experience—the system that had prevailed up to 1764. In addition to historical experience, moral prudence taught that governors should rule in accordance with the temper and beliefs of the governed, with full regard to circumstances, and not by abstract theories of government or the mere arbitrary will and reason of those in power.

When the contrary policy was resumed, after the fall of Rockingham's government, under the Chatham and North administrations, it led to the series of conflicts which culminated in war and the independence of the colonies. It is noteworthy that Burke never referred to these events as "the American Revolution," but only as "the American war." The conflict was not over rival theories of government, such as democracy and monarchy; rather, it was a *civil war* within the British empire, brought on initially by the political imprudence of Parliament. He regarded the colonies as wholly on the defensive in this war, and he did not believe that their original intention was to secure independence from Britain. On 19 April 1769, he stated in Parliament that irrational fears, backed by sincere convictions on both sides of the Atlantic, were creating and accelerating a mutual distrust between Britain and her colonies that had led to a disastrous psychological impasse: "The Americans have made a discovery, or think they have made one, that we mean to oppress them; we have made a discovery, or think we have made one, that they intend to rise in rebellion. Our severity has increased their ill behaviour. We know not how to advance; they know not how to retreat. . . . Some party must give way."[18]

Although Burke refused to discuss any theory of sovereignty in the abstract, in his early response to colonial resistance he clearly accepted the legitimacy of Parliament's sovereignty over the colonies. Even in his *Speech on American Taxation*, he argued that Parliament "as from the throne of Heaven . . . superintends all the several inferior legislatures, and guides and controls them all, without annihilating any. As all these provincial legislatures are only co-ordinate to each other, they ought all to be subordinate to her. . . ." But he then added a significant principle: "She is never to intrude into the place of the others, whilst they are equal to the common ends of their institution."[19] This added principle clearly differentiated between the "idea of the constitution of the British empire, as distinguished from the constitution of Britain."[20] In short, while Burke continued to recognize the general sovereignty of Parliament, at the same time he came to hold that it should "never . . . intrude" into the sovereignty of the chartered rights of colonial legislatures as long as they fulfilled "the common ends of their institution" in domestic affairs. The function of Britain as the superior central government in its empire was to supervise, not to supersede, colonial governments.

Burke was convinced that the Grenville and North policies had encouraged conflict because they had been based not on historical experience, nor on a strict regard for the character, temper, and beliefs of the Americans, nor on the infinitely complex circumstances of their historical development, but on "mere abstract principles of government." He believed that this form of ideology was a kind of political and metaphysical insanity; it applied speculative abstract concepts to practical social and political affairs. In his *Speech on American Taxation*, he attacked the ministry's appeal to an abstract "right" of sovereignty in order to justify their "right" to tax the colonies as fatal in its practical consequences:

> Leave America, if she has taxable matter in her, to tax herself. I am not here going into the distinction of rights, nor attempting to mark their boundaries. . . . Do not burden them by taxes; you were not used to do so from the beginning. Let this be your reason for not taxing. These are the arguments of states and kingdoms. Leave the rest to the schools, for there only they may be discussed with safety. But if, intemperately, unwisely, fatally, you sophisticate and poison the very source of government, by urging

subtle deductions and consequences odious to those you govern, from the unlimited and illimitable nature of supreme sovereignty, you will teach them by these means to call that sovereignty itself in question. . . . If that sovereignty and their freedom cannot be reconciled, which will they take? They will cast your sovereignty in your face. Nobody will be argued into slavery.[21]

In refusing out of moral prudence to enforce sovereignty as an abstract absolute "right" without regard to the empirical circumstances in America, or to the political consequences of ideological theory, Burke was following a precept laid down by his party chief, the Marquis of Rockingham: "Such a right was irrelevant unless the Americans chose to acknowledge it."[22] Burke saw that the attempt by the ministry to enforce its "rights" of sovereignty in America would result in the loss of the colonies.

By 1775, Burke realized that the problem of harmonizing British sovereignty and American freedom was at a critical stage. He noted later in his *Letter to the Sheriffs of Bristol*: "I am . . . deeply sensible of the difficulty of reconciling the strong presiding power, that is so useful towards the conservation of a vast, disconnected, infinitely diversified empire, with that liberty and safety of the provinces which they must enjoy."[23] On 16 November 1775, in his proposed *Bill for Composing the Present Troubles in America*, Burke told the House that Britain should officially give up her rights of sovereignty in taxation to the colonial assemblies, thus granting the Americans full constitutional rights in representation, taxation, and all of their domestic affairs. He observed that "sovereignty was not in its nature an abstract idea of unity, but was capable of great complexity and infinite modifications." Thus Burke proposed a giant step towards granting American nationhood, freedom without independence, and came close to the nineteenth-century concept of a British commonwealth of free nations. Parliament rejected his bill. Yet within two years, after Britain's defeat at Saratoga, North's administration offered the Americans substantially the same proposal, only to have it rejected. By the end of 1775, and irrevocably after the Declaration of Independence, Burke was convinced that North's insistence upon "unconditional submission" guaranteed American independence, which he himself preferred to conquest by force.

It follows that, after military conflict had begun between the colonies and Britain, Burke felt compelled to change his original position regarding sovereignty within the empire. The first explicit sign of his transition from empire to federalism occurs in November 1775 in the provisions of *A Bill for Composing the Present Troubles in America*. This bill and his speech of about three and a half hours in support of his motion on how to conciliate America have been largely ignored or minimized by historians, and even by Burke scholars. Yet, together with his *Address to the King* and his *Address to the British Colonists in North America* (1777), it sets forth the major change in his conception of sovereignty within the empire.

Burke first laid it down as a principle that "sovereignty was . . . capable of great complexity and infinite modification, according to the temper of those who are to be governed and to the circumstances of things: which being infinitely diversified, government ought to be adapted to them and to conform itself to the nature of things, and not to endeavour to force them."[24] In essence this is Burke's principle of moral prudence, the first of political virtues, applied to sovereignty. It stands in total contrast to King George's declaration on 18 November 1774, that "blows must decide whether they are to be subject to this country or independent." Neither the King nor North's majority in Parliament could conceive of any modification in sovereignty as an alternative to unconditional submission to Britain or independence for America. This narrow and rigid conviction illustrated what Burke meant by his aphorism that "magnanimity in politics is not seldom the truest wisdom; and a great empire and little minds go ill together."[25] Conciliation through moral prudence and a change in sovereignty within the empire meant that Britain should grant total self-rule to the colonial assemblies and limit its sovereignty to foreign affairs. Burke's proposal was a giant step towards granting the Americans nationhood within a federated British empire that retained this limited authority. It provided constitutional freedom but not legal independence, and it had the basic rudiments of the concept of a commonwealth of free nations united through the Crown to Britain.

A more refined measure of Burke's vital change in his conception of sovereignty is apparent in the companion pieces addressed to the King and the American colonists. In both works, Burke reviewed the "misconduct of government" that resulted in the alienation of America, and noted the "repeated refusals to hear or to conciliate" colonial complaints, followed by the British use of force. Parliament constantly oscillated between enforcement and concessions. In both addresses, he emphasised "the vital principles of the British constitution" contained in the colonial charters, and their violation by statutes of Parliament, often without cause or provocation. In the *Address to the King*, he observed that "the cause of inflaming discontent into disobedience and resistance into revolt" was centred in "the subversion of solemn fundamental charters on the suggestion of abuse, without citation, evidence, or hearing . . . ."[26] He referred to the policy of taxing the colonies for revenue as "an attempt made to dispose of the property of a whole people without their consent."[27] This violated the provisions in the colonial charters, and resulted in rebellions.

In his *Address to the British Colonists in North America*, Burke again lamented "the invasion of your charters." Quite distinct from his position early in the conflict with the colonies, he now argued that the constitutionally established chartered rights of each colony took legal precedence over parliamentary statutes: "Because the charters comprehend the essential forms by which you enjoy your liberties, we regard them as most sacred, and by no means to be taken away or altered without process, without examination, and without hearing, as they have lately been."[28] In this work, Burke treated the colonial charters as the constitutional foundation for colonial liberties and rights. In essence, this is his case against the "arbitrary" and "unconstitutional" acts of Parliament in American colonial affairs.

In retrospect, as the troubles in America mounted, Burke's reiterated appeals to past historical experience and to moral prudence on the part of Parliament became increasingly inadequate to quiet the fears and resistance of the colonies. A new arrangement in legal and political sovereignty was urgently required. Between 1774 and early 1778 Burke gradually developed a plan for a federal type of sovereignty within the British empire. On 2 December 1777, the day before news reached London that Burgoyne had surrendered at Saratoga, he said in the Commons: "We must and ought to treat with [the colonies] on the terms of a federal union."[29] But by the time the North administration repealed the punitive legislation of 1774, amended the Declaratory Act, and gave up the "right" of taxation, many colonists had declared in favor of independence. This development was confirmed when the Continental Congress rejected the offer made by the Carlisle Commission of a greatly enlarged colonial sovereignty, and by April 1778, Burke favored an end to the war and independence for America. After news of Cornwallis's surrender reached London three years later, and Parliament knew that America was lost, Burke bitterly and ironically reminded his colleagues in the House: "We did all this because we had a right to do it: that was exactly the fact."

Yet Burke never arrived at a full-fledged theory of a commonwealth incorporating independent nations that would be legally connected with Britain. The closest he came to such a concept was in his second speech on conciliation in his appeal for "a federal union." That appeal remained in a rudimentary form. He failed to follow up the obvious necessity to maintain the legal connection of the colonies to Britain through the monarchy. Apparently, he could not imagine that the role of Britain's limited constitutional monarch could be extended to an overseas empire. Moreover, behind his omission was his long-standing fear as a Whig that the monarchy might again aspire to absolute power, and that too much patronage in the hands of the Crown would corrupt Parliament. Despite this serious restriction in his revised conception of empire, Burke was far more perceptive than any of his British contemporaries regarding the political problems of empire and the need for a new conception of sovereignty. That historical development remained to be worked out during the nineteenth and twentieth centuries.

Burke and Human Rights

F. P. Lock

Ours is "the Age of Rights."[1] Claims to rights have been advanced on an unprecedented scale and solemnly recognized in such international documents as the United Nations Universal Declaration of Human Rights of 1948. Since then, appeals to "human rights" have achieved increasing prominence in political argument and rhetoric. Indeed, the question of individual human rights is now so central a preoccupation of political discourse that one scholar has asserted that "the value of studying Burke today depends in large measure on his treatment of it."[2] Such an affirmation may initially provoke incredulity. Even to introduce Burke into the debate on so distinctively modern a topic as "human rights" may appear an anachronism. Admittedly, the terms which Burke used ("natural rights," and after 1789 "the rights of men" and "the rights of man") are not synonymous with "human rights." Yet the difference is philosophical and rhetorical rather than practical.[3] A more serious barrier is Burke's reputation as an enemy of such rights. Today, most readers first encounter Burke as the antagonist of Thomas Paine, the great champion and popularizer of the "rights of man." A recent anthology, for example, presents Burke, together with Jeremy Bentham and Karl Marx, as one of the three great enemies of the concept of "human rights."[4]

How Burke earned his place in this triumvirate is no mystery. Abusing the French *Déclaration des droits de l'homme et du citoyen* of 1789, he excoriated it as "madness," a compound of "childish futility," "gross and stupid absurdity," and "palpable falsity."[5] These phrases, however, do not fairly represent Burke's views on "human rights." All his opprobrious epithets are directed against what he regarded as "the pretended rights of men," not what he acknowledged as their "*real* rights" (R 86).[6] Far from denying the existence of what are today called "human rights," Burke regarded respect for these "*real* rights" as a mark of the good and just society. Burke thus differs from the "liberal" tradition not in rejecting rights but in what he recognizes as a right.[7]

The French *Déclaration* of 1789, so vilified by Burke, is the foundation document in the modern history of "human rights."[8] Previously, such claims had typically been framed as lists of grievances. Notable examples include Magna Charta and the Bill of Rights of 1689. Even the American Declaration of Independence, while advancing some universal propositions, retained much of the form of a bill of complaint. The French *Déclaration* marked a significant innovation. Dropping the complaint mode entirely, it asserts a series of universal "rights" to which not only the French but all humanity are entitled.[9] Its modern successors, such as those promulgated by the United Nations, have followed this pattern. Critics of these documents have charged that they are too abstract and rationalistic, that in seeking to express "universal" rights they fail to respect differences between cultures, as well as the different ways in which societies may legitimately conceptualize and protect the "rights" they accord to individuals. Outsiders, these critics claim, should not seek to impose an alien code of doubtful universality.[10] This objection relates chiefly to "human rights" as an international issue.

A further charge is that "human rights," at least as commonly conceived and asserted, are excessively individualistic, destructively privileging the atomized individual at the expense of the group and the community. Their pursuit authorizes, even encourages, the renewal within society itself of the Hobbesian "warre of every man against every man" that society was instituted to supersede.[11] Combining both charges, Third World critics have argued that "human rights" are an agent of a Western imperialism that seeks to impose its values and objectives (especially in-dividualism) in the guise of ideas that claim universality but which are in reality the product of Western capitalism.[12] These are serious criticisms, which advocates of global "human rights" have endeavored to address.[13]

By what may at first appear a paradox, Burke's treatment of "the rights of men" may prove unexpectedly relevant to the problem of "hu-man rights" in today's world. For the French *Déclaration,* while advanc-ing universalist claims, is founded on a concept of popular sovereignty and "democracy" that is palpably a product of a distinctively Western tradition. Even a friendly critic has acknowledged that the United Na-tions Universal Declaration may look like "an attempt to universalize Canadian social democracy as it stood in the bright dawn of victory after 1945."[14] If this desideratum is a theory of rights that can credibly be presented to Africa, to Islam, and to China as genuinely "human" rather than parochially Western, Burke is decidedly relevant to its construction. His approach to politics is anti-individualistic. Wary of attributing inde-feasible "rights" to atomized individuals, he preferred to treat them as part of a system of social duties and obligations.[15]

Furthermore, without eschewing principles, he was always ready to modify generalized concepts (such as rights) according to local and par-ticular circumstances. His long and intense concern with India forced him to confront the reality of cultural difference not as an armchair an-thropologist but as a practical lawgiver. Inclined by temperament to re-spect such differences, Burke might have become a relativist. Instead, he sought the universal human needs and values that find expression in that cultural diversity.

Admittedly, Burke was not a systematic philosopher, and never wrote a formal treatise on "human rights," or even a comprehensive exposition of his own ideas. His opinions have to be deduced from a variety of writ-ings and speeches, each avowedly addressed to a particular problem rather than a general question. This process of extraction is liable to the two fallacies identified by Quentin Skinner as "the mythology of doctrines" and "the mythology of coherence."[16] To mine Burke's works for his thoughts on a topic of urgent contemporary interest, such as "human rights," is a procedure that may appear particularly likely to commit both fallacies.

Burke, however, while he deprecated the tyranny of "abstractions and universals," claimed to follow "the guide and light of sound, well-understood principles," without which political argument would be no more than a "confused jumble of particular facts and details."[17] To adumbrate the principles that governed his attitude to "human rights," and to illustrate them with some of the "particular facts and details," is the purpose of this essay.

Burke's most sustained treatment of "human rights" occurs in his *Reflections on the Revolution in France* (1790). In opposition for most of his career, Burke was habituated to developing his own ideas through the refutation of his opponents' case. The *Reflections* is no exception. Burke begins by demolishing the theory of popular sovereignty advanced by Richard Price in his sermon of 4 November 1789. Having disposed of Price, he proceeds to a more general consideration of the early events of the French Revolution (Price's inspiration). In the course of his analysis, Burke frequently has occasion to attack the principles enshrined in the French *Déclaration*. His rhetorical strategy is to appear as the champion of "the *real* rights of men," which the "pretended rights" espoused by the National Assembly would actually subvert (*R* 86). As part of this strategy, Burke often gives the phrase "rights of men" an ironic or negative edge. Thus he dubs Price "the archpontiff of the *rights of men*," and stigmatizes "the rights of men" as a "grand magazine of offensive weapons" in which Henry VIII would have found a fit "instrument of despotism" (*R* 16, 172).[18] In 1790, when the phrase "rights of men" was associated with a levelling populism that most of Burke's intended audience found distasteful, these ironic uses were rhetorically effective. For modern readers, however, they are likely to create an appearance of unmitigated hostility towards such rights.

This impression is misleading. What provoked Burke's ire were false claims and abstract formulations. In his *Appeal from the New to the Old Whigs* (1791), he deplores "the madness of their declaration of the pretended rights of man" and deprecates "the mischievous tendency of all such declarations to the well-being of men and of citizens, and to the safety and prosperity of every just commonwealth."[19] Burke did not deny the validity of the "rights of men." Indeed, such rights are integral to his philosophy of politics. As a philosopher, he acknowledged their derivation from the natural law. As a statesman, however, he preferred to derive them from positive laws. The value of such enactments as Magna Charta and the Bill of Rights of 1689 was in declaring and recognizing such "natural rights" in a form that made them effective and enforceable. The framers of the Petition of Right of 1628, for example, rejected the "theoretic science" that would have given them merely a "vague speculative right" and "exposed their sure inheritance to be scrambled for and torn to pieces by every wild litigious spirit." Instead, guided by a "practical wisdom," they chose a "positive, recorded, *hereditary* title" (R 45–6). Burke defends the value of inherited liberties through characteristic metaphors drawn from the law of property. Inheritance provides "a sure principle of conservation, and a sure principle of transmission; without at all excluding a principle of improvement." Inherited liberties "are locked fast as in a sort of family settlement; grasped as in a kind of mortmain for ever." This veneration of rights as an inheritance derived not from "the superstition of antiquarians" but from "the spirit of philosophic analogy" that treated the state as a kind of extended family (R 47–9). Rights so enshrined are likely to be respected.

Abstract formulations of right, Burke believed, were delusive guides to "*real* rights of men" as they existed in actual societies. Characteristically, he expressed this idea through a metaphor drawn from the laws of physics: "these metaphysic rights entering into common life, like rays of light which pierce into a dense medium, are, by the laws of nature, refracted from their straight line. . . . [I]n the gross and complicated mass of human passions and concerns, the primitive rights of men undergo such a variety of refractions and reflections, that it becomes absurd to talk of them as if they continued in the simplicity of their original direction" (R 90–1). The "*real* rights of men" exist in "a sort of *middle*, incapable of definition, but not impossible to be discerned" (R 92). Instead of defining, Burke therefore chose rather to describe some of them:

> If civil society be made for the advantage of man, all the advantages for which it is made become his right. It is an institution of beneficence; and law itself is only beneficence acting by a rule. Men have a right to live by that rule; they have a right to justice; as between their fellows, whether their fellows are in politic function or in ordinary

occupation. They have a right to the fruits of their industry; and to the means of making their industry fruitful. They have a right to the acquisitions of their parents; to the nourishment and improvement of their offspring; to instruction in life, and to consolation in death. Whatever each man can separately do, without trespassing upon others, he has a right to do for himself; and he has right to a fair portion of all which society, with all its combinations of skill and force, can do in his favour. [In this partnership all men have equal rights; but not to equal things. He that has but five shillings in the partnership, has as good a right to it, as he that has five hundred pound has to his larger proportion. But he has not a right to an equal dividend in the product of the joint stock; and] as to the share of power, authority, and direction which each individual ought to have in the management of the state, that I must deny to be amongst the direct original rights of man in civil society; for I have in my contemplation the civil social man, and no other. It is a thing to be settled by convention.[20]

This passage is Burke's fullest account of "the *real* rights of men" as they are enjoyed and limited in actual societies—what are today called "human rights." Its rhetorical purpose in the *Reflections* is to advance a strong negative argument: participation in the political life of a society is not a "natural right." This it does eloquently and unambiguously. Only as a counterpoise does Burke adumbrate what he thought were the "*real* rights of men" in society. Nevertheless, as his nearest approximation to an enumeration of these rights, the passage merits close analysis.

By modern standards, Burke's concept of the role of the state is minimalist.[21] So too is that implied by the French *Déclaration*. Yet the two versions of minimalism could hardly be more different. The French document regards the state, and especially its agents, with suspicion—it is a necessary evil. Many of its provisions are designed to protect the individual, treated as a discrete and ideally self-sufficient unit. Each individual is endowed with "rights," articulated in terms of freedom from various kinds of "oppression." Society exists only to protect those rights, among which "*la résistance à l'oppression*" is prominent (Article 2). In brief, government is the enemy. Burke's "rights," in contrast, are imagined less as protections against the oppression of others than as "advantages" that accrue from co-operation with others. These advantages are less easily defined than legal "rights," perhaps are not susceptible to legal definition at all. For the most part, they are reciprocal, requiring the co-operation of others. In Burke's view, society exists not to protect individuals from each other but to facilitate their happy interaction.

What then, for Burke, were these "*real* rights of men," which comprise "all the advantages" for which society was instituted? The fundamental right implied by membership of a society is the right to live under an equitable system of law, a right to justice. All members of society are entitled to protection by the law, against violence and oppression, whether on the part of the state itself or its officers, or on the part of other individuals. The law should, for example, prohibit arbitrary arrest or detention, and guarantee the secure inheritance, quiet enjoyment, and free transmission of property. Such basic legal rights figure prominently in all formulations of "human rights" and are largely uncontroversial.

A second, more contentious group of rights governs economic relations within society. Because the economic role of the state has changed much more than its legal function, these rights are easily misinterpreted. Burke was no doctrinaire market liberal. Strongly believing in freedom of enterprise as a general principle, he was nevertheless willing to abridge it when the public interest so demanded.[22] Hence the individual's right to "do for himself" whatever he can do without "trespassing upon others" implies a *laissez-faire* freedom from regulation, while the "right to the fruits of their industry" offers protection against confiscation and arbitrary taxation.

Yet other rights imply a more interventionist state. An example is the right of "making their industry fruitful." In a modern context, this would be taken to imply that the state should provide work.[23] Likewise, a modern reader may interpret the right "to the nourishment and improvement of their offspring" as mandating a system of provision or subsidy by the state of food and education for the young. Burke meant nothing of the kind. He consistently objected to any attempt to interfere with a free market in foodstuffs.[24] In 1795, which saw the most serious food shortages in his lifetime, Burke vehemently opposed any attempt to supplement or subsidize wages from taxes, insisting that charity, not the state, must preserve the poor from starvation.[25]

What then did Burke understand by these particular "rights"? To illustrate the distinction between theory and practice, he cites "a man's abstract right to food or to medicine." Conceding the rights themselves as beyond dispute, Burke turns immediately to "the method of procuring

and administering them." In one of today's welfare states, the acknowledgment would be taken as recognition of a social right to food and medi-
cal care. What Burke meant, however, was much more limited. To satisfy
the right to food and medicine, he advises invoking "the aid of the farmer
and the physician, rather than the professor of metaphysics" (R 89–90).
These rights are best understood in conjunction with the right to "a fair
portion" of whatever society can do in favor of an individual. They imply
an active, benign paternalism on the part of the state, but nothing so
specific as a make-work program. This portion, significantly, is "fair," not
equal. Society should seek to create, to foster, and to maintain, so far as
human endeavors can, conditions favorable to economic enterprise, prosperity, and security. All will benefit from these conditions, though not all
equally.

Society's efforts on behalf of the individual are thus general rather
than particular. In the case of agriculture, the state should not intervene
in the free market. Left to itself, the market will (with rare exceptions)
best provide abundance of foodstuffs. This is the context within which
men's "right to the nourishment and improvement of their offspring"
should be understood. The state encourages provision, but does not directly provide. Even this role, however, goes beyond the distinctly
minimalist concept of the economic provisions (Articles 13–15) of the
French Déclaration, which seem designed primarily to equalize and minimize the burden of taxation. More generally, the French Déclaration declares that the end of society is no more than "la conservation des droits
naturels et imprescriptibles de l'homme" (Article 2). Burke, on the contrary, follows the Aristotelian tradition of attributing to the state a moral
purpose.[26]

The contrast with the French Déclaration is even more striking in
the matter of religion. The French document says nothing about education, and treats religion only as a subheading of opinion, free expression
of which is guaranteed (Article 10). Attributing a more active role to the
state than as a mere neutral guarantor of freedom of expression, Burke
offers more, a right to "instruction in life, and to consolation in death."
Later in the Reflections, he endorses the institution of an established church
as the best way of providing religious teaching and comfort (R 134–40).

Membership of such a church should not be compulsory, but may properly confer civic privileges. Burke limits the personal "right" to freedom of religion (such as envisaged in the French *Déclaration*) to its private practice. Society, acting through the legislature, had equally a "right" to establish a particular religion, and for Burke such an establishment was no infringement of the "rights" of those who chose not to belong to it.

These are the two principles on which Burke decided all the questions relating to religion and society that arose during his career. On the one hand, and against many of his usual associates in the Whig Party, he consistently championed the privileges of the Established Church. On the other, he supported with equal consistency the right to private dissent.[27] He broke with the dissenters when he thought that their aim had ceased to be toleration, and encompassed the destruction of the Established Church.[28]

Again, the paternalist nature of Burke's concept of the state is evident. For Burke, the legislative power had not only the right but the responsibility to provide, according to its best lights, a religion for the people, and to confer whatever civil or political rights they saw fit exclusively on the adherents of that religion. Individuals who dissent from the doctrine or practice of that Church are entitled "to instruction in life, and to consolation in death" according to their own mode. But the precise limits of that toleration, like the extent of the franchise, is within the competence of the legislature to determine.[29]

Burke did not, however, believe that a legislature was free to make any regulations it chose. To be morally valid, legislative power must be exercised "according to that eternal immutable law, in which will and reason are the same" (*R* 140). The most flagrant case known to Burke of a system of law that violated this requirement was the Penal Code that the Protestant minority had imposed on the Irish Catholics after 1689. Having grown up in Ireland, Burke knew at first hand the misery and the degradation that these laws had caused.

About 1761, in response to a wave of anti-Catholic agitation that he regarded as hypocritical and factitious, Burke began work on a *Tract on the Popery Laws* that was intended to expose both their injustice and their rashness. These laws had been imposed by a legislature that represented only a small part of the population. Burke does not, however, argue that they were on this ground morally invalid. Instead, he advances arguments drawn from natural law. Indeed, the *Tract* provides some of the most convincing evidence for the natural law interpretation of his thought.[30] As clearly as anywhere in his writings, the *Tract* suggests just which "natural" rights Burke thought were preserved when men entered society. Overwhelmingly, these are the rights to inherit, to acquire, and to transmit property.[31]

The Penal Laws were not directed only against Catholic ownership of property. Other provisions abridged the right to bear arms; to freedom of education, religion, and marriage; to eligibility for public employment; and to the franchise. Burke's treatment of these topics exhibits interesting variations. The more "private" rights he treats with the same indignation as the laws against property. In discussing the "right of *self defence*," admittedly, he concedes that although the "first" of the laws of nature, "many wise communities have found it necessary to set several restrictions upon it, especially temporary ones, on some imminent danger to the publick from foreign invasion." Yet Burke's recitation of the draconian provisions of the Penal Laws shows that they went far beyond what the public interest could conceivably require. Indeed, some of the provisions were manifestly intended rather to humiliate than for any rational purpose.[32]

Far different is Burke's treatment of the exclusion of Catholics from public life. On the franchise, Burke is silent. Their exclusion from "all Offices in Church and State" he accepts as "a provision just and necessary."[33] The sincerity of this statement has been questioned, as a concession designed to make the other arguments more palatable.[34] Much later, in the 1790s, Burke did indeed argue in favor of admitting Catholics to civil and military offices. But this need not mean that he thought so in the different climate of the 1760s. He never regarded participation in public life as a "right." All members of society are not entitled to equal "rights." Not to have a vote, or to be eligible for public office, is no grievance against the laws of nature. But since people first entered into society the better to protect their property, society cannot, consistently with its primary purpose, arbitrarily deny the fundamental human right to inherit, acquire, and transmit property, "the first origin, the continued Bond, and the ultimate End" of society.[35] The worst that Burke can say against the Penal Laws is that they are "a Law against property," and therefore "a Law against industry," a law that subverts the fundamental purpose of society itself.[36]

Acts of 1778 and 1782 largely repealed the Penal Laws so far as they affected property, though Catholics remained excluded from public life.[37] After 1789, in the aftermath of the French Revolution, Catholic agitation to have their remaining disabilities removed greatly increased. Burke was particularly disturbed by a development about 1791, when (mainly) Dissenting reformers sought to draw the Catholics into an alliance. Much troubled by this possibility, Burke worked hard to prevent it by advocating timely concessions to the Catholics. Early in 1792, he wrote a public letter to Sir Hercules Langrishe, a moderately pro-Catholic Irish M.P. This letter confirms the evidence of the earlier *Tract* that, for Burke, the worst injustice of the Penal Laws was their trespass on the rights of property. Burke was convinced that the franchise should be extended to the Catholics, as a matter of equity and as highly expedient to prevent their jacobinization. Even so, he explicitly avoids claiming the franchise as a "right." Instead, he calls it a "civil privilege." This privilege should be extended to freeholders, as in England, so as to create as responsible an electorate as possible. Such a moderate and timely reform would defuse the clamor of the excluded Catholics for "a right of voting by the head," which for Burke was the "real evil." [38]

Thus, for Burke the fundamental "human right" was the right to protection of property. In the *Reflections*, he argues that not even Parliament has the right "to violate property, to over-rule prescription or to force a currency of their own fiction in the place of that which is real, and recognized by the law of nations" (R 224–5). In notes for a later speech, putting a strong but hypothetical case, he asserts: "Slavery is contrary to Nature. True, but you would not instantly manumit all slaves. Property is to be secured."[39]

In giving primacy to the protection of such rights, of course, Burke was doing no more than following Locke and the mainstream of eighteenth-century thought.[40] Yet his emphasis is significantly different. Burke's is a more paternalistic model of society and its organs. Among the "rights of men," he argued in 1792, is the right "to a wise protecting parental Government."[41] For Locke, participation in the political process was the individual's best guarantee that he would in fact receive the benefits for which he had given up his "natural" rights and accepted the social compact. Burke was less concerned with protecting the individual from the potential tyranny of the state, and more concerned with protecting the property of the few from the folly and the rapacity of the many. To prevent this, Burke posited a "right" to "a sufficient restraint upon their passions" by "*a power out of themselves*." The nature and extent of this restraint could not be "settled upon any abstract rule," and certainly should not be determined by those who were to be subject to it. The "rights" which individuals were to enjoy was to be determined by the "constitution," the perfection of which was "a matter of the most delicate and complicated skill" (R 88–9). Such a task called for the collective wisdom of ages, and should not be rashly undertaken by a mere temporary body of inexperienced men, such as the National Assembly. For Burke, the idea of a partnership across time circumscribes the moral, if not the legal, rights of a single generation to remake society according to its will and pleasure. Since the construction and preservation of a balanced constitution called for insight and reflection, Burke condemned what he called "this vile scheme of altering the principles of election to a right of voting by the head."[42] Many contemporary problems in "human rights" concern the protection of "minority rights" against the tyranny, or the potential tyranny, of a majority.[43] Burke's warnings against the abuses of majority rule are therefore timely and relevant.

Government, Burke insisted, is not "a problem of arithmetic" (R 76). While acknowledging that government was instituted for the benefit of the governed, he had no faith in the wisdom of the many. He therefore distrusted electoral democracy as a mode of government, and had little faith in popular elections, even with an electorate as narrow as that of eighteenth-century Britain. Popular elections were a "mighty Evil," only necessary because the alternative was worse.[44] He therefore opposed successive attempts to make elections more frequent, or to widen or reform the franchise. Most existing governments discharged their trusteeship responsibly. In the last resort, the people would rise to overthrow any government that became intolerably and incurably vicious. For such an extreme necessity, which would be a law unto itself, political wisdom could not provide. He therefore dreaded the destabilizing influence of French principles, which would unsettle established governments for an advantage that would be at best theoretical and might prove wholly chimerical. In his view, the test of a legitimate government was its practical efficacy, not its theoretical basis. A constitution that could plead prescription, and under which an equitable system of law was equitably administered, served every purpose of society.

Thus, all members of society, in Burke's view, are entitled to certain rights. Some of these correspond to modern individual rights: for example, the right to equal treatment before the law, and to security for the inheritance, acquisition, and transmission of property. Another kind of "right" is both less determinate and less individual, being exercised through participating in society itself. This is the right to "fair portion" (but not an equal portion) of the advantages that society offers, such as the conditions of social stability that encourage economic enterprise. These are Burke's "human rights." Participation in politics is another matter, the preserve of a subset of citizens, membership of the group being settled by convention. For Burke, a just society is one in which individuals, protected by equality before the law, are free to pursue their own economic advantage. Since society is not a collective of equals, but rather a partnership between greatly unequal partners, "human rights" are a necessarily unequal system of privileges and obligations, not a set of individualistic claims against each and all. This reciprocity is best codified in positive laws, privileges, and immunities, rather than being expressed as abstract, general truths. "Human rights" as he conceives them are thus legal, unequal, and apolitical.

In a passage that is often quoted, Burke distinguished the point of view of a "Professor in an University" from that of a "Statesman." A professor seeks the "abstractions and universals" of politics. A statesman, as Burke counted himself, must govern himself by "circumstances," which are "infinite" and "infinitely combined."[45] This is a recurrent *leitmotiv* in Burke's political thought, present as early as his advocacy of the repeal of the Stamp Act in 1766. Parliament had an undoubted right to tax the colonies, a right "clear beyond contradiction as an absolute, clear and speculative opinion." But the moment this right is "blended with the happiness and misery" of the real world, its exercise becomes a matter of prudence.[46]

After 1789, Burke's opposition to theory intensified, because in France theory was being applied to politics on an unprecedented scale. Burke condemned the French *Déclaration* as mischievous and delusive, inapplicable to real problems and impotent to protect actual rights in real societies. In pursuit of the abstract "rights" described in the *Déclaration,* the French had plunged into an anarchy that violated on an unprecedented scale the basic rights to property, to liberty, and even to life. Before the Revolution, the French enjoyed the rule of law. Although their system was deficient in protecting personal liberties, the *parlements* guaranteed a high degree of security of property (*R* 238–9). Wise reformers would have built on this inheritance, not destroyed it. By refusing to make any use of the old materials, the French had acquired paper liberties that could not be enforced and therefore could not be enjoyed. Repudiating the rule of law, they had fallen prey to the arbitrary will of the temporary majority of the National Assembly, itself subject to the caprices of the Parisian mob. Despite the right to property enshrined in a strongly worded article of the *Déclaration,* property rights had been subverted on an unprecedented scale.

The example of France did not, however, lead Burke to repudiate the concept of "natural rights." Their pre-existence was no less important for him than for his opponents. Individuals surrendered their "rights" to society, in trust. Society has no "right" to be unjust towards any individual. This is no mere theoretical concession. Eager to avoid the chaos of anarchy, Burke was equally averse to the chains of Hobbesian despotism. The fear of arbitrary power was part of Burke's Whig inheritance. Nor was arbitrary power the preserve of tyrants. It could equally be usurped by a tyrannical majority, or pretended majority. Burke was keenly aware of the convulsion in property caused by the English Civil Wars, and in the *Reflections* he accused Price of praising 1689 but being really inspired by 1649 (*R* 21). The populist pretensions of the National Assembly were thus no unprecedented aberration. The French *Déclaration* explicitly defines the law (which is charged, among much else, with the final determination of the rights of property) as "*l'expression de la volonté générale,*" to which all citizens, either directly or indirectly, are entitled to contribute (Article 6). This idea (which derives from Rousseau rather than Locke) was anathema to Burke. In the first place, he denies the "right" to participate. Second, even those who by convention possessed the "right" to determine what was law in a particular society have no "right" to make their will and pleasure the standard of that law.

Burke repeatedly denied that even Parliament has the "right" to be unjust. In the course of his attack on the Irish Penal Laws, for example, he argues that "a Law against the majority of the people" cannot be valid. Even if, he imagines, such a law were to be enacted not by representatives but by the people themselves, it would still be "null and void." Even the people themselves have no right to make a law "against the principle of a superior Law, which it is not in the power of any community, or of the whole race of man, to alter—I mean the will of Him who gave us our nature, and in giving impressed an invariable Law upon it." No laws, Burke continues, "can derive any authority from their institution, merely and independent of the quality of the subject matter."[47] Thus for Burke, the Penal Laws were morally invalid not because the majority had not consented to them, but because they denied to a majority of the population a share in the "advantages" for which society was constituted.

The question of the moral competence of a theoretically sovereign legislative power arose in an even more acute form in relation to France after 1789. Opponents of British intervention claimed that the internal government of France was a matter that solely concerned the French. Rejecting this notion that "men in possession of the ruling authority are supposed to have a right to act without coercion in their own territories," Burke argued that "as to the right of men to act any where according to their pleasure, without any moral tie, no such right exists."[48] In a world in which strong assertions of national autonomy are increasingly perceived as inimical to peace and international order, and as a barrier to the universalizing of "human rights," Burke's theory of "weak sovereignty" is decidedly relevant and is attracting renewed interest.[49]

Burke believed that some values were indeed universal. Believing that the way in which "natural rights" were embodied and given practical effect would vary from one society to another, as well as over time, Burke had no difficulty in assimilating India within his paradigm. In his Speech at the Opening of the Impeachment, he repudiated what he called "geographical morality," the idea (which he attributed to Hastings) that the nature and meaning of values such as justice might vary from place to place. "Arbitrary power," exercised at the mere pleasure of an individual or a group, could never be legitimate anywhere.[50] But Burke nowhere suggested that representative institutions were needed, or would even be desirable, in India. Indians were as much attached to their "ancient constitution" as the British were to theirs. Under their institutions, as Burke imagined them, whether Muslim or Hindu, the people enjoyed the benefit of living under known and equitable laws. Under such dispensations societies had flourished for thousands of years. Burke's critique of British rule in India, and of the Hastings administration in particular, was that it had subverted a beneficent system of government and substituted nothing more than arbitrary power exercised for the personal advantage of the governing few.

Yet Burke was no relativist. Indian laws and customs were legitimate not just because they were established in India, but because they (for the most part) embodied universal principles of justice. Law is not merely the will of a national legislative body, nor the will of the majority of the population of a state. Respectful as Burke was of hallowed cultural practices, he was unafraid to condemn what he thought offended against the universal principles of justice. An instance that remains contentious is the Islamic practice of mutilation as a judicial punishment. This surfaced as a practical problem for Burke in 1781, when he helped frame the Bengal Judicature Act. Drafted in response to complaints against the Supreme Court of Calcutta, which had been charged with administering English law with insufficient regard to local susceptibilities, this Act sought to ensure that Muslims and Hindus would be tried by their own laws and practices. Significantly, however, the Act prohibited mutilation as a punishment.[51] Yet Burke accepted (though reluctantly) the death penalty. The debate continues: both the death penalty and mutilation remain in use, and remain controversial. In the real world, agreement to prohibit "cruel, inhuman or degrading treatment or punishment" (as provided in Article 5 of the United Nations Declaration) may be easier to achieve than a consensus about exactly what treatment or punishment should be so defined.[52] Burke's example counsels caution, but not despair, in the search for a genuinely universal code of "human rights."

Most present-day readers of Burke live in one of the Western-style democracies, in which the franchise has been extended to virtually all adults. Habituated to regard the vote as a "right," such readers may doubt the relevance of Burke's ideas to their kind of society, or to the model of society they would like to propose to the world beyond the West. Limited as it may appear, however, Burke's concept of "human rights" has at least a descriptive validity that approaches the universal. His "rights" represent not a theoretical ideal that only a few constitutions (and those modern) have ever approached, but a practical prescription for a "well-ordered" society, such has often been approximated. Nor, in practice, even in the modern West, is the franchise actually treated as a "human right." All societies regulate it in some way, usually making it a privilege of citizenship. This accords exactly with Burke's principle that political rights are to be "settled by convention."

In the 1790s, Burke had good reason to fear the sudden and indiscriminate extension of the franchise. His gradualism prevailed. No reform was undertaken until 1832, and not until 1929 were all adults (with some few exceptions) entitled to vote. Burke's attitude to the franchise, far from standing in the way of an acceptance of his concept of "human rights," is actually what makes them so readily exportable. A nearly intractable problem in the international "human rights" debate is how to interpret the concept to non-Western cultures. In large parts of the world, including much of Africa, many Islamic countries, and China, democratic traditions of the Western kind are either weak or absent. Yet these societies possess alternative modes of governance and ways of thinking about the individual and the state that are well established and sanctioned by long and powerful traditions. To achieve any meaningful agreement about the nature of "human rights" will not be easy.

A Burkean theorist of rights would question whether the franchise is so unambiguously a "human right" that it should form part of the same package of rights as freedom from torture. Further, even to those who think it is such a right, a Burkean might retort that, in practice, more progress with the promotion of human rights might be obtained by divorcing them, so far as possible, from political considerations. Two leading authorities have suggested something of the kind, though without explicitly invoking Burke. R. J. Vincent has argued that rights should come before politics.[53] Even closer to Burke in spirit is the argument of John Rawls that since "basic human rights express a minimum standard of well-ordered political institutions for all peoples," they can be adequately protected in a "well-ordered hierarchical state with its consultation hierarchy." In such a state, a "system of law" can ensure "the right to life and security, to personal property and the elements of the rule of law, as well as the right to a certain freedom of conscience and freedom of association."[54] The suggestion that an effective and respected system of law can serve as an adequate substitute for representation, and the phrasing of religious freedom as "a certain freedom of conscience," are in the spirit of Burke. India before the advent of the British (at least as Burke idealized it) might qualify as a "well-ordered hierarchical state," whereas the Ireland of the Penal Laws would not.

If international formulations of "human rights" are to have any chance of achieving universal acceptance, they need to be minimal rather than maximal. Burke's "*real* rights" seem in principle achievable. Burke, like Rawls, offers a middle way, neither imposing alien norms on the strength of their presumed universality, nor admitting the excuse of local exceptionalism as a means of shielding tyranny and oppression from inspection and control. Values such as justice are indeed universal, but justice can equally well be administered in a hierarchical society as in a democratic one. As Rawls recognizes, the cause of what he calls "basic human rights" (Burke's "*real* rights of men") may be retarded rather than advanced by an insistence on linking it to Western-style democracy. That Burke, who was no liberal, should so nearly coincide with a leading modern theorist of liberalism suggests that the search for a genuinely universal concept of "natural rights" or "human rights" need not be doomed. The friends of "human rights" should certainly not be deterred by Burke's primary reputation as the antagonist of Paine and his *Rights of Man* from studying his writings, where they will find an unexpectedly fertile source of ideas, encouragement, and inspiration.[55]

Edmund Burke on Tradition and Human Progress: Ordered Liberty and the Politics of Change

Joseph Pappin III

Even though Edmund Burke never, to my knowledge, used the word "tradition"—he did at least once use the word "traditionary"[1]—there seems to have been a natural connection established, for many persons, between Burke's "traditionalism" and what they see as the essence of modern conservatism. "Traditionalism," Anthony Quinton argues, is one of the three pillars of conservatism, and Burke is the father of modern conservatism.[2] Isaiah Berlin once went so far as to claim (at least before Connor Cruise O'Brien secured a begrudging and qualified retraction from him) that Burke's traditionalism was so unqualified that it could be labeled as "reactionary."[3]

Alfred North Whitehead, when he sets out to give meaning to the appellation "pure conservative," argues that "the pure conservative is fighting against what is the essence of the universe."[4] If we can surmise from Whitehead's magisterial philosophical work, *Process and Reality*, that the essence of the universe and of reality itself is "process," it is easy to conclude that the "pure conservative" is one who resists change, the invariable procession of reality, and, moreover, all possibility of progress. The "pure conservative" for Whitehead, it would seem, is one who supports tradition for its own sake. And it would seem that Berlin's "reactionary" Burke is just such a "pure conservative."

However, to characterize Burke as one who supports tradition for its own sake, as one who resists all change, as one who rejects the possibility of progress, is to distort Burke. A closer analysis of Burke's metaphysical and political commitments (and of his analyses of human nature and tradition, of ordered liberty and change, and of the possibilities for human progress) reveal that, even if we accept Whitehead's definition of a "pure conservative," Burke does not fit the bill.

Burke's Metaphysics

Any attempt to discern the nature of Burke's metaphysical commitments (and to respond to Whitehead's caricature of conservatism) must begin with the ancient philosophical problem of being and becoming, or of the "one and the many." We all recall that the grand pre-Socratic philosopher of pure flux and pure change was Heraclitus, and that Parmenides held the opposite position of Being as One, permanent and immobile. It took Aristotle to cut through this virtual Gordian knot and divide being into being-in-act and being-in-potency, and it was upon Aristotle whom Burke relied. For Aristotle, to whom Burke referred as the "Great Master of Reasoning," reality was a "union of permanence and change" that entailed hierarchical levels of beings in existence, each of which had the capacity to actualize their potentialities, to realize their essential natures.[5] For Aristotle, change is possible, but it is structured change within the dynamics of one's own nature or essence.

Now it so happens that the phrase "union of permanence and change" is Burke's own, and he utilizes the phrase in extolling a principle of renovation as applied to Parliament.[6] And his use of this phrase indicates that Burke's politics of tradition, conservation, liberty, change, and progress has a firm philosophical foundation that is compatible, consistent, and in basic union with the perennial philosophical realism of Aristotle and Aquinas. Without some acknowledgment of Burke's philosophical realism, we run the risk of allowing Burke to fall prey to the label of "reactionary" conservative, with the pejorative use of the term "conservative" that Whitehead employs. We thereby fail to grasp the foundations of Burke's authentically developmental conservative politics, of his dynamic conservatism, if you will.

Now we know that Burke frequently speaks out vociferously against metaphysical speculation. For example, when addressing the realms of morals and politics, Burke bluntly states that "pure metaphysical abstraction does not belong to these matters."[7] In his *Speech on the Petition of the Unitarians* he declares that "no rational man ever did govern himself by abstractions and universals."[8] He found the corruption of manners, lewdness, and the loss of virtue that took place during the French Revolution to be in part a result "of metaphysical speculation blended with the coarsest sensuality."[9] And in the *Reflections on the Revolution in France* he warns against becoming "entangled in the mazes of metaphysic sophistry."[10]

Despite his seeming principled hostility to all types of "metaphysical speculation," it is my contention that the metaphysics against which Burke fulminates is the abstract, disembodied rationalism of much of Enlightenment thought and the application of that thought to the contingent, particularized realm of politics. This does not make him, I shall argue, an opponent of all metaphysical systems. Throughout his life Burke consistently embraced the classical natural law tradition, and it would have been impossible for him to do so without at the same time embracing the metaphysics which necessarily must support it. That he most certainly did hold to the natural law tradition is ratified in his *Speech in the Impeachment of Warren Hastings* in which he argues that "We are all born in subjection—all born equally, high and low, governors and governed, in subjection to one great, immutable, pre-existent law . . . by which we are knit and connected in the eternal frame of the universe, out of which we cannot stir."[11] In his earlier *Tract on the Popery Laws,* he argues that for both positive law and tradition to be justified, both must ultimately be grounded not in the mere "statutes of the people" nor the force of arms, but in a superior law, "which," according to Burke, "it is not in the power of any community, or of the whole race of man, to alter,—I mean the will of Him who gave us our nature, and in giving impressed an invariable law upon it."[12]

The elements of a vibrant metaphysics are present in Burke's thought. There is a creative, transcendent being who has created an "eternal frame of the universe," and an invariable "pre-existent law," prior to any human actions, a law which is written in the nature of each individual person. Burke assumes the reality of an essential human nature and of a moral law that guides and directs the ethical lives of individuals. While the *Tract on the Popery Laws* was an early work, left unpublished, much later in Burke's career, during the trial of Warren Hastings, he refers to "those eternal laws of justice which are our rule and birthright" and to the "primeval, indefeasible, unalterable law of Nature and of nations."[13] Throughout his *Correspondence* as well, we find numerous references to such things as the "Law of Nature"; to the "rights of humanity and Laws of Nature"; to "the God of Law and order"; to the "instinctive principles of self defence and executive powers under the legislation of nature, enforcing its first law"; to the "established Laws of Nature"; and to the "immutable Laws of Nature and the principles of Essential Justice as well as to all reason and good policy."[14]

There is, thus, a natural law for Burke. This natural moral law is implanted by God, reflected in our common human nature, recognized by human reason with all its frailties, and secured by faith. It is the application of abstract theory directly to concrete, contingent social and political matters without regard for circumstances that Burke disparages, not a metaphysically grounded natural law.

On the one hand Burke denies the efficacy of acting solely on the basis of abstractions and universals, as the "rights-of-man" theorists such as Thomas Paine would have it; their politics calls for a direct democracy, here and now, as the only polity in conformity with natural rights. On the other hand, Burke qualifies his criticism of the reliance upon abstractions and universals by claiming that "I do not put abstract ideas wholly out of any question; because I well know that under that name I should dismiss principles, and that without the guide and light of sound, well-understood principles, all reasonings in politics, as in everything else, would be only a confused jumble of particular facts and details, without the means of drawing out any sort of theoretical or practical conclusion."[15] What Burke reviles is a mathematicized, deductive metaphysics that, when arbitrarily applied to the complex mass of human affairs, disregards the traditions and habits of a nation. In by-passing the virtue of prudence, that virtue which perfects man's practical reason, this type of metaphysics leads invariably to chaos.

In fact it is Burke's adversaries, the French *philosophes,* who, in their radical, deductive empiricism, deny the ability of the human mind to obtain objective, essential knowledge about the nature of man and the political good. One need look only at the thought of Jean LeRond d'Alembert, Baron d'Holbach, and Denis Diderot to uncover the natural trajectory of Enlightenment rationalism. For example, d'Alembert assailed "metaphysics," declaring "that this title will soon become an insult for our men of intelligence."[16] If metaphysics encompasses a realm of being beyond the purely material and observable, then it receives d'Alembert's rebuke. He speaks of metaphysical essences or natures as "occult qualities," and in arguing so, radicalizes Locke's empiricism, which considered essences and substances to be substrata that underpin and support various accidents and qualities, substrata that we can infer but never *really* know. D'Alembert dismisses as superfluous such inferences. For d'Alembert these are only the facts of the mind, of the "physics of the soul," as he calls them, resulting in perceptions, and philosophy is relegated to an analysis of these facts.[17] Baron d'Holbach, in his *System of Nature*, echoes d'Alembert's conclusions, "Matter is eternal, and necessary, but its forms are evanescent and contingent."[18] Of man he asks, "Is he any thing more than matter combined, of which the form varies each instant?"[19]

For these French *philosophes*, who advance the metaphysics against which Burke rails, there is only matter and motion; they thus exclude the possibility that the mind can grasp an essential structure of reality. So radical is this materialism, and so reductive of existence to sheer change and flux, that any knowledge of the nature of things, including of ourselves, is beyond our powers. It is Denis Diderot who draws the stark conclusion from this depiction of existence as pure flux and change, and also its consequences for philosophy and, ultimately, politics: "But if the state of this world of phenomena is one of perpetual change, if nature is still at work on it, then despite the chain that links all phenomena, there can still be no philosophy."[20] To Diderot we owe a debt of gratitude for drawing the logical conclusion from the *philosophes'* radical materialism, which is a strict nominalism that does not permit for the existence of any forms, natures, substances, or stable essences that can be grasped to any extent by the human mind. This is an unbridled metaphysical skepticism that, in the hands of these philosophic atheists, opens the door to the primacy of the arbitrary will and individual choice in human affairs. It allows for a politics that can continually start things anew, disregarding the customs and traditions of a nation, imposing new enterprising designs on a population with no connection to essential reality, since reality itself is nothing more than pure and constant change.

Burke seizes immediately on the dilemma of the *philosophes* and their failure to grasp the intelligible structure of reality. Because they reduce the Aristotelian list of ten categories to only two (i.e., those of substance and quantity, those categories that can be perceived and quantified), they reduce reality to the sheer repetition of numbers. Burke concludes: "The troll of their [i.e. the *philosophes'*] table might have informed them that there was something else besides *substance* and *quantity*." And then, without direct attribution to Aristotle, he recommends the Stagirite's complete table of categories: "They might learn from the catechism of metaphysics that there were eight heads more in every complex deliberation which they have never thought of." [21] Thus, the *philosophes* are rebuked for a failure to utilize the abiding metaphysics of Aristotle, whose philosophy is the foundation of philosophical realism, which holds for an intelligible structure of the universe. This is the same Burke who clarifies his position on theory thus: "I do not vilify theory and speculation—no, because that would be to vilify reason itself. . . . No; whenever I speak against theory I mean always a weak erroneous fallacious unfounded or imperfect theory; and one of the ways of discovering that it is a false theory is by comparing it with practice." [22]

As opposed to the British empiricists and French *philosophes*, Burke argues in his *Philosophical Inquiry into the Sublime and the Beautiful* that we can discover the existence of God through his effects, though with considerable difficulty. Unlike the British empiricists, he advances a cosmological argument for God's existence. He writes: "It is by a long deduction and much study, that we discover the adorable wisdom of God in his works." [23] Burke also refers to that "great chain of causes which, link . . . one to another, even to the throne of God himself," a throne we can ascend to through reason, and faith, even though the nature of God remains a mystery to us.[24] Also in the *Inquiry* he states, "The more accurately we search into the human mind, the stronger traces we everywhere find of His wisdom who made it."[25] These arguments for God's existence emerge from within the tradition of philosophical realism, which clearly affirms the capacity of the human mind to reach metaphysical conclusions by the sheer light of reason, in so far as this realm is the realm of the metaempirical.

It should be no surprise that for Burke the order of the universe is real and discoverable by the human mind, as he concludes in a letter in 1791: "I love order so far as I am able to understand it . . . for the universe is order."[26] And just as there is an order to the universe and an orderer, there is also a social order into which man is born, an order in which he is placed by the Providence of God, an order that brings with it not only stability but also a sense of self through a great mosaic of social strands, ties, and connections. It is an order that includes a great train of duties and obligations that infuse human life with meaning and continuity that does not preclude but rather serves to guide and direct gradual, slow, and almost imperceptible, but no less real, change. This is an "ancient order into which we are born. . . ." Moreover, "The place that determines our duty to our country is a social, civil relation."[27]

The radical materialism of the *philosophes,* conjoined with their abstract theory of rights, serves to atomize man and strip him of his sociality, as reflected in various "state of nature" and "social contract" theories. Burke, on the other hand, acknowledges the social nature of man, in which "[a]rt is man's nature." He maintains that "men are not tied to one another by paper and seals. They are led to associate by resemblances, by conformities, by sympathies. It is with nations as with individuals. Nothing," Burke continues and emphasizes, "is so strong a tie of amity between nation and nation as correspondence in laws, customs, manners and habits of life."[28] So crucial is this social dimension of human nature that Burke claims that "[m]en are never in a state of *total* independence of each other. It is not the condition of our nature."[29] Moreover, "Man, in his moral nature becomes, in his progress through life, a creature of prejudice, a creature of opinion, a creature of habits, and of sentiments growing out of them."[30] For Burke, these elements of prejudice, opinion, habits, and sentiments "form our second nature as inhabitants of the country and members of the society in which Providence has placed us."[31]

Human Nature and Tradition

Burke does not posit some presocial state of nature from which humans emerge by choice to form a society and from which they can as easily elect to defect if they withdraw their consent. This is to place the cohesion of society in an act of human will, and to predicate a social contract as the precondition for society. While Burke utilizes the language of "contract" at times, it is with a much-altered meaning from that of Locke or Rousseau. His notion of contract is not one into which we enter voluntarily, but one which, as a partnership, finds us already placed, rooted, and connected, for our own good and for the good of those with whom we are connected.

Burke's distinction between a first and second nature places the reality of human nature squarely within the context of the social fabric within which human beings fulfill their destiny, and in this regard it is in agreement with Aquinas, who writes, "Custom, and especially custom in a child, comes to have the force of nature. As a result, what the mind is steeped in from childhood it clings to very firmly, as something known naturally and self-evidently."[32] The development of a second nature through habit, custom, and the social weight of tradition lends ontological ballast to our being, socializing us, giving us a sense of order and purpose, and yet allowing for an existential freedom, permitting man, within the framework of tradition, to become, according to Burke, "in a great degree a creature of his own making, and who when made as he ought to be made is destined to hold no trivial place in the creation."[33]

This last statement is crucial if we are to understand Burke and the role of tradition in his thought. Clearly, through custom and habit, our social selves are shaped. But we are never simply creatures of our social environment, simply sponges upon the tradition of which we are a part. It is through an appreciation of the natural law, and of the tradition-transcending notion of natural justice, that tradition is for Burke capable of being judged and found wanting. We know that in the Hastings trial Burke repudiates a situational, geographical morality that would excuse the tyrannical, despotic behavior of the East India Company on the premise that the Indian subjects required repressive treatment in order to be governed. Burke argues that "the duties of men, in public and in private situations, are . . . to be governed by their relation to the great Governor of the Universe, or by their relation to mankind."[34] When addressing the Lords, Burke held that they are bound by the rules of "natural, immutable, and substantial justice."[35]

Thus, the real Burke stands in sharp contrast to the portrayal of Burke offered by Alasdair MacIntyre in his work *Whose Justice? Which Rationality?* MacIntyre argues that Burke's politics are completely bound to the traditional order to which Britain found itself tied at the end of the eighteenth century, and that all political judgments are internal to that order and permit for the application of no external standard.[36] Obviously, Burke's case in the Hastings trial rests almost exclusively on the premise that there *is* an external standard by which any tradition or practice can be judged. This is not to disavow the normal functioning of tradition and prescription in the determination of rights and duties and actions, for Burke did contend that "the British Constitution is a prescriptive Constitution, whose sole authority is that it has existed time out of mind."[37] When prescriptive government serves the benefit of the people and does not violate the purpose for which it exists, time does confer authority upon that government. Nonetheless, he also says explicitly that "the doctrine of prescription . . . is a part of the law of nature" and we know that this law is impressed immutably upon our human nature, coming as it does from God.[38] So, "*prescription* . . . gives right and title,"[39] and "[p]rescription is the most solid of all titles, not only to property, but . . . to government."[40] For example, Burke's opposition to slavery shows distinctly that the mere historical endurance of an institution does not provide sufficient warrant for it to claim the protective, moral mantle of prescription. No institution, however enduring, can claim justification if it violates and excludes an entire people based on arbitrary principles. Justification of any sort can only be granted when an institution serves "the good of the whole."[41]

We know that institutions and their practices may no longer serve the common good of a nation and therefore require reform. Certainly this was the situation that Burke set about to correct upon becoming Paymaster General, as he argued in his *Speech on Economical Reform*. Here he claims that when the reason for a practice no longer survives "it is absurd to preserve nothing but the burthen of them. . . . There is a time," Burke concludes, "when men will not suffer bad things because their ancestors have suffered worse. There is a time, when the hoary head of inveterate abuse will neither draw reverence, nor obtain protection."[42]

Returning to the earlier point concerning man being "a creature of his own making," Burke qualifies this in a manner that preserves a certain "existential freedom" within the parameters of custom and tradition: "Every sort of moral, every sort of politic institution, aiding the rational and natural ties that connect the human understanding and affections to the divine" assist in building "up that wonderful structure, Man."[43]

Ordered Liberty and Change

It was the tradition of freedom that the Americans brought with them, by and large, from England that Burke defends when he states, in his *Speech on Conciliation with America,* that "the people of the colonies are descendants of Englishmen. England, Sir, is a nation which still, I hope, respects and *formerly* adored, her freedom. The colonists emigrated from you when this part of your character was most predominant; and they took this bias and direction the moment they parted from your hands."[44] Burke defends a living, vibrant tradition of liberty with deep historical roots. He reveres this tradition not merely because it is historically rooted but because it has protected, and will continue to protect, the chartered rights of Englishmen.

Yet Alasdair MacIntyre, who seems to have a running battle with Burke, levels a further charge against the "Philosopher in Action." MacIntyre maintains that Burke embraces a tradition that is "dead," not living, and which, of all things, champions a "liberal individualism." (MacIntyre claims to find such a "liberal individualism" reflected especially in Burke's economics.)[45] And what is the difference between a "living tradition" and a "dead tradition"? "A living tradition," according to MacIntyre, "is an his-

torically extended, socially embodied argument, and an argument precisely in part about the goods which constitute that tradition." Moving to
the fundamental point, MacIntyre holds that "[t]raditions, when vital,
embody continuities of conflict. Indeed," he concludes in dramatic fashion, "when a tradition becomes Burkean, it is always dying or dead."[46]

Perhaps MacIntyre is right. After all, in the *Reflections on the Revolution in France* one indeed finds Burke extolling the "ancient, permanent
sense of mankind."[47] Elsewhere Burke contends that "our country is not a
thing of mere physical locality. It consists, in a great measure, in the
ancient order into which we are born."[48] Is this a static, retrogressive
concept of tradition, bound to the past for the sake of the past and fearful
of human liberation?

MacIntyre, however, misreads Burke. Not only does Burke hold to a
living, vibrant tradition, but he also holds that a horizon of intelligibility
and meaning transcends all traditions, that these traditions may be pru-
dentially judged thereby, as is made clear by his positions on the natural
law and the eternal laws of justice. His concept of a living tradition is,
indeed, developmental, a dynamic conservatism that is open to and seeks
the natural improvement of human society. In *A Letter to Sir Hercules
Langrishe on . . . The Roman Catholics of Ireland* he urges the enfran-
chisement of Catholics as something just and right, but he urges that this
process proceed by "*degrees.*"[49] He writes: "We must all obey the great
law of change. It is the most powerful law of Nature, and the means
perhaps of its conservation. All we can do, and that human wisdom can
do, is to provide that the change shall proceed by insensible degrees. This
has all the benefits which may be in change, without any of the inconveniences of mutation."[50]

What could be more reasonable? Ossified practices that violate the
"eternal laws of justice," such as the exclusion of a whole category of
people—even the majority, in Ireland—from the franchise, subjecting
them to abject penal laws, are an abomination. Yet, even here, Burke
urges gradual change. What could be more pointed about Burke's high
regard for both tradition and change than his fight for justice in America,
in Ireland, and in India? His fight for justice in the latter two countries is
based more directly and immediately on the claims of justice and natural

law, while his defense of America is grounded in a call for the restoration and recognition of the freedom that is part of the tradition of liberty Americans brought with them from England. But there is no necessary contradiction between these two contextually differentiated arguments.

In a letter to Adam Smith, Burke wrote that "the Nature of man . . . is always the same."[51] Even more pointedly, in his *First Letter on a Regicide Peace* he wrote that "men are not changed, but remain always what they always were."[52] If Burke were to speak for himself in this matter of whether he was defending a "dead tradition," he might reply to MacIntyre in the following manner: "The animating principles both of my philosophy of human nature and politics are those of change and stability. We have a common human nature. A stable feature of our common human nature is our capacity to reason as well as our tendency to submit to our passions. But I wish to emphasize also our second nature, which is shaped and formed by our prejudices, our opinions, our habits, and the sentiments that emerge from these. As I argued in the Hastings trial, all of these together 'form our second nature, as inhabitants of the country and members of the society in which Providence has placed us.'"[53]

Still, there is MacIntyre's further point, noted above, that "[t]raditions, when vital, embody continuities of conflict. Indeed when a tradition becomes Burkean, it is always dying or dead." Does Burke himself provide evidence to support MacIntyre's claim, since, as we noted earlier, he states that he "loves order" so far as he is able to comprehend it?

Burke might, again, reply that "I quite agree with MacIntyre's characterization of a 'living tradition,' as long as we recognize some bounds to the argument. There should be some measure of commonality between prescription on the one hand and the boundaries provided by the natural law and timeless laws of essential justice on the other. In fact, in the *Reflections* I referred to 'that action and counteraction which, in the natural and in the political world, from the reciprocal struggle of discordant powers, draws out the harmony of the universe. These opposed and conflicting interests . . . interpose a salutary check to all precipitate resolutions. They render deliberation a matter, not of choice, but of necessity; they make all change a subject of *compromise*, which naturally begets moderation.'[54] How, in all fairness, could my position be described as an embrace of a 'dead tradition'? Rather, I endorse the 'reciprocal struggle of discordant powers' as providing for checks and balances, insuring moderation and reflecting the actions of the universe."

Burke defends a moderating conservatism. He proclaims, quite rightly, that freedom is the birthright of all, or of none. He also recognizes that the spirit of freedom without restraint leads to excess. He argues that "society cannot exist, unless a controlling power upon will and appetite be placed somewhere."[55] For Burke, the best kind of liberty is ordered liberty, a liberty through which we establish bonds and ties not only with the living, but also with the dead and those yet to be born. Progress and improvement are possible, but not without minding the lessons and the goods bequeathed to us from the past. As Burke asserts, "People will not look forward to posterity who never look backward to their ancestors."[56] Tradition, habit, and customs, while undoubtedly sometimes the bearers of shackles and blinders, provide us with a storehouse of ancestral wisdom. The progress of the human mind is slow, and it assimilates the lessons and experiences of history in a deliberative, experimental manner.

For MacIntyre and other Burke detractors, it may appear that so venerable is the past to Burke that it is sufficient for a practice to have survived for it to be legitimate. It may appear to them that Burke believes that a *prima facie* argument can be made that a practice is good and venerable *because* it is old. Burke does in fact contend that the origins of particular societies and governments are frequently couched in violence and that "there is a sacred veil to be drawn over the beginnings of all governments."[57] Further, "those who pull down important ancient establishments, who wantonly destroy modes of administration, and public institutions . . . are the most mischievous, and therefore the wickedest of men."[58]

But this objection against Burke flounders when we insert the deleted portion of this oft-cited quotation: "Those who pull down . . . public institutions *under which a country has prospered* are . . . the wickedest of men" [emphasis added].[59] It is not the sheer weight of time elapsed that hallows traditions and institutions. While there is a Burkean presumption in favor of institutions and constitutions that have endured for a long period of time, Burke wishes to place this presumption within the context of a larger normative horizon (i.e., whether these institutions and constitutions have actually benefited a country).

An interpretation of Burke that places Burke's commitment to tradition within this larger normative horizon helps to explain Burke's analysis of abusive governments and the practicality of revolutions against them. Burke remarks in the *Reflections* that "governments must be abused and deranged indeed, before it [revolution] can be thought of; and the prospect of the future must be as bad as the experience of the past."[60] Indeed, to conclude that revolution is justified is not an easy judgment to render. But Burke's further remarks in the context of the Hastings trial provide some normative assistance in the matter. "Despotism," he says, "if it means any thing that is at all defensible means a mode of government, bound by no written rules, and coerced by no controlling magistracies, or well settled orders in the state. But if it has no written law, it neither does, nor can, cancel the primeval, indefeasible, unalterable law of nature, and of nations; and if no magistracies control its exertions, those exertions must derive their limitation and direction either from the equity and moderation of the ruler, or from downright revolt on the part of the subject by rebellion, divested of all its criminal qualities."[61] In other words, the normal societal presumption against the radical surgery of revolution can be overcome under the duress imposed by a truly despotic government.

Similarly, Burke's defense of ordered liberty can be understood only in light of Burke's larger metaphysical commitment to a moral realist conception of the human good, not to a "dead" historicism. Burke contends that our freedom flows from our nature as intelligent and reasoning beings. Burke writes of "the rational and moral freedom of individuals," of "that personal liberty" that contributes so much "to the vigor . . . and dignity of a nation."[62] Not only is freedom natural to all persons, it is their birthright. In Burke's *Letter to the Sheriffs of Bristol* he makes clear that "[l]iberty, if I understand it at all, is a *general* principle, and the clear right of all the subjects within the realm, or of none. Partial freedom seems to me a most invidious mode of slavery."[63] Yet our freedom is not meant to be unbridled because we are created by God to be social beings. Burke remarks that "[l]iberty, too, must be limited in order to be possessed."[64] For liberty to flourish it must have "wisdom and justice for her companions," Burke writes in his *Reflections*.[65] Moreover, he claims that "among a people generally corrupt liberty cannot long exist."[66] Thus, freedom is not true freedom if it is unbounded, unrestrained, and unlimited. Burke concludes that "[s]ociety cannot exist, unless a controlling power upon the will and appetite be placed somewhere; and the less of it there is within, the more there must be without. It is ordained in the eternal constitution of things that men of intemperate minds cannot be free."[67]

While Burke argues against the social contractarianism and individualism of figures such as Hobbes and Locke ("Men are never in a state of *total* independence of each other. It is not the condition of our nature"),[68] there is still a sense in which the individual, for Burke, is prior to society, and it is this sense that protects Burke from any charge of being a collectivist. For Burke, the individual is prior to society in the sense that society exists for the express purpose of aiding each person to perfect his moral nature. In this sense, the person does not exist for society and is prior to society in the order of final causality. Certainly, the text that so admirably pulls together Burke's resolution of the matter resides in that timeless passage for which Burke is so well known: "[Society is] a partnership in every virtue and in all perfection. As the ends of such a partnership cannot be obtained in many generations, it becomes a partnership not only between those who are living, but between those who are living, those who are dead, and those who are to be born."[69] This captures well Burke's notion of a "living tradition," one that provides the context for the realization of the individual's moral perfection through a partnership with society at large and, more specifically, through the small platoons within which we all live our lives. Burke thus committed himself to defending authentic progress and improvement based on a prior metaphysical commitment to a notion of the common good that eschewed both collectivism and liberal individualism.

Human Progress

It remains for us to consider whether for Burke genuine human progress is possible, or whether his is a politics of resignation, one that seeks to prevent the bad from becoming worse still.

Michael Freeman, in his *Edmund Burke and the Critique of Political Radicalism*, holds that the "dominant ideology of the Western World today" is quasi-perfectionism, and he attributes this ideology to Burke.[70] After all, Burke proclaimed, "In the long series of ages which have furnished the matter of history, never was so beautiful and August a spectacle preserved to the moral eye as Europe afforded the day before the Revolution in France."[71] And yet the French Revolution exploded on the scene, and ushered in, for Burke, the greatest evil and tyranny the world had yet witnessed. Burke bemoaned the advent of this revolution as the "subversion of that order of things under which our part of the world has so long flourished, and indeed been in a progressive State of improvement, the Limits of which, if it had not been thus rudely stopped, it would not have been easy for the imagination to fix."[72]

In truth, all human contrivances, whether individual or corporate, are flawed. In his *Speech on . . . the Duration of Parliaments*, Burke warned "[t]hat man thinks much too highly, and therefore he thinks weakly and delusively, of any contrivance of human wisdom who believes that it can make any sort of approach to perfection." Burke invokes the principle of unintended consequences, noting that every political good pursued will be attended by unintended "inconveniences," and that countervailing actions are required to overcome them.[73] Elsewhere, Burke declares that "[t]hose who expect perfect reformation, either deceive or are deceived miserably. . . . Indeed, all that wise men even aim at is to keep things from coming to the worst."[74]

If anything, the history of human society appears for Burke to manifest a cyclical movement rather than inexorable progress. He compares society "to a permanent body composed of transient parts" and notes that the whole appears to follow "the disposition of a stupendous wisdom moulding together the great mysterious incorporation of the human race," moving "in a condition of unchangeable constancy . . . through the varied tenour of perpetual decay, fall, renovation and progression."[75] In Burke's *First Letter on a Regicide Peace,* he forthrightly denies a science of history, holding that it is impossible to ascertain the "internal causes which necessarily affect the fortune of a state." He doesn't deny that there are such causes, but the full comprehension of them infinitely exceeds the powers of the human mind, and, even if they exist, they do not preclude the efficacy of human action. After all, "The death of a man at a critical juncture," Burke reminds us, "his disgust, his retreat, his disgrace, have brought innumerable calamities on a whole nation. A common soldier, a child, a girl at the door of an inn, have changed the face of fortune."[76] Indeed, human action, both individual and collective, is vital to the gradual progress and reform of the human condition.

We may reasonably conclude that for Burke progress is possible, has occurred at times, and has been undermined at others. And all this has taken place within the order of Providence, an order that will remain something of a mystery to us. Certainly Burke regarded God's providential design as mysterious in that, as he notes, God's "wisdom is not our wisdom, nor our ways his ways."[77] This design is not completely impenetrable, for there is what Burke refers to as "the known march of the ordinary providence of God," upon which are found "the rules of prudence" according to which we are to make both our ethical and political judgments.[78] But it is sometimes the case that we see demonstrated the extraordinary providence of God, as Burke refers to the ways of "the all wise but mysterious Governour of the world" who sometimes intervenes in history "to snatch nations from ruin."[79]

We cannot, however, rely on such occasional interventions to absolve us of our responsibilities. Instead, we "may assume that the awful author of our being is the author of our place in the order of existence; and . . . having disposed and marshalled us by a divine tactick, not according to our will, but according to his, he has, in and by that disposition, virtually subjected us to act the part which belongs to the place assigned us."[80] Thus, according to God's ordinary providence we find our assigned place in the order of existence; and we often find ourselves in situations that are the result of gradual, historically conditioned changes that in turn determine what our duties are towards each other. As Burke records, "But there we are; there we are placed by the Sovereign Disposer; and we must do the best we can in our situation. The situation of man is the preceptor of his duty."[81] Burke writes in *Reflections* of that "wonderful structure, Man; whose prerogative it is, to be in a great degree a creature of his own making"—and when so made and shaped in part by his own choices "is destined to hold no trivial place in the creation."[82] While we are in important respects creatures of our own making, providence calls us to a high standard: "We ought to elevate our minds," Burke declares, "to the greatness of that trust to which the order of Providence has called us."[83]

God calls us to greatness, and to realize this greatness we must exercise our freedom in a manner such that our nature is perfected, so that we might progress humanly in the order of virtue and in pursuit of the common good. To this end, God ordains the existence of the state: "He who gave our nature to be perfected by our virtue willed also the necessary means of its perfection. He willed therefore the state."[84]

If the order of providence has called us to greatness and, with the aid of the state, to the perfection of our nature, then obviously human progress is possible but not inevitable. Even if there is historical causation at work, the complete intelligibility of those causes escapes human comprehension, thus undermining the arguments of the eighteenth-century apostles of progress. Says Burke, "I doubt whether the history of mankind is yet complete enough, if ever it can be so, to furnish grounds for a sure theory on the internal causes which necessarily affect the fortune of a state." Burke does not deny "the operation of such causes, but they are infinitely uncertain, and much more obscure, and much more difficult to trace, than the foreign causes which tend to raise, to depress, and sometimes to overwhelm a community."[85]

Obviously, for Burke, the French Revolution took on an almost predetermined character as it appeared to march inexorably toward the Reign of Terror. Still, no matter how despairing the current thrust of events or history may be, we finally cannot comprehend the actions of the "Supreme Director of this great drama," who may dethrone kings and humble the great "under the dispensations of a mysterious wisdom."[86] While Burke concludes that we would be wise "to conform ourselves to that State of things which providence is pleased to direct or to permit,"[87] we must nonetheless do our best in whatever situation we find ourselves, "and leave the rest to the disposer of Events."[88] As he states in his *Correspondence*, "You perform a present Duty—and as to the future it must be committed to the disposal of Providence."[89] Thus, we do know that God wills the good, and yet permits evil to occur, and we continue to struggle within that providential order. Our obligation is not to discern God's complete providential design but rather to act in such a manner as to realize the goods appropriate to our nature as rational animals.

It is clear that progress requires change, and humans adapt best to change—that most powerful law of nature—gradually. "The march of the human mind," Burke declares, "is slow."[90] In his *Letter to the Sheriffs of Bristol*, Burke states that "nothing in progression can rest on its original plan. We may as well think of rocking a grown man in the cradle of an infant."[91] Burke reminds his constituents that without embracing reasonable change, consistent with the principles of liberty that are the inheritance of Englishmen, they risk permanently rupturing the "special relationship" between Britain and America.

Burke's defense of gradual change applies to the British Constitution as well. Burke chides those who "would settle the ancient Constitution in the most remote times exactly in the same form in which we enjoy it at this day—not considering that such mighty changes in manners, during so many ages, always must produce a considerable change in laws, and in the forms as well as the powers of all governments."[92] But proper change is not achieved by way of abstract theorizing, creating constitutions totally *de novo*, irrespective of the accretions of time. For Burke, the Constitution is the result not of one action, nor of the action of legislators at one moment in history. Instead, "the parts of our Constitution have gradually, and almost insensibly, in a long course of time, accommodated themselves to each other, and to their common as well as to their separate purposes."[93]

When it comes, however, to the ultimate principles of justice and morality, there *are* eternal, timeless truths. For Burke there are no new discoveries in the area of moral principles, in the principles of liberty that lay the foundation for just governance. And this will be the case well "after the grave has heaped its mould upon our presumption, and the silent tomb shall have imposed its law on our pert loquacity."[94] Burke remarks in his *Speech on Conciliation with America* that basic justice is indeed timeless: "Men are every now and then put, by the complexity of human affairs, into strange situations; but justice is the same, let the judge be in what situation he will."[95] Burke elsewhere refers to the "stable and eternal rules of justice and reason."[96]

There is a law of nature entailing change, and change, if it is to result in genuine human progress, must contribute to human flourishing. But, for the most part, Burke's philosophy of change, or reform, or human progress, basically involves preserving what has already been achieved over time and recognizing it as good. Applying this doctrine to the political realm, he explains that "I would not exclude alteration neither; but even when I changed, it would be to preserve. . . . I would make the reparation as nearly as possible in the style of the building."[97] A distinction is called for between the essential and the accidental in matters of change and reform. Renovation and reform entails the "union of permanence and change," leading Burke to declare "that in all our changes we are never wholly new." At the same time there must be "enough of the new to invigorate us," that we "may have the advantage of change without the imputation of inconstancy."[98]

In his *Speech on the Plan for Economical Reform* Burke contends that it is incumbent on wise governance "well to know the best time and manner of yielding what it is impossible to keep."[99] Burke scorns "those gentlemen [who] argue against every desire of reformation upon the principles of a criminal prosecution. . . . They are proud of the antiquity of their house; and they defend their errors as if they were defending their inheritance."[100] Burke urges "timely reform. Early reformations are amicable arrangements with a friend in power; late reformations are terms imposed upon a conquered enemy."[101] Thus for Burke, reform should be early (as the abuse is recognized to be the bearer of corruptible fruit) and temperate, "because a temperate reform is permanent; and because it has a principle of growth,"[102] hence sustaining the dynamic "union of permanence and change."

Political change through gradual reform ensures progress of a sort— a type of progress that embraces continuity and yet accommodates the necessity for change that inheres in the order of things, which is the order of nature. Still, Burke's philosophical realism rejects the unfettered optimism of the liberal progressivism of the eighteenth-century rationalist.

He recognizes in his *Letter to Monsieur DePont* in 1789 that "[t]here is, by
the essential fundamental constitution of things, a radical infirmity in all
human contrivances."[103] Once again we are reminded of Burke's admonition that "change shall proceed by insensible degrees,"[104] rather than by
the effort to eliminate all human infirmities.

Finally, the virtue of prudence must prevail if human progress is to
be secured. In fact, prudence is the first among the political and moral
virtues. "Prudence is not only the first in rank of the virtues political and
moral," Burke argues, "but she is the director, the regulator, the standard
of them all. Metaphysics cannot live without definition; but Prudence is
cautious how she defines."[105] And Burke's understanding of prudence provides a ready refutation of Freeman's claim that Burke is a "quasi-perfec-
tionist": "Prudence . . . will lead us rather to acquiesce in some qualified
plan that does not come up to the full perfection of the abstract idea, than
to push for the more perfect, which cannot be attained without tearing to
pieces the whole contexture of the commonwealth. . . . In all changes in
the state," Burke continues, "moderation is a virtue, not only amiable, but
powerful. It is a disposing, arranging, and conciliating, cementing virtue
. . . . Moderation . . . is the virtue only of superior minds. It requires a
deep courage, and full of reflection, to be temperate when the voice of
multitudes . . . passes judgment against you."[106]

Burke calls for a "public-spirited prudence." Such prudence includes—
and I utter this Burkean proclamation with some mixture of hesitation
and candor—"[t]oleration," which, "being a part of moral and political
prudence, ought to be tender and large." But the spirit of toleration must
be accommodated to a larger concern: "The good of the commonwealth is
the rule which rides over the rest; and to this every other must completely submit."[107]

For Burke, authentic human progress and development, politically
considered, is a necessarily imperfect and flawed movement towards the
realization of the "common good," a good which is not static, but dynamic, in that it can never be finally achieved in its entirety under our
temporal condition. Politically, progress is measured by political reason
in pursuit of the common good, which entails justice. "For," according to
Burke, "where there is no sound reason there can be no real virtue; and

madness is ever vicious and malignant."[108]

Finally, progress must be tempered by realism about the human condition. There will never be, nor should there be, a completely egalitarian society, if by this we mean a leveling of all distinctions and subordinations within society. In this regard, Burke calls upon "the great primaeval contract of eternal society, linking the lower with the higher natures, connecting the visible and invisible world, according to a fixed compact sanctioned by the inviolable oath which holds all physical and all moral natures, each in their appointed place."[109] We must recognize, Burke holds, "the happiness that is to be found by virtue in all conditions; in which consists the true moral equality of mankind, and not in that monstrous fiction which, by inspiring false ideas and vain expectations into men destined to travel in the obscure walk of laborious life, serves only to aggravate and embitter that real inequality which it can never remove, and which the order of civil life establishes as much for the benefit of those whom it must leave in a humble state as those whom it is able to exalt to a condition more splendid, but not more happy."[110]

Ultimately, for Burke the moralist, human progress is found in the moral perfection of each individual, each of whom is a member of a larger, historically grounded society with its own specific common good. History is the stage upon which the human drama unfolds, under the guidance of God's ordinary, and, at times, extraordinary providence.

The Problematic Relation between Practical and
Theoretical Virtue in Aristotle's Nicomachean Ethics

GERMAINE PAULO WALSH

One of the most intensely debated interpretive issues of Aristotle's
Nicomachean Ethics is the relation between practical and theoretical
virtue. In seeking to define the human good, which he associates with
happiness (*eudaimonia*), Aristotle examines a whole range of human
virtues or excellences, both moral and intellectual.[1] Aristotle indicates
that there is a tension, if not an inconsistency, between practical and
theoretical virtue, which has led scholars to dispute what Aristotle
ultimately poses as the role of practical and theoretical virtue in the good
life.

Throughout most of the *Ethics*, Aristotle asserts that there are a
variety of goods necessary to the achievement of happiness, including
wealth, honor, friends, and the particular moral and intellectual virtues.
Human happiness, Aristotle seems to argue, is achieved through a balanced acquisition of these goods, which satisfy various human needs and
capacities. However, in X.7–8, Aristotle seems to alter his position by
arguing that there is really only one good that brings about happiness:
theoretical wisdom or "contemplation" (*theoria*).[2]

The deepest disagreement among scholars concerns the reconciliation of X.7–8 with the rest of the *Ethics*. While the enigmatic statements

in X.7–8 have sparked much debate, two general interpretations have emerged.[3] According to one interpretation, generally referred to as the "exclusive" interpretation, X.7–8 contains Aristotle's definitive word on the highest form of human happiness. In light of Aristotle's statements in X.7–8, it is evident, according to adherents of this interpretation, that he presents two kinds of happiness: best is the theoretical or contemplative life (*bios theoretikos*), devoted to the perfection of intellectual virtue—or, more specifically, to the activity of strictly theoretical thinking—and "secondarily" good is the practical or political life (*bios politikos*), devoted to the exercise of moral virtue. According to supporters of the "exclusive" interpretation,[4] Aristotle's ultimate explanation of human happiness is based on the possession of one good, theoretical wisdom, given that in X.7–8 he clearly relegates the activity of moral virtue to a subordinate position.[5]

According to a second interpretation, referred to generally as the "inclusive" interpretation, Aristotle's statements in X.7–8 do not really signify a break with his earlier arguments, and thus do not imply that he presents two different explanations of happiness. Rather, human happiness is a composite achievement, requiring the development of a variety of capacities and the possession of a variety of goods. According to supporters of the "inclusive" interpretation,[6] Aristotle claims that the achievement of happiness must reflect the compound nature of the human person, and thus that all of those objects that he mentions throughout the *Ethics*, including the various moral and intellectual virtues, have some share in the happy life.[7]

My objective here is to cast light on this ongoing debate by examining Aristotle's presentation of "practical thinking" or "prudence" (*phronesis*) and "theoretical thinking" or simply "wisdom" (*theoria* or *sophia*).[8] The focus of my analysis is Aristotle's presentation of the intellectual virtues of practical and theoretical thinking in Book VI and Book X (specifically, X.7–8). Although I support the "inclusive" interpretation, I agree with those scholars who accept the "exclusive" interpretation in believing that Aristotle's arguments about theoretical activity in X.7–8 are in fundamental tension with his overall account of happiness. That is, I think it undeniable that Aristotle argues in X.7–8 that happiness, in its highest and most perfect form, consists solely in theoretical activity, whereas in the *Ethics* as a whole he argues that happiness consists in a range of choiceworthy activities that includes both practical and theoretical virtue. Although I agree with advocates of the "exclusive" interpretation in this regard, I maintain that Aristotle's account of theoretical activity in the *Ethics*, particularly in X.7–8, is presented in a way that invites critical reflection. In the first place, Aristotle invites his readers to compare the claims he makes in X.7–8 about the intrinsic goodness of theoretical activity with the claims he makes elsewhere about the intrinsic goodness of practical activity. In the second place, careful attention to X.7–8 reveals that Aristotle presents an argument about the nature of theoretical activity that, in certain respects, he subtly undermines. As such, rather than interpreting X.7–8 as Aristotle's clearest statement of the superiority of theoretical activity to practical activity, I argue that Aristotle's description of theoretical activity in X.7–8 is a kind of caricature of philosophic activity.[9]

The Book VI Account of Practical Thinking

Aristotle begins his examination of the "intellectual" virtues of practical and theoretical thinking in Book VI by stating that we need to define more fully what the attainment of virtue really requires. As Aristotle explains in his discussion of the moral virtues, the development of virtue requires more than having the proper habits. To have the kind of character necessary to respond correctly to the various circumstances of life, one must also have some kind of reasoning ability that guides one's actions. This is the ability that Aristotle refers to as "right reason" (*orthos logos*, 1138b18–21).[10] It is right reason, Aristotle maintains, that enables the virtuous person to "hit the mean," to keep his "eyes fixed on the target,"[11] particularly when it comes to situations in which general rules of action cannot deal adequately with particular circumstances. Yet as the description of right reason thus far ascertained "lacks clarity" (1128b24–25), the task at this point is to examine right reason more closely (1138b34–35).

In examining the sense in which reason directs the exercise of moral virtue, Aristotle reintroduces the theme of the "parts" of the human soul. In Book I, Aristotle remarks that we can best begin to understand the soul by distinguishing, "in speech," between its "rational" and "nonrational (*alogos*) part" (1102a27–31). By the opening of Book VI, Aristotle maintains, having completed our study of the nonrational part of the soul and its corresponding moral or ethical virtues, i.e., those of "character" (*ethos*), we may now move on to investigate the rational part and its corresponding "intellectual" virtues, i.e., those of "thinking" (*dianoia*, 1138b35–39a3).

Aristotle posits in Book I that we consider the soul to consist of two parts, but at the opening of Book VI he asks us to "assume" that the rational part of the soul is itself composed of "two rational elements" (1139a4–6): with one of these elements, we are able to apprehend or study (*theorein*) "the kinds of things whose principles (*archai*) are invariable," and with the other, "the kinds of things whose principles are variable" (1139a7–9). Our supposition that the soul can be divided in this way, Aristotle states, is based on another, more fundamental assumption: that a person can gain knowledge of a thing only if that thing, or something very similar to that thing, is already present in the person. That is, according to this theory, there is a certain likeness between the things whose principles are invariable and one part of our rational soul, and between the things whose principles are variable and another part of our rational soul (1139a10–13). In the *De Anima*, Aristotle discusses this theory of knowledge at length, and determines that although the theory does seem to hit upon some truth, it is nevertheless seriously flawed. For example, in the *De Anima* Aristotle attributes to Empedocles the theory that knowledge is possible only through an affinity between subject and object, and pokes fun at it by saying that according to this theory, Empedocles himself would be forced to "conclude that his god is the least intelligent of all beings, for of god alone is it true that there is one thing, strife, which he does not know, while there is nothing which mortal beings do not know, for there is nothing which does not enter into their composition" (*DA* 410b4–7).[12]

After stating that we should assume that the soul itself is composed of a rational and a nonrational part in Book I, Aristotle remarks that the truth of this theory is "irrelevant for our present purposes" (1102a32). Yet as Aristotle asks us to make another assumption about the parts of the soul—this time, regarding the two parts of the soul's "rational" part—it certainly seems plausible to assume that the truth of this theory has become quite relevant. Aristotle's tentative language about the divisibility of the soul in the *Ethics*, together with his criticism of the accompanying theory of knowledge in the *De Anima*, suggest that the assumptions he asks us to make about the various parts of the soul, and the specific virtues that accompany them, should be made conditionally. That is, we must try to determine whether this theory really corresponds to the facts, as Aristotle reminds his readers to do again and again.[13]

Since Aristotle indicates the tentative nature of this theory, one may wonder why he raises such suppositions about the soul's "parts" at all. One reason may have to do with the difficulties involved in studying things that are complex in nature. In making the analogy between studying a circle and studying the human soul in I.13 (1102a30–32), Aristotle suggests that because of the difficulty we face in trying to grasp things that have complex natures, we often have to posit the existence of distinct "parts" in order to get at the whole. As the example indicates, although a circle is really indivisible, one way by which we can come to understand it is by distinguishing between its "convex" and "concave" sides or "parts." Similarly, although the human soul is really indivisible, one way by which we can come to understand it is by distinguishing between its "rational" and "nonrational" parts. Even though we cannot see the whole of the human soul when we focus on one or another of its parts, we can at least begin to learn about the soul by studying it in this way.[14]

There may be, however, another reason for Aristotle's supposition about the soul's divisibility. It is on the basis of this assumption—i.e., that one "part" of the intellect is different from another—that Aristotle, in X.7–8, distinguishes theoretical activity from practical or political activity, and argues that the former is superior to the latter. That is, this "separability" of the intellect into theoretical and practical aspects enables Aristotle to present the possibility of an activity, indeed, of a way of life, that is free of the vulnerabilities and instabilities of practical activity. By arguing that theoretical thinking is superior to practical thinking, and thus more definitive of happiness, if not the essence of happiness itself, Aristotle may be attempting to save the study of the human good from being twisted or even destroyed by those who would be satisfied with

nothing less than absolute precision.[15] Given that practical activity is almost always imprecise and susceptible to error, it cannot be satisfying to
those who seek precision and certainty. I shall return to this theme in the
last section of this article.

In defining practical thinking, Aristotle explains that it is not simply
an intellectual achievement. The perfection of practical thinking is the
attainment of truth in regard to action (*praxis*, 1139a26–27). In describing the way in which we acquire the virtue of practical thinking, Aristotle
explains that since "thinking (*dianoia*) alone moves nothing" (1139a36), it
cannot, in itself, account for human action. In III.2, Aristotle states that
action is sparked by choice (*proairesis*), but in Book VI he explains that the
starting point of choice itself is "desire (*orexis*)[16] and reason (*logos*) for the
sake of something. That is why choice cannot exist without intellect
(*nous*) and thinking (*dianoia*) or without some characteristic (*ethikos*) or
disposition (*hexis*); for good action (*eupraxia*) and its opposite in action
cannot exist without thinking and character (*ethos*)" (1139a33–35). Only
with the combination of thinking and desire are human beings moved
toward an end, an end that is realized by "good action" (1139b5).

Aristotle's arguments in the opening chapters of Book VI suggest that
it is very difficult to acquire the virtue of practical thinking. To do so, one
must both understand and desire the good life, and this can come about
only over time, through much learning, discipline, and experience. Although Aristotle does provide a rudimentary explanation of theoretical
thinking in the opening chapters of Book VI, he does not explain how it is
that a person becomes theoretically wise, or the way in which the theoretically wise person's activity reflects the good life. Since theoretical
thinking involves a kind of knowledge that is distinct from knowledge of
human affairs, and has no bearing on action, it would seem that theoretical thinking, unlike practical thinking, does not depend upon desire, or on
one's overall character, since it involves only the "higher element" of the
soul's rational part, that element which is least tainted by the part of the
soul with desire. By the end of VI.2, it is thus unclear as to how one might
acquire the virtue of theoretical thinking.

Perhaps it is for this reason that, at the opening of VI.3, Aristotle asks
that we make a "new beginning," and proposes that we now assume there

to be five abilities or aspects of the soul that affirm or deny truth: art (*techne*), scientific knowledge (*episteme*), prudence (*phronesis*), wisdom (*sophia*), and intellect (*nous*, 1139b15–18). In explaining each of these intellectual abilities, Aristotle states that prudence, on the one hand, shares a certain similarity with art,[17] while wisdom, on the other hand, includes scientific knowledge and intelligence.[18] It thus becomes clear even after this "new beginning" that Aristotle's focus continues to be the distinction between practical and theoretical thinking.

The prudent person, Aristotle states, is said to "deliberate well with respect to what is good and expedient for himself," i.e., with respect to "living well" (1140a26–28).[19] The prudent person's deliberative abilities are not, however, limited to his own good, since he apprehends or studies (*theorein*) what is good for human beings in general, and thus is said to be "capable of managing households and cities" (1140b8–11). Thus the prudent person understands the political nature of the human person, recognizing that his own good, or the good of any one individual, "cannot exist without household management nor without politics" (1142a9–10). There is a connection, Aristotle suggests, between understanding human nature, i.e., the "political" nature of the human person, and the ability to deliberate well about what living the good life entails (1140a25–28).

Aristotle is careful to distinguish prudence, which is always associated with virtue, from "cleverness" (*deinotes*). While it is true that one cannot be prudent without also being clever, cleverness itself is not a virtue (1144a24–30; 1152a7–13).[20] What distinguishes the prudent person from the merely clever person, Aristotle argues, is that the prudent person's deliberative abilities are directed by an understanding of the proper end of human life, i.e., the good life, and of the means that are appropriate to this end (1144a34–38; 1142b23–25). The clever person's deliberative abilities, on the other hand, are used for bad purposes, such as plotting a murder, or a robbery, or a seduction. Aristotle's references to Priam in Book I suggest that there are cases in which a person may be genuinely prudent, and thus good, but nevertheless unable to obtain happiness.[21] That is, due to the role of fortune or chance in human affairs, goodness and happiness do not always coincide. Hence there is always a degree of vulnerability attached to practical activity. Aristotle maintains, however, that in most cases, the prudent person will attain happiness, since intentions and abilities are linked with results. Hence in general, the prudent person succeeds in achieving the ends he seeks. As Aristotle states,

> One may deliberate well either in an unqualified way, or relative to a qualified end. Good deliberation directed toward some unqualified end succeeds (*katorthoun*) with reference to that unqualified end; good deliberation directed toward some particular end succeeds with reference to that particular end. Accordingly, if to deliberate well is a mark of a prudent person, good deliberation is rightness with respect to what is expedient in reference to an end (1142b29–35).[22]

Aristotle argues that the attainment of both prudence and theoretical wisdom requires experience (*empeiria*). However, the experience required for prudence, Aristotle indicates, is more extensive in its nature, and hence requires more time to acquire, than the experience required for theoretical wisdom.[23] It is possible for "the young" to become theoretically wise in certain respects, such as in mathematics, since "the objects of mathematics exist by abstraction" (1142a8–17). However, it is not possible for "the young" to become prudent, since prudence, being "concerned with particulars," requires familiarity with experience, and this "requires much time" (1142a8–16). Experience is in fact so important to prudence, Aristotle states, that one should pay as much attention to the "undemonstrated assertions and opinions of experienced and older and prudent people," as one does to demonstrated truth, "for such people observe rightly because they have gained an eye from experience" (1143b12–14).

Aristotle refers to the complexity of prudence in remarking that those reputed to be prudent are said to have a variety of other intellectual capacities as well, such as judgment (*gnome*),[24] understanding (*sunesis*),[25] and insight (*nous*)[26] (1143a25–28). Aristotle's characterization of the prudent person as having insight is especially significant for one seeking to understand the difference between practical and theoretical thinking since insight, Aristotle states, "deals with ultimates at both ends of the scale" (1143a35–36). That is, with insight one grasps both "primary terms and concepts," which are unchangeable or invariable, and "ultimate particulars," which are contingent or variable (1143b1–5). By defining prudence as combining a certain kind of knowledge of universals—that is, knowledge of the general principles of ethical action—with knowledge of particulars, Aristotle suggests that the radical separation between theoretical and practical thinking, at least in regards to the human good, may not be absolute. In any case, after having characterized the prudent person in this way, Aristotle's statement that one may be "wise" without being prudent—that prudence, in short, is not an essential part of wisdom—seems incomprehensible.

In the final explanation of prudence as a virtue given in Book VI, Aristotle begins by offering an analogy between prudence and cleverness, on the one hand, and "natural virtue" and virtue proper, on the other hand. Before examining Aristotle's analogy, it may be helpful to consider Aristotle's remarks in Book III, where he introduces the notion of "natural virtue." In III.5, Aristotle considers the theory that the achievement of virtue does not come about through one's own efforts, but rather that each human person is inherently endowed with some kind of power or ability, like vision (*opsis*), which determines the goal or aim of his actions (1114b3–8). Aristotle rejects this theory as insufficient, arguing that if natural virtue alone directs human action, then it would not be possible for human beings to learn from each other about the proper aim of human life, or for them to redirect their vision in any way (1114b5–25). Aristotle recognizes that if this theory were true, virtue would be no more voluntary than vice; that the achievement of "virtue," if one were still to call it that, would have nothing to do with learning, effort, and personal choice. According to Aristotle, the type of character that a person develops is, at least in some way and to some extent, due to himself, and thus the theory that "natural virtue" alone determines each person's character is insufficient.[27] With this discussion in the background, we now turn to Aristotle's discussion of the relation between natural virtue and virtue proper presented in VI.13.

According to Aristotle, the difference between natural virtue and virtue proper is analogous to the difference between cleverness and prudence. Just as cleverness alone is similar to prudence though not identical to it, so too natural virtue, though similar to virtue proper, is not virtue (1114b2–4). While beasts and children are not blamed for acting on the basis of whatever natural virtues they possess, such behavior in an adult should be criticized, since "without insight (*nous*), they are harmful"

(1144b8–9).

> Just as a strong body in motion but without vision stumbles heavily because of its lack
> of vision, so it is in the matter we are considering. If a person acquires insight (*nous*) it
> makes a great difference in his action. It is only then that his disposition, though similar
> to the corresponding natural disposition, will be virtue in the full sense. Just as there
> are two kinds of dispositions in the part of the soul which forms opinions, cleverness and
> prudence, so also in the moral part of the soul there are two dispositions, the one being
> natural virtue and the other virtue in the full sense, and of these the one in the full sense
> cannot come into being without prudence (1144b11–18).

Because the achievement of virtue requires prudence, Aristotle goes
on to argue, "some thinkers," Socrates in particular, mistakenly assert
that "every virtue is a species of prudence" (1144b18–19). The Socratic
account of virtue is thus "partly right and partly wrong," Aristotle claims;
while Socrates "was wrong in regarding every virtue as prudence," he
was "right in saying that without prudence virtues cannot exist" (1144b19–
21). Our account of virtue, Aristotle states, "must go a little beyond that
of Socrates" (1144b26). In explaining the development of virtue throughout the *Ethics*, Aristotle takes care to show that no one human capacity
or "part" of the soul is alone sufficient to achieve virtue, not even the
"intellectual part" of the soul. Virtue involves intellectual abilities, desires, and dispositions, which combine in each individual to form character. If any one of these is lacking or defective, a person will not be virtuous in the complete sense of the word.

With all of this in the background, Aristotle is now in the position to
state the fundamental difference between his understanding of virtue and
that of Socrates. Virtue is not merely a disposition "in accordance with
right reason" (*kata ton orthon logon*), as Socrates maintains, but one
which is "accompanied by right reason" (*meta tou orthou logou*, 1144b27–
28). That is, while Socrates attributes one's action, and the overall state
of one's character, to the guiding force of reason or knowledge alone,
Aristotle attributes the development of character to reason along with
other capacities. In other words, Aristotle would say that one cannot understand the character of any particular person without grasping the extent to which the various capacities of reason, desire, and disposition are
developed, and the way in which these various capacities interact.[28] Thus
Aristotle recognizes an alternative that Socrates did not think possible:

the "parts" of the soul can achieve a kind of "friendship."[29] For Aristotle, the achievement of virtue entails the *cooperation* of the various "lower" capacities *with* reason, rather than their being simply *mastered by* reason.[30]

With this account of virtue, Aristotle, unlike Socrates, attributes "qualified" senses of virtue to various human beings, depending on the "natural virtues" with which they are endowed, the way in which they are educated, the extent to which they appropriately train their desires, and the extent to which they develop their intellects. For Aristotle, these various capacities, though distinct, are related in such a way that each affects, and is affected by, the others.

The Book VI Account of Theoretical Thinking

In VI.7, the only chapter devoted solely to wisdom (*sophia*)[31]—"the most accurate form of knowledge" (1141a16)—Aristotle begins to make his case that theoretical thinking is superior to practical thinking, and that the exercise of this seemingly amoral and apolitical activity is the most definitive expression of human happiness. At the opening of VI.7, Aristotle remarks that there are two different opinions about what wisdom is. According to one opinion, those who excel in art or craftsmanship (*techne*), i.e., those with skill in regards to the production of particular things, are said to be wise (1141a9–12). According to a second opinion, those who are "wise in general" rather than in any "particular or qualified sense" are called wise (1141a13–14). One may be surprised to note that Aristotle does not mention that according to another common opinion, those who excel in politics and legislation are said to be wise, even though he does report this opinion elsewhere.[32]

Furthermore, while one might expect that Aristotle would eventually follow his usual procedure of showing how the various opinions are in some sense correct and in others incorrect, he does not do so. Rather than going on to argue that to be wise in the fullest sense, one must have abilities that combine aspects of both opinions given, Aristotle accepts only the latter opinion. He rejects the first opinion, which maintains that to be wise, one must understand something about variability and particularity, and accepts only the second, which maintains that to be wise, one need understand only invariability and universality. The truly wise person, his argument indicates, grasps and focuses most intensely on the "highest things," those things that are absolutely unchanging or static.

The arguments supporting the claim that theoretical thinking is the highest kind of intellectual virtue, that it is wisdom properly speaking, are first developed in Book VI, though they are more fully expressed in X.7–8. The claim begins with an identification of superiority with permanence or immutability. "It would be absurd," he comments, "to regard politics or prudence as the best since a human being is not the best thing in the world" (1141a22–23).[33] As evidence of the inferiority of practical thinking to theoretical thinking, Aristotle remarks that even some nonrational animals seem capable of prudence. In making this point, Aristotle defines prudence as the ability to apprehend (*theorein*) what is good for oneself and for others of "one's own kind;" we can observe that even a nonhuman animal is "prudent" when it "entrusts itself" to another animal that "observes its interests well" (1141a25–27). For this reason, according to Aristotle, prudence is often attributed to those nonhuman animals "that display a capacity of forethought in matters relating to their own life" (1141a27–28).

This argument is strange in several respects. First, Aristotle makes it clear throughout the *Ethics* that prudence is an intellectual virtue, and hence a uniquely human capacity, essential to the good life. How then could any nonhuman animal possess an intellectual virtue? When comparing the capacities of human beings with other animals elsewhere in the *Ethics*, Aristotle is careful to state that we attribute certain human abilities to other animals only metaphorically.[34] The fact that Aristotle states such a strange opinion here without any refutation or qualification is quite puzzling.[35] Secondly, if one considers which animals most readily "entrust themselves" to others, one might think of "the young" of many species, and they tend to do so only until they mature. After having stated several times that "the young" are not fit to study the human good, could Aristotle now be suggesting that "the young" are in fact prudent after all? Finally, Aristotle has just defined prudence as the ability to deliberate well about one's own good, and yet the example he gives here is that prudence entails entrusting one's good to others.

To return to Aristotle's strange argument that one may be wise without being prudent, we turn now to the examples he gives of certain wise men. Because wisdom, it seems, is concerned only with invariable things, a person may be wise without being prudent. Some who are wise, in fact, such as Anaxagoras and Thales, seem to be totally lacking in prudence, since "they do not know what is advantageous to themselves" (1141b5–6). While Aristotle acknowledges that they possess knowledge that is "extraordinary, wonderful, difficult, and even superhuman," it is nevertheless "useless," he maintains, "because the good they are seeking is not human" (1141b7–8). Yet while prudence may be superior in usefulness, Aristotle indicates, it can never have the comprehensiveness or precision of wisdom, and hence is inferior.

Immediately after characterizing the wise person in this way—i.e., as someone who grasps unchanging, universal principles—Aristotle compares him to the prudent person, whose knowledge is tied to particulars. It is only with prudence, Aristotle says, that a person has the ability to understand and achieve the human good, to both "aim at and hit the best thing attainable by action" (1141b13–14). One who is prudent in the complete sense of the word grasps both the universals and the particulars that have to do with action. However, since good action depends on knowledge of particulars more than it does on knowledge of universals—since experience is more vital to the prudent person than abstract knowledge—certain individuals may lack the "universal knowledge" of the human good, and yet be "more prudent than those who have universal knowledge only" (1141b17–18). In arguing that knowledge of particulars is more important than knowledge of universals when it comes to the human good, Aristotle remarks, again rather mockingly, that a person who knows that light meat is wholesome, without knowing what sort of meat is light, will not produce health (1141b17–19); like "wise men" such as Anaxagoras and Thales, the kind of knowledge this person has is useless.

The Book X Account of Theoretical Thinking

As discussed in the previous section, there are some very unusual twists involved in Aristotle's analysis of prudence and wisdom in Book VI. He defines prudence as being essential to the achievement of the human good, yet goes on to claim not only that wisdom is superior to prudence, but that a person may be wise without being prudent, while simultaneously portraying certain "wise men" as being rather ridiculous.

At the close of X.6, Aristotle restates that happiness consists in "activities that conform with virtue" (1177a10) and goes on in X.7–8 to describe practical activity and theoretical activity as being incompatible. He repeats the claim made in Book VI that theoretical activity—or perhaps more accurately, a certain kind of theoretical activity—is superior to practical activity. He supports this claim with several arguments, then goes on to compare the theoretical or contemplative life with the practical or political life on the basis of the amount of external goods required by each. I shall examine each of these arguments in turn, and then comment on the significance of the closing statements Aristotle presents in X.8, where he asks a crucial question: Are the conclusions we have reached in harmony with the actual facts or deeds (ta erga) of life (1179a17–23)?

According to the first criterion, theoretical activity is of greater worth than practical or political activity because in engaging in the former, we are exercising our "best part" and hence our "highest virtue" (1177a12–14). We know that this is the activity of our "best part," Aristotle remarks, because it is with this part of the soul, i.e., the "theoretical intellect" (nous),[36] that we study the "highest things" (1177a19–20). Aristotle refers to this part, i.e., the "theoretical intellect," as the "divine part of the soul," and remarks that it is vastly superior to the "compound soul" (1177b27–32). While practical activity, Aristotle states, is inextricably linked with the passions and the compound soul, the theoretical intellect is "separate from" the compound soul and its merely "human" virtues (1177b28–78b23).

However, as discussed previously, although Aristotle's supposition about the soul's divisibility was made conditionally, and was presented as being very problematic, it is upon this supposition that Aristotle's entire defense of the "theoretical life" rests.[37] Furthermore, even if one does accept the supposition that the soul is composed of distinct parts, one must nevertheless acknowledge that the higher part, however "divine" it might be, is still only a part, not the whole. The compound nature of the human soul, Aristotle indicates elsewhere, cannot be completed or ful filled by engaging in any one activity. Aristotle has made it clear through-out the *Ethics* that the perfection of practical activity is essential to the completion of human life, particularly in his discussions of justice and friendship. By arguing that justice and friendship are essential to the achievement of the human good, Aristotle indicates that acknowledging the "political" nature of the human person is essential to the human good, and thus that any person who devotes himself solely to theoretical activity cannot fulfill his potential for virtue.

The next two arguments Aristotle presents to prove that the activity of theoretical contemplation constitutes human happiness are first, that such contemplation is the "most continuous" activity in which a person can engage (1177a22), and second, that this activity brings pleasures of marvelous "purity" and "permanence."[38] Upon considering these arguments, we may recognize a certain similarity between them and the description of the Platonic notion of the good that Aristotle criticizes in Book I. In criticizing the Platonic position, Aristotle redirects the focus of philosophic attention from abstract universals to particular instances of the good by showing that goodness and permanence do not necessarily coincide.[39]

While it may be true that "we are able to contemplate (*theorein*) continuously," as Aristotle asserts in X.7, "more easily than to perform any kind of action" (1177a22–23), it is also true, as this very argument tacitly acknowledges, that there is no one activity that human beings can engage in continuously. In calling attention to our compound nature, which makes it impossible for us to enjoy either perfect continuity or pure and permanent pleasure, Aristotle's statements in X.7 urging us to strive to have "divine thoughts" and to "become immortal as far as possible" have a particularly ironic ring (1177b27–78a4).[40] While it may be true that a simple being always engages in a single activity, such is not the case for a compound being (1154b24–27). As Aristotle states at the close of Book VII, "there is no single object that continues to be pleasant forever, because our nature is not simple" (1154b21–22).

Furthermore, in a well-known passage in X.4, Aristotle repeats this claim, explaining that human beings cannot experience pleasure continuously because pleasure always accompanies activity, rather than being separate from it, and no one activity can be engaged in continuously by a human being (1175a3–20). Some scholars—including many of those subscribing to the "two lives" version of the "exclusive" interpretation[41]—maintain that Aristotle's account of pleasure in Book X is not genuinely philosophic, unlike the account of pleasure he presents in Book VII. In the words of one noted supporter of the "two lives" view, the Book X account of pleasure is subordinated to the "moral-political horizon."[42] One of the reasons cited in support of this view is Aristotle's supposed "dismissal" in X.4 of a genuinely philosophic question: "the question whether we choose life for the sake of pleasure or pleasure for the sake of life" (1175a17–19).[43] However, the claim that Aristotle's treatment of pleasure in Book X is not philosophic is unwarranted. Aristotle argues that we need not answer the question by choosing between pleasure and perfect activity because "[pleasure and activity] are obviously interdependent and cannot be separated" (1175a19–20). That is, like the convex and concave aspects of a circle, and the "parts" of the soul, the two (i.e., choosing activity for the sake of pleasure, and pleasure for the sake of activity) are distinct "in speech," but inseparable "by nature."

For those who wish to live a life that is continuously pleasant, a life of pleasure without pain, the compound nature of the human person may be a source of dissatisfaction, and even contempt, since it obstructs continuity. For others, however, this compound nature can be a source of satisfaction, and even admiration, since hand in hand with the difficulties of life is the opportunity to overcome those obstacles and risks that stand in the way of human fulfillment. However harsh the results of having a compound nature may be, Aristotle points out that these difficulties can in some sense be overcome by the pleasure and permanence offered in friendship.[44] Simply being in the presence of one's friend, Aristotle states, brings pleasure (1170b3–11). Furthermore, it is friendship that provides human beings with the highest degree of permanence or continuity, since by "sharing each other's words and thoughts" over the course of a lifetime (1170b13), friends remain friends throughout all the changes in their lives.

Not even with friendship, however, can human beings wholly overcome vulnerability. Since one's happiness is dependent upon one's friend, who, unlike the "invariable things," may change—e.g., one can lose a friend through death—the stability that friendship offers is not without certain risks. In the face of such risks, some people may prefer a life devoted to theoretical contemplation to one that embraces these inevitable risks and difficulties. It is significant that, after devoting two whole books to the centrality of friendship in the good life, Aristotle never speaks of the theoretical contemplator of X.7–8 as having or needing friends, only "co-workers" (1177b1). By neglecting or refusing to love any person more than they love theoretical contemplation, those who engage in the kind of theoretical activity described in X.7–8 can avoid these risks. But while it may be true that those who avoid friendship and practical activity avoid certain risks and pains, it is also true that such people fail to experience the greatest pleasures that are available to human beings, the pleasures inherent in the shared lives of friends.

The fourth argument Aristotle presents to show that happiness is found in the activity of theoretical contemplation is that such contemplation is the most self-sufficient activity available to human beings. "The wise person," Aristotle states, "is able to study by himself, and the wiser he is the more he is able to do it" (1177a27–34). However, the definition of self-sufficiency that Aristotle gives in Book I (1097b8–12) and reconfirms in Book V (1134a26–27) is not that of a solitary or isolated individual. The person who is self-sufficient possesses all of those objects that are required for happiness, including both a certain level of material goods, and relationships with other people—parents, children, friends, etc.— all of which are necessary for human beings to fulfill their "political" nature (1197b9–12).[45]

As several scholars have pointed out, the self-sufficiency that Aristotle ascribes to the contemplator of X.7–8 invites comparison to the similar, though seemingly "less perfect" self-sufficiency of the magnanimous person described in IV.3.[46] While it is true that Aristotle's remarks invite such comparison, one who understands Aristotle as arguing that self-sufficiency is free of dependency and association with others is mistaken. It is precisely this erroneous understanding of self-sufficiency that ultimately undermines the virtue of both the magnanimous person and the theoretical contemplator. Aristotle's arguments in IV.3 suggest that magnanimity that does not acknowledge the "political" nature of the human person leads to a kind of paralysis that is an obstacle to moral action and friendship, which are essential to human fulfillment. Similarly, his arguments in X.7–8 suggest that a kind of theoretical activity that does not acknowledge the "political" nature of the human person is an obstacle to human fulfillment.

Aristotle's fifth argument in support of the claim that theoretical contemplation is the activity most conducive to happiness is that it is loved for its own sake, producing nothing beyond itself (1177b1–3). This argument, however, like that about the permanence offered by contemplation, is in pointed tension with the arguments Aristotle makes in Book I that criticize the Platonic notion of the good.[47] In Book I, Aristotle criticizes the Platonic understanding of the good for failing to recognize that both those goods that fulfill a final end and those goods that fulfill an intermediate end are intrinsically good.[48] It is for this reason that Aristotle can claim that moral action is intrinsically good, desirable both for its own sake and for the sake of happiness.

In making the claim about theoretical contemplation being loved for its own sake and producing nothing beyond itself in X.7, Aristotle calls attention to the fact that human action cannot exist in a vacuum, separate from effects or consequences of any kind. Virtuous actions, after all, affect both the agent who performs them and those with whom the agent associates. It may strike one as strange to consider that Aristotle states explicitly in Book I that the exercise of moral virtue is good because it fulfills an intermediate end, and then argues in X.7 that it is not intrinsically good because it aims at an intermediate end, rather than a final end.

There are some striking parallels that become especially noticeable at this point: the relation between pleasure and activity, the discussion of the circle's convex and concave aspects, and the examination of the soul's parts. All of these, Aristotle indicates, are separable "in speech" but not "by nature." Yet Aristotle's arguments in X.7 about contemplation being loved for its own sake and producing nothing beyond itself imply, to the contrary, that knowing and doing, or theoretical activity and practical activity, are separable. Again we may recognize a similarity between Aristotle's claim that the highest human activity has nothing to do with results, and his previous arguments about the continuity and permanence that contemplation offers. Since theoretical contemplation neither affects nor is affected by others, but rather is completely self-contained, it is an activity that provides the contemplator with a way to escape from the possibility of misfortune. In other words, Aristotle again describes contemplation in such a way that it is particularly appealing to those who would rather not accept the inevitable vulnerabilities of human life, or who are unwilling to risk the pain one experiences when one's intentions prove unsuccessful, be it due to error in deliberation, or the effects of chance.

In Book VI, as discussed previously, Aristotle argues that although intended results are sometimes beyond one's own control, it is nevertheless true in general that goodness and happiness coincide, that intentions and effects are linked.[49] But Aristotle's arguments about the complete self-containment of contemplative activity suggest his recognition that for some people, such generalities are not satisfactory. For such people, indeed, contemplative activity may be satisfactory, since it is beyond the realm of failure or disappointed expectations. Yet even after describing contemplation in this way, as an activity that supposedly provides supreme pleasure, continuity, and self-sufficiency, Aristotle subtly indicates that even the contemplator is subject to vulnerability, since his happiness requires "a complete span of life" (1177b24–25).

In making his sixth argument to demonstrate that happiness is found in contemplation, Aristotle remarks that contemplation is the only activity in which genuine leisure is found. This claim, like the previously discussed criteria presented in X.7, relies on some assertions that are in stark contrast with arguments Aristotle makes elsewhere. In the first place, part of Aristotle's argument about the inferiority of politics to contemplative activity with respect to leisure is based on an association of political action with military pursuits (1177b6–7). In the *Politics*, however, Aristotle harshly criticizes those regimes that make this very association. By collapsing political and military pursuits together, such regimes, according to Aristotle, are able to preserve themselves in times of war, but come to ruin when war ceases, since they do "not know how to be at leisure" (*Pol* 1271b5–6 and 1334a 2–10).

Secondly, in *Politics* VII.15, Aristotle states explicitly that philosophy, justice, and moderation are all activities of leisure.[50] The only distinction he makes in regards to them is that philosophy is always an activity of leisure, whereas justice and moderation are activities both of leisure and of occupation. This dual function of justice and moderation—i.e., the fact that they are not always activities of leisure—does not lead Aristotle to conclude that they are in any way less essential than philosophy in the achievement of the good life. To the contrary, Aristotle argues quite emphatically that justice and moderation are particularly crucial for those enjoying good fortune and the opportunity for leisure, since such blessings can lead to excessive pride (*hubris*).

> There is, then, a need for much justice and much moderation on the part of those who are held to act in the best way and who have all the gratifications that are regarded as blessings, like those—if there are such—whom the poets assert are "in the islands of the blessed." For these will be most particularly in need of philosophy, moderation, and justice to the extent that they are at leisure in the midst of an abundance of good things of this sort (*Pol* 1334a25–34).

Aristotle's argument about leisure in *Ethics* X.7, however, suggests that it is precisely this dual character of justice and moderation that makes them inferior to theoretical activity. While Aristotle goes on to retreat somewhat from his association of politics with military pursuits further along in X.7 (1177b8–13), he nevertheless claims that political activity is "unleisurely" and inferior to theoretical contemplation because the end it serves is intermediate, rather than final. This is evident in his claim that statesmen—i.e., those who are most actively engaged in political activity—unlike contemplators, seek things beyond the activity in which they are engaged. Statesmen pursue "advantages such as power, honor, or at least happiness for the statesman himself and his fellow citizens, and that is something other than political activity" (1177b13–15).

Aristotle's argument here about the inferiority of political activity seems to be based on the fact that politics serves an intermediate end, rather than a final end. Yet the logic of this argument, as discussed previously, undermines one of the most fundamental principles of Aristotle's whole theory of the human good. Aristotle quite explicitly criticizes the Platonic understanding of the good for failing to adequately distinguish between final and intermediate ends. For Aristotle, unlike Plato, both

those goods that serve an intermediate end and those that serve a final
end are intrinsically good. It is for this reason that, for Aristotle, the
intrinsic goodness of political activity is assured. By identifying philosophy, justice, and moderation as appropriate activities of leisure, Aristotle
indicates that the human good is a complex achievement. In linking these
three, Aristotle suggests that the human good can be destroyed or ob-
structed by the absence of any one.

The theoretical activity described in X.7–8 is at odds with the political nature of the human person, and for this reason is fundamentally flawed.
To correct this flaw, Aristotle seems to suggest, those engaged in theoretical activity must find a place for the moral virtues, particularly justice and moderation. In his portrayal of theoretical contemplation,
Aristotle indicates that the desires for certainty, self-sufficiency, pure and
continuous pleasures, and invulnerability, can be so misdirected that they
induce human beings to seek satisfaction in some realm beyond that of
human imperfection. By emphasizing the importance of the virtues of
justice and moderation along with theoretical activity, Aristotle indicates
how these potentially destructive desires can be checked. With justice
human beings remember their political nature and their dependency on
others, while with moderation human beings are able to rein in those
very drives that often make it difficult to accept the fragility of human
happiness.

After presenting these arguments to indicate the kind of happiness
that is available to those who devote themselves to theoretical contemplation, Aristotle makes the well-known remark that the practical or
political life is happy only in a "secondary" sense, since it can offer only
"human" happiness (1178a8–9). The virtues of the person who leads the
practical or political life are inferior, Aristotle states, because they belong
only to our compound nature (1178a19–23). Yet Aristotle calls this extraordinary claim into question immediately after he states it, acknowledging that everyone, including even the contemplator, is subject to the
needs of a compound nature, since everyone is dependent upon the neces-
sities of life.[51] It is impossible, Aristotle states, to achieve even the most
supreme form of happiness without external goods (1178a24–27 and
1178b34–37). He then compares the amount of external goods required

by the contemplator with the amount required by the person who leads the practical life. Although Aristotle initially indicates that the practical person needs more than the contemplator, since the performance of virtuous acts is always dependent on external goods, whereas theoretical study is not, he ultimately concludes that it is possible to live the practical or political life even if one's means are moderate (1179a3–5). In reporting that both Solon, a "wise" statesman, and Anaxagoras, a "wise" contemplator, acknowledge that the achievement of happiness requires only moderate means (1179a10–17), Aristotle points to the common ground between theoretical and practical activity immediately after having argued as to their radical separateness.

Near the end of X.8, Aristotle states that we must now judge the theory we have reached in light of the actual deeds or facts (*ta erga*) of life, "for it is in them," he says, "that the decisive element lies.... If they are in harmony with the deeds we must accept them and if they clash we must assume that they are mere words" (1179a18–23). That is, theory must pass the test of sound experience, of the deeds of life, to be considered valid. It is in these final statements that the claim that happiness consists solely in contemplative activity is most directly called into question.[52]

The deeds or experiences of life to which Aristotle refers in order to test this theory about contemplative happiness are the "rewards" that the gods grant to those human beings who imitate divine activity by engaging in contemplation. That is, if this theory that contemplation is the highest, most godlike activity were true, according to Aristotle, one would expect certain actions on the part of the gods. The gods would rejoice in that which is best and most akin to themselves, namely, the activity of the theoretical intellect (*nous*), and they would requite with good those human beings who love and honor this aspect of their intellects (1179a25–29).

This expectation is strange for several reasons. First, it attributes moral activity to the gods, implying that the gods act to requite good with good. Yet the description of divine activity that Aristotle has presented thus far makes this expectation impossible. Shortly before making this argument, Aristotle remarks that attributing moral actions to the gods is ridiculous (1178b8–18). Divine activity, he maintains, is completely self-contained—"thought thinking itself" (*nous noesis*), as he says in the *Metaphysics* (1074b15–1075a11). The gods then could have no awareness, let alone concern, for human beings.

We must try to understand why Aristotle ends his examination of theoretical contemplation by attributing action—that is, other-regarding moral action—to the gods. Does he really mean that the gods act in this way? If this is the case, then divine activity does not consist merely in self-contained contemplation, but also in the exercise of the moral virtues, such as justice and generosity, in which case the theory about happiness being found solely in contemplative activity is not sound. If, on the other hand, Aristotle does not really mean that the gods engage in moral action, then why does he make their action, their requiting good with good, the "proof" of his theory? What Aristotle's final remarks in X.8 suggest, I believe, is that in considering what we know from experience, from the "deeds" of life, the "highest" activity, at least for human beings, must combine thinking and doing. The best activity cannot be one that radically dissociates knowledge from action, or theoretical activity from practical activity. The best activity, the good life, includes both.

The Evolution of Catholic Social Thought in the Last Two Centuries

GERALD A. McCOOL, S.J.

Father Francis Canavan has devoted a great deal of his energies to the study of Edmund Burke and the exposition of what is known today as Catholic social thought. From the point of view of their content a certain resemblance between Burke's political philosophy and contemporary Catholic social thought seems obvious enough. As the late Sir Ernest Barker once remarked, in a conversation with Father Canavan, "Burke's thought had a Catholic cast." For example, the conception of representative government that Burke defended in his statement on the role of a member of Parliament does not differ very greatly from the proper role of an elected representative elaborated in the philosophy of Jacques Maritain, the twentieth-century Thomist whose defense of democracy influenced the teaching of Paul VI.[1] Like Leo XIII, the great pioneer of modern Catholic social thought, Burke refused to accept the rationalist conception of society entertained by Enlightenment philosophies. For Leo XIII, as for Burke, rejection of the Enlightenment theory of government was based upon a shared pre-Enlightenment conception of practical reason, human nature, and historical tradition. Burke and Leo also believed that a legitimate place should be granted to its traditional religion in a nation's life and culture, a place that Enlightenment social theory was unwilling to concede.

Burke at times was considered to be sympathetic to Catholicism. In fact, in his own lifetime, he was suspected on occasion of being a crypto-Catholic. Whether that suspicion was justified or not, the similarity between Burke's political philosophy and Catholic social thought as we know it today is not likely to be traced to the influence upon Burke's thinking of the eighteenth-century Catholicism with which he would have come into contact. For, as is Burke's own approach to politics, modern Catholic social theory is built upon an older form of thought that the Catholics of Burke's own generation had generally abandoned and which they had practically forgotten. After the French Revolution, Catholics would be obliged to revive that forgotten form of thought and develop its speculative resources before they would be able to enter into serious dialogue with the liberal culture of the bourgeoisie or with the revolutionary socialism of the nineteenth century. The Catholic Church that would go about that work in the second half of the nineteenth century would be a Church notably different from the Church of the *ancien régime* in which Burke's own contemporaries had lived. Its ultramontane ecclesiology, the influence within it of a restored Thomist philosophy, and the radically different context in which the Catholic Church was forced to come to terms with the nineteenth-century liberal state would have been quite foreign to the Catholics of Burke's own generation.

The first major difference between the Catholic Church of Burke's generation and the Church with which present-day Catholics are familiar is the position of legal and moral leadership possessed by the contemporary papacy. A second significant difference is the change in Catholic theology and canon law brought about by the revival of pre-Enlightenment Catholic philosophy and the consequent decline of the Enlightenment ecclesiology that had been normative during much of the eighteenth century. A third important difference, connected with the second, is the disappearance of eighteenth-century episcopalism, Gallicanism, and Josephinism from mainstream Catholic thought

The end of the *ancien régime* seemed at first to be the final blow to a papacy that had been progressively weakened by the anti-papal religious policy of eighteenth-century Europe's absolute monarchies.[2] As the result of the French Revolution, venerable legal forms, long-established ecclesi-

astic principalities, and a multitude of established religious and educational institutions, which had slowly come into being through long centuries of Christian history stretching back beyond the reign of Charlemagne
to the earliest days of medieval Europe, were completely destroyed. In
1801, Napoleon forced the papacy to make its peace with France in a
concordat whose terms were favorable to the emperor. In 1803, the French
emperor secularized the German prince bishoprics, whose origin went
back to feudal times Finally, in 1806, Napoleon brought the Holy Roman
Empire itself to an end, thereby forcing Catholics into a lasting position
of political and cultural inferiority in the new German states. The ultimate indignity to the papacy was inflicted when, in 1809, Napoleon,
annoyed by the refusal of Pius VII to ally the papacy with the emperor in
his religious policy, occupied Rome, arrested the pope, and carried him
off as a prisoner to France.

We are aware today that the captivity of Pius VII was a turning point
in the history of the papacy. The patience and dignity with which Pius VII
endured his ordeal provoked a reaction of sympathy for him. That reaction was the starting point for the nineteenth-century devotion to the
pope as the symbol of a suffering Church unjustly persecuted by anti-
Catholic secular regimes. In that devotion, the person of the pope was
identified with the Church in the Catholic imagination with a directness
that eighteenth-century popular devotion had not stressed. Thus, in the
second half of the nineteenth century a number of strong popes were able
to assume a leadership position in the Church from which the institutional structure and legal forms of the *ancien régime* would have excluded them. The nineteenth-century Church was weaker in resources
than the Church of the *ancien régime* but it was stronger in its unity.
Freed, to a large degree, from its former identification with secular institutions, it became more conscious of itself as a purely religious society
distinct from secular society, with which its relations, at times, were
very difficult. The increased independence of the papacy, freed from the
restrictions that the eighteenth century had placed upon it, gave the pope
an immediate influence upon the Church that eighteenth-century popes
did not possess. From the pontificate of Pius IX until the present day,
Roman pontiffs have been very much aware of that authority and of the

obligation that it has placed upon them to assume a leading role in Catholic social teaching.

The Church of the *Ancien Régime*

On the intellectual level, the greatest help that the popes received in assuming a larger teaching role came from the revival of St. Thomas's social and political philosophy. In the sixteenth and early seventeenth centuries a brilliant Thomistic renaissance had taken place. Dominican theologians and moralists of major stature, Cajetan, Banez, and Vitoria for example, and equally distinguished Jesuit theologians, moralists, and political philosophers, like Bellarmine, Suarez, and Lessius,[3] turned their attention to the new and pressing problems of modern Europe and its colonies. Whatever may have been the deficiencies of Baroque scholasticism, the work of its great representatives resulted in a distinctively Catholic theology of grace that granted an intrinsic goodness and intelligibility to fallen nature, something the Augustinian theology of the Reformers could not give. Thanks to St. Thomas's philosophy of man and being, Baroque scholastics granted greater freedom to the human will under grace than either the Reformers or the Jansenists. Because he was a disciple of St. Thomas, Bellarmine could argue that the Church was a visible, perfect society with its own juridical structure distinct from the legal structure of the state. Bellarmine's Church was neither the invisible Church of the Reformers nor the purely private association that later liberal legal theory considered the Church to be. Thanks to St. Thomas, Bellarmine could also argue that, through their consent, the subjects of the state designated the legitimate possessor of the divine authority to rule it. Kings could not rule absolutely independently of that designation, as James I had claimed, through their immediately given divine right. Furthermore, even a king's legitimate authority was not unlimited in its scope. It could be restricted, for example, by the indirect power of the pope to intervene in matters that touched upon religion.[4] Relying on the social ethics of St. Thomas, the great Dominican jurist, Vitoria, was able to defend the natural rights of unbaptized Indians against their exploitation by Spanish colonists, and, on the basis of the same social ethics, the great Jesuit jurist, Suarez, produced his remarkable philosophy of law.[5]

After 1630, however, Baroque scholasticism fell into disfavor. The new physics of Galileo and the Cartesian revolution in philosophy called into question the Thomistic philosophy of knowledge, man, and being which had supported Baroque social theory. The Thomistic metaphysics of form and finality was excluded from the purely mechanical post-Cartesian world. Neither was there any place for Thomas's Aristotelian practical intellect in the post-Cartesian philosophy of knowledge that had as its ideal an impersonal, mathematical reason uninfluenced in its operations by the moral dispositions of its possessor. In reaction to the hostile pressure of the age, scholastic philosophy weakened and distorted its content in an unsuccessful effort to come to terms with contemporary rationalism. Ultimately, by the end of the century, even Jesuit theologians, like Benedict Stattler, were no longer using it.[6] Newer theologies inspired by Malbranche's amalgam of Cartesianism and Augustinianism became popular in France, and, since their metaphysics were incompatible with the metaphysics of St. Thomas, these seventeenth century theologies could no longer support the social teaching of the great Baroque theologians.

Nor indeed, except for Jesuits and Dominicans, were many theologians interested in doing so. In the seventeenth century, especially in France, a great resurgence of Augustinian theology and spirituality had taken place. Pierre de Berulle, the founder of the French Oratory, whose spirituality influenced great saints like Vincent de Paul, was profoundly Augustinian, and his thought ran counter to the Baroque humanism of Jesuit moralists like Suarez and Lessius. Jean du Vergier de Hauranne, abbe de Saint Cyran, was influenced by Berulle, and through Saint Cyran, so was the devout community of Port Royal, with which the name of Blaise Pascal will always be associated. In Pascal, the spirit of radical seventeenth-century Augustianism can be clearly seen: profound distrust of natural reason, an anti-Aristotelian philosophy of nature, moral rigorism, and a sense of human sinfulness that could have led to despair were it not for a profound trust in the saving love of Christ. Nothing could be farther from Pascal's thought than the optimistic philosophy and theology of Baroque social theory.

The "Augustinus" of Cornelius Jansen, Bishop of Ypres, rather than *The Spiritual Exercises* of Ignatius Loyola, provided the intellectual justification for his form of radical Augustinism and gave its adherents their name of Jansenist. Although, in its early days, Jansenism was a pious movement in the Church rather than a dissident one, Jansenist conflicts with the French crown and the Holy See over time engendered in its adherents a spirit of extreme hostility toward the Holy See. Anti-papalism joined to an increasingly sectarian habit of mind became a mark of eighteenth-century Jansenism, especially after Clement XI condemned its leader, Pasquier Quesnel, in the papal bull, *Unigenitus Dei Filius.* Since Jansenist lawyers were very often found among the judges and government officials in both France and Germany in the eighteenth century, their anti-papalism and their fanatical hatred of the Society of Jesus made them very dangerous enemies of both.

Jansensist anti-papalism was strengthened by its alliance with Gallicanism. Disputes between the theologians and canon lawyers of the pope and of the emperor had been frequent in the late Middle Ages, and the authority of the pope was seriously weakened during the Great Western Schism, when three rival claimants contended for possession of the papal office. The Council of Basle was able to end the Schism but, as a result, conciliarism emerged as a significant force in Catholic ecclesiology. Supreme authority in the Church, conciliarists claimed, was vested in her councils, and, apart from their decrees, the pope possessed little or no teaching authority of his own. By restricting the legitimate authority of the pope to the power conferred on him either by an ecumenical council or by the unanimous consent of her episcopate, conciliarism, and its associated movement, episcopalism, encouraged Europe's civil governments to impose restrictions of their own upon the Church, including the very effective exsequatur. A monarch's exsequatur was the explicit permission required for the promulgation of a papal bull within his kingdom. Thanks to the exsequatur, any civil government which wished to do so was able to forbid the publication of any authoritative papal teaching in its territory.

Modern France, however, was not content with the exsequatur. In 1505, Francis I forced the pope to grant the king of France the permanent right to nominate her bishops and abbots and the right to confer the greater part of her ecclesiastical benefices, and, in the early seventeenth century, Richelieu tried to bring the whole French Church under his own control with the aim of making himself, in effect, the Patriarch of France. In 1684, Bossuet helped Louis XIV have an assembly of French prelates issue the Declaration of the French Clergy; according to that famous document, France's civil government was independent of the Church in secular matters and, in religious matters, a council was superior to the pope. The pope's authority to teach was rigidly limited by the Church's canons and, even in matters of faith, papal teaching had no validity without the consent of the entire Church.

The practical anti-papalism of royal Gallicanism was given theoretical support by the systematic Gallicanism of Edmond Richer. For Richer, the Church's authority to teach was vested primarily in her parish priests rather than in her diocesan bishops. Consistent with that anti-hierarchical position, Richer associated himself with the Jansenist contention that exempt religious orders like the Society of Jesus had no legitimate place in the Church's ministry. As eighteenth-century Gallicanism spread beyond France and its influence was more widely felt, Catholic ecclesiology gradually became more compatible with the ecclesiology of the established Church of England than with either the older Baroque ecclesiology of Bellarmine or the newer ecclesiology of the nineteenth-century Catholic Church.[7]

Rationalism affected all sections of the educated classes in the eighteenth century, and, in their different ways, Jansenists, Gallicans, and the partisans of royal absolutism showed the effects of its influence. Working in coordination with each other, Europe's Bourbon monarchies engaged in an aggressive campaign to weaken the authority of the pope and bring Catholic institutions in their countries, as far as possible, under their own control.[8] One of the major obstacles preventing them from doing so was the Society of Jesus. The international network of Jesuit schools was controlled by an exempt religious order directly responsible to the Holy See. Consequently, Jesuit schools were, to a large degree, exempt from state control in their operation. For that reason, among others, in the last third of the century the Bourbon monarchies began their ruthless campaign of pressure on the pope to secure the suppression of the Society of Jesus. Hostile to the Jesuits for their own reasons, influential Jansenists worked effectively with the Bourbon governments toward the same end.

The force of their combined pressure proved to be too strong for the pope to resist and, in 1773, after the Jesuits had already been expelled from France, Spain, Portugal, and Sicily, the Holy See suppressed the order. With the loss of Jesuit resources, the papacy found itself without an influential defender and the political theory of Bellarmine was left without any influential base of support.[9]

The way was now open for state control of Catholic schools, as there was little or no counterweight to be found against the dominance of Gallican political and social theory. German Gallicanism took the form of Febronianism, so named after its leading proponent, Justinus Febronius, alias Nikolaus von Hontheim, suffragan bishop of Trier. Hontheim vested the Church's teaching authority in her bishops rather than in her priests, as Richer had done, but he was equally hostile to the Holy See. He allowed the pope no more than a primacy of honor and placed rigid restrictions on his right to teach. Without the collective consent of the whole Church, Hontheim claimed, papal teaching had no force.

The ecclesiologies of Bellarmine and Hontheim were as different in the philosophies that inspired them as they were in their aims. Bellarmine had been a scholastic theologian whose social thought was nourished by the philosophy of St. Thomas. Hontheim was a canon lawyer whose legal thinking had been shaped by eighteenth-century anti-Aristotelian epistemology and metaphysics. Bellarmine, as a Jesuit, set out to make the case for the pope's authority against the arguments mounted against it by Europe's absolute monarchies. The aim of Hontheim's ecclesiology, on the other hand, was to protect the powerful prince-bishops of the German Imperial Church against the efforts of Austria, Bavaria, and the Holy See to encroach upon their governing authority. For, as well as being prelates, the great archbishops were prince electors of the empire and, as such, secular rulers. They were drawn exclusively from the most powerful noble families of Germany, and the cathedral chapters that elected them were rigidly restricted in their membership to the aristocracy.

As secular rulers influenced by the Enlightenment in their own religious thinking, the prince-bishops, for political reasons, were sympathetic to the eighteenth-century movement to unite the Protestant and Catholic Churches in a single national Church and therefore showed little interest in clarifying the doctrinal differences between them. Jealous of their independence as princes of the empire, the prince-bishops also resented any endeavor by the Holy See to assert its authority in Germany and considered any such activity hostile interference by a foreign power in matters that should be reserved to them. For that reason, until the outbreak of the French Revolution active opposition to Rome was a consistent element of their policy. In 1786, for example, almost on the eve of the Revolution, under the influence of the archbishop electors of Mainz, Cologne, and Trier, the Congress of Ems officially approved the major theses of Hontheim's ecclesiology. Papal power, the Congress declared, must be stringently restricted. Exempt religious orders, like the Jesuits, Dominicans, and Franciscans, must be abolished, and appeals to Rome from Germany must be forbidden. In the Congress of Ems, in other words, the German Imperial Church proclaimed itself to be a Gallican national Church.[10] Preservation of the political status quo—and its own legal, social, and religious privileges—was about all the Imperial Church had to offer in the way of social theory.

The Jansenism and Febronianism manifested by the Congress of Ems showed itself as well in the social policy of Austria and Bavaria. Enlightenment rationalism and moralism, which had penetrated the thinking of Germany's educated classes, both clerical and lay, were also evident in the reforms these two governments imposed upon both Church and state through their absolute authority. The suppression of the Society of Jesus left the network of its schools and universities open to its control, and government officials lost no time in exercising their authority over it. The universities of the two monarchies became state institutions and their faculties, even of theology, were appointed by the state and subject to its control in their teaching activity. Under these circumstances their philosophy and theology became increasingly rationalistic, and, in Bavaria, under the ministry of Montgelas, university theology became extremely so.[11]

Thus, at the end of the *ancien régime,* the intellectual foundations on which the older Catholic social theory had been built had been effectively destroyed. In Austria, Joesph II made full use of his authority over the Church to carry out the Josephinist program of educational, cultural, and religious modernization that bears his name.

Although the emperor did not suppress religious orders, as the Congress of Ems had recommended, he did secularize a considerable number of monastic institutions and used their property to finance his program of social, educational, and religious modernization. The whole of the Austrian Church's intellectual, liturgical, and devotional life underwent a radical program of eighteenth-century updating, and many popular devotions, such as pilgrimages and public processions of the Blessed Sacrament, were forbidden. The number of students studying for the priesthood was determined by the state, and the curricula of the seminaries that educated them required state approval. Although very much a man of the Enlightenment, Joseph II was far from being an enemy of the Church, and his efforts at modernization and reform were benevolent in their intention and often beneficial in their effect. Nonetheless, the verdict of Church historians has been that, on the whole, Josephinism had an extremely damaging effect upon the Church; a great many of her irreplaceable religious and cultural resources were destroyed, and Enlightenment thought was enabled to penetrate the German Church. Intellectually and institutionally impoverished, German Catholics were placed even more deeply in that state of cultural inferiority in which they found themselves during the nineteenth century.[12]

At the end of the eighteenth century, therefore, neither in Germany nor in Latin Europe were there many signs from which the emergence of modern Catholic social thought might have been predicted. The influential modern papacy would have seemed inconceivable. The Catholic confessional states had acquired a legal authority over the Church that the contemporary Church would never want to grant them. The Jansenist and Febronian ecclesiology of that era, an almost universal ignorance of traditional scholastic philosophy and theology, the lack of strong independent institutions under the Church's own control, and the uncritical acceptance of Enlightenment social theory by its own educated members left the Catholic Church of Burke's day without the intellectual resources required for the creation of a well-grounded independent system of Catholic social teaching.

The Progressive Revival of Catholic Social Thought

Time would be required for the recovery of those resources. The Romantic reaction against Enlightenment individualism and rationalism favored the Catholic intellectual revival in Europe in the early nineteenth century, and in Germany, particularly in the Catholic Tübingen school, that revival produced a theology of very high intellectual quality. It did not, however, point at first toward a return to the older Catholic social theory. The anti-Roman attitude of the German Imperial Church was still alive in the new German theology, and the commitment of its best representatives to post-Kantian idealism precluded their return to the scholastic social philosophy of Vitoria and Bellarmine. Germany did not seem to share the enthusiasm shown by Joseph de Maistre and Felicite de Lamennais for the pope as supreme ruler of the Catholic Church.[13] Febronianism was still an influential force there in the first half of the nineteenth century and, after the restoration of the Bourbon monarchy in 1815, the French episcopate was still predominantly Gallican in sentiment.[14] The distinction between Church and state was looked upon by Catholics as an anti-clerical liberal program, and, even for enthusiastic partisans of papal independence, like Joseph de Maistre, the alliance of throne and altar remained an ideal in Catholic political theory.

Nevertheless there were some indications that propping up authoritarian European monarchies might not be the only alternative to anti-clerical liberal democracy. Daniel O'Connell's successful political agitation for Catholic emancipation in 1829 showed how effective a remedy parliamentary politics could provide for social injustice, even when, as in Ireland, democratic political activity required that Catholics work together with middle-class liberals toward a common goal. Felicite de Lamennais saw the merits of Catholics in France following the same line of action, and advised his coreligionists to turn their backs on the discredited monarchy of Charles X and give their support instead to his democratic liberal opponents.

Unfortunately, however, neither the French bishops nor Gregory XVI were farsighted enough to see that the Church's future might lie in that direction. Such breadth of vision could hardly be expected of them in 1830, when anti-Catholic liberals had launched their revolutions in France and in the Papal States on the basis of an Enlightenment understanding of the rights of man. Lamennais was condemned, and in papal teaching the legitimacy of an established government rather than the rights of man was still claimed to be the moral basis of its right to rule. The industrial revolution was in its infancy in France and Germany, and, for many years to come, middle-class Catholics were blind to the social injustice that liberal capitalism inflicted on the working class. Outstanding individuals, like Frederic Ozanam, were deeply concerned about the condition of the urban poor and devoted themselves heroically to the work of Christian charity. For all of that however, as Henri de Lubac has pointed out, the indifference of the Catholic middle class as a whole to the social injustice of an exploitative economic system could not fail to alienate Europe's industrial workers from the Catholic Church.[15]

In 1891 Leo XIII condemned the iniquity of liberal capitalism by establishing the right relationship between capital and labor with the help of St. Thomas's Aristotelian theory of social justice. Nevertheless, when Leo made that move in *Rerum Novarum* a number of middle-class Catholics were still disturbed by what they took to be his papal advocacy of socialism.

Rerum Novarum would not have been possible without a number of historical developments that took place during the troubled pontificate of Pius IX. Between the revolutionary years of 1830 and 1848, the Catholic intellectual revival continued. Religious orders, notably the restored Society of Jesus, were able to place their resources once again at the disposal of the Holy See. Liberal attacks on the Church provoked many European Catholics to turn to the papacy as their most effective defender. Gallicanism began to decline in France, and, after 1848, although Febronianism remained influential in German state bureaucracies, individual German Catholics began to challenge it. If Catholics were turning to the pope for protection against their own governments, the pope's intervention was harder to condemn as a threat to the liberty of their national Church. Aware of his new status and of the pastoral responsibility which came with it, Pius IX responded vigorously, albeit negatively, to the challenges which he had to meet both in the Church and in the surrounding liberal society. A number of unsatisfactory nineteenth-century systems of Catholic philosophy and theology were censured by the Holy See, and, in his famous *Syllabus of Errors*, Pius IX took a stand against the century's liberal culture and the government policies inspired by it.

Pius was also aware that condemnation alone would not suffice to counteract the influence of nineteenth-century liberalism on the educated Catholics of modern Europe. The nineteenth century was the time in which periodicals and newspapers came of age, and Pius was very conscious that Italian Catholics needed influential journals of their own. For that reason, he sponsored his own Catholic journal of opinion, *Civilta Cattolica*, and recruited a team of Jesuits to edit it.

Among them was Matteo Liberatore, one of the small group of Jesuits deeply committed to the revival of St. Thomas. His position on *Civilta Cattolica* gave Liberatore the opportunity to publish a widely read series of articles, which later appeared in book form. Their unifying theme was that in St. Thomas's pre-Enlightenment philosophy of knowledge, man, and being Catholics would find an intellectual instrument much better equipped to structure a coherent and comprehensive Catholic theology than any of the modern post-Cartesian philosophies. Only when Catholics reappropriated St. Thomas's philosophy and used it, rather than deficient modern philosophies, to structure their experience of the world, would they be able to engage in effective dialogue with their contemporaries. In a second series of articles, which proved to be very important in the development of Catholic political theory, Liberatore also argued that St. Thomas could provide the intellectual basis required for a sound social ethics. The series of articles in *Civilta Cattolica* was one of the first major efforts to link the revival of St. Thomas to the restoration of Catholic social theory.[16]

Behind Liberatore, moreover, stood an even more influential Jesuit disciple of St. Thomas, Luigi Taparelli D'Azeglio. As one of the early Thomist pioneers in Italy, Taparelli had helped to win Liberatore over to Thomism. Even before that, however, as Rector of the Gregorian University, Taparelli had made a Thomist of the future Leo XIII. He was the author of the first original and comprehensive Thomist work on natural law theory and social ethics written in the nineteenth century, a work which still deserves careful study.[17]

Pius IX's successor, Leo XIII, was thoroughly convinced that a return to the philosophy and theology of St. Thomas was needed before the Church could dialogue successfully with the modern world, and, in his landmark encyclical, *Aeterni Patris*, he threw the whole weight of his authority behind that revival. *Aeterni Patris* did more than stimulate the remarkable revival in medieval studies that followed it. It also fostered, particularly in France and Germany, a flourishing development of Thomistic ethical theory and its application to the social problems of modern Europe.[18] It is not surprising therefore that when Leo's encyclical, *Rerum Novarum*, the magna carta of modern Catholic social teaching, was issued in 1891, its philosophical framework was Thomistic. The notions of natural law, private property, social justice, and the diverse types of natural societies, which have become familiar to students of papal social teaching, made their appearance in *Aeterni Patris*, and all were appropriated from St. Thomas. The link between Thomistic ethics and Catholic social teaching established in *Rerum Novarum* has not been broken in the many papal encyclicals issued since, through which more than a century of social teaching from Leo XIII to John Paul II has been articulated.[19]

That continuity is evident in the titles chosen by Leo's successors for their own social encyclicals. On the fortieth anniversary of *Rerum Novarum*, Pius XI confirmed and updated its teaching in his own *Quadrigesimo Anno* and, sixty years later, John Paul II returned to Leo's groundbreaking encyclical in his *Centestimus Annus*. Two reasons can account for this unbroken continuity. One of them is that the ethical and social philosophy of St. Thomas, refined and extended over a century of historical and systematic development, can justify the Church's claim to be a perfect society in her own right and, by doing so, can expose the injustice of the radical privatization of religion required by liberal political theory and deny the totalitarian state the moral right to force the Church to submit to its own authority.

Thomas's philosophy of man also provided the intellectual foundation for the notion of a complex, subordinated series of societies, described in papal encyclicals. Each of these societies is distinguished from the others by the diverse natural or supernatural ends toward which its

activities were directed. That affirmation, of course, entailed the existence of natural ends, which Thomas's metaphysics of final cause, as opposed to eighteenth-century empiricism and rationalism, could justify.
As a social being endowed with free will by his human nature, man
possessed the inviolable right of immunity from undue interference by
others in using the means required to reach the ends of the societies in
which his nature placed him. This, as we have seen, was the conception
of society through which Leo XIII had defended the right of the Church
to deal with secular states as one perfect society to another in its concordats, even though, in the positive law of nineteenth-century Europe,
the Church's relations with Europe's states were not the same as they
had been in the legal system of the *ancien régime*. This philosophy of
society supported Leo XIII and his successors in their rejection of both
liberal capitalism and Marxist collectivism on the basis of an understanding of social justice derived from the ethics of St. Thomas.

Much as it gained from that theoretical justification, however, papal
social teaching could not have become as influential as it did after *Rerum
Novarum* if the First Vatican Council had not invalidated eighteenth-
century Gallican and Febronian ecclesiology by its formal definition of
the pope's infallibility and of his primacy of jurisdiction within the Church.
Febronian rejections of papal authority, such as the one made at the Congress of Ems, could no longer make any claim to Catholic orthodoxy.
Nonetheless, the increased authority of the pope would not have been
welcomed, as it frequently was, if, in the course of the nineteenth century,
the episcopate had not become much closer to Europe's working classes,
more pastoral in its approach, and considerably more apostolic in its
mentality than the Catholic episcopate had been at the end of the *ancien
régime*.

In fact, Catholic social teaching was not the work of the papacy alone.
It had come into being through an interplay between the papacy and a
number of socially conscious bishops. The influence of the famous bishop
of Mainz, Wilhelm von Kettler, and of Cardinal Manning on the composition of *Rerum Novarum,* for example, is now rather generally accepted.
In later years, Leo's successors would turn for assistance not to bishops
alone but also to recognized experts in Thomistic social theory.[20] Hence

the composition of papal encyclicals was generally a team effort. None-theless, despite their being the work of many hands, an observable thread of unity ran through that remarkable series of papal documents. A gen-erally Thomistic philosophical framework in their theoretical analysis linked to empirical observation of contemporary society was commonly used to justify the papal teaching contained in them. The result has been, of course, that, since the actual state of society is continually changing, the papal estimation of contemporary social relations has been required to change as well. That is an important point, which readers of the papal encyclicals should keep in mind, and one that, at times, some of the encyclicals' critics appear to have overlooked.

Some change can be seen, for example, in the papal response to the development of democratic government during the twentieth century. As papal nuncio in Belgium, Leo XIII had recognized the important role of political parties influenced by Catholic principles in modern liberal soci-ety, and he was by no means unaware of the contribution to social justice made by organized political parties in Ireland, England, and America. Far from being a threat to religion and the social order, political parties made it possible for individual Christian citizens to shape the course of public policy through their votes. And, as the number of educated citizens increased, more and more of them had the ability—and indeed the duty—to take part in government in this way. Civil society was no longer the monarchical society of the *ancien régime,* in which the majority of the population had no voice in the direction of public policy.

Leo XIII therefore was anxious to explore the possibility of a rap-prochement between the Catholic citizens of France and the government of the French Republic, which had succeeded the Empire of Napoleon III. Neither the royalist Catholics nor the anti-clerical rulers of the Republic were ready as yet for that type of mutual cooperation, and Leo's hopes for it turned out to be premature. Political activity by Italian Catholics in the newly unified Italian state had already been ruled out, when, in protest against Italy's seizure of the Papal States, the papacy had forbidden Catholics to take any part in Italian politics. That veto would remain in force until the pontificate of Pius XI, when the Lateran Treaty finally resolved the status of the Papal States.

Thus, in Mussolini's fascist Italy, party politics were not permitted, meaning that Pius XI could not support the Christian Democratic party Don Luigi Sturzo had founded before Mussolini's rise to power. Only after the fall of Mussolini could Sturzo's sucessor, Alicide de Gaspari, who had been protected by the Vatican during World War II, emerge from obscurity and make the party a major force in Italy. If the compromise between the Holy See and Mussolini's Italy in the Lateran Treaty delayed the emergence of Christian Democracy there, it assured the international recognition of the Holy See as a sovereign state and freed the Church from her long involvement in European power politics. The Church could now be seen as a purely religious community.

Although it is not always sufficiently recognized today, the influence of Pius XI on the evolution of Catholic social theory was quite remarkable. It was Pius XI who prepared the way for Paul VI's later defense of democracy and for the support that Paul would give to the United Nations. His pontificate covered most of the period between the two world wars. The old Europe of the Empires was dead and the new Europe that had succeeded it was divided between secular liberal democracies and their totalitarian rivals. By the 1920s Russia and Italy were already totalitarian, and by 1933 Germany was totalitarian too. In the eighteenth century, before the French Revolution, no matter how anti-papal civil governments might be, they still considered themselves Christian confessional states. But twentieth-century governments did not always consider themselves thus, and Pius XI realized that the Church was now obliged to interact with a society whose dominant ideologies were hostile not only to Catholicism but often to Christianity in general. Concordats with secular states, which Pius used extensively, might protect the Church against aggression by hostile governments, but concordats, of themselves, had little direct influence on public opinion. Education by papal word and action was needed for that.

The Church's disapproval of secular liberalism was already known, but Catholics, especially right-wing Catholics, could still be blind to the anti-Christian nature of some movements opposing secular liberalism. Pius XI was not blind, as he made very clear in two strongly worded encyclicals. *Non Abbiamo Bisgno* was directed against Italian fascism and

Mit Brennender Sorge contained a strong condemnation of Hitler's National Socialism. Pius's intention to reach as large an audience as possible can be gathered from his unusual use of the vernacular in place of the curial Latin in which encyclicals are customarily written. An unpublished encyclical condemning the immorality of Hitler's anti-Semitism was still in the drafting stage at the time of Pius's death.[21]

Relations between capital and labor were no longer what they had been when Leo XIII published *Rerum Novarum,* and a number of models other than individualistic capitalism and Marxist socialism were being proposed in several European countries. It was time to update Leo's teaching and, in order to do so, Pius published his own encyclical, *Quadragesimo Anno,* on the fortieth anniversary of *Rerum Novarum.* One of the most significant and influential contributions *Quadragesimo Anno* made to Catholic social thought was the stress it placed on the notion of subsidiarity. In St. Thomas's philosophy of society, subordinate or imperfect societies have their own natural ends and, because of that, members of those societies have the moral right to pursue those ends without undue interference from the state. St. Thomas's theory of society therefore was more subtle and complex than either the individualistic theories of society proposed by Locke and Rousseau or the collectivist theory of society defended by the advocates of the modern totalitarian state.

Subsidiarity did more than simply defend the family against state interference, as Catholics already knew. It could also serve to justify the existence of smaller cooperative groups, involving both capital and labor, working together freely inside the larger industrial complex of a modern civil society. Made up, as it was, of many groups of free individuals working toward their own legitimate, though limited, common ends, modern society need not and should not be monolithic. Civil society is not a single unit composed of isolated individuals and the state. Neither is its economic system made up of single social entities made up of workers and their employers. Both civil society and its economic system consist of an ordered hierarchy of natural societies subordinated to each other by the ends that specify them. The notion of subsidiarity, to which *Quadragesimo Anno* gave a prominent place in Catholic social theory, truly came into its own after World War II, when Catholic politicians like Maurice

Schumann and Konrad Adenauer used it to reconcile national sovereignty with membership in a larger European economic union and popes, like Paul VI, employed it to justify their support of the United Nations.

The institution of the feast of Christ the King during Pius XI's pontificate was an explicit reassertion of the Catholic theology of society and authority in the face of the anti-Christian political theories of the time. As Incarnate Son of the creating God, Christ is the legitimate head of both civil society and the Church. Although distinct and possessed of their own legitimate authority, both Church and state are under grace, and in each of them free human agents are bound to make their personal contribution to the common good under the guidance of God's natural and positive law. Civil societies receive their legitimate authority from the creating and redeeming God and no reasons of state can free their governments from the constraints of God's commandments.

Pius's awareness of the increasing level of education in modern society and his appreciation of the principle of subsidiarity inclined him to approve of democratic states in whose governance a mature electorate, guided by Christian principles, and working together at times through the recently established lay Catholic Action groups, could take a responsible part. Democratic governments had their faults but, despite their attraction for conservative Catholics, totalitarian antidemocratic movements were often thoroughly anti-Christian in their inspiration and hence more dangerous. Pius's realization of that fact caused him to issue his unequivocal condemnation of *Action Française,* the anti-democratic movement whose founder, Charles Maurras, was far from being Christian. That condemnation caused a sensation in France. Prominent French royalists, including a number of distinguished Jesuits and Dominicans, had given their support to *Action Française* and made no secret of their displeasure at its condemnation.[22]

One former supporter of the movement, however, reacted in a very different way. Convinced that Pius XI's condemnation of *Action Française* was justified, Jacques Maritain abandoned his opposition to democracy and defended his decision to do so in *The Things Which Are Not Caesar's,* the first of the many influential works which he was to write on political philosophy. Over time, Maritain and his disciples were destined to become highly influential Thomistic defenders of representative democracy. Maritain's personal influence on Paul VI was deep and far reaching, and the Christian Democratic parties that emerged in Europe after World War II drew a great deal of their intellectual inspiration from him. The admiration Paul VI explicitly expressed for the political philosophy of Jacques Maritain became evident in the sympathy he was to show for the attempt made by the United Nations to draft an international declaration of the rights of man.

Vatican II and the Pontificate of John Paul II

The revival of Catholic intellectual life, which Leo XIII had encouraged, bore fruit in the Second Vatican Council. The pope who convoked the Council, John XXIII, was on excellent terms with the president of the restored French Republic, and Paul VI, who presided over the Council's second half, was an open supporter of Christian Democracy. The understanding of her own social nature, which the Church expressed in the *Dogmatic Constitution on The Church (Lumen Gentium)*, and the understanding of the Church's relation to contemporary society, found in the *Pastoral Constitution on the Church in the Modern World (Gaudium et Spes)*, are very different from the understanding of the Church and her relation to the world prevalent among eighteenth-century *ancien régime* Catholics. The emphasis the Council placed on the responsible role assigned to individual free agents in both the Church and civil society, and the value the Council placed on independent group initiative by educated Catholics in contemporary society, is clearly in the line of development that led Pius XI to stress the principle of subsidiarity. Both could also find support in Jacques Maritain's Thomist defense of representative democracy as a contemporary demand of the natural law.[23]

The Council's commitment to religious liberty might have seemed a radical innovation to conservative Catholics. Nevertheless, that commitment was an authentic extension of St. Thomas's philosophy of knowledge, man, and being. Indeed, it was an extension that became necessary once the ethics of St. Thomas was applied to the developed state of contemporary society. The freedom of man's will, St. Thomas had taught, was inseparable from the natural orientation of the human intellect to the truth of being. For that very reason, every moral agent must have the right to choose the good as his intellect presents it to him. If the claim truth has upon the intellect is grounded on the being of God Himself, as Thomas teaches, it follows that no external authority may infringe upon man's moral freedom, even though, through no fault of his own, the judgment of an individual agent may be erroneous.

John Paul II was one of the bishops actively involved in drafting the *Declaration on Religious Liberty (Dignitatis Humanae)*. As a theologian, he was conversant with the extension of papal social teaching to the problem of human rights, in the context of the economic and social problems of the Third World during the pontificates of John XXIII and Paul VI,[24] and, as a philosopher, he was also aware that the understanding of human rights and the philosophical justification for them found in the writings of these two popes depended on a very different philosophy of knowledge and man than the one the eighteenth-century philosophies had used to justify their own Enlightenment understanding of the rights of man. The philosophy of rights that guided John Paul's activity at Vatican II was basically Thomistic. As a theologian, John Paul was also guided by a conception of grace and nature and an understanding of faith and reason very different from the skeptical epistemology and pessimistic Augustinianism theology of the seventeenth-century Jansenists and eighteenth-century Febronians.[25]

It was obvious to John Paul as well that the understanding of society that guided the Council's teaching on the nature of the Church and the Church's relation to the modern world was richer, deeper, and more complex than the conception of society presupposed by Febronian ecclesiology and eighteenth-century canon and civil law. The difference between the two conceptions involved far more than the increased authority of the pope within the Church after Vatican I. It was due to the recovery of the older notion of Church and state as two distinct societies, each autonomous in its own order, yet both in the order of grace and nature subject in their own way to the authority of Christ. This was the vision of the free individual's relation to society that had moved Pius XI to institute the Feast of Christ the King, and it was the vision that would later move John Paul II to speak of the redeeming Christ as the meaning-giving center of human life, human work, culture, and social action in the first encyclical of his pontificate, *Redemptor Hominis*.

The eighteenth-century Church, like the eighteenth century itself, was not enamored of history. Reflecting the culture that nourished it, Enlightenment Catholic thought was profoundly individualistic. On the contrary, Vatican II, like the society it confronted, was preoccupied with both history and community. The communal historical consciousness that manifested itself in the Council's documents is reflected also through the focus on the acting person, community, and culture that characterizes the writings of the present pope. John Paul's appreciation of modern philosophy and his use of Scheler's phenomenology as the starting point for his own metaphysics of the acting person manifest the difference between John Paul's personalist approach to philosophy and the ideal of impersonal reason embodied in Enlightenment thought and culture. They also manifest the difference between the starting point of John Paul's philosophy, his insight into the inner experience of the human subject, and the strictly objective starting point of nineteenth-century scholasticism. Nevertheless, despite the subjective personalism of its starting point, the unabashedly metaphysical framework of John Paul II's *Veritatis Splendor* reveals the abiding influence of St. Thomas on the pope's philosophical and moral thinking. *Fides et Ratio*, John Paul's remarkable encyclical on the importance of philosophy for sound Catholic theology, is intended to carry forward the philosophical project of Leo XIII's *Aeterni Patris*. Yet the same encyclical consciously extends and modifies Leo XIII's conception of Thomism in the light of more than a century of intellectual and social development. John Paul, for example, has made it clear that he no longer desires to give St. Thomas the almost exclusive role in structuring Catholic theology that Leo XIII had given him, and, in John Paul's historical account of nineteenth-century Catholic thought, the present pope speaks highly of the contributions made by Catholic philosophers and theologians whose orientation was not Thomistic.[26]

The author of *Fides et Ratio* has also shown that he is conversant with the history of Catholic social thought sketched out in this article. In his writings we find an accurate appreciation of both the Enlightenment ideal of reason and of the eighteenth-century theology of grace and nature on which the ecclesiology and social theory of the *ancien régime* were based. John Paul's encyclicals have been written in light of the protracted effort made by the modern Church to counteract the individualism of Enlightenment rationalism through the historical revival and speculative development of the social teaching pioneered by the great sixteenth- and seventeenth-century scholastics.[27] As is evident from *Fides et Ratio*, John Paul, like many contemporary philosophers, is convinced that the Enlightenment reason that challenged the theology and social teaching of the Catholic Church during the last two centuries has now become a spent force.

Unfortunately, however, as *Fides et Ratio* points out, the widespread abandonment of Enlightenment reason characteristic of contemporary culture has not brought with it a return to the Christian faith. On the contrary, it has created the skeptical postmodernist mindset that is pervasive in contemporary culture, a generalized, unreflective conviction that no attempt to find meaning or purpose in human life can possibly be successful. In our contemporary intellectual climate, social problems now seem to be rationally insoluble by their very nature, and the Church's social teaching, rather than being intellectually challenged by Enlightenment reason, as it was in the past, can now simply be dismissed out of hand as meaningless.

For John Paul II, therefore, the Catholic Church now finds herself confronted with a new culture in a new society. In our postmodern contemporary culture, a new set of problems confronts the Church. But John Paul believes that, as she has done in the past, the Church must deal with these new problems by drawing on her inherited philosophical resources and developing them through creative extension and modification as she applies the social theory structured by those resources to the changing culture and society in which the Church must always live. Continuity and change, creative fidelity to a sound philosophical inheritance combined with empirical observation of a constantly changing society, will continue to be the source of authentic Catholic social teaching.

Defending Authority in a Cynical Age

JOSEPH KOTERSKI, S.J.

The combination of individualism and egalitarianism that has stirred the hearts of Americans from the earliest days of our existence can often make us unthinkingly accept anything that goes by the name of "democracy" as preferable to "authority," and majority vote as preferable to decree. The rhetorical force of appeals to individual liberty should not, however, be confused with the genuinely ordered liberty and real (but restricted) rights that our republican form of government and democratic ideals were intended to protect. Absent the exercise of authority that is both steadfastly committed to the protection of legitimate social privileges and able to decide on what courses of action serve the common good, the rising chant of rights in conflict will push us perilously close to a form of paralysis in which rights talk seems to trump any other consideration of what constitutes that common good.[1]

Contemporary defenses of such authority, however, seem to be sadly missing from political discourse. Flagrant abuse of the power vested in authorities has made the very idea of authority deeply suspect for people of good will across the ideological spectrum. Whether the issue be the corruption of public figures, the draft during an unpopular war, court-ordered school busing for purposes of desegregation, the tax system, or apartheid, the same fear haunts liberals and conservatives alike, namely, that there is considerable danger in the power wielded by authority. Even when some bureaucrat manages to make a fair and generally helpful decision, we tend to feel a bit of surprise and delight that none of the interested parties managed to co-opt the system. Personal experience at the hands of some governmental official or bureaucrat acting in an arbitrary way joins with resentful memory of the great totalitarian regimes that dominated the history of the last century to reinforce the general suspicion that authority is simply a synonym for the possession of power.

In *The Origins of Totalitarianism* Hannah Arendt notes that the world is in our era ruled almost exclusively by power. The cynic would add that this has probably always been the case. Even those who think of their lives as ordered primarily by religious beliefs are prone to cynicism, finding it easier to say either "Throw the bums out" or "Wouldn't it be better if our own guys, rather than the bad guys, held the reins of power?" But as comforting as cynicism may seem, it detracts from the effort to understand the moral nature of the institutions necessary for social happiness. It is my thesis here that social happiness depends on the careful balancing of enlightened authority and ordered liberty, a balance that can be shaken as easily by the reduction of authority to power as by the substitution of anarchy for ordered liberty.

To put it simply, power is not authority. In fact, they are quite different, and the tendency to confuse the two is at the root of what gives authority such a bad name today, on both the political Left and Right. Authority is not equivalent to totalitarianism or dictatorship, although the authoritarian character of these forms of government has smeared their semantic kin, authority, with a frightful reputation.

To think straight about the matter, it will not do simply to prefer to have "our own" in power rather than "the bad guys," as if power were all that authority is. To conceive the battle over authority as merely a tug of war between competing interests is to reduce the question of authority to one of power. There can be justifiable uses of power by legitimate authority but there can also be authoritarian abuses of power that render the conduct of the person holding an office immoral, or perhaps even make the office an illegitimate usurpation of power, if the structure of rule assumes a tyrannical form. Since our experience of authority in normal life is so often identified with public office, the scandal of corruption in public figures makes it very hard to preserve respect for certain offices.[2] But the resentment we feel at a betrayal of trust, whether the massive betrayal of the totalitarian regimes or the puny pettifoggery of small-minded bureaucrats, is a resentment explicable only in light of our moral expectations that proper authority rests on law, not on power, on reasonable decision making for the common good, not on willful assertion of private interest.

To maintain such a distinction between power and authority it is necessary to consider the general nature of authority as a positive and essential feature of social living, and not just a necessary evil that functions as an indispensable corrective for what goes wrong in social relations. To this end it will be useful to examine differences such as those between public and private, means and ends, society and government, authority and law; and to reflect on the nature of the particular institutions where authority-relations are found, including families, societies, states, churches, businesses, voluntary associations, prisons, and so forth. What the analysis of particular institutions shows is the importance of a substantive and not merely a procedural notion of the good, and the overriding need for authority not just as a final arbiter in disputes but as a firm guiding hand throughout the decision-making process.

The absence of a substantive notion of the good—upon which authority depends—is revealed in the contemporary dispute among liberals and conservatives over the meaning of terms such as "liberty" and "equality." The libertarian leanings found among some conservatives incline them to the view that less government is better and that the government that governs least, or if possible, not at all, governs best. Liberals, on the other hand, insist that there cannot be genuine liberty until significant progress is made in redressing the discrepancies of earning-power and opportunity between some social classes and social groups. In truth, both seem to value liberty and both can make a good case against the arbitrary exercise of raw power that makes authority authoritarian and excludes some parties, *de jure* or *de facto*, from free participation. The argument to be made here is not that a general theory of authority will answer all substantive questions about how to balance liberty and equality in particular circumstances. Rather, it is that, despite the fact that authority has a bad name today, society in principle needs authority for the progressive resolution of these and other social questions. The idea of authority may connote restriction, oppression, and even servitude, but in fact, authority is an essential concomitant of ordered liberty with genuine but limited rights.

What Sort of Thing Is Authority?

To remove the confusion between power and authority that generates so much hostility toward authority today, it will prove helpful to have a good definition. What sort of thing is authority? To use the classical approach to definition (i.e. by way of genus and species), to what larger group does it belong and what is its specific trait? What sort of quality is it that lets us say that a person is acting with authority in a certain case? Many persons in different walks of life are called authorities, whether by virtue of the office they hold or the knowledge they have. In fact, it is a curious phenomenon that many academics are quick to condemn arguments from authority as the weakest of arguments even while they scurry around to become recognized by their peers as authorities in their own chosen fields. But it is not from the desire to be the source of the weakest of arguments in their fields that they do this; it is out of a latent sense of the real definition of authority that they exert themselves so vigorously in their pursuits, namely, the connection of a person with authority to some truth prior to and superior to the person bearing witness to that truth. Because of the existence of this truth, we are able to decide about the correctness of an assertion or the advisability of an action to be taken in light of the truth.

The chief task of authorities is to be a witness to a truth superior to themselves, by which they make the decisions they do and by which they are entitled to judge whether and how to use the power at their disposal. It is this intrinsic relation of authority to a higher truth that allows authority to command obedience and prevents the decisions of authorities from seeming or being partial and arbitrary. This is the case whether we are talking about the truths of physics (about which someone like Stephen Hawking is a recognized authority and competent judge), or the truths embodied in the founding documents of a nation (about which a Supreme Court Justice is expected to be a juridical authority). We expect from a Supreme Court justice, for example, a learned opinion, showing the chain of reasoning by which a decision was reached, and not the raw assertion of judicial will. If we disagree with a decision, the burden falls on us to point out the missing or misinterpreted premises, or to identify some faulty step in the logic, and to do it in a form that is reasonable, argued as cogently as we can for all to consider.

Questions related to the nature of authority may be subtle and hard to answer, but so they also seemed during the early years of our schooling. When we were in the third grade, our teachers needed to make authoritative judgments about how we handled the addition of fractions and to decide which of our answers were right and which were wrong (even if the answer was counterintuitive, as when one-third and one-sixth were said to add up to one-half and not one-ninth!). These authoritative judgments were only possible because there existed a truth with which the authority had experience *as truth*, a truth to which every judgment handed down must bear witness. Where the material authority of the truth of arguments is not produced for our inspection, we must rely on the formal authority of the teacher, and we are then immediately alert to the dangers of an arbitrary decision. But this very possibility points to the need for genuine authority to be related to some higher truth, and in the best of all possible worlds, to present the case for the decision in a way that rests the burden entirely on the material authority of the arguments. The difficulty, or even the impossibility, of doing so in many circumstances makes it clear that there is a sociological necessity for formal authority.

J. M. Bochenski raises the question: to what category does "authority" belong?[3] Is it a thing, a quality, or some kind of relation? This division is at the heart of most philosophical schemes for the classification of the types of being that make up the whole of reality, however much the advanced details of these schemes may vary. A planet, for example, and any of the objects on it, are clearly "things" that have various "properties" or "qualities" (e.g., spherical, solid, watery, blue, green) and stand in various "relations" to other things (e.g., near a certain star or at a certain position on the globe, revolving on its axis at a certain speed, experiencing and exerting a gravitational attraction with respect to other objects, more or less dense than other objects, etc.). Invariably, philosophers who attempt to categorize the types of things that constitute reality possess different temperaments; some are inclined to lump together what others prefer to split. But the useful insight at the basis of this sort of discussion is that there is an interwoven texture of reality. "Thing" covers the set of entities that can each be called a whole entity, one having a certain unity and relative independence, but admittedly existing within the larger whole that is the universe and as part of many other regional groupings. "Quality" is intended to designate some kind of property intrinsic to a "thing," while "relation" refers to some kind of connection between things or qualities.

Ordinary speech allows us to designate various persons as authorities, so there is a sense in which authority is a thing, for persons fall under the general category of "things." Since we can also correctly speak about the authority with which a given person answered a question or settled a dispute, it may be classified as a quality possessed by a person. But at the foundation of both these usages is a relation. "Authority" is an intrinsically relational word like "parent" or "friend" rather than a proper name for any one person or the name of some inner characteristic. Psychologically, some individuals seem to bear a kind of personal authority, such that they need only enter a room to become the center of attention; their demeanor and gravity may shift the center of conversation in a particular direction; their cleverness or learning predominates. There is some quality within them that is the ground of the sociological authority they possess. But even here their authority is exhibited by the way others relate to them.

There are any number of cases where what we mean by "authority" is neither an individual person nor some personal quality but rather an office held, as when we speak of the "authority of the office" and mean to indicate the obligation of the governed to obey the governor, regardless of who occupies the office or whether the occupant possesses any personal charisma. A scholar with no personal magnetism with which to attract a school of disciples could thus have authority in a certain field (the sociological relation of knowledge) just as an air traffic controller whose personality would make him the kill-joy of a party deserves the complete attention of pilots approaching an airport (the sociological relation of action).

Bochenski is presumably right that it is the operative relations that justify the legitimate psychological and sociological uses of the word "authority" for both persons and qualities.

We might consider family structure as one of the most obvious natural cases of an authority-relationship. Children need the guidance of parents, and we try to place orphans in the care of foster parents. The authority appropriate to parents comes from the special relation in which they stand to their children. The point here is not that parental supervision of dependent children is the central paradigm for understanding authority, as if political authorities were simply *in loco parentis* for the general populace, but simply that the structure of authority is relational. This is true not only of a natural association such as a family, but also of a voluntary association such as a baseball team, where the manager has authority over who plays and what the strategy is going to be at any point in the game. He is more likely to be successful if he has special talent for the job (within the philosophical category of "quality"), but he is in charge regardless.

Granting the legitimacy of the use of the word under all three possible categories, the claim here is that the relation involved is a connection between authority and a higher truth. This is not to say that all parents are natively gifted with knowledge of what it takes to be good parents any more than that all managers are good managers. The actual situation is sadly otherwise. But it is precisely by looking at health that we can discuss disease; and it is by looking at the example of a successful family structure that we have the grounds for diagnosing the problems of dysfunctional families where, among other problems, we find individuals unable or unwilling to exercise the authority proper to their parental roles. And what is true for the family is also true, by way of analogy, of the baseball team. Serious study of the sports page over the years reveals the wisdom of sportswriters in finding fault with managerial style for at least some of the disastrous seasons experienced by teams loaded with star athletes.

The same connection to truths superior to one's own decisions or preferences can be seen in other normal experiences of authority-figures as well, for example, in the case of a person deemed an expert in some area of professional competence or in the case of someone holding public office. Were some experience to disabuse us of the conviction that a given person really had the knowledge he claimed to have, our respect for the learning that constituted his authority would diminish as quickly as our respect for a person in high office found to have abused the power placed at his disposal. Should the official retain the office, fear or even terror might suddenly fill the gap, but our moral outrage would make it clear that authority had passed over into authoritarianism. The naked use of raw power would replace its tempered use in the service of a higher truth and thus further the confusion between power and authority that gives authority the terrible reputation that plagues its steps today.

My claim that there are truths that authorities must inspect and respect in their use of power is not intended in some vague, mystical sense. It is often the case that these truths are hard to formulate, or too complex to be stated in short compass, but they nonetheless exist and are the subject of much of our conversation about know-how and common sense. What does it take to be a good parent or a good manager? It is not at all clear that the advice of the experts is always or regularly right. What determines whether the experts are right (e.g., whether we praise or blame the influential brand of child nurture championed by Dr. Benjamin Spock) will necessarily be certain truths (e.g., about child-rearing), so far as we can figure them out. For example, the entire sphere of childhood education has seen "experts" constantly challenging traditional authorities with their advice about breast-feeding, quality-time, interpersonal skills, the best ways of dealing with siblings and young friends, etc. "By their fruits ye shall know them" applies to expert authorities in this area as much as to any other field of life.

It is not enough for our purposes to identify authority as primarily relational, for there are many types of relations. A useful device for further classification of the general types of relation is to count the number of terms employed. Mathematical formulas, for instance, are classified by the number of variable terms involved, so the straight line described by the equation $y = 5x + 3$ is a second-order equation in a single plane. The distance between two points, like the distance between two cities, shows the significance of introducing additional terms. New York and Boston are about 240 miles apart, a simple two-term relation. But to traverse the distance from one city to the other requires the introduction of a third term related to one's moving in a particular direction at a particular speed. Given the mathematical ability to express speed as a correlation of distance and time, it is just as easy to say that the two cities are four hours apart, and it sounds at first as though we have a two-term relation, but actually an additional relation has been added here, "by Amtrak" or "by a car travelling at 60 mph" (and, of course, headed in the right direction), and it is vital to specify this factor.

Initially, authority too sounds as if it were basically a two-term relation between the *bearer* of authority and those *subject* to the authority, but here likewise it will prove useful to identify a third crucial relation, the *area* in which authority is being exercised. "Gladly wolde he lerne and gladly teche," Chaucer said of the Clerk,[4] and here the case of a teacher's authority provides an example. In the ordinary classroom, the teacher is not expected to know "everything," but to know quite thoroughly the day's lesson. What a joy it was during a recent semester to have a student from one of my philosophy classes stop by my office, admire the rock collection of this very amateur geologist, and start to instruct me on the geological significance of what I had gathered merely for beauty's sake. Where I am the authority for him in philosophy, his knowledge of rocks makes him an authority to me in geology. This provisional authority (by way of *area*) is different from the type of authority exercised over children. Earlier in our respective educations, by contrast, a single person, a parent or a grade school teacher, had responsibility for the whole of our studies, for that person knew more than we did in all areas of life.

Even within one's field, there is much point to reminding oneself in Socratic fashion how much one doesn't know. (In fact, I have never had a class where the very effort of preparing the lectures and leading the discussions didn't result in learning far more than I ever did in class as a student.) Cultivation of some humility here does nothing to remove the duties or the prerogatives of authority. If anything, it deepens the general point of this essay, that authority is a truth-relation, for, as Bernard of Clairvaux wisely insisted, the real definition of humility is reverent love for the truth.[5] Real humility will resist the temptation falsely to belittle one's genuine strengths as well as to boast of accomplishments one doesn't actually have. A person without mature humility can even find it hard to take a compliment without some embarrassment, but from authentic humility a profound gratitude flows that will find a graceful way to acknowledge praise without letting honor go to one's head.

The exercise of authority also provides scope for humility on the part of the person in authority. This may be seen in the contrast between the case of an employer whose power has gone to his head and the case of an employer who enhances the confidence of an employee who is unsure of himself by assigning work that is so graduated in challenge as to leave the employee unaware of how he has become able to complete a task that might have seemed impossible at the start. Both the bossy and prudent employers have claimed certain prerogatives in assigning tasks and have tried to fulfill their duties in getting the work of the office done. Yet the bossy employer has probably done more to hamper that work by making his authority resented, whereas the prudent, perhaps unheralded, employer has subtly gotten the work done by the good use of her authority, exercising both command over, and respect for, those subject to this authority.

The Ethics of Authority

By taking note of the intrinsic relation of any authority to some truth outside and above itself, we lay the foundation for an ethics of authority. Authority is present in all aspects of social life; and authority, of any type whatsoever, has duties that define its purpose. Failure to live up to those duties perverts its effectiveness, either by failing to protect persons under its charge against other invasive, powerful forces or by dominating, in its own self-interest, those over whom it is supposed to rule. In the first case it exhibits some form of cowardice or weakness or indifference, while in the second it errs by aggressiveness, greed, or selfishness.

To avoid these extremes is precisely why in regard to politics we prefer the rule of law to autocratic regimes. The idea of an autocratic regime suggests rule by force alone, a regime inevitably subject to the arbitrary decisions of personal agency if not to outright whim. The idea of the rule of law, on the other hand, suggests the predominance of impersonal and reasonable decision-making. But rule by law cannot escape making a place for authority, that is, the creation of offices that persons must occupy. Even when power is divided, for instance in the tripartite scheme of the American experiment in democracy, there remains the problem of authority vested in the offices charged separately with making or executing or interpreting the law. The separation of powers has proved a wise strategy for balancing competing forces but should not be construed as having eliminated the need for an ethics of authority, for authority is an essential concomitant of liberty, an indispensable principle for holding liberty and order in balance.

The relationships involved in authority regularly involve the communication of something from the bearer of the authority to those subject to the authority. Systems of social life that operate by extensive dependence on persuasion and consent, goodwill, mutual understanding, or tolerance might seem to be able to do without authority, but deeper observation regularly reveals that it is only their smooth operation that conceals the presence of this other indispensable factor. Even in societies blessed with a spirit of generous cooperation and goodwill, and which try to proceed by consensus whenever possible, there is still a need for authority. In other words, there is a need for authority beyond those societies whose members for one reason or another cannot be trusted to decide for themselves what the best course of action is. It is only our distrust of abusive authorities, nurtured by the optimistic experience of living in a free society, that often makes us blind to the vital directive role that authority has.

What is it that authority communicates? Ultimately, what it imparts is a decision about how to proceed, but this is a point that needs careful consideration, for it is precisely this prerogative of decision making that makes authority suspect. To some extent it is a question of style: Will the conduct of authority be authoritative or authoritarian? But to

say that it is *only* a question of style is not enough. Even a gruff adminis-
trator can be fair and prudent in decision making, and pleasant manners
is no guarantee of a backbone firm enough to make the tough and even
unpopular choices without which a society will flounder. The difference
between authoritative and authoritarian conduct is founded, rather, on
whether the authority makes decisions in justice and fairness and on the
basis of the truths small and large that pertain to the area in question.
Paradoxically, it is the intrinsic subordination of any human authority to
a standard higher than itself that renders the bearer of that authority
genuinely authoritative.

The relation between those who bear authority and those subject to
it can be disrupted by various imbalances. Yves Simon lists possible conflicts with justice, life, truth, and order as likely to give authority the
bad name it often has today.[6] If, for instance, the relationship becomes
one where the bearer of political authority asserts some privileged position, some right to goods and services or to lower prices, resentment
will easily spring up. And this will be so whether the privilege is asserted by those who make congressional junkets or by those who are
members of Politburo dachas, for the fairness of exchange that generally
characterizes justice seems to have been violated.

If political authorities emit propaganda and expect quiet submission,
our sense of truth is offended. Cynicism can set in and make us suspect
that "authority" is merely a pragmatic tool for pacifying or arousing the
masses. Even at those times where the decisiveness of authority seems to
be attractive primarily as an easy alternative to the distressing inactivity
of prolonged deliberation, we should expect more of authority than the
following formalistic logic: Our present troubles demand that we do
something, x is something, therefore we should do x. We have a right to
expect more from those in positions of authority.

In the sphere of academic life, nothing so quickly rouses the ire of the
professoriate than any challenge to autonomy of thought. Academic freedom has become the battle cry on many a campus, even when the cry
emanates from those motivated by political correctness rather than the
discipline of rigorous argument moving ineluctably at the command of
truth. But once again there is something missing in the cry for autonomy:

the true liberty of thought in the search for truth. The books Karl Jaspers published on the life of the university before and after the Second World War illustrate the conflict with searing honesty.[7] As the new rector of his own beloved University of Heidelberg after the war, Jaspers reflected on the broken academic ranks. Those who had been outspoken against tyranny were silenced or even killed; those who had collaborated as propagandists were now shamed; and the commitment to truth of those who said nothing was questioned. As he labored to restore confidence in German institutions of higher learning, he voiced a sounder philosophy of education than those who speak only of academic freedom. He argued that the universities must be absolutely free from the ideological pressures of civil authority, but those who abide within the ivory walls must be resilient in the pursuit of the truth.

The freedom from civil authority granted to universities is a recognition of the need for universities to be places where any idea at all may be expressed so that its consequences may be rigorously and impartially examined. A prerogative preserved only by constant renegotiation of the inevitable town-and-gown disputes, such security from outside interference does make possible an unwavering commitment to the search for truth. But it is no more true here than anywhere else in life that freedom is a guarantor of achieving truth. What the rhetoric of academic freedom can obscure is that freedom is not an end in itself, not the primary goal of a liberal education but only an intermediate end. It is worth fighting for in the service of a higher end, but it is the higher end of truth-seeking in which the university serves the needs of a larger community that does not have the time or leisure to pursue that end.

Just as in the academy, parental (or even political) authority can easily seem an obstacle to the exercise of freedom and the achievement of truth vital to the spiritual nature of the human person. Inevitably the decisions of authority come from a source outside the person subject to that authority, and even if the actions commanded are objectively for the good, the mere fact of being commanded detracts from the spontaneity and voluntariness we cherish as marks of our freedom. Perhaps the case of teenagers will prove useful here, for with their increasing bodily strength, size, and energy come strong and healthy desires to make their own decisions. Their parents must walk a delicate line of guiding them decisively and leaving them room to act independently, even if they make some painful mistakes. What this example suggests is not that authority will always look like the care of good parents, subtle but solicitous. The point is, rather, that authority has to size up the capacities and maturity levels of those subject to authority in order to determine the proper mode of its exercise. If an error in one direction leaves those who ought to be subject to authority untrained in self-control and eventually bored and restless with their energies unharnessed and uncultivated, an error in the opposite direction will keep those who are no longer children at the level of perpetual adolescence, unable to deal maturely with legitimate authoritative decisions and continually alienated by any demand for obedience.

By the vagaries of political history, the change undergone by the term "liberalism" reflects this same ambivalence about authority at the level of political life. It also reveals the failure to ground the notions of "liberty" and "equality" in any substantive view of the human good, thus making any justification for the exercise of authority more problematic. Classical liberalism emphasized freedom and personal autonomy, and to this end developed a sophisticated theory of private property, a politics focused on personal autonomy and on popular self-determination. The consequence: the rhetoric of rights predominant in our political discourse since the revolutions of the late eighteenth century.

Modern liberalism has swung, however, from an emphasis upon individual self-determination to state-enforced redistribution and empowerment, highlighting *egalité* instead of *liberté*. The clash of desires here is evident even in the constraints liberals are willing to place, through high marginal tax rates, upon persons' disposable incomes to pay for social programs. But *liberté* still prevails in other areas, most notably those related to certain "lifestyle" issues such as abortion. The freedom of choice campaign associated with claims about abortion rights has generated a popular theme throughout the advertising industry that equates needs and desires, that is, that creates the perception of "needs" that are hardly more than inflamed desires. Further, there is the problem with arbitrariness in governmental policies about which choices are to be given legal protection and preference, as evident in the tangled debates over the integration of schools and neighborhoods. Liberalism's attempt to "empower" some will mean for others a change in the type of education available, common living patterns, and the free use of goods and property. Out of concern to provide universal access, the debates over healthcare reform somehow remain oblivious to the reduction of choices that plague the programs of socialized medicine in Canada, England, and Scandinavia.

Weighing these matters shows that it is just as important that authorities defer any personal whim or private prejudice to the common good as that they simply get things done. We do not mind speed limits when the authority imposes them for the common good, but where the need for such speed limits decreases (e.g., on the vast stretches of straight road in the western states), the law would be brought into contempt by scrupulous enforcement of a standard designed for the congested traffic flow of the eastern seaboard. The common good of safety on the roadway should not permit individual drivers to do what they like, but authorities are expected to display a degree of common sense in planning for genuine regional differences.

At the root of the confusion about the idea of authority is the view that power alone guarantees the liberty that is equality of opportunity. There is considerable truth in the observation that freedom to act presupposes the power to act, but to judge the matter aright requires a profound sense of what freedom is and what it is for. In the mood cycle of a given culture, there often comes a period of romanticism and the conviction that only activity that flows spontaneously from passion is worthwhile, but this is as debilitating to the spiritual nature of persons as is the stoic distrust of all passion. As mentioned earlier, liberty and equality (and the authority upon which both depend for realization), suffer absent a substantive notion of the goods that liberty and equality are intended by nature to serve.

The Difference between Power and Authority

It may require the threat of a nightstick or even the use of physical force to cow a hardened criminal, and it may simply be fear of apprehension and punishment that keeps some people from breaking the law. But in people of even ordinary virtue respect for the value of social order and the common good testifies to the reality of moral authority distinct from the power of enforcement. The directives of a person whom we credit with moral authority, e.g., a teacher who has won the trust of his students, or an elder whom we consult for advice, have forcefulness not because of physical strength, but because of knowledge or character or proven ability. Where power implies some attempt to master the given, to have control over reality,[8] true authority suggests respect for the truth about things as they are given and the direction of activity in accord with that truth.

While the word *power* could certainly be used to describe the forces of nature (e.g. the energy of a storm), to speak of *human power* adds the note of awareness of directing energy and strength to specific goals, and thus implies responsibility for its use. The attempt to control the reality power encounters, is (for better or worse) coercive, but not all coercion is bad. It may indeed be for the better: witness the work of the Army Corps of Engineers devising a systems of locks and dams to control flooding. But as floods and mudslides in populated areas from time to time remind us, developers need a healthy respect for natural flood plains, and sometimes what the Corps has to control is not the river so much as human desires to build wherever persons happen to fancy.

Authority, when operating according to the ethic here proposed, is rooted in discovering the truth about reality. It works by a kind of reverence for the truth about things. To some this will immediately suggest passive submissiveness to the status quo, but trying to be respectful of the fact that things have natures no more implies a stodgy reluctance to change than it does a meddlesome eagerness to tamper and adjust. What is required is the prudence to determine how closely the status quo is attending to the nature of things and how much pressure and disruption of the existing order would be required to bring about any significant change. Authority has a legitimate but restricted right to use the power at its disposal—and sometimes the duty to use it—but, except when it polices the incorrigible among us, it works best by issuing a call for moral respect. All power rests on the ability to "control" persons or things, but genuine authority ought to evoke ready obedience by those under it, whether they fully understand or not.

Etymological explanations go only so far, but the roots of the word authority in *auctor*, author, suggest the need for present authority to look to a past founding event, whether it be jurists returning to the authors of our Constitution or moralists pondering the plans of the author of human nature and of creation as a whole. The root verb *augere* means "to grow, to increase," and what the *auctor* is supposed to do is to make what has been founded grow and increase. In our politics, for instance, it implies a careful cultivation of balance by preserving a genuine but restricted set of liberties, with neither anarchy and license on the one hand nor total conditioning and the abolition of freedom on the other. Political authority achieves this goal by the legitimate use of certain powers, not by the arbitrary use of the force at its disposal, which would be regarded as violence. The juridical power vested in a head of state exemplifies this distinction. While the formal origin of his power is the legal constitution of the society, history has shown the persistent need for checks and balances to be written into this constitution to help restrain the head of state from accumulating too much power and becoming arbitrary and forgetful of the purposes to which his powers are ordered.

In contrast to the rule of law, rule by power is limited only by something outside the possessor of the power: another power which it fears. Instead of taking the measure of things, including the nature of human beings and well-balanced social institutions, power-driven forms of government prefer to fashion things to the measure of their own liking, whether for ideological reasons (e.g., the Marxist vision of man championed by some twentieth-century totalitarian governments) or for private aggrandizement, as has been the custom of tyrannies down through the ages. Hannah Arendt describes the difference between the desire to respect reality and the desire to dominate reality as a difference in temporal focus.[9] Rule by power sees the past as a source of reality it wants to control, and so looks to the present and future as opportunities where it can exercise domination. By contrast, authority governs present and future by fidelity to the origin, allowing the foundations to set limits to political power. To refuse to give assent to legitimate authority is ultimately to align ourselves with power, and, ironically, the most radical existentialists end up in the same place as the totalitarian regimes they deplore, since both resort to a philosophy of will in denying the existence of natures and essences. They both reject higher truths to which present authority must be subordinate in order to preserve human freedom.

The point is more general than these political examples at first suggest. Teenagers, for example, can easily come to see the world as largely a clash of forces, where power decides all. Suddenly finding themselves taller than their parents, they might resent still being treated like children. Their developing body strength can surprise them, and getting a car can appear to represent their long-awaited empowerment. Swift growth can surprise parents, too, but perhaps memory of their own experiences will be a helpful guide. Beyond the occasional moments of teenage rage at what seems like indentured servitude and of adult panic watching what seem like underprepared flights from the nest, the real task is negotiating the relations of power and authority to freedom. Every teenager needs somehow to learn how to deal with walls and resistances and limits. In the normal course of events, it is parents who have to provide the firmness of a moral and psychic wall so that their growing children will learn to love and respect walls in life: the walls of a home that give privacy and security, the walls of a school that shelter the free play of the mind, and the walls of the city that enable commerce and participation in civic life. Excessive use of parental power that crushes young spirits does them just as much a disservice as the insufficient use of parental power that never teaches children how to depend on a wall.

The recognition that there are higher truths that genuine authority must recognize allows us to make a useful distinction between an authority's "decisions" and its "determinations." I take "decisions" to refer to the choices, good or bad, an authority makes by its own power; I use "determinations" to refer to statements an authority makes not by its own choice but in recognition of the way things are. However easy it would be to lump together all the activities of authority under the same heading, it is better to recognize that there is a legitimate sphere of *decisions*, whose binding force comes precisely from the power at the disposal of authority to choose a course of action for the common good; they are binding wholly and entirely because they are so decided. On the other hand, there is also a sphere of *determinations*, whose binding force arises from a source higher than the authority, but which an authority may have to recognize, respect, or make known to those it governs. This is part of the speculative activity of authority and is well exemplified by Plato's philosopher-kings, who were to look to the world of forms for the fundamental patterns and structures of reality. The truths they labored to learn were in no way their decisions, but simply what they had determined already to be the case, and thus quite distinct from policies they subsequently chose to follow in light of what they had already determined to be true. This is not at all to suggest that we employ a Platonic model of authority, but simply that we use Plato's striking image to illustrate the real differences afoot when we try to distinguish between deciding and determining.

Summary

Authority in general consists in the moral prerogative of someone with a right to receive obedience. This right flows from a twofold duty on the part of authority, the duty to witness to the truth and to unify common action by determining rules all are to observe. The truth in question could well be a truth about the common good of a society, like the protection of innocent life or the safeguarding of private property, the organization of energy and resources for some project individuals or small groups alone could not manage, or, more generally, maintenance of the order and stability in which personal freedom can be exercised. But it could also be the truth to which a scholarly authority stands as a witness in the theoretical domain, whether it be the nature and configuration of the stars or the history of a remote civilization. Here the aspect of action could be limited to deciding on the proper procedures of a research project or weighing the merits of an article for publication and thus directing in a small way the progress of a field of learning. Whatever the degree to which control of action in common may be relevant, the structure of authority remains relational, conveying the decisions of those in authority to those who are subject to it. But unless the authority preserves its own relation to truths higher than itself, it runs the risk of contempt by devolving into an authoritarian exercise of raw power.

VII

Questioning the New Natural Law Theory: The Case of Religious Liberty as Defended by Robert P. George in Making Men Moral

Keith J. Pavlischek

Although most well known in academia as an Edmund Burke scholar, the deeper theological, philosophical, and political commitments that inform Francis Canavan's work are easily discernable.[1] He can be characterized as a political theorist with a deep commitment to Catholic orthodoxy in theology and to Thomistic natural law doctrine in philosophy and metaphysics. His essays in *The Pluralist Game* on the relation between religion, morals, law, and public policy reflect the best of that tradition.[2] Moreover, Father Canavan has inspired a host of his students and others influenced by his work to take their Catholic and—in the case of we "separated brethren"—Protestant commitments seriously as political theorists. Along with his students, Canavan has in no small measure contributed to the revival of serious reflection on the implications of Catholic social teaching as well as the political implications of natural law.

In this essay, I want to pay tribute to Canavan's scholarly contributions by engaging in a friendly yet critical debate with one of today's most important contemporary American Catholic political and moral philosophers, Professor Robert P. George. Widely recognised as a leading public intellectual among American cultural conservatives, he is particularly noted for his vigorous public opposition to the abortion license, the legalization of physician-assisted suicide, the legal recognition of same-sex marriages, and, more generally, "political correctness" on American university campuses.[3] Canavan, of course, has no quarrel with George on any of these issues. Indeed, for the most part, the above description of Fr. Canavan applies equally well to Professor George. In addition, while both are committed to the Catholic teaching on religious liberty in *Dignitatis Humanae*, both are concerned with exploring both the implications and philosophical grounding of that teaching more fully. Like Canavan, George is most concerned that pluralism in matters religious not be confused with, or collapse into, pluralism in matters moral.

Despite these obvious similarities, there is one notable difference. Trained as a Jesuit in the old days, Canavan's work is informed by a more traditional natural law doctrine. Professor George, on the other hand, is perhaps the most prolific American proponent of the "new natural law theory," as articulated most notably by John Finnis and Germain Grisez. While George and his mentors have, not surprisingly, found allies among American conservatives alarmed by the juridical and political manifestations of relativism, subjectivism, and proportionalism, they have nonetheless encountered strong criticism from traditional Christian theologians and philosophers who remain unpersuaded by their attempts to provide a coherent moral philosophy and an objective morality without appealing to metaphysics and teleology.

Particularly problematic in the new natural law theory is the understanding of religion as a "basic good." The most withering criticism of this aspect of the theory as articulated by Grisez and Finnis still remains Russell Hittinger's *A Critique of the New Natural Law Theory*.[4] This essay seeks to extend Hittinger's critique of the work of Grisez and Finnis to one particular aspect of George's position, namely, his defense of religious liberty in his book *Making Men Moral: Civil Liberties and Public Morality*.[5] By connecting George's defense of religious liberty with deeper structural criticisms of the natural law theory, I hope to show how George's position in particular, and the new natural law theory in general, generates profound and unacceptable theological difficulties.

The largest part of George's book *Making Men Moral* (hereafter *MMM*) consists of a dialectical engagement with the political and legal theorists

Ronald Dworkin, Jeremy Waldron, David A. J. Richards, and Joseph Raz. The main point of this engagement, George tells us, "is to challenge various liberal arguments that purport to show that political communities cannot be justified in limiting liberty for the sake of upholding public morality." And indeed, George presents powerful, and I think compelling, arguments insisting that "the legislator ordinarily cannot be freed from the need for moral deliberation and judgment in considering a proposal to enforce moral obligations. His enquiry cannot legitimately be restricted in such a way as to avoid the question whether an act proposed for legal prohibition is morally right or wrong" (*MMM*, 7). If someone has good reasons to believe that a certain act is immoral, argues George, he "may support the legal prohibition of that act for the sake of protecting public morals without necessarily violating a norm of justice or political morality" (*MMM*, viii). This does not mean, however, that a person ought always (or ever) support such legislation, for there are often compelling reasons for legally tolerating moral wrongdoing. These reasons are, however, prudential (*MMM*, vii).

In addition to the chapters in which he directly engages liberal theorists, George devotes a chapter titled "Social Cohesion and the Legal Enforcement of Morals" to the famous Hart-Devlin debate. This debate grew out of the Wolfenden Report (1957) in Great Britain, which insisted "it is not the duty of the law to concern itself with immorality as such" (*MMM*, 48). Lord Devlin, of course, argued in favor of morals legislation but defended such laws in the interest of maintaining social cohesion and avoiding social disintegration. Against Devlin, however, George maintains that "the truth of the morality a society would enforce . . . is a *necessary* condition for the legitimacy of its enforcement," and that "a concern for social cohesion per se is not a *sufficient* ground for enforcing moral obligations" (*MMM*, 71, emphasis mine). Devlin's error, like that of the liberals George criticizes in his book, was to prescind from the question of "moral truth" when considering morals legislation.

Thus, over against Devlin's "communitarian" position, which argues that social cohesion is sufficient to enforce morals legislation, on the one hand, and the liberal position, which denies it in principle on the other, George appeals to what he calls the central pre-liberal tradition of thought on morality politics and the law. "Aristotle and Aquinas," claims George, "whatever the defects of their views, were correct to suppose that the truth or the falsity of their claim that a certain act is immoral is often relevant to a sound determination of whether the act in question should be forbidden by law" (*MMM*, 7). George argues that the central tradition is superior to liberalism in that it allows room for the law to encourage virtue and to combat vice.

Nevertheless, George finds the central tradition flawed in one significant respect. What is the principal "defect" of the central tradition represented by Aristotle and Aquinas? "There are certain respects, especially those touching upon religious liberty, in which the influence of liberalism on the tradition has been salutary" (*MMM*, 38). The problem with Aquinas, according to George, is that he "assumes the propriety of legislating not only morals, but also faith, and indeed of legislating morals precisely in so far as they are accepted on religious authority and are the means to an end (i.e., heavenly beatitude) that religious faith puts forward but reason by itself cannot identify. Aquinas makes the first principle of politics a matter of religious belief, thus proposing a radical establishment of religion that is entirely inconsistent with a due regard for religious liberty" (*MMM*, 41). George hints at his proposed solution to this defect early in the book: "I shall later argue that religion, considered as a basic human good within the grasp of practical reason, can indeed provide a reason for political action. It cannot, however, provide a reason for compelling or forbidding religious belief or practice. Aquinas's approach, in so far as it imperils religious freedom, jeopardizes (for reasons that I shall later identify) the value of religion itself" (*MMM*, 41).

Early in the book, George identifies himself as a defender of natural law theory associated with the work of John Finnis and Germain Grisez. George is among those modern Catholic protagonists of natural law who have claimed that we can fully understand and obey the natural law without any knowledge of God.[6] Clearly, he follows John Finnis in his attempt to construct an account of natural law and our knowledge of it without needing to avert to the question of God's existence, nature, or will.[7] Not surprisingly, then, George's critique of Aquinas on religious freedom resembles closely Grisez and Finnis's departure from Aquinas's more traditional understanding of natural law theory, and incorporates their revised understanding of the "good of religion."

The Grisez-Finnis revision of the natural law tradition, and its understanding of the good of religion in particular, has been criticized by a number of Catholic theorists, most notably and compellingly by Russell Hittinger in his *Critique of the New Natural Law Theory*. In this chapter, I ask whether George's modifications to "the central tradition" required to defend religious liberty involve only slight modifications in that tradition (or at least its Thomistic inheritance), or whether they require something much more substantial. Religious liberty, according to George, can be defended on a number of different grounds:

> Some argue for religious liberty on the basis of the controversial view that all religions are (equally) true or untrue; or the equally controversial religious view that religious truth is a purely subjective matter; or the pragmatic political ground that religious freedom is a necessary means of maintaining social peace in the face of religious diversity; or the political-moral view that religious liberty is part of the right to personal autonomy; or the religious-political view that "religion," if a value at all, is a value with which the government lacks the jurisdiction or competence to deal. (*MMM*, 219–220)

George, by contrast, holds that the right to religious freedom is grounded precisely in the "value of religion, considered as an ultimate intelligible reason for action, a basic human good" (*MMM*, 220).

Hittinger, whose critique focuses on the problematic notion of religion as a basic good, concedes that the Grisez-Finnis system of natural law includes many of the same components as that of a traditional natural law theory: the content of the basic goods is derived from inclination; the goods are regarded as principles themselves; the difference between goods as means and as ends is objective, prior to choice and situation; and the goods are principles that are universally binding.[8] But it departs in one important respect: According to Hittinger, Grisez and Finnis argue that their theory "does not require a speculative doctrine of nature in order to establish the foundational principles. The nature and proper ends of human inclinations, for instance, are not the objects of theoretical reason, but are objectives of practical evaluation. The *ratio* of the goods does not require an *ordinatio* derived from the philosophy of nature at work in the older natural law systems."[9]

Hittinger argues that the Finnis-Grisez system of natural law "substitutes intuitions for a philosophy of nature" and that they "want the results of a natural law theory but are unwilling to defend and deploy the theoretical apparatus necessary to sustain it."[10]

To enter the details of this debate would take us too far afield, although I must confess that I find Hittinger's critique quite compelling. However, since George explicitly grounds his defense of religious liberty in the good of religion, it is necessary to summarize the modifications required to the more traditional approaches to natural law, and specifically to the good of religion, if George wants to make his argument for religious liberty in this way.

What, then, is the fundamental difference between the Grisez-Finnis-George understanding of religion and that of Aquinas? According to the former, religion is a good that should be evident to any rational agent since it is, literally, one of the foundational principles of practical rationality. As such, prior to choice, the agent has a categorical obligation to respect and promote, or at least never to act against, religion as a basic form of human flourishing. The good of religion, like the other basic goods, is an "intrinsic" aspect of human flourishing. Religion, like the other basic goods of life—knowledge, play, aesthetic experience, sociability (i.e., friendship broadly conceived), and practical reasonableness—is an *end in itself*. The first characteristic of all these goods, including religion, "is that one can act for their sake and their sake alone."[11] They are not merely "instrumental goods." Moreover, "the goods are irreducible, in that they cannot be reduced to another or to some still more basic, ultra-fundamental good or purpose."[12] "As first principles of practical thinking," George summarizes,

> basic reasons for action are, as Aquinas held, self-evident (*per se nota*) and *indemonstrable*. The human goods that provide basic reasons for action are fundamental aspects of human well-being and fulfillment, and, as such, belong to human beings as parts of their nature; basic reasons are not, however, derived (in any sense that the logician would recognize) from methodologically antecedent knowledge of human nature, such as is drawn from anthropology or other theoretical disciplines. Rather, they are grasped in non-inferential acts of understanding by the mind working inductively on the data of inclination and experience. (*MMM*, 12–13)

They "are not Platonic forms," George adds, "that somehow transcend, or are in any sense extrinsic to, the persons in whom they are instantiated." Nor are they "means to human flourishing as a psychological or other state of being independent of the basic human goods that provide reasons for action." Rather they are *"constitutive"* aspects of the persons whom they fulfill. Religion as one of these basic goods is "a value that practical reason can identify as an intrinsic aspect of the integral good of all human beings" (*MMM*, 222).

Following Grisez, George insists that the good of religion is intelligible, even if we prescind completely from the problem of a theistic referent or belief in God's existence. The philosophical-religious quest begins in the universally shared recognition that it is necessary and desirable to find a more-than-human source "of meaning and value" and "enter into a relationship with it." As a reason for acting, according to Grisez, "religion is the good of harmony with the more-than-human ultimate source of meaning toward whom (or which) the philosophical–religious quest is directed."[13] Similarly, George:

> We human beings have always wondered whether there is anything greater than ourselves, that is to say, an ultimate, or at least more nearly ultimate, source of meaning and value which we must take into account and (if personal) with whom we can enter into a friendship and communion. The question is both sensible and important. If there is a God (or gods, or non-deific ultimate realities), and if harmony and communion with the ultimate is possible for human beings, then it is obviously good to establish such harmony and enter into such communion. (*MMM*, 220)

The good of religion is nothing more, it seems, than an inclination, desire, or longing to be ordered to, or in relationship with, some undefinable something. But what makes religion valuable?

> Is religion a value? Irrespective of whether unaided reason can conclude on the basis of a valid argument that God exists—indeed, *even if it turns out that God does not exist*— there is an important sense in which religion is a basic human good, an intrinsic and irreducible aspect of the well-being and flourishing of human persons. Religion is a basic human good if it provides an ultimate intelligible reason for action. But agnostics and even atheists can easily grasp the intelligible point of considering whether there is some ultimate, more-than-human source of meaning and value, of enquiring as best one can into the truth of the matter, and of ordering one's life on the basis of one's best judgment. *Doing that is participating in the good of religion.* (*MMM*, 221, emphasis mine)

According to George, even an atheist or agnostic engages in a "religious act" when he simply "considers" whether there is or is not a "more-than-human" source of meaning. Because "searching, believing, and striving for authenticity are interior acts of individual human beings" they cannot, as interior acts, be compelled. "If they are not freely done, they are simply not done at all. Compelled prayers or religious professions, or other apparently religious acts performed under compulsion, may bear the external marks of religious faith, but they are not in any meaningful sense 'religious.' If religion is a value, the value of religion is simply not realized in such acts" (*MMM*, 220–221).

This is true enough, but it is worth noting that this argument misses the crux of controversies over religious liberty. If religion simply involved "interior acts," religious liberty as a public legal matter would hardly be an issue. Even preconciliar Catholic traditionalists held that interior acts could not be coerced. Pope Leo XIII, for instance, insisted "that it is not lawful for the State, any more than for the individual, . . . to hold in equal favor different kinds of religion," and that "the State is acting against the laws and dictates of nature whenever it permits the licence of opinion and of action to lead minds astray from truth, and souls away from the practice of virtue."[14] Like all nineteenth-century Popes, Leo XIII regarded it entirely just for a Catholic state to place restrictions on the propagation and public worship of non-Catholic religions. But this was entirely consistent with his admonition that "the Church is wont to take earnest heed that no one shall be forced to embrace the Catholic faith against his will, for as St. Augustine wisely reminds us, 'Man cannot believe otherwise than of his own free will.'"[15] The issue is more precisely enjoined around a proposal for governmental suppression of a religious practice. The issue arises over whether government may legitimately prohibit certain acts labeled religious (e.g., public worship, proselytizing, promulgating heresy, etc.).

George does engage this issue, however, for he insists not only that government may never legitimately coerce religious belief, nor require religious observance or practice, but in addition, that it "may not forbid them for religious reasons." And it should "protect individuals and religious communities from others who would try to coerce them in religious matters on the basis of theological objections to their beliefs and practices" (*MMM*, 222). Public "religious" acts are, in principle, for George, never to be subject to legal proscription. But why?

The first thing to observe about this is that "theological reasons" or "religious reasons" seem to be epistemologically inferior reasons regardless of whether they are true. I tend to think that this itself is problematic.[16] But my objection to this way of stating the problem has less to do with the purported epistemic inferiority of (even true?) theological reasons. My concern has to do with the implications of this position for Thomistic natural law teaching on more fundamental questions. George indicates that Aquinas, for instance, would forbid certain religious observances or practices for theological reasons. But this is somewhat misleading as it implies that the good of religion for St. Thomas is a supernatural rather than a natural virtue.

Hittinger points out that the difference between Aquinas and the new natural law theorists lies not in the distinction between the good of religion, with its attendant obligations, and the good of the supernatural relationship with God. Aquinas explicitly distinguishes between them (ST II, II, 81). Aquinas conceives of one's relationship to God not just as an end but as a personal communion that does indeed require theological explication and the practice of the supernatural virtues. However, according to Hittinger, Grisez uses "the Thomistic distinction to reinforce his own position that the basic goods, including religion, are incommensurable, and that there does not exist, prior to choice, a hierarchy among them." He overlooks, Hittinger points out,

> the theoretical apparatus that Aquinas employs in order to justify the *natural* virtue (or, good) of religion and its place in the natural law system. Not only is it presupposed that certain aspects of God's being are demonstrable . . . but Aquinas's discussion of religion likewise presupposes a philosophy of human nature—in particular a hierarchical and teleological account of the intellect and the will's relation to objects and ends. Indeed, Aquinas argues that the virtue of religion is superior to other natural virtues precisely because it governs man more immediately with regard to his final end. It is not one categorical among others, but an architectonic [natural] virtue (emphasis mine).[17]

Throughout Aquinas's discussion of religion he assumes the natural knowledge of God reached in the *prima pars* and assumes that religion is not simply one good among the foundational goods but is, rather, a superordinate good. The Thomistic virtue of religion is decidedly less formal than the Grisez-Finnis-George understanding. Also, unlike theirs,

Hittinger points out, it is architectonic and superordinate.

Moreover, it should be noted that Aquinas discusses the virtue of religion in II-II, q. 81, where he argues that the virtue of religion is a species of the natural virtue of justice, which entails rendering to God what is his due in terms of reverence and obedience. There are three reasons for this. First, "because God is the first principle of the creation of all things," a debt is owed to his being; second, honor is due "under the aspect of his excellence," and it is the proper response of a created will to this kind of being; and finally, religion is a good because the human soul is ordered to God as an end. This is why Thomas can hold, in strikingly Augustinian fashion, that religion "commands all the other virtues" (II–II, 81, 3, 4).[18]

Whatever may be the problems of this approach, it is at least possible for Aquinas to affirm the good of religion and still retain criteria that would allow one to ascertain whether a particular religion and its practices satisfy the formality of that good. That is simply because, for St. Thomas, the religious act is ordered to an object, God. The essence of the natural virtue of religion is *latria*, the giving of total submission and service, outwardly through sacrifice, and inwardly through devotion. For Grisez, Finnis, and George, however, it would seem to be impossible to disqualify religion or its practices per se as participants in the good of religion. At best a particular religious action may be morally condemned because *per accidens* it violates one of the other basic goods (e.g., human sacrifice, chattel slavery). In short, whereas Aquinas roots the virtue (or good) of religion in the natural obligations all human beings have to *God*, George, following Grisez and Finnis, roots it in the openness of the human subject to some overarching "value," whether or not that value is divine. As Hittinger puts it, "Atheists and agnostics, as well as theists, are bound by a universal form of the good that is defined simply as a need to establish good relations with unknown higher powers."[19] Thus, while George may avoid religious indifferentism by claiming to reject an argument for religious liberty based on the notion that all religions are equally true or equally false, it is hard to avoid the conclusion that his own argument for religious liberty is grounded in a similar notion that all religions are equally *valuable per se*.[20]

Moreover, religion seems to be the one good in the Grisez-Finnis-George system that cannot be judged morally good or bad, except by reference to the intention of the agent. Thus, while George speaks much of the good of religion, he does not consider corresponding vices. For Aquinas, devotion, prayer, adoration, sacrifice, offerings in support of the institutions of religious observance, and praise in words and music are required by the natural justice owed to God. The vices that correspond to the virtue of religion include superstition, dabbling in divination, tempting God, perjuring ourselves, committing acts of sacrilege, and trying to purchase spiritual goods with money. As counterintuitive as it may seem to the Christian, for George, "dabbling in divination" or, say, "witchcraft" would not constitute a vice per se but rather would constitute a genuinely valuable participation in the good of religion, providing the actions were performed sincerely and in good faith.

This, I'm afraid, will inevitably have serious implications for how we understand something as basic as the Decalogue. As Alasdair MacIntyre observes, "according to Aquinas all the moral precepts of the Old Law, the Mosaic Law summed up in the Ten Commandments, belong to the natural law, including those which command us as to how we are to regard God and comport ourselves in relation to Him. A knowledge of God is available to us from the outset of our moral enquiry and plays a crucial part in our progress in that enquiry."[21] St. Thomas never doubts that the First Table of the Decalogue is indispensable. The duties to God are the epitome of absolute precepts (ST I-II, 100, 8). One of the implications of this line of reasoning for pre-modern Christians was that, in principle, the First Table of the Law could legitimately be the subject of civil legislation. Public idolatry, blasphemy, etc. could legitimately be proscribed.

Now, one typically modern way to deny the legitimacy of proscribing idolatry is to deny the very possibility that one could actually worship a created thing. One could redefine the vice of idolatry as simply being the vice of worshiping whatever thing you worship in bad faith. Thus, all worship is implicitly true worship.

Is this what George is doing here? Recall that he insists that for the legislator to proscribe an action, it is a necessary condition that the action be immoral. All immoral actions are, in principle at least, subject to morals legislation. George holds that if someone has good reasons to believe that a certain act is immoral, he "may support the legal prohibition of that act for the sake of protecting public morals without necessarily violating a norm of justice or political morality" (*MMM*, viii). Thus, it would seem, no one can have good reasons to believe that idol worship is immoral.

According to the central tradition, says George, laws forbidding certain powerfully seductive and corrupting vices can help people to establish and preserve a virtuous character by (1) preventing further corruption; (2) preventing the bad example by which others are induced to emulate them; (3) helping to preserve the moral ecology; and (4) educating people about moral right and wrong (*MMM*, 1). Unless he were to modify his main thesis and say that some public vices are not, in principle, subject to legal proscription (that is, certain types of vices, like idolatry) it would seem, then, that George is faced with a dilemma. Either (a) concede that the tradition is correct in understanding the Decalogue as a reflection of the natural law (and hence as moral precepts) and thus allow, in principle, the proscription of public actions such as idolatry; or (b) maintain his position that public actions such as idolatry cannot in principle be legislated, but reject the traditional teaching that the First Table of the Decalogue is a part of the natural law (perhaps by saying the tradition had, in fact, no good reason to believe violations of the precepts were "immoral"!). If he chose (a), he could say of legislation proscribing, say, idolatry, precisely what he says of other types of morals legislation: whether or not it would be permissible to proscribe this or that "religious activity" is a matter of prudence. As it stands, one cannot help think that George opts for (b) and does not consider the negative precepts of the First Table of the Decalogue as moral! If they were moral precepts, they could, in principle, be subject to morals legislation. But, since such things as idolatry, false worship, proselytizing a false religion, etc., cannot in principle be subject to morals legislation, it would seem to follow that such actions cannot be immoral per se.

Moreover, for George, it would seem, as long as the action (say, engaging in a Satanic or Wiccan ceremony) meets the formal requirements of the good of religion, that is, if it "provides an ultimate intelligible reason for action," involving an attempt to consider if "there is some ultimate, more-than-human source of meaning and value," it is a valuable enterprise that would, strangely enough, *fulfill the requirements* of the natural law. Thus, what Aquinas and the tradition call a vice (e.g., violations of the First Table of the Decalogue—see also St. Paul's reflections on this in Rom. 1:21–22), George would call a moral obligation of natural law, provided the action was done in good faith and did not *per accidens* violate another basic good.

Finally, it should be briefly noted how George's treatment of the virtue of prudence differs from the Thomistic understanding, although not, perhaps, from the Aristotelian one. MacIntyre points out that Aquinas followed Aristotle in holding that the exercise of *prudentia* is required for the exercise of the other moral virtues, and that it is the one moral virtue without which the intellectual virtues cannot be exercised (ST Ia–IIae, 57, 5). But Aquinas adds a dimension to his discussion of *prudentia* that is not Aristotelian. *Prudentia*, for Thomas, is to be exercised with a view to the ultimate end of human beings (ST II–IIae, 47, 4). This has political ramifications. For Aristotle, the good legislator must exercise *phronesis* in legislating for a polis. For Aquinas, however, the good legislator needs *prudentia*, "but that *prudentia* is exercised so that human law accords with the divine law, more especially in respect of the divinely ordained precepts of the natural law. Thus *prudentia* always has for Aquinas a theological dimension, even when it is exercised as an acquired natural virtue rather than as a supernatural virtue."[22] If George is embracing the premodern tradition, then it is fair to say that it is not a pre-modern Christian one, at least not to the extent that the virtue of prudence excludes *a priori* a consideration of the ultimate telos of human beings.

Conclusion

George embraces an important aspect of Aristotelian–Thomistic thought about morality, politics, and law (the central tradition), specifically its defense of morals legislation. By contrasting this position with that of contemporary liberal theorists, he gives the impression that the adjustments he makes to the central tradition are merely minor alterations or slight adjustments. I have tried to suggest that George's grounding of the right to religious liberty in "religion" as a basic, noninstrumental, intrinsic, incommensurable "good" involves not simply a minor tinkering or adjustment in Thomism, nor even a "development of the tradition," but rather a profound and radical reconstituting of the metaphysical and epistemological roots of the tradition. This results, I think, from allowing the moral-political (practical reasoning) cart to pull the metaphysical-theological (speculative reasoning) horse.

This is not a problem unique to George but is a typically modern temptation. As MacIntyre has observed, for instance, modern readers of Aquinas are tempted to read questions 90–97 of the *Summa* Ia–IIae, the so-called treatise on law, in relative isolation from other writings of Aquinas, and indeed, from the rest of the *Summa*. But, MacIntyre argues, the various disputes over the meaning of the principium of the natural law indicate that questions 90–97 are not self-interpreting. Aquinas's discussion has to be read in terms of some structure and principles beyond what is said in answer to these particular questions.[23] There is a progression in the Summa, MacIntyre maintains, "from what must be presupposed about God and nature in the First Part, through the sequences of moral enquiry of the first and second parts of the second part, to the recognition in the third part of the revealed truths which define for us the Kingdom of God."[24]

To put it another way, the hallmark of Catholic philosophy has been its effort to show the congruence between faith and reason. We may ask, generally, whether the Grisez-Finnis-George theory of natural law does that, or whether it leads to an emasculation of the theological tradition to fit the philosophy. More specifically, we may ask if, in order to make an argument for religious liberty, George must call a virtue (e.g., divination, idolatry) what St. Thomas calls a vice, we have in this case more of a contradiction between faith and reason than a congruence.

To accept a defense of religious liberty styled after George's attempt in *Making Men Moral*, I would argue, *necessarily* requires one to read Aquinas in the truncated manner about which MacIntyre warns. All this would be of little import if this were simply a textual matter or a question of historical quibbling over this or that interpretation of Aquinas.

But more is at stake here, for this type of reading necessitates a radical change in how we should understand our obligations to God, the nature of "religion," the virtue of prudence, and even how we understand something as fundamental to the Christian life as the Ten Commandments. One may reasonably ask if such changes constitute more of a challenge to any recognizably orthodox Christian doctrine than a "development" of it. Correspondingly, if one holds on to the more traditional understanding of religion, of the Ten Commandments and prudence, one must necessarily reject George's specific argument for religious liberty.

What I wish to respectfully suggest, in short, is that Christian theorists, Catholic or otherwise, must carefully weigh the costs of grounding a right to religious liberty in the "good" of religion as understood by George, Finnis, Grisez, and other defenders of the new natural law theory. I am inclined to think that it isn't worth the metaphysical and theological price.

This is not to suggest, of course, that the defense of religious liberty be abandoned. One can, after all, accept the more traditional understanding of religion and natural law, and still offer a defense of the conception of religious liberty affirmed by *Dignitatis Humanae*. Indeed, Francis Canavan's work is an example of just such an approach. It begins by affirming that an adequate defense of liberty requires a "realistic" metaphysics encompassing "a universal human nature whose natural tendencies and needs are knowable to the human mind" and "the existence of God who is truth, and the truth about whom answers to the deepest human needs." At the same time, insisting that neither "an abstract ethical argument" nor an argument from the "rights" of "conscience" in support of religious liberty are sufficient to ground the conclusions of *Dignitatis Humanae*, it argues that a convincing defense of these requires a systematic account of "the nature of a just political and legal order in human society."[25]

More specifically, it insists that such a defense involves the recognition that a rightly ordered society is "organized in different ways for different purposes."[26] It involves the recognition, in other words, that although it "is the highest community in its limited sphere," the state "is not the only community" in which man's social nature finds expression, and "its purposes are not the only or highest goals" of "human life and human society."[27] "The state and its organs of government have limited powers," in short, "because they have limited goals and functions"[28] in the overall scheme of human social life. A robust defense of religious liberty, therefore, must center on the incompetence of the state—its lack of jurisdiction—in religious matters, and thus must take its bearings from a social ontology sufficiently complex to do justice to the full range of social jurisdictions and responsibilities, and their relations.[29]

VIII

Catholicism, Liberalism, and Religious Liberty

ROBERT P. HUNT

One of the central questions confronting scholars who work from within the Catholic intellectual tradition is the relationship between Catholicism and liberalism. For those persons who, like the late Rev. John Courtney Murray, S.J., describe the "liberal tradition of politics" as a tradition committed to "constitutionalism, the rule of law, the notion of sovereignty as purely political and therefore limited by law, [and] the concept of government as an empire of laws and not of men,"[1] the relationship is not a particularly problematic one. Because both Catholicism and this "liberal tradition" display a practical political orientation in support of constitutionalism and limited government, the relationship between the two traditions is a friendly and perhaps even complementary one.

When the word "liberal" is used in a narrower sense—to designate a particular and highly individualistic model of man and society—the relationship becomes more problematic, especially given the Roman Catholic emphasis on man's intrinsically social nature. There are many scholars who argue, however, that the developments in Roman Catholic social teaching inspired by the Second Vatican Council make rapprochement between Catholicism and liberal individualism still possible. Since the

Second Vatican Council, so the argument goes, Roman Catholics have come fully to embrace human rights and religious freedom, not merely as prudential accommodations to the empirical fact of religious diversity but as exigencies of the moral order that reflect an ever-deepening Catholic commitment to personal dignity. In fact, because Catholics have abandoned the thesis/hypothesis distinctions of an older "confessionalist" perspective, rapprochement with the liberal tradition of politics becomes more than the establishing of a *modus vivendi* between two somewhat incompatible worldviews. It becomes a *sine qua non* of our principled commitment to constitutional government, a dynamic "working out" of the principles embedded—but for so long latent—within the Catholic tradition itself.

R. Bruce Douglass provides an articulate defense of this integrationist perspective in his introduction to *Catholicism and Liberalism: Contributions to American Public Philosophy.*[2] According to Douglass, the days of antagonism between Catholicism and liberalism are pretty much over. "Both traditions have changed: they have undergone, in fact, a whole series of changes that have had the effect of redefining rather fundamentally what they stand for."[3] This is not to say, Douglass argues, that there are no disagreements between Catholics and liberals, but the areas of disagreement would become increasingly insignificant if only "both sides . . . [would not allow] themselves to become obsessed with certain particularly divisive issues on which they continue to have deep, abiding differences."[4] In other words, if only we could "get over" our differences on issues that lead to unnecessary culture wars (e.g., abortion, homosexuality, etc.), rapprochement would be a fairly easy thing.

In his own contribution to *Catholicism and Liberalism,* Paul E. Sigmund argues similarly that the differences between Catholicism and liberalism "are not that great" if one does not engage in "excessively reductionist" efforts to turn liberalism into a defense of value neutrality (of the sort championed by Ronald Dworkin and Bruce Ackerman). Rather, Catholics in particular ought to appreciate the value-laden commitments of "substantive liberals" to a view of the human person that is quite similar to the Catholic perspective. Says Sigmund:

> [T]here is a convergence of contemporary Christian Democrats and those liberals who
> argue that something more than a commitment to individual freedom is necessary to
> undergird social cooperation in a democracy, namely a moral and social view of the
> human person. In the case of the Christian, this view of the person sees the human being
> as endowed with an immortal soul and a special right and duty to make moral and social
> choices for which he or she is responsible to God. In the case of "substantive liberals"
> it is a conception of the human person as moral, free, and aware of his/her responsibility
> to respect the equal moral rights of other human beings.[5]

Central to Sigmund's explicit argument—one that describes Locke, Kant, and Joseph Raz as "substantive liberals"—is the implicit assumption that one of the "moral rights" that all human beings possess is the right of religious freedom. Since the Catholic tradition, particularly in the wake of *Dignitatis Humanae*, and the "substantive" liberal tradition both embrace the right of religious freedom, something more than a *modus vivendi* between the two traditions is possible.

This essay will argue, however, that the integrationists' assumptions regarding overlap between the two traditions are too sanguine. And it will do so not by "obsessing over" those issues where there is clear substantive disagreement between Catholics and liberals (e.g., abortion and homosexuality). Rather, it will look at an issue on which there seems, at first glance, to be principled agreement, namely, religious freedom. I will show that the U.S. Supreme Court's defense, since *Everson v. Board of Education of Ewing Township, New Jersey* (1947), of the "liberal" neutrality principle in matters of religion makes any sort of "deep" rapprochement between the two traditions morally and politically problematic. The Supreme Court's religion clause jurisprudence has been grounded not in a principled commitment to limited constitutional government and religious freedom but rather to the *conscientia exlex* of nineteenth-century liberalism. This liberal individualist view of the human person, of society, and of church-state relations differs markedly from the conciliar argument of *Dignitatis Humanae*.

This chapter will consist of three parts. First, I will analyze the development of *Everson*'s "neutrality" principle. I will argue that a jurisprudence based on that principle must, of necessity, (a) create unnecessary tension between the non-establishment and free exercise clauses of the First Amendment; (b) resolve that tension by diminishing the signifi-

cance of the religious component of free exercise, thus creating a secularist view of what constitutes the public good; and (c) lay the foundation for
the defense of what Gerard Bradley has described as the "superneutrality"
of autonomous selfhood. Second, I will argue that the logical *terminus ad
quem* of this effort to conflate liberal political morality and constitutional
jurisprudence is found in the work of legal scholar David A. J. Richards,
not in any reputedly "substantive" form of liberalism. Third, I will discuss
briefly the Second Vatican Council's movement away from a defense of
religious freedom based on the right of conscience and toward its defense
on more properly juridical—yet distinctively Christian—grounds. This
juridical defense of religious freedom, as John Courtney Murray points
out, clearly avoids the Catholic "confessionalist" alternative. More importantly, within the context of the current "Catholic" effort to appropriate aspects of what Sigmund calls "substantive liberalism," it avoids the
antiperfectionist liberal effort to conflate ethics and constitutional jurisprudence in defense of the sovereign self. In sum, the political theory of
Dignitatis Humanae, even though not as developed as some of its critics
(and its defenders) might like, provides a better defense of constitutionalism, the rule of law, and religious freedom than does the liberal alternative.

The Logic of *Everson* and the Emergence of a New Moral Principle

The most memorable words of *Everson v. Board of Education of Ewing
Township, New Jersey* are not those in which a bare majority of five
justices upheld a program of reimbursing the parents of parochial school
children for the cost of bus transportation to and from school. They are
those in which Justice Hugo Black (with none of his confreres writing to
the contrary) asserts that the First Amendment's non-establishment
component means that "Neither a state nor the Federal Government can
set up a church. Neither can pass laws which aid one religion, aid all
religions, or prefer one religion over another. . . . In the words of
Jefferson, the clause against establishment of religion by law was intended
to erect 'a wall of separation between church and state.'"[6]

A dissenting opinion written by Justice Wiley Rutledge echoes Black's
separationist claim, arguing that the purpose of the First Amendment

"was to create a complete and permanent separation of the spheres of religious activity and civil authority by comprehensively forbidding every form of public aid and support for religion."[7] Rutledge and the other dissenters attempt to make short shrift of Black's claim that the statute is a facially neutral general welfare statute that neither advances nor hinders religion. Here, Justice Black's argument *in support of the law* is significant because it sets the parameters within which the Court will be forced to operate at the level of juridical principle in future religion-clause cases. The First Amendment, Black argues, "requires the state to be neutral in its relations with groups of religious believers and non-believers; it does not require the state to be their adversary. State power is no more to be used to handicap religions, than it is to favor them."[8]

There is much in Justice Black's practical effort to resolve the case that would not, at first glance, fly in the face of what *Dignitatis* later lays down as the proper foundation for religious freedom, particularly as the conciliar document is interpreted by John Courtney Murray. First and foremost, Black attempts to set limits to the constitutional powers of federal and—more controversially for those who reject incorporationist arguments—state authority. Moreover, in affirming limits on the power of government in religious matters, Black maintains that such limits should in no way be construed as displaying hostility to religion. Finally, and assuming for present purposes that Black's argument for incorporating the non-establishment prohibition through the due process clause of the Fourteenth Amendment is correct, state public welfare statutes that treat religionists as eligible for the same benefits as others can in no way be said to violate the non-establishment provision.

Why then did Murray, who took an active part in supporting the statute, soberly claim after the Court's *Everson* decision that "We have won on busing, but lost on the First Amendment"?[9]

The problems that most anti-*Everson* constitutional and/or legal scholars encounter center around Jefferson's "wall of separation" metaphor and Justice Black's selective reliance upon the Virginia debates on religious freedom in the mid-1780s in general and Madison's *Memorial and Remonstrance* in particular. These scholars would agree that the debates conducted in the First Congress over the scope and nature of the religion clauses are more determinative of the framers' intent than was Madison's more grandiose and controversial argument several years earlier, made in a decidedly different political context.[10] Furthermore, Black's "separationism," to the extent to which it relies upon Madison's views on the proper role for religion within a liberal society, is rooted in what Stephen Monsma has accurately described as an "Enlightenment worldview that is itself anything but neutral and universal. If the great world religions such as Catholicism and Judaism are 'sectarian'—as the Supreme Court's opinions have often referred to them—the worldview in which *Everson* is rooted is surely no less sectarian. As John Courtney Murray wrote two years after the decision, it was rooted in 'an irredeemable piece of sectarian dogmatism.'" Monsma goes on to explain that "in the effort to prove that 'no establishment of religion' means 'no aid to religion' the Supreme Court proceeds to establish a religion—James Madison's."[11]

Clearly, the "no aid to religion" thrust of Black's (and the dissenters') opinion has the practical effect of undermining *Dignitatis*'s later claim "that the right of all citizens and religious bodies to religious freedom should be recognized *and made effective in practice*".[12] *Dignitatis* contends that the state must "show religion favor" as an aspect of its general concern for the common welfare. Black is forced to define the "general welfare" in such a way as to exclude, in principle, any support for religion whatsoever. An article of Enlightenment dogma that would wall off matters of state from "sectarian" influences is manifestly inconsistent with the right of religious bodies to make their faith "effective in practice," unless the religious bodies themselves accept as true the same piece of Enlightenment dogma and seek to privatize all matters of religious belief and practice. In short, Black's reading of "non-establishment" as legal shorthand for Jefferson's or Madison's larger philosophical agenda turns the religion clauses into precisely what Murray believes the clauses were intended to avoid. They are hardened into an "article of faith" with a specific secularist content.

Monsma chastises the Court for this "wrong road taken." Given what Monsma sees as the mixed signals of *Everson* (i.e., the practical upholding of the reimbursement plan despite the Court's extreme separationist rhetoric), he contends that the post-*Everson* Court should have adopted the less hubristic course of true neutrality, thus making it possible for states to assist religionists and non-religionists in matters of education, for example, in a truly even-handed manner. The right road would comport with a pluralistic, religion-friendly social and cultural environment. The wrong road that the Court actually marched down (i.e., the "secularist" path) created an environment hostile to plural forms of religiosity, especially those of a more communitarian nature. For Monsma, a chastened and "neutralized" *Everson* shorn of its radical separationist rhetoric might lay a proper juridical foundation for American church-state relations. The way to combat the separationist orthodoxy (or, to use Murray's phrase, "article of faith") is to eschew orthodoxy and embrace true neutrality.

Monsma's effort to embrace neutrality while rejecting "no aid" separationism is reflected in the plurality opinion of Justice Clarence Thomas in *Mitchell v. Helms* (2000). The Court upheld, against an Establishment clause challenge, the constitutionality of the Education Consolidation and Improvement Act of 1981 and the ability of state and local agencies, with the support of federal funds, to lend educational equipment and materials (including library and media materials and computer software) to public *and private* (including religious) elementary and secondary schools. Justice Thomas attempts to prove that if a state's purpose is secular (i.e., has neither the purpose of advancing nor inhibiting religion), the lending of such materials meets constitutional muster even if those materials could later be diverted to advance the religious missions of some of the schools. Says Thomas:

> In distinguishing between indoctrination that is attributable to the State and indoctrination that is not, we have consistently turned to the principle of neutrality, upholding aid that is offered to a broad range of groups or persons without regard to their religion. If the religious, irreligious, and areligious are all alike eligible for governmental aid, no one would conclude that any indoctrination that any particular recipient conducts has been done at the behest of the government.[13]

In sum, neutrality between religion and irreligion—Black's phrase— should not be construed as hostility to religious institutions, and the "secular purpose" test should not be construed as constitutional shorthand for liberal political morality. What remains of *Everson,* however, is the debatable proposition that the Constitution commits us to some form of "neutrality" in matters of religion and that governmental endorsement of religion in general is, perhaps, constitutionally problematic.

And therein lies the difficulty with *Everson's* "neutrality" principle, even when it is shorn of its more radical separationist applications. Can a purely juridical principle that explicitly seeks to say nothing whatsoever about the merits (or demerits) of religion affirm a type of public order that is open to the positive good of religious freedom? In other words, does juridical "neutrality" of the sort that Monsma endorses lead inexorably to the type of sectarianism that Monsma properly deplores? Can the "neutrality" principle and a more expansive religiously pluralistic notion of the general welfare coexist together? There seems to be little basis for optimism when one focuses on the trajectory of American church-state relations since *Everson,* especially in light of how the "neutrality" principle has been interpreted by even the more "moderate" members of the Court. Consider the following:

1. Black's own idiosyncratic constitutional literalism and desire to avoid becoming a self-ordained moral philosopher-jurist probably assists Black in avoiding the logic of his own position: a desire to privatize *all* fractious religious and moral issues. Black most certainly does advance a view of religion itself that would constitutionally privilege a liberal Protestant brand of religiosity. (For example, in *Engel v. Vitale* [1962], Black claims that "the Establishment Clause . . . stands as an expression of principle on the part of the Founders of our Constitution that religion is too personal, too sacred, too holy, to permit its 'unhallowed perversion' by a civil magistrate.")[14] At the same time, however, his fidelity to what he perceives as "the text" of the Constitution does not permit him to "personalize" fractious moral questions (e.g., contraception) at the level of constitutional principle. Where Black finds constitutional warrant to do so (e.g., in his reading of the explicit provisions of the Bill of Rights), he naturally reads constitutional provisions in a highly individualistic manner. Where he does not find warrant to do so (i.e., when the text is silent on a subject), he remains silent. Thus, his own conception of what would be a constitutionally legitimate "general welfare" statute would not be

completely eviscerated by the demands of liberal individualism. If the "general welfare" statute in question did not directly implicate questions of religion, Black would give it wider operative scope and, thereby, give state legislatures broader reserve powers in matters of public health, safety, and morals. Liberal "philosopher"-jurists such as Brennan, Douglas, and Blackmun would have little difficulty in expanding Black's textually grounded, albeit idiosyncratic, individualism into a more comprehensive article of faith.

2. If the principle of "liberal neutrality" expands beyond what Monsma wishes for it to be—that is, an article of peace that establishes a limited form of government under which religionists and non-religionists are treated equally—it runs the danger of eviscerating any "thicker" notion of the common good or general welfare. It also runs the danger of subordinating the free exercise clause, and thus religious freedom itself, to the demands of the non-establishment clause. The supposed "tension" that jurists such as Warren Burger see in the commands of "non-establishment" and "free exercise" is dissolved in the name of a larger (but by no means constitutionally grounded) right: the right to freedom of conscience, construed in liberal individualist terms. For example, in *U.S. v. Seeger* (1965), the Court argued that any set of beliefs in ultimate reality, whether grounded in religion or a purely ethical creed, might serve as grounds for exemption from facially valid federal laws: "A sincere and meaningful belief which occupies in the life of its possessor a place parallel to that fulfilled by the God of those admittedly qualifying for [conscientious objector status] comes within the statutory definition."[15] Justice Black, in *Welsh v. U.S.*, extended the logic of *Seeger*, claiming that "beliefs that are purely ethical in source and content," if held strongly, are sufficient to justify exemptions from military service.[16]

The logic of the Court's argument is certainly consistent. The overarching neutrality principle of the non-establishment clause requires that the state make no judgments about the veracity, or even the utility, of religious convictions. If the free exercise clause protects anything, then, it protects not religious exercise but, rather, individual beliefs, whether religious or not. Francis Canavan captures the ruthless logic implicit in this line of argument:

The Court's insistence on governmental religious neutrality is . . . manifested in the tendency it has sometimes shown to take all ultimate beliefs, of whatever nature, as religious beliefs that are equal before the law. Thus it is the position of the belief in the individual's conscience, not the substance of that which is believed, that makes a belief religious for legal purposes. Government must accept as religious beliefs whatever an individual holds as his deepest convictions, even though he himself may deny that they are religious beliefs in the ordinary sense of the term. The result is to formalize and individualize the definition of religion used by the Court. The definition is purely formal inasmuch as it requires only that a belief be ultimate; it is individualized inasmuch as its content is supplied by the individual alone.[17]

How do we accommodate religious practices without acknowledging, per *Everson*'s "neutrality" principle, that religious belief is a "good" thing that, to paraphrase *Dignitatis*, is worthy of respect? By accommodating them, as Gerard V. Bradley points out, not as religious practices *per se* but as activities that flow from deeply held beliefs. For example, "moderate" Justice Sandra Day O'Connor, in *Board of Education of Kiryas Joel v. Grumet* (1994), maintains that "[w]hat makes accommodation permissible, even praiseworthy, is not that government is making life easier for some religious group as such. Rather, it is that government is accommodating a deeply held belief."[18] Or, as Justice David Souter, a more ardent separationist, argued in *Employment Division v. Smith* (1990), "in freeing the Native American Church from federal laws forbidding peyote use . . . the government conveys no endorsement of peyote rituals, the church, or religion as such; it simply respects the centrality of peyote to the lives of certain Americans."[19]

Thus, when the principle of "governmental neutrality" is elevated to the status of a liberal article of faith, it exercises a particularly deleterious effect on the religion clauses of the First Amendment. In questions of non-establishment, "neutrality" comes to mean no support for religion over irreligion. In the area of education, for example, this means, as Canavan argues, that "the public school, . . . having been 'neutral on the side of God,' is now commanded to be neutral between God and whatever His opposite may be."[20] Neutrality between religion and non-religion becomes a defense of liberal individualism. Similarly, in questions of free exercise, as Bradley states, "the coherent rationale for a 'superneutral' religious liberty is this: it's about liberty, not religion."[21]

The practical effect of this "retheoretizing" of the religion clauses of the First Amendment is that the clauses are transformed from politico-juridical principles that *limit* the powers of government in religious matters out of *respect for the good of religious freedom* into something quite different: an exhaustive philosophical defense of something quite similar to the *conscientia exlex* argued for by nineteenth-century laicists—a position against which the Church fathers addressed their argument for religious freedom in *Dignitatis Humanae*. Nowhere is this defense of the *conscientia exlex* expressed more clearly than in the ethical and constitutional arguments of David A. J. Richards.

David Richards and the Logic of Liberal Neutrality

In *Toleration and the Constitution*, David A. J. Richards lays out a "metainterpretive" theory of religious liberty that is, properly speaking, not a theory of religious liberty at all. Rather, it is an argument for "the egalitarian interpretive independence of each person" and "the inalienable right to conscience."[22] In making this argument, he provides us with a clear example of the trajectory that must be taken by the "liberal neutrality" model of American church-state relations. His argument is not a perversion of Black's arguments in *Everson* and *Welsh*, but rather a playing out of the philosophical principles embedded in Black's embrace of separationist neutrality.

Richards argues for the "contractarian" moral foundations of American constitutional law in general and the religion clauses of the First Amendment in particular. Citing Jonathan Edwards, who he believes was arguing in terms consistent with "the spirit of the Lockean epistemology of experience and the theory of the moral sense," Richards maintains that early American religious thinkers believed that ministerial diversity advanced "the kind of choice, expression, and change of religious conscience which alone dignified its religious and moral integrity."[23] The power to choose, and not the potential object of choice, is what gives the conscience whatever degree of dignity it may be said to possess. This contractarian voluntarism is the "motivating idea of Lockean principles" that finds its way into our reflections on the religion clauses through Jefferson and Madison. It also underlies a "conception of ethical independence" that allows us to read the religion clauses in a truly philosophical, as opposed to sectarian, manner. Thus, Richards's explicitly exhaustive reading of the religion clauses begins with an antiperfectionist, neo-Kantian philosophical stand that denudes Locke's, Jefferson's, and Madison's political theory of substantive moral commitments to anything other than respect for the freely formed conscience.

Implicitly rejecting Murray's "articles of peace" reading of the religion clauses, Richards turns the First Amendment into a legal shorthand for a comprehensive deontological moral code: "The challenge to interpretation offered by the religion clauses is, thus, implicitly philosophical: it turns on controversies that ask how we may understand and delineate the ideal of free conscience in a way that properly expresses the regulative moral conception of equal respect. We need an account of equal respect that expresses such respect in an acceptably content-neutral way, one that does not prejudge the substance of belief that free and rational people may entertain."[24] Acceptable content-neutrality (as opposed, we must imagine, to unacceptable content-neutrality) makes no distinctions based on the substantive merits, or non-merits, of any particular teleological conception of human goods. The religion clauses should be read in such a way as to establish the moral priority of rights over goods. "[The] state must guarantee and secure to persons a greatest equal respect for the rational and reasonable capacities of persons themselves to originate, exercise, express, and change theories of life and how to live it well. Thus, the concerns of the religion clauses are instantiated at every stage in which the state may bear upon the process of forming such conceptions, the exercise and expression of such conceptions once achieved, and the changes and revisions of such conceptions."[25]

The supposed tension between the non-establishment and free exercise clauses is eliminated. The phrases "non-establishment" and "free exercise" are expressive of two distinguishable moments within the regime's larger commitment to the rights of conscience, whether religious or not. "The free exercise clause focuses on the coercion of the specific form of one's rational and reasonable conscience, which leads to a more general concern for any coercion of conscience; the antiestablishment clause attacks the corruption of the state's educational role by sectarian conscience."[26]

The sectarian conscience, we must assume, is the conscience that would impose upon others some alternative to the neutral, contractarian model that Richards provides. In short, the religion clauses become the primary vehicles through which liberal antiperfectionism will be impressed upon us as that moral, political, and jurisprudential philosophy that most comports with the true human good: free choice. Religious freedom is protected not because religion is a substantive human good but because it happens to be a component of a larger freedom, that of the rational (i.e., freely formed) conscience. Similarly, the prohibition of religious establishments is part of a larger prohibition of any sectarian effort to impose a substantive conception of the human good on others. Remarkably, Richards describes his account of rationality and reasonableness as "neutral in the sense that it is procedural."[27]

Richards's "procedural," "neutral" perspective provides an intellectual foundation for the Supreme Court's jurisprudence on church-state relations since *Everson*. Unlike the conciliar fathers who wrote *Dignitatis Humanae*, Richards is not primarily concerned with developing a theory of constitutionalism that juridically limits the powers of government in religious matters and yet provides conditions of public order within which religiosity will flourish. Rather, he is attempting to develop a comprehensive metapolitical theory of "equal respect" for autonomous persons that must rely for its enforcement upon those persons charged with the duty of interpreting the U.S. Constitution—the Justices of the Supreme Court. This metapolitical theory must, by definition, be given privileged status over "sectarian" (i.e., perfectionist) counterclaims. In short, Richards's argument for personal autonomy—echoed, even if they are not aware of having done so, by Justices O'Connor and Souter—is a recipe for the comprehensive reordering of our public life, and of the social institutions upon which the state exercises an impact, consistent with a liberal, individualist model of man and society. But whereas seventeenth- and eighteenth-century liberals such as Locke and Jefferson were attempting to develop a political theory that would limit the power of the state, Richards's antiperfectionist liberalism must, by its very nature, embrace the power of the state as a means to impress its highly individualistic view of man and society upon those who would disagree. Francis Canavan captures the paradoxical nature of this brand of statist individualism:

> Recent constitutional law in the United States has limited government by insisting more and more upon individual rights. Still more recently, so has civil rights legislation enacted by Congress or by the several state legislatures. This undoubtedly limits what government may do to individuals, but by the same token, and necessarily, it increases what government may do for individuals and institutions.
>
> Consequently, government today is obligated to be, at one and the same time, individualistic and statist. It is individualistic when it serves an expanding array of rights. But insofar as it uses the power of the state to impose those rights upon institutions, government is statist, and the fingers of the bureaucracy reach more and more into all of the institutions of society.[28]

Dignitatis Humanae, Religious Freedom, and the Juridically Limited State

Dignitatis Humanae is acknowledged to be the centerpiece of the Second Vatican Council's reflections on the political-juridical order, the nature of constitutional government, and the proper foundations for religious freedom in the modern world. While the document is not itself, as Kenneth L. Grasso aptly points out, a systematic treatise of political theory, its content has become fodder for both integrationists and neo-confessionalists.[29] Integrationists such as David Hollenbach and Michael Novak embrace the document for what they see as its support for liberal political institutions; neo-confessionalists such as Ernest Fortin criticize it for what they see as its insufficiently Catholic view of human society and overly cribbed view of the common good. However strongly their substantive views of the proper role for the Church in society may differ, integrationists and neo-confessionalists seem to agree on one point: By embracing human rights and religious freedom, the Second Vatican Council embraced some variant of liberalism.

Hollenbach goes so far as to maintain that the Second Vatican Council embraced not only liberal political institutions but also a semi-Rawlsian vision of human dignity:

> In many ways, Rawls's work has strong affinities with the emphases of Catholic social

thought as it developed since the Second Vatican Council. Rawls stresses the importance of freedom as an essential expression of human dignity. His "difference principle"—which maintains that inequalities in the distribution of primary human goods can be justified only when they are to the advantage of the least advantaged—bears a notable resemblance to what recent Catholic thinkers, including the present pope, have called "the preferential option for the poor."[30]

Thus, in their "practical implications" (if not in their underlying premises) Rawlsianism and Catholicism have much in common, especially in regard to the idea that fundamental human dignity is the wellspring of rights-talk.

On the other hand, and possibly to counter the effort of those Catholics who, like Hollenbach, seem to embrace practical Rawlsianism, Ernest Fortin wonders whether any Catholic defense of human rights—and, more importantly for purposes of this essay, a principled defense of religious freedom—might not place contemporary Catholic social teaching in conflict with its historic commitments to "virtue, character formation, and the common good." For Fortin, this might produce within the Catholic tradition "a latent bifocalism that puts it at odds with itself and thereby weakens it to a considerable extent."[31]

Thus, for both Hollenbach and Fortin, a defense of human dignity and religious freedom is a concession to the claims made upon us by the liberal model of man and society. Since *Dignitatis Humanae* embraced both concepts, it is liberal in orientation.

The problem here is that these accounts fail to appreciate fully the distinctiveness of Catholic social thought. As a result, they find it difficult to appropriate "the sacred tradition and doctrine of the Church—the treasury out of which the Church continually brings forth new things that are in harmony with the things that are old" (*DH*, 1, 163). The Church's social teaching embodies neither a form of baptized Aristotelianism nor a neo-Kantian embrace of radical personal autonomy. The monisms implicit in Aristotelian archaism (i.e., neo-confessionalism) and accommodationist futurism (i.e., neo-Kantian or antiperfectionist liberalism) are both rejected. The thread of the conciliar argument regarding religious freedom relies upon a moral realist defense of a juridically limited state.

In drafting *Dignitatis*, the Second Vatican Council attempted to move away from a defense of religious freedom based on the human conscience's abstract right to follow its own dictates, toward a defense of human freedom based on the human person's concrete right to be free from governmental coercion in religious matters. The Council's own final argument and John Courtney Murray's analysis of the trajectory of that argument are instructive in this regard. They help us to differentiate the Church's developing social teaching from those arguments that would force the Church to choose between a complete rejection or a complete embrace of modernity.[32] (Murray's analysis in particular also makes it clear, however, that further work needs to be done on this aspect of the Church's social teaching.)

Murray contends that the third schema and final draft of *Dignitatis* move away from arguments for religious freedom grounded in the right of conscience. These arguments would seem to force us to choose between two undesirable positions, one of which inclines toward statist individualism and the other toward the confessional state. The first position would seem to embrace the proposition that a sincere conscience, even if it is erroneous, is the bearer of rights that trump the demands of truth and the temporal common good. This alternative has unfortunate overtones of a privatized religiosity and might result in a form of statist individualism. The second alternative would advance the counterclaim that, since an erroneous conscience has no rights, there is no obligation in morality and law to recognize that the person whose conscience happens to be formed erroneously is a bearer of rights. Thus, "in the name of the moral order," a person whose conscience is formed properly "can deny the rightfulness of the erroneous conscience's claim and absolve [himself] of all duties with respect to it."[33] On this argument, religious truth must be affirmed and safeguarded by that particular instrument responsible for promoting the temporal common good—the state. Roman Catholics who wish to remain loyal to sacred tradition must endorse some form of confessional state *at the level of principle*.

Murray contends that the third schema and final draft of *Dignitatis* move away from these false alternatives in the direction of solid ground. They move tentatively toward a more properly juridical defense of limited constitutional government and religious freedom that depends for sustenance upon a Christian view of the dignity of the human person. And in so doing, they argue for a view of the state that prevents it from becoming, as Murray elsewhere described the false alternatives, either "*episcopus externus* or amoral policeman."[34]

A study of the nature of the juridical order, Murray argues, reveals it to be "the order of rights, [having] to do with intersubjective relations among men." Within the juridical order—a deliberately limited order—man faces "'the others,' who also have their own duties and rights. No one may ever urge 'rights' against the truth; the very notion is nonsensical. Rights are urged against the others."[35]

A juridical approach to the problem of religious freedom makes no exhaustive claim for the rights of conscience. It tries "to set outside limits to a sphere of human activity, and to guarantee this sphere against forcible intrusion from without, but not to penetrate into the interior of this sphere and to pronounce moral or theological judgments of value on the activity itself."[36] The "sphere" in question is that of religion, and the politico-juridical theory appropriate to this sphere is one that places limits on the coercive power of government, not on the compulsory moral power of the truth itself. Conceived in juridical terms alone, religious freedom is a freedom from coercion by "the others," especially from those who, by giving the concept of religious freedom positive juridical content (that is, by adopting a comprehensive political "article of faith"), are quite willing to advance a comprehensively statist notion of the common good or public order.

Is Murray's argument that government not be permitted "to pronounce moral or theological judgments of value" on the free exercise of religion similar to the argument that government must be "neutral" on the question of whether religion constitutes a social good? In other words, would the trajectory of Murray's juridical argument, assuming for the moment that it accurately captures the trajectory of the conciliar argument, force the Church to embrace liberal neutrality in practice? Is Murray arguing for Hobbesianized "articles of peace" and a truncated view of the common good? In fact, Murray's argument seems to assume that this negative juridical notion of religious liberty provides a positive foundation upon which society will display respect for the affirmation of persons' (and faith communities') religious sensibilities. Murray contends that

> by reason of its negative [juridical] content [religious freedom] serves to make possible and easy the practice of religious freedom for men and society. It serves to assure full scope for the manifold manifestations of freedom in religious matters. . . . It is to create and maintain a constitutional situation, and to that extent to favor and foster a social climate, within which the citizen and the religious community may pursue the higher ends of human existence without let or hindrance by other citizens, by society, or by government itself.[37]

Murray believes that the state, in pronouncing no "moral or theological judgments of value on the activity [of religious freedom] itself" is not being "neutral" between religion and irreligion; to do so would be to imply a conception of government that is completely ahistorical. Rather, in its very *limitedness* the state expresses a preferential option for religious freedom and provides for those conditions of social life within which the higher ends of life can be pursued. The state, while limited to pursuing the requirements of a moral public order, cannot adopt a truncated, Hobbesianized view of civic life if it is to create those conditions under which "the higher ends of human existence" can develop. The concept of "public order" must be seen against the backdrop of a more comprehensive conception of the temporal common good if true public order and religious freedom are to be achieved. In short, the success of Murray's political "articles of peace" depends upon a societal "article of faith" that is open to religion as an aspect of human flourishing.

In fact, the conciliar document seems to be clearer on this point than is Murray's analysis of it. *Dignitatis Humanae* advances a distinctively Christian differentiation on political things by moving in the direction of a principled defense of limited constitutional government and religious freedom. Unlike the liberal model of man and society, it recognizes "the social nature of man." Rather than endorsing a privatized religiosity in the name of civil peace, it acknowledges that man "should give external expression to his internal acts of religion; that he should participate with others in matters religious; that he should profess his religion in community"(*DH,* 3, 170). Rather than attempting to be neutral between religion and irreligion, "government . . . ought indeed to take account of the religious life of the people and show it favor, since the function of government is to make provision for the common welfare" (*DH*, 3, 170). This favoritism is displayed not through the state's establishment of a particular confessional perspective, but by its maintaining a morally grounded public order within which religious freedom (construed by the public as a positive good), and those social institutions that support such freedom, can flourish. In fact, the confessional state is to be discouraged in principle not because religion is a private matter but because religious freedom is an intrinsic human good that the state advances indirectly through its juridical commitment to constitutional limits and forms. Robert P. George captures the truly Christian dimension of *Dignitatis*'s argument for religious freedom when he contends that "[c]oercion can only damage that possibility of an authentic religious faith, a true realization of the human good of religion. Coercion deflects people from really choosing that human good, for it seeks to dominate their deliberations with the prospect of a quite different good—of freedom from imminent pain, loss, or other harms, or of some other non-religious advantage."[38]

But, as Francis P. Canavan properly notes in a commentary on *Dignitatis*, the success of constitutional government depends upon more than a commitment to juridical norms and procedures. It depends upon a people's commitment to a higher order of morality and law. Canavan says, "But, at least under a constitutional form of government (which the declaration [on religious freedom] seems to consider normal), the moral order and the public order derived from it will be effective restraints on government insofar as they are accepted by the collective conscience of the larger and sounder part of society and are upheld by constitutional organs, such as the courts of law."[39]

George's and Canavan's apt, but cautionary, words capture the essence of the teaching of *Dignitatis Humanae*: (1) religious freedom is an intrinsic human good and the Church's developing commitment to its protection reflects its larger commitment to personal human dignity; (2) limited constitutional government is that form of government which most comports, in principle, with the Church's commitment to human dignity; (3) the politico-juridical notion of religious freedom as a freedom from coercion in religious matters reminds the state of its own intrinsic limitations and lays the foundation for the attainment of larger human ends and purposes; (4) these larger human ends and purposes are attainable only when a society commits itself to preserving not only constitutional forms and structures but also the moral law upon which those forms and structures depend for sustenance.

The politico-juridical notion of religious freedom toward which *Dignitatis* seems to be moving, albeit tentatively, is similar then, for both Murray and Canavan, to the view of religious freedom embraced by the First Amendment of the U.S. Constitution. The First Amendment must be read, according to Murray, as "a prejudice in favor of the method of freedom in society and therefore the prejudice in favor of a government of limited powers, whose limitations are determined by the consent of the people."[40] Or, as he puts it in extending the analogy, "the freedoms of the First Amendment, including the 'free exercise of religion,' were understood to be certain specified immunities; . . . not claims on society and government for positive action, but assurance against positive coercive action by government and society."[41]

Angela C. Carmella observes that "religious liberty, not separation or parity, is the goal of the religion clauses."[42] The problem is that this view of the religion clauses no longer informs the constitutional law governing American church-state relations, especially since the *Everson* case. Those who subscribe to *Everson* and its progeny cannot logically maintain either (a) that the First Amendment's primary purpose was to protect religious freedom, or (b) that the non-establishment component of the religion clauses must be subordinated to the free exercise component. Rather, *Everson* has the effect of laying a foundation for the supremacy of the sovereign self. In so doing, *Everson*'s politico-juridical norms become articles of faith for a thoroughly "retheoretized" (to use Murray's term) view of church-state relations that is, in many respects, hostile to the arguments advanced by the Church fathers in *Dignitatis Humanae*. Monsma's argument for a chastened (and less secularist) reading of the "neutrality" principle opens the public square to persons of religious sensibilities, but it must be supplemented at the philosophical and social level by a theory of man and society that grounds a defense of religious freedom (and the state's juridical role) in something other than liberal premises.

Conclusion

Robert P. George has noted that religious opponents of what he describes as "orthodox [liberal] secularism" adopt two lines of response to the liberal reading of American public life and law (and, by implication, of the religion clauses of the First Amendment). The first, necessary though not sufficient, is to prove that "secularism itself is based on a nonrational faith" that is not consistent with our country's founding traditions. The second is to claim in addition that "religious faith, and especially religiously informed moral judgment, can be based upon and defended by appeal to publicly accessible reasons . . . provided by principles of natural law and natural justice."[43]

One might extend George's argument to the politico-juridical order of church-state relations. The first step on the road to a rhetorical and practical victory over liberal antiperfectionism is to highlight, as Monsma has done, its own "articles of faith" and statist implications. But a further step must be taken beyond the rubric of "neutrality," and those who argue from within the Catholic social tradition are well situated to take that step.

It would be ironic indeed if the Church, having come to embrace religious freedom and constitutionally limited government as a matter of principle, were to seek rapprochement with a model of man and society that undermines the religious, social, and cultural foundations required for the true flourishing of religious freedom. Rather than seeking common ground with individualistic liberalism, the Church ought to commit itself to developing a political theory that, at one and the same time, affirms the limited and yet invariably moral nature of constitutional government. John Courtney Murray's interpretation of the trajectory of the Second Vatican Council's efforts emphasizes the limited juridical nature of the state in religious matters—possibly because of his desire to fend off the claims of Catholic "confessionalists." Those who wish to develop further the Church's teaching in these matters must show clearly how this commitment to juridical limits can in no way be construed as an endorsement of the type of "liberal neutrality" that has encumbered American church-state relations for the past fifty years.

Church and State in Liberal America:
Locke and Tocqueville Revisited

THOMAS A. SPRAGENS JR.

In his *Letter Concerning Toleration*, John Locke admonished his readers that it was "above all things necessary to distinguish exactly the business of civil government from that of religion and to settle the just bounds that lie between the one and the other."[1] It was necessary to make the appropriate distinctions and draw the proper boundaries, in his view, because doing so offered the only realistic means of escaping the devastating religious fratricide that had plagued Europe since the Reformation. From the Wars of Religion to the Puritan-Anglican-Catholic strife of seventeenth-century England, policies of enforced religious conformity produced warfare among the contending sects. Since no sincere believers would be willing to abandon their faith at the behest of some secular authority, the only way out of this quagmire seemed to be a policy of state neutrality in matters religious. At least insofar as different religious sects did not advance doctrines incompatible with civil society, doctrines that rendered them subservient to foreign rulers, or doctrines that led them to persecute other faiths, the civil magistrate could avoid religious warfare in his realm by tolerating them all in the peaceful practice of their worship and their pursuit of salvation. For this kind of tolerance to be feasible, however, it had to be possible to draw a clear line between the proper business of religion and civil government and to demonstrate that neither had the right or the need to tread upon the domain of the other.

Fortunately, Locke argued, it was quite possible to accomplish this feat and to effectuate the institutional disentanglement of church and state "because the church is itself a thing absolutely separate and distinct from commonwealth. The boundaries on both sides are fixed and immovable. He jumbles heaven and earth together, the things most remote and opposite, who mixes these two societies, which are in their original, end, business and in everything perfectly distinct and infinitely different from each other."[2]

Locke could insist upon this separability by depending upon reinforcing dualisms between the inner and outer realms of human life, between the temporal and the eternal, and between compulsion and persuasion. The church's proper business was the conduct of worship and the procurement of salvation for its members. These tasks were intrinsically inward, oriented toward eternity, and attainable only by voluntary acquiescence. The state's proper business, in contrast, was limited to the protection of the lives, liberties, and properties of its citizens. These were outward and worldly matters enforceable if necessary by law and force.

The most difficult area in which to draw the requisite boundary between the different enterprises of church and commonwealth, Locke recognized, came in the area of what he called "practical opinions." "Speculative" doctrines like those concerning God's trinitarian nature or the belief in transubstantiation governed beliefs rather than actions. But "practical" doctrines were ethical and moral beliefs that carried consequences for the behavior of those who held to them. And since behaviors occur in outward actions, here arose "great danger lest one of these jurisdictions entrench upon the other and discord arise between the keeper of the public peace and the overseers of souls." But even here Locke's final word is one of reassurance: "if what has been already said concerning the limits of both those governments be rightly considered, it will easily remove all difficulty in this matter."[3]

A century and a half after Locke offered these words of advice and reassurance, Alexis de Tocqueville traveled to Jacksonian America to get a glimpse of what the world's future looked like. He believed that democratization was historically inevitable and that the former British colonies were currently farthest along this curve. As a keen observer of manners and mores, he took interest in the intersection of religion and politics in this country; and he offered some interesting claims and predictions regarding what he saw here. In many other places, he wrote, the spirit of religion and the spirit of liberty had been "in frequent hostility." But that was not the case in America, where the settlers of New England "were at the same time ardent sectarians and daring innovators." In America, then, the spirit of religion and the spirit of liberty "have been admirably incorporated and combined with one another."[4]

This pattern of association in which "liberty regards religion as its companion in all its battles and its triumphs," Tocqueville believed, was not adventitious but was instead grounded in the logic of psychological and spiritual complementarity. Human beings, he argued, required some fixity in their first principles and their most fundamental conceptions about the world and their place in it. Without such fixity, they would be seriously disoriented: "doubt on these first principles would abandon all their actions to chance, and would condemn them in some way to disorder and impotence." The moral reference points provided by religion, therefore, were particularly indispensable in the emerging political universe of democratic liberalism. For in such a political universe, everything in the secular world was fluid, mobile, and indeterminate. There, people "broke down the barriers of the society in which they were born; they disregarded the old principles which had governed the world for ages; a career without bounds, a field without a horizon was opened before them."[5] It seemed to follow, then, that the vitality of religious belief and commitment could be expected to continue into the American future out of a kind of psychological necessity: peculiarly without social "bounds" or a set historical "horizon," the citizens of this brave new democratic world would, for that very reason, find it most necessary and desirous to maintain the fixed points for identity and action that religion alone seemed able to provide.

Prompted by these observations and arguments, Tocqueville then went on to hazard a prediction about the likely pattern of religious and sectarian affiliation that would characterize the American future. Some members of the ever-changing and basically antinomian democratic society would conform their moral lives to the political order. These people would become fully secular and largely protean selves swimming along in the seas of democratic contingency. But others would find such a protean existence unbearable and would seek the guidance and security of the most settled and "dogmatic" religious authority available. And in this respect, the deep historical roots and settled hierarchy of Catholicism would seem particularly attractive. Thus, "the men of our days," wrote Tocqueville, "are naturally little disposed to believe; but as soon as they have any religion, they immediately find in themselves a latent instinct which urges them unconsciously toward Catholicism." As a consequence, he opined, "our posterity will tend more and more to a division into only two parts—some relinquishing Christianity entirely, and others return-ing to the Church of Rome."[6]

It would seem safe to say that today, another century and a half later, neither Locke's assurance that the domains of religion and politics can be cleanly and easily disentangled and kept from each other's turf nor Tocqueville's predictions about patterns of sectarian affiliation have been fully borne out. A quick look at the U.S. Constitution Annotated or even at the daily newspaper will make it clear that we are still troubled and in some cases deeply divided about the proper location of the line between church and state, religion and politics. And although Catholics certainly play a significant role in American society, they have not become the statistically dominant denomination Tocqueville predicted. Indeed, Catholic leaders and social thinkers exhibit an understandable sense of increasing embattlement and marginalization.[7] What events or forces have made Locke's assurance and Tocqueville's speculations seem obsolete?

Locke's sanguine expectation has, in a very fundamental sense, actu-ally been vindicated. Recall that he was writing within historical sight of the Wars of Religion and the Saint Bartholomew's Day Massacre. By comparison with these bloody fratricides, our current politico-religious strife seems fairly tame. We have in fact much to be grateful for in terms of the practical consequences of constitutional innovations such as the English Act of Toleration of 1689 and the First Amendment provisions of the U.S. Constitution regarding the free exercise and establishment of religion. But a number of causal factors have kept the entente between religious commitments and liberal regimes perpetually vexed.

The first of these factors is not surprising. And in fact it could have been anticipated from a careful reading of Locke's *Letter*. For he recognized and conceded in that essay that the greatest danger to the success of his principles in maintaining comity between church and state—keeping each of them happy and safely out of the other's hair—arose from religious beliefs that carry implications for behavior and not merely for professions of faith. I can believe that God is trinitarian, you can believe that God is a unity, and a third can believe that God is female; and we can all hold fast to those beliefs without being compelled toward conflicting deeds. But it is otherwise with practical beliefs, which impinge directly upon moral claims and conduct. "Moral actions," acknowledged Locke, "belong to the jurisdiction both of the outward and inward court, both of the civil and domestic governor; I mean both of the magistrate and conscience. Here, therefore, there is great danger."[8]

Indeed, these dangers and difficulties are unceasing. The leading examples today, because of the salience of "cultural" issues in our political battles, are probably abortion and homosexuality. And this contemporary salience of arguments about proper sexual conduct (in the broad sense of the phrase), and about appropriate legal practices related to them, is what accounts for the current tendency to see religious commitments as ancillary to conservative politics—e.g., the "Religious Right." In earlier decades of this century, when the salient battles were over the welfare state and civil rights, it was more common to see religion as a force behind the liberal and progressive social conscience—e.g., the "social gospel" and "liberation theology."

A second cause that contributes to making it more difficult rather than easier to draw lines that produce peaceful coexistence among religions and between the state and religious denominations is increased moral and religious pluralism. Locke's conception of toleration was in effect a political entente among Protestant sects ranging from Anglicans on the Right to Quakers and Anabaptists on the Left. Atheism, he wrote, did not warrant toleration because "the taking away of God, though but even in thought, dissolves all. . . . Promises, covenants, and oaths, which are the bonds of human society, can have no hold upon an atheist."[9] And Catholics were also excludable on the grounds that by their allegiance to the Pope they "delivered themselves up to the protection and service of another prince" and were ipso facto subversives.[10] But these latter suspicions were largely rendered impotent by the presidency of John Kennedy. And few of us today seriously entertain the idea that religious skeptics cannot be moral people and good citizens. So we now inhabit a society more deeply and widely pluralistic than Locke's England—not only ethnically and racially but morally and religiously as well. Rather than ranging only from Anglican to Anabaptist, contemporary American society encompasses a moral and religious spectrum that runs from Islam to militant secularism.

The impact of this more extensive pluralism upon the problems addressed in Locke's *Letter* is twofold. First, toleration has to run deep. Both the state and its citizens are required to accept beliefs and behaviors that diverge more and more profoundly from those they endorse. The second consequence is to force more and more religious expressions and symbolism outside the public domain. For whatever toleration and the boundary between church and state mean in the abstract, in concrete terms they mean the privatization not so much of religious beliefs and commitments per se as the privatization of *contested* religious beliefs and commitments. Where the range of pluralism encompasses only Christian sects, no one will regard manger scenes on the courthouse lawn at Yuletide as a violation of the separation between church and state. Today, such religious displays occasion protest; and the public square becomes increasingly naked from the standpoint of Christian believers.

The other major development affecting the boundary-drawing between church and state has been the considerable expansion of the scope of governmental activity under the aegis of the welfare state. Drawing the line between church and state is one thing when the role of the magistrate is essentially confined to the police function of protecting life, liberty, and estate. It becomes quite a different task when the state is extensively involved in the provision of social services. What families, local communities, and churches once did, the state now has largely colonized: providing relief for the poor, assisting the aged, and educating the young. The major consequence of the welfare state in this context, then, is to expand the public domain at the expense of the private realm. The line between church and state has to move, and the space occupied by religious institutions grows smaller.

The compound effect of these two developments is to force the role and visibility of religion ever more completely into an ever shrinking private domain. Not too surprisingly, many of the religiously committed wind up protesting what they experience as their increasing marginalization. Alarmed not only by the diminution of the public presence of religion but also by what they see as a concomitant process of moral decline in society at large, some religious leaders—especially those in the evangelical and fundamentalist camps—pull out their cudgels and do battle with the forces of "secular humanism." And even those religious leaders who do not aspire to what H. Richard Niebuhr characterized as a "Christ of culture" voice a sense that serious and dedicated Christian believers increasingly fall into the status of "resident aliens" in liberal America.[11]

If Locke's reassurance about the relative ease and benign effect of drawing a clear boundary between church and state has not entirely worked out, what can be said about the fate of Tocqueville's prediction about the shape of religious commitment and affiliation in democratic society? His forecast, you will recall, was that the citizens of fully democratized cultures would "tend more and more to a division into only two parts— some relinquishing Christianity entirely, and others returning to the Church of Rome."[12] On the face of it, this prediction has not been borne out, since adherents of the Church of Rome number only about twenty percent of the population, while Protestant denominations retain a larger share of adherents.

But if we attend to the reasoning behind Tocqueville's prediction, we might conclude that his judgment has been vindicated at its core, even though the specific details of the prediction have not proved accurate. For his reasoning was based in his reading of the psychological and spiritual effects of living in a culture dominated by powerful forces leading people toward materialism, egoism, skepticism, and social mobility. Since religion pushes in the other direction along each of these dimensions—toward idealism, community, dogmatism, and fixity—people will react psychologically and spiritually to social and cultural democratization in one of two ways, Tocqueville thought. Those who find a life of protean individualism and hedonism fully congenial, he reasoned, would find religion fundamentally anomalous to their spiritual bent and would abandon it altogether. These are the dynamics that lead Stephen Macedo to write that democratic liberalism "holds out the promise, or the threat, of making all the world like California,"[13] with its dynamism, fluidity, and tendency toward narcissistic self-indulgence. On the other hand, some would react to the cultural kaleidoscope of liberal culture with a sense of psychic vertigo and moral revulsion. They would therefore seek a religious home that offered the sense of certainty, fixity, community, and discipline they found lacking in the larger society.

A good case can be made, I believe, that Tocqueville's analysis remains quite pertinent today, telling us much about the current relationship between religion and democratic culture as well as about the causal forces that shape it. It seems reasonable to conclude that Tocqueville quite presciently saw the decline of the mainline Protestant denominations. These denominations assimilated more easily and fully to the surrounding liberal culture than did Catholicism, and they therefore lost much of their moral distinctiveness and their social function as time went on. Thus many of the children of these denominations could, as Tocqueville predicted, drift fairly easily into secular liberalism and relinquish their religious affiliation altogether. But others who resisted this assimilation reacted not by becoming Catholic, for the most part, but by joining fundamentalist or evangelical denominations that seemed to offer greater religious vitality and a way of life more clearly distinguished from the putatively demoralized secular culture.

In speculating that most people find it difficult "to keep their minds floating at random between liberty and obedience" and in predicting that "our posterity will tend more and more to a division into only two parts" when it comes to religion, Tocqueville can arguably be credited with anticipating the basic configuration of today's "culture wars." In the presidential election of 2000, the television electoral map was blue on both coasts and red throughout the center of the country. Put tendentiously from the point of view of their adversaries, the red area represented the benighted bigots of "fly-over country," whereas the blue areas along both coasts represented Sodom and Gomorrah. It wasn't simply "the economy, stupid," this time out. Instead, cultural allegiances competed with and sometimes trumped economic logic. How else to account for the fact that the Democratic candidate won among upper-class married women and lost among lower- and middle-income married women? And in many of our political and cultural battles, it's Pat Buchanan and Jerry Falwell against the ACLU and People for the American Way. We also face a rather odd class-cultural demographic in which, as Peter Berger has pointed out, an elite as secular as Sweden governs a non-elite as religious as India.

Thus, when it comes to church and state in contemporary liberal America, the problem can be framed in the following terms: *How can we successfully draw Locke's boundary line in a democratic society that is more profoundly pluralistic and has a much larger domain of state action than in Locke's day—and that also is marked by the kind of cultural bifurcation Tocqueville anticipated?* Are we doomed to live forever in the midst of pitched battles between those who champion school prayer and those who want the public schools to engage in a kind of religious deprogramming? Between those who seek a quasi-theocracy and those who would wall off religious communities like creatures in a zoo? I hope not. There are viable, legitimate, and more productive ways to institutionalize the relationship between church and state. Tension there will always be, but it can be the creative tension of a genuine and respectful pluralism rather than zero-sum warfare between antithetical crusading armies.

That kind of creative entente between church and state would not be possible in all historical and political settings. A faithful church would have to become de facto subversive under regimes that refused to respect human rights, failed to treat its people with dignity, or engaged in aggressive military ventures abroad. And a liberal regime could never fully accommodate religious organizations seeking to conduct holy wars against the infidels in their midst. But these constraining conditions on both sides are generally respected in contemporary democracies. The liberal state is informed by an ethos and usually bound by constitutional imperatives that require respect for civil liberties and human dignity. And even the most militant denominations in contemporary democratic societies don't seek to persecute or disenfranchise their fellow citizens, however heretical or pagan they may consider them. In our own time and place, then, it should be possible for both the church and the liberal state to remain true to their prevailing moral commitments and obligations without infringing upon the legitimate needs and obligations of the other party.

For the relationship between the church and the liberal state to be one characterized by constructive and creative engagement rather than by mutual hostility, paranoia, and aggression, however, a number of rules of engagement need to be kept in mind. At times in recent years, these rules have not been recognized or have been honored more in the breach than in the observance. So let me conclude this essay by framing these rules of engagement in the form of admonitions to both sides—first to religious believers and the institutionalized church, and then to secular citizens and the authorities of the liberal state.

The first admonition to the faithful is that they must relinquish any residual hopes or aspirations toward some form of Constantinian settlement between church and state. In the explicit political sense, of course, this admonition seems obvious and unexceptionable. But it must be understood that in a broader cultural sense it is also true that, as Locke put it several centuries ago, "there is absolutely no such thing under the Gospel as a Christian commonwealth."[14] Because this country has from its inception been predominantly Christian, much of the public culture— even in official and governmental environs—has been de facto sectarian even in the face of the constitutional prohibition against religious establishment. School prayer is the obvious example here, but there are many other instances that could also be enumerated. As these come under attack, the embattled faithful often rally to the defense of crosses or mangers on the courthouse lawn or the posting of the Commandments in a courtroom.

But these atavistic crusades are neither proper nor worth pursuing. They should be abandoned as a form of nostalgic cultural imperialism whose day has gone. The public square need not be entirely naked, but it certainly must be broadly ecumenical and inclusively pluralistic. It is also neither wise nor appropriate for the faithful to expect secular public institutions to serve as agencies of religious socialization, and that includes the inculcation of moral norms distinctive to or predicated upon religious commitments. It violates the liberal state's obligation to treat all of its citizens equally and with respect for it to endorse, much less enforce, modes of behavior particular to one conception of a humanly good life—except insofar as these modes of behavior coincide with the civic virtues of liberal regimes.

The abandonment of Constantinian yearnings, both political and cultural, should not be viewed by the faithful as tragic ostracism or as craven capitulation to the heathen. Instead, it should be welcomed as the liberating relinquishment of a dangerous temptation. When the church cohabits too cozily with the state, liberal or otherwise, the result is not that the state becomes regenerate so much as that the church becomes too worldly. The usual result is not that politicians become saintly, but that bishops lead troops into battle. The church needs always to remember that it follows one who once said that birds had nests and foxes had holes, but the Son of Man had nowhere to lay his head. If the church succumbs to the lure of the throne, it loses its integrity, its authenticity, and, thereby, its distinctive mission.

Accepting disestablishment with good cheer does not equate, however, with meekly acquiescing in social marginalization. The church has every right to resist the efforts of those whom Stephen Macedo has dubbed "evangelical atheists," that is, those who attempt to turn religion into something that is done only in private by consenting adults. Indeed, the church is obligated to resist this pressure if it is to fulfill its charge to "bear witness to the Gentiles." To do that, the church must be clearly visible. It is the real "city on a hill" of which John Winthrop spoke, an intimation of the blessed community and an example to the world. The church should, therefore, not be at all bashful about doing its work and conducting its ministry in a very public way.

In holding resolutely to its legitimate public presence, the church also should resist pressures to hold its tongue. Some influential liberal theorists have recently undertaken to set boundaries to what they regard

as proper public discourse—or "public reason"—in pluralist democracies. The basic claim here is that whenever anyone engages in public advocacy in a pluralistic and well-ordered democracy, he or she is bound by
the norms of civility and fairness to eschew justifications that draw upon
comprehensive moral or religious doctrines. The argument is that the use
of public power in such a society is legitimate only when it is grounded in
principles that "all citizens may reasonably be expected to endorse in the
light of principles and ideals acceptable to them as reasonable and rational."[15] Since all are not of the same religion, it follows that the faithful
should not invoke their religious beliefs or obligations in discussing matters of public policy.

Now it is true that considerations of democratic legitimacy, civility,
and prudence all dictate making a genuine effort to justify political policies one advocates in terms that can appear compelling to all reasonable
fellow citizens. Not only the ideal of government by consent but the
canons of good rhetorical strategy strongly counsel the invocation of reasons all could conceivably accept. But both norms of candor and the obligations of bearing witness are also relevant here, and these push us in a
somewhat different direction. They would lead us to come clean, as it
were, and be explicit about, rather than seek somehow to hide, the deeper
moral imperatives that impel us to support policies conducive to keeping
the peace, defending human dignity, succoring the needy, and so on.

Contributors to public discourse in a well-ordered democracy, I would
argue, need not choose between being "political" (i.e., constrained by
the limits of the society's moral consensus) or "comprehensive" (i.e.,
explicitly grounded in more distinctive and extensive moral or religious
views). Religiously committed citizens can and should speak at appropriate times with a prophetic voice. It is not only fidelity to divine
injunction, but better—even if not wholly welcome—service to the
larger society for the faithful to reference the theological sources of
their political judgments. It is not some breach of democratic civility,
then, but a thoroughly proper and legitimate contribution to public discourse when, say, the Catholic bishops or the Council of Churches issue
political pronouncements that invoke God's will as they perceive it. Their
fellow citizens are free to reject or ignore their admonitions on the grounds

that they depend upon beliefs they do not share. But they at least are candidly informed about the ultimate convictions that shape the views and aspirations of some of their peers. And they are properly reminded that, however legitimate it may be by the standards of democracy, the popular will is not immune to condemnation on more universal and transcendent moral grounds.

The Church's adherents should also resolve to be good citizens, whenever the obligations and virtues of citizenship do not run directly counter to the demands of faith. In some historical situations, good Christians would be morally obligated not to be "good citizens" insofar as that means remaining obedient to the laws and carrying out the policies of their government. In Hitler's Germany, for example, it is hard to see how any serious believer could avoid being de facto treasonous or subversive. The true Church there inhabited Dietrich Bonhoeffer's jail cell. But the tensions between the demands of faith and liberal regimes are usually not so stark. To the extent that the idea of natural right—as set forth in the preamble to the Declaration of Independence, for example—provided the moral foundation for the development of liberal regimes, these polities are in effect grounded in a secularized and attenuated version of Judeo-Christian ethics. If they remain true to their own articulated principles, therefore, these regimes must base their institutional practices and policies upon a respect for the fundamental dignity and the moral equality of all their citizens.

Hence it does not conflict with the demands of faith for believers to embody what secular liberalism sees as its " political virtues." It is consonant with their deeper comprehensive commitments for believers to exhibit "the virtues of fair social cooperation such as the virtues of civility and tolerance, of reasonableness and the sense of fairness."[16] More than that, their religiously based belief in the sanctity of life and the dignity of personhood should lead church members to be among the most determined defenders of human rights. And their acceptance of the obligations of *caritas* should make them the best of neighbors and exemplars of the liberal ideal of "fraternity." It was no accident that the church and its adherents were at the center of the civil rights movement in this country, for example. And in this instance, the believers were the best of citizens precisely because they lived up to the demands of their faith. In their insistence upon according respect and the full rights of citizenship to all members of our society, they not only fulfilled their religious obligations but at the same time forced the liberal regime to live up to its own ideals. Perhaps this is what it means to live up to the biblical admonition to be the salt of the earth.

In a phrase favored by the Reverend William Sloane Coffin and the Christian social ethicist William Lee Miller, the church should conduct an ongoing "lover's quarrel" with the liberal regimes it inhabits. It can be a *lover's* quarrel because of the genuine moral aspirations of liberalism and because liberal regimes accord the faithful protected space within which to live as God would have them live. It is a *quarrel* because no society lives as God would have it live, and believers can never forget or be silent about that. *In extremis,* that quarrel may turn into outright opposition or civil disobedience. Thoreau, Martin Luther King, and the Berrigans spent time in jail. Sometimes it comes to that. Religious believers in this world are inescapably subject to two masters; so although in some respects they can be model citizens of liberal regimes, they can never be fully obedient subjects of earthly powers. When the tensions between obligations to divine and worldly authority turn into perceived contradictions and outright opposition, one can only hope that liberal regimes remember their respect for the moral and religious commitments of their citizens and that the religiously inspired disobedients remember both the procedural legitimacy of democratic authority, however contingent it may be, and the fallibility of their reading of God's will.

To summarize, then, my admonitions to the faithful who live under liberal regimes are: relinquish atavistic yearnings for political or cultural Constantinian arrangements and learn the freedom and authenticity of living as "resident aliens"; resist those who would silence or marginalize the Church or religious faith; bear witness and speak to the larger society with a civil and respectful but prophetic voice; be good citizens and the best of neighbors within the constraints of the lover's quarrel that all believers must carry on with even the best civil society. These admonitions need to be paired, however, with a correlative set of admonitions directed to the liberal state. For contemporary transgressions of the proper boundaries between church and state by no means issue from only one side of the divide.

To the liberal state and its secular citizens, then, I offer the following unsolicited advice. First, it would be well to abandon reliance upon the metaphor of a "wall of separation" between church and state or religion and politics as expressing the proper model for regulating their relationship. This metaphor was even in its inception purely a dictum from Jefferson's pen, and although it has upon occasion been invoked in opinions of the Supreme Court it has no constitutional provenance. Moreover, in the context of the vast extension of state activity over the past century, this metaphor is peculiarly inappropriate as a guideline for negotiating the institutional interface at issue. Indeed, since the extent of state action is so ubiquitous these days, converting that entire territory into a space to be surrounded by a wall within which religious institutions can have no legitimate presence or function is a recipe for the outright ostracism of religion from public life. This was hardly what Locke or the framers of the Constitution had in mind. And it effectively converts a plan for a tolerantly evenhanded pluralistic society into a blueprint for an exclusionary secularist society in which any religious references and ecclesiastical activities are forced behind closed doors.

The proper standard is instead expressed in the specific prohibition of the First Amendment: to wit, Congress shall not *establish* any religion. This standard is something other than a directive to erect a wall beyond which religion is banished. It simply prohibits the government from placing its authority and coercive powers at the service of either religion generally or one particular religion. This constitutes a significant limitation upon majoritarian and state power, but it prohibits only government favoritism, endorsement, or use of force on behalf of religious groups— not the public presence and public functioning of religious organizations within society. Indeed, given the conjunction of the establishment clause with the free exercise clause, the state is not only permitted, on a nonprejudicial basis, to accord religious groups and institutions space and liberty to conduct their enterprises, however public these might be, it arguably is positively required to do so.

The policy consequences of this difference between the "wall of separation" and the "non-establishment" standards can be significant. For example, the former standard would make it inappropriate for a public school to permit a student religious group to use its building for an after-school meeting, whereas the latter standard would make it not only acceptable to do so but mandatory, if other student associations were accorded that opportunity. The former standard would prevent any tax-funded educational subsidy from being used at a school run by a religious organization or affiliated with a religious denomination, whereas the latter standard would allow that to happen, so long as the subsidy were available to all schools performing the same educational role and so long as no students were forced into attendance. My contention, then, is that in both of these instances it is the second policy that is appropriate. The liberal state has the right, as I have argued elsewhere, to foster the capacities and virtues necessary for its survival and success.[17] And that gives the state the right to promote these capacities and virtues in the context of the education of the young. But that legitimate authority neither necessitates nor justifies a project of attempting to create a homogeneous cadre of wholly secularized little civic republicans. Those educated at religiously affiliated institutions—say I, writing at a place sometimes called "Methodist Flats"—can be socialized as good democratic citizens, too. Rather than being driven toward a program of financially coercive secularist homogenization in education, then, better for us to recall the pointed counsel of John Stuart Mill, who was himself a religious skeptic and one who was concerned to defend genuine pluralism, diversity, and autonomy.

> All that has been said of the importance of individuality of character, and diversity in opinions and modes of conduct, involves, as of the same unspeakable importance, diversity of education. A general State education is a contrivance for molding people to be exactly like one another; and as the mold in which it casts them is that which pleases the predominant power in the government—whether this be a monarch, a priesthood, an aristocracy, or the majority of the existing generation—in proportion as it is efficient and successful, it establishes a despotism over the mind, leading by natural tendency to one over the body. An education established and controlled by the State should only exist . . . as one among many competing experiments, carried on for the purpose of example and stimulus to keep the others up to a certain standard of excellence."[18]

Mill's worries about state education may be overstated, but his basic point should be well pondered by those who believe it appropriate for a liberal state to create a de facto state monopoly over secondary education for all children not fortunate enough to have chosen wealthy parents.

Second, a liberal society should not try to silence its faithful citizens nor should it seek to drop a veil of ignorance over the role of religion both historically and in the contemporary world. Although a liberal society must thwart any and all Constantinian aspirations harbored by its religious citizens, that does not require adopting the kind of "don't ask, don't tell" policies favored by some devout secularists who insist that state neutrality dictates the closeting of religion. A society genuinely dedicated to pluralism, diversity, human dignity, and autonomy should not try, for example, to browbeat a Joseph Lieberman from openly affirming his religious commitments and their role in shaping his political views. More secular citizens may decide to oppose him at election time out of wariness about what they see as a political stance too closely entangled with religion. But they should not try to hush his honest acknowledgment of his "comprehensive" views by characterizing this candor as a breach of democratic propriety.

Similarly inappropriate is the notion that a democratic, secular, public education should seek in curricular terms to hide or ignore the role that religious beliefs and affiliation have played in the world. At times, this official silencing resembles the way that the former Soviet Union used to write its *personae non gratae* out of history. From my perusal of my children's high school American history texts, I can tell you that many students enter college believing that American constitutional thought was significantly influenced by the practices of the Iroquois but that the Founders' theological beliefs were irrelevant. Similarly, American students are often left with little or no understanding of how central the enterprises and identities of the various religious denominations have been to much that has happened in our history. (I have a vivid memory of attending a lecture given by the sociologist of religion, Robert Bellah, that made me realize how important this understanding is to a sound grasp of American history and how little my own education had done to produce such an understanding. My ignorance is not atypical and should not be surprising upon reflection. Even at the university level, I find the word "religion" or a cognate only one time in the course descriptions of the fifty American history courses in my own university's bulletin.)

Third, it needs to be insisted that a genuinely pluralistic liberal society must not embrace a philosophically and morally tendentious construction of "tolerance" that renders it incompatible with belief in an objective or transcendent human good. To make this misstep, whether out of naïveté or malice, effectively derogates all religious believers as "bigots" *ab initio*. Properly understood, the liberal virtue of tolerance requires citizens to respect the political rights of those fellow citizens who do not share their comprehensive moral or religious beliefs and to treat them as civic equals. It does not require acquiescing in the genial nihilism of affirming all beliefs and behaviors as just as true and morally worthy as any other. As Patrick Neal has tellingly noted, this kind of confused and misguided understanding of the meaning and demands of toleration does not embody but rather violates the requisites of liberal state neutrality vis à vis the comprehensive moral and religious beliefs and affiliations of its citizens. For it endorses one specific *conceptualization* of the human good above other important and incompatible ways of understanding what a "conception of the good" is. Specifically, this position misidentifies liberal state neutrality as the de facto endorsement of a moral meta-theory that sees having a conception of the good as equivalent to having a set of preferences or desires rather than as believing the world to be such that it imposes moral claims upon us.[19] This faulty and tendentious way of understanding toleration is itself intolerant. It privileges moral decisionism over moral cognitivism. And, in practical terms, it thereby is intolerant of religious believers in the very act of construing them as the intolerant ones. It is necessary to insist, therefore, that the liberal state must remain neutral about *conceptualizations* of the good rather than claiming to embody moral neutrality at the same time as it decisively privileges a non-neutral conceptualization of the good incompatible with serious religious belief.

Finally, it is not only proper by reference to its own constitutive norms but also wise and prudent for a liberal society to recognize and respect the religious denominations in its midst as valuable components of a healthy democratic civil society. That is so for several reasons. In the first place, it is generally the case that religious believers make good neighbors and good liberal citizens. There is a great deal of overlap between the ethical imperatives most religions place upon their adherents and the liberal civic virtues. Both adherents of the major religious faiths and good liberal citizens, for example, are under moral obligations to be responsible agents, to treat others with care and respect, and to lend a helping hand to those in need.[20] Second, religious congregations in this country conduct an enormous array of very important social services. Were these services to wither away, our social safety net would be damaged far more drastically than most people realize. In cities like Boston, New York, and Philadelphia, many of the most successful inner-city projects are church run. In my own locale, churches not only provide major support for youth programs, "tough love" groups, Alcoholics Anonymous, and the like; they also work closely with county social service agencies and run the largest soup kitchen in town. And when Hurricane Floyd ripped through part of our state, church congregations probably provided more assistance to its victims than FEMA and the Red Cross put together.

Finally, it is worth recalling Tocqueville's argument for why religion is important to societies dedicated, as liberal regimes are, to liberty and equality. For religion provides a moral anchor arguably needed to prevent the restless mutability, the antinomianism, the materialism, and the privatistic individualism endemic to capitalist liberal democracies from becoming self-destructive. Religion reminds liberal societies of the eternal verities in the context of their mutability, of the need for lawfulness and self-restraint in the context of their drift toward self-indulgence, of higher goods than the material gain they prioritize, and of the need for communal bonds in the face of their individualism.

Given the self-understanding of religious people as being "in but not of the world," the relationship between church and state can never be entirely frictionless. The criteria that should govern the interface between the two institutions and regulate their respective jurisdictions will always be contestable and likely will always remain contentious. If the wider recognition and acknowledgment of our epistemic fallibility on matters

moral and religious has eased the difficulties of managing this relationship since the passage of the Act of Toleration in 1689, the wider scope of
the state and the deeper doctrinal pluralism of our own society have
created new problems. If we can proceed on the basis of the admonitions
and reciprocal restraints I have recommended here, however, hope remains that we can do better than descend into a pattern of interminable
pitched battles between extremists on both sides. We need to shun those
who seek to enlist us in supposedly new but in fact old, improper, and
counterproductive crusades either to establish a "Christian commonwealth" or to "*ecrasez l'infame*." We should avoid reenacting the destructive and divisive politics of post-revolutionary France in which animosi-
ties between believers and anticlerics have been a constant obstacle to
social progress and comity. Instead, we should remember what Tocqueville
taught us about the productive synergy between de-established religion
and a democratic society. For, as William Galston, with a nod to that
perspicacious nineteenth-century visitor, recently has said: "In some
measure, religion and liberal politics need each other. Religion can
undergird key liberal values and practices; liberal politics can protect—
and substantially accommodate—the free exercise of religion. But this
relationship of mutual support dissolves if the respective proponents
lose touch with what unites them."[21]

Liberalism and Marriage:
The Pluralist Game Revisited

GERARD V. BRADLEY

Fifteen years ago, in a phrase that served as the title of his important book, Richard John Neuhaus advanced the paradoxical proposition that America's current moral crisis—characterized by the cultural and legal acceptance of moral infamies like abortion—can nevertheless be characterized as the "Catholic moment." Why? Because the Roman Catholic Church can and should take the lead in proclaiming moral truth, thereby regenerating our culture and changing our law. Again, why? Because the Catholic Church is the most formidable and most resolute repository and defender of traditional moral beliefs in the United States.

Father Neuhaus is appropriately credited with bringing this odd but true thesis to wide public attention. The thesis was anticipated, however, by another Catholic priest-scholar more than twenty years before Neuhaus wrote in 1987. In 1965, Father Francis Canavan, in an essay entitled "Law and Morals in a Pluralist Society," wrote about the point when changing Western societies in general, and America in particular, would undergo a moral meltdown. He described that "moment" in the following manner: "The tide is not flowing in favor of traditional Christian morality; the sound we hear today is the melancholy, long, withdrawing roar of the sea of faith."[1] This pessimistic, yet prescient, appraisal came at precisely the same time that many sober Catholics were celebrating the Second Vatican Council's release of Catholics and Catholic thought from what they considered to be a pre-Vatican II ghetto. In celebrating this release, they embraced what they perceived to be the Church's rapprochement with the practices of the liberal, pluralist state.

Unlike many of those who celebrated, however, Canavan recognized that the tide that flowed against traditional Christian morality had in fact been at least partially brought into being by the underlying philosophical commitments of the liberal intellectual tradition, most especially in that tradition's seeming elevation of "choice" to the highest of moral and political goods. And Canavan, like Jeremiah (but without the brimstone), calmly but correctly prophesied as to where those commitments, dressed up in the garb of "moral neutrality," would take us: "[O]ne need not be excessively pessimistic to predict that euthanasia and homosexual relations will become the subject of acrimonious public debate within the lifetime of most of those who read this article" (9).

Legal euthanasia has indeed arrived in Oregon, and (we may speculate) has been incorporated into the ethos of many, if not most, doctors practicing in the United States. We also may legitimately wonder what effect the legalization of "gay marriage" in Vermont will have on our constitutional law and on the public support, encouragement, and protection of family life. The time is ripe for a discussion of how liberal political morality (under the rubric of "neutrality") has brought us to this "moment" and what the proper response on the part of Roman Catholics should be. There is no more reliable guide on these questions than Francis Canavan.

In this essay, I intend to explore and extend Canavan's insights into contemporary political liberalism, specifically its claim to a "moral neutrality," and the current debate over abortion and gay marriage.

Canavan and Ratzinger on Law in a Pluralist Society

Commenting recently on what he perceives to be a crisis in law, Joseph Cardinal Ratzinger lamented what he calls the "end of metaphysics."[2] Naturally he places that phrase in quotation marks: given what metaphysics is, it cannot die; indeed, it cannot be killed even by men rebelling against it. By "metaphysics," Ratzinger means objective moral truths that ought to serve as the foundation for the positive law. His claim is that positive law has been disconnected from its foundation in the natural moral law and has been replaced by some variant of judicial positivism. Canavan would, I think, be counted as a herald of these observations. In the aforementioned 1965 essay, Canavan seemed to regard the loss of a popular moral consensus as the immediate instigator of the tidal crisis he described. He lamented the loss of a "moral consensus that once existed, and which supported laws [about divorce and pornography, for example] still [then] on the statute books" (13).

But here, seemingly, is an interesting tension between Canavan and Ratzinger. Canavan was cautious about grounding the positive law directly in moral truth, holding that "Catholics should be hesitant to enact laws that impose more than the generally accepted standards of public morality" (13). Ratzinger, on the other hand, argues that where metaphysics is ignored, or thought to be a corpse, the state, "can only refer to the common convictions of its citizens' values, convictions that are reflected in the democratic consensus." Law, he continued, is then exposed to the whims of the majority, a disastrous result. This effect is "manifested concretely by the progressive disappearance of the fundamentals of law inspired by the Christian tradition."[3] Ratzinger seems eager to embrace what Canavan seems hesitant to enact: laws grounded directly in the Christian tradition rather than in "generally accepted standards of public morality." And Canavan seems to embrace what Ratzinger rejects: a legal positivism in which generally accepted standards of public morality become the foundational norm for law.

The conflict or tension between Ratzinger and Canavan on the relation of the positive law, especially the positive law of a pluralistic democratic society, to the natural law is more apparent than real. When we look more closely at Canavan's thoroughgoing critique of liberal neutrality, as advanced for example in "The Pluralist Game" (1982), we see that he anticipates the trenchant warnings of Cardinal Ratzinger, warnings that have deservedly drawn much interest among Catholics and other moral traditionalists. Canavan, as usual, was there first.

The "pluralist game" is the "way in which we [i.e., late-twentieth-

century Americans] attempt to resolve the problems arising out of our
pluralism through the political, which includes the judicial process" (ix).
Canavan has consistently argued that, in his words from a 1992 article,
liberalism's "purely procedural and substantively neutral model of civil
society . . . is a flim-flam and a confidence game"(153). There is, Canavan
has shown convincingly and often, no such possibility of a purely procedural and substantively neutral model of civil society. "There is," Canavan
writes, "no such thing as a society that is simply neutral on all questions
of substantive human good" (153). Those who would argue that the state
should take a position of "neutrality" on all questions related to what gives
value to life are really engaged in a kind of intellectual con game. And to
what end? "[T]o lure us into agreeing to a highly individualistic and secularist agenda, which has its own substantive content" (153)—a content
that elevates the norm of "choice" to the highest of individual and social
goods and charges the state with the responsibility of enforcing this norm.
In this construal, liberal rhetoric is just the carnival barkers' huckstering,
used to separate passersby (especially those with non-liberal sensibilities)
from their moral convictions about how society ought to be run.

Canavan gives us a splendid example of this con game: "[T]he public
decision to protect areas of conduct regarded as private can and does vary
with time and circumstance. In New York today people may legally appear naked on the stage, but the people in the audience may not smoke
while looking at them. There is a time within living memory when the
reverse was true. Drawing the line therefore is a political issue and one
that inevitably will often have to be argued in moral terms" (153). Canavan
thus makes two extraordinarily perceptive moves. The first has to do
with the inevitable "partiality" of any political society. No society, however much it might try, can free itself of metaphysics and philosophy.
Every political order relies upon philosophical presuppositions. One can
deny that these presuppositions exist but they are never in fact eliminated. Canavan insists—rightly—that "political issues" eventually raise
"moral questions that must be answered in the light of some conception
of human nature, its basic needs, and its common social welfare" (154).
Canavan's cogent critique of liberalism is consonant with and indeed rooted
in the insights of the Second Vatican Council, yet it steers clear of explicit

reliance upon theological premises: "I am not proposing a Catholic, Christian, Judeo-Christian, or any other religious orthodoxy for the pluralistic society of this country" (154). But a substantive orthodoxy of some sort it must have, and we would play the "pluralist game" more honestly and forthrightly if we all, including liberals, admitted this fact.

The second perceptive move undermines the claim that Canavan and Ratzinger are at odds on the proper foundation for positive law. It need not—and should not—be said that morality represents nothing but the will of a majority imposed on the minority who may disagree with it. Canavan approvingly cites Professor Paul Weiss, of Yale University:

> A respect for the rights of minorities is but a respect for the individuals who form the minority. It means that they are to be acknowledged to have the same rights as those who form the majority. Plural marriages, incest, human sacrifice, free love are to be denied to the minority, not because they are not liked by the majority, but because it would be wrong for anyone to engage in them. The representatives elected by the majority ought to act representatively even for the minority, and therefore ought to urge only what all ought to accept. (10)

Thus, Canavan finally does sound like Cardinal Ratzinger. He warns us of the demise of a metaphysically enriched view of the human person and of the rise of an alternative "metaphysics" that engenders public support because it claims to be an alternative to "deep" views of the human good. Canavan helps us to see that liberalism's claim to "moral neutrality" on the question of the good life is a transparent disguise for the imposition of liberal morality.

Sexual Ethics and American Public Morality

The constitutionalization of abortion rights is probably the greatest injustice in American society today, but it could be argued that the late-twentieth-century disintegration of marriage is more epoch-defining, and more hazardous to persons' moral health. Marriage is the grounding principle of sexual morality. Immoral sexual acts are often wrong for reasons other than that they are non-marital—for example, it is unjust to impose oneself sexually upon another without that person's consent. But non-marital sexual activity is wrong for precisely that reason: that it is non-marital.

That marriage supplied the unifying force in questions of sexual morality was, until a generation ago, the common morality of Americans of diverse religious beliefs. And it was the central viewpoint of American public law. As Justice John Harlan wrote in 1961 (in an opinion favoring a constitutionally grounded legal immunity for contraceptive use by married couples): "The laws regarding marriage . . . provide both when the sexual powers may be used and the legal and societal context in which children are born and brought up. . . . [L]aws forbidding adultery, fornication and homosexual practice . . . express the negative of that proposition."[4] In other words, laws that encourage certain sexual practices, prohibit others, and immunize still others from legal coercion are made, and properly so, with an eye to the commonly shared view that marriage is a public good. Indeed, one might argue that the common morality that served as the basis for laws regarding marriage and sexual morality extended beyond this. A social commitment to marriage entailed a wide pattern of restraint upon the part of all persons, married and unmarried alike. Simply put, marriage is not only a lot of work for married couples. It is a high-maintenance deal for any society that recognizes it as a unique opportunity for human flourishing.

But what happens when this societal consensus begins to disintegrate? What if a large number of people come to believe that marriage as traditionally construed is not the unifying force in matters of sexual ethics? Or that they are entitled to regular sexual satisfaction regardless of the willingness of their spouses, if indeed there are spouses at all? It is not necessary to imagine what this asserted right to sexual satisfaction would do to a society. The drift of the past thirty years bears witness to the consequences. We merely have to recall the sexual revolution of the sixties, attended by increasing rates of illegitimacy and divorce, and soon thereafter, by the legalization of abortion.

Abortion as a legal liberty may find some of its roots in the economic needs and aspirations of contemporary women. That is, the abortion license is often thought to be a necessary corollary of the quest for women's economic and political equality. And it may find other roots in certain aggressive arguments for human eugenics. *Roe* v. *Wade* was nevertheless a decision midwifed by the notion of sexual freedom. Abortion was seen by many of its supporters as back-up contraception.

But the constitutional imprimatur that *Roe* v. *Wade* provided for abortion (and the 35 million abortions that have followed in its wake) has, paradoxically enough, not eroded the staunch pro-life commitments of more than half of this country's inhabitants. We may live in a culture of death, but many persons have managed to escape its corrupting influence. Indeed, the vast majority of Americans, whether avowedly pro-life or "pro-choice," know that abortion is wrong. If there is a classic case proving the Apostle's vision of a natural law written on the hearts of all, abortion is that case. Even many of those who support abortion rights obligingly cite their "personal" opposition to the practice, and even a pro-abortion president expressed hope that it could be made "rare." How commonly do we hear people address pregnant women as "moms" or "expectant mothers" carrying "babies." No one asks a pregnant woman how her "fetus" is doing. They ask how the baby is.

Why does abortion have so little traction upon our consciences? That abortions kill babies is undeniable; it is obvious; it is there for all to see. Every birth, every sonogram, puts the lie to "pro-choice" arguments. That the choice to abort is therefore a stark choice between life and killing is undeniable. We have endured a whole generation of attempts to disguise abortion rhetorically, to redescribe it or to deflect attention from its baby victims to its adult "victims." But abortion on the ground is a stubborn thing; it makes unshakable demands upon our consciences. Many, including a pro-abortion president and pro-abortion congressmen, run from the moral reality of abortion, but none can hide. The moral truth, at least in this case, is a tireless pursuer. The rhetorical brandishing of "choice" as the principle to be defended (rather than abortion itself) makes this quite clear.

Abortions cast a thin shadow over the moral culture. They are performed in private, out of view and only here and there, behind bland facades—e.g., at the "Women's Health Center," in that unadorned building just off the strip mall. But once done, they are not forgotten, especially by the women who have had them. For almost all of them, their abortions are a matter of regret, if not of shame or self-contempt. And abortions are rarely discussed. Very few women are widely known to have had abortions. There are few visible effects of abortions, save for the occasional ghastly discovery of "remains."

The pro-life position, even when taken up in the academy, where one would expect to encounter the greatest resistance, is often accorded a respectful hearing. Being "pro-life" may not win friends in some quarters, but pro-life arguments are generally considered to be responsible and reasonable, even if mistaken. And these arguments are accessible to those who wish to ground their principles in some source other than religious authority or revelation. Reason is, at least by and large, believed to offer ample support, if not cogent or conclusive arguments, for the wrongness of abortion. One can be demonstrably pro-life with respectability. More-over, despite the salience of choice or autonomy as the foundation of ethical decision making in other realms of life—especially with regard to sexual activity—few give choice a very wide berth in the ethics of life. That there is an inalienable right not to be killed that accrues to (regular, full-fledged) persons is hardly questioned. That persons at the edges of life are denied that right upon the basis of diminished capacity is a grave injustice. But each argument against their right not to be killed implicitly concedes the existence of that right for many, many others.

Therefore, because of the thin shadow cast by abortion and the recognizable frailty of the one simple principle of choice in the area of life and death, the liberal "neutrality" principle cannot fully exercise its charms. And, thus, the possibility of being respectably pro-life.

Not so, however, in the current debate over same-sex marriage, where opponents are branded as intolerant hate-mongers. In this area, the liberal shell game of "neutrality" over competing conceptions of the good life holds sway. Why is this so, even among those who profess to be personal supporters of a more traditional view of marriage?

Choice *is* very widely held to be the successor to marriage as the principle of morally permissible sexual activity. That choice is miscast in this role is surely true, but it is not obviously true in the same sense that it is miscast in the realm of abortion politics. There is no sexual sonogram that demonstrates to all but the least sensitized among us the wrongness of mutually agreeable, emotionally intense, pleasurable non-marital sex. In addition, there appears to be no victim where choice becomes the prevailing norm. At least where unmarried adults consent, as in fornication or prostitution, there seems to be, in truth, no injustice. Or at least this is the view of those who make choice the principle of morally permissible sexual activity.

Fornication and prostitution are indeed morally wrong, but they are not wrong by dint of applying the Golden Rule alone. That uncontracepted marital intercourse is the only morally upright genital sexual act is not obvious, though it is true. That marriage itself is indissoluble is not obvious, though it is also true. But why is it held to be true by fewer and fewer persons? And what should a person with these traditional sensibilities do when confronted by the demands of a pluralist society?

In regard to the first question, the temptation to rationalize sexual misbehavior is so great because the emotions are so powerfully engaged in the acts themselves. Where the (emotionally appealing, physically exciting) act appears to have no victim, the elusiveness of the reasons for the act's immorality makes for only a very faint pang of conscience, a light tug from one's better self. And where at the same time religious authorities speak diffidently and equivocally, for fear of giving offense, many people almost cannot be blamed for thinking it is all okay.

This is true especially where the meaning of marriage has been transformed. What *could* it mean to say that marriage is the principle of upright sexual activity where "marriage" has come to include same-sex couples? Under such a dispensation, marriage *cannot* be understood to be essentially related to children and reproduction, for no issue from the marriage is possible. Children are entirely optional. Indeed, marriage itself could hardly be understood as sexually exclusive: where sexual acts are not, morally speaking, necessarily reproductive in kind, then the ends of sex (friendship, pleasure, intimacy) simply do not imply or entail exclusivity.

In regard to the second question, one must remember that our legal tradition, including constitutional law, has not supported extension of marriage to same-sex couples. Nor have a majority of the American people been disposed to support such an extension either. But, then, there is the filtering device of liberal neutrality. And it is at this point that Canavan's analysis of the suppressed metaphysics of contemporary liberalism becomes helpful to those who seek to take responsible positions on this crucial public question.

Marriage and the Pluralist Game

Many people say that they personally believe that marriage is a union of one man and one woman. Many such people are married to persons of the opposite sex, and cannot really imagine the attraction some persons have for others of the same sex. They would be vastly disappointed if one of their children decided that he or she wanted to marry someone of the same sex. They often also say, however, that it would be wrong, perhaps even a grave injustice, for the state to base its law of marriage on a controversial moral judgment—in fact, theirs and that of most people—that marriage is the union of one man and one woman. Their thought is that the state ought to be *neutral* between competing understandings of what marriage is. It would be wrong, these persons say, for the state to impose *anyone's* moral code for marriage—that is, to make my, or your, morality the template impressed upon all, especially through the instrument of law.

Sometimes this viewpoint is elaborated along the following lines. Marriage is, in truth, the union of a man and a woman, as Scripture teaches. Marriage is also a sacrament (or an analogous sacred relationship) in many religions. But, although this constitutes the truth about marriage, the religious provenance of this definition makes it an inappropriate basis for civil law. One could thus say that marriage really is permanent and that divorce is impermissible or even, strictly speaking, impossible. But one could coherently say as well that civil law ought not to track this view, thus making provision for the possibility of divorce under certain circumstances.

About this way of viewing the relationship of the truth about marriage and the civil law, I make the following three preliminary points. First, on no one's account of it (as far as I am aware) is the civil law supposed simply to reproduce the moral truth about marriage. Much of what is truly good in and about marriage is beyond effective legal assistance. The endless self-giving that is required of spouses cannot be enforced. Everyone is a bad spouse sometimes, and some persons are bad spouses most of the time. Still, no one suggests that there should be legal penalties for being a bad (ungenerous, self-centered, indifferent) spouse. Men who see more of professional football than they do of their wives and children combined will have a lot to answer for on Judgment Day—in the hereafter, not here. In short, the civil law, recognizing its own intrinsic limits, cannot create perfect marriages. But does this mean that the civil law must be completely "neutral" on the question of what constitutes marriage in the first place?

Contra the "neutralist" claim that those who adopt a "deeper" view of the relationship between marriage and civil law are statists, the most that any reasonable person proposes is that the civil law ought to reflect some basic or defining features of marriage, and only where that serves political society's common good.[5] To what extent the law ought to make provision, for example, for civil divorce is, it seems to me, a question permitting a range of answers consistent with the moral truth that a valid marriage is indissoluble. A legal regime of "no-fault divorce," though, seems outside that range. But one need not take a strong view of the permanence of marriage to hold that no-fault divorce has worked great harm to innocent people in our society, and that some type of "fault" regime would constitute a great improvement over the current state of affairs.[6]

Second, the common mindset described above suffers from what I call the "transparency" problem. When speaking of the judgment that, for example, same-sex marriage is wrong or impossible, one is often heard to say that it is "my" view, or part of "my moral code." This way of speaking is often an innocent locution for the proposition, "same-sex marriage is simply wrong, objectively." This way of speaking is harmful, however, when casually (often unthinkingly) joined to ambient notions of moral subjectivism or emotivism.

There is justice in the claim that coercion based simply upon "my" morality would be an unfair imposition on "your" morality. The mere *fact* that a judgment is *mine* is not a *reason* for the state to act in a certain way, perhaps especially to the detriment of others who do not share *my* view. That one feels repulsed by what homosexuals do does not constitute a reason for this or that public policy regarding same-sex marriage. It does not constitute a reason for anything. It is just a feeling.

But no one really thinks that the mere fact that one holds a particular view on any subject is, taken alone, a reason for action, apart from the *reasons* why one holds the view to be true. In contrast to the opaque or intransitive quality of moral judgment evident in the common view expressed above, conclusions about the morality of same-sex marriage usually are, and should generally be seen as, *transparent* for the reasons *why* the view is held. Some people may be able to give no account of their reasons. They will make uninteresting conversation partners. Other people really are moral emotivists or relativists, and *would* be unfairly imposing upon others if they called on the state to act coercively simply on the basis of their feelings on the subject at hand. But these facts about some people do not support the proposition that opposition to same-sex marriage is necessarily, or even commonly, subjectivist or emotivist.

Most people believe and mean to say that same-sex marriage is simply wrong for everyone, that it is objectively and categorically immoral. This view could be false. If it is false, its falsity constitutes a sufficient reason to discard it, particularly insofar as a false view should not provide the basis for civil law. Therefore, doctrines about political "neutrality" or unjust imposition are simply unnecessary. If the view is true, however, it is not quite as easy to discard political arguments flowing from this moral judgment. Doctrines *of* neutrality, in this case, are either inapposite or require arguments in their favor as to *why* the law should be neutral on this important question.

Third, the common mindset often asserts or implies that certain truths about marriage (such as its permanence or heterosexuality) can be based *only* on revelation or the authority of a sacred text or religious personality. This view asserts or implies that these truths, even if they are truths, are *not* knowable by reason alone. Some defenses of the legal recognition of same-sex marriage, notably the recent decision of the Hawaii Supreme Court, appear to take this view. If this claim about the nonrational basis of any judgment about the illegitimacy of same-sex marriage is true, I agree that the civil law should not be founded upon such esoteric truths. But mere assertions that such judgments are nonrational will not suffice, nor will simple dismissals of them as somehow grounded in nothing more than religious bigotry.

Nor, for that matter, will it suffice to claim that political determinations based on such judgments violate the principle of "neutrality," for, as Canavan has ably pointed out, the law cannot be neutral on these issues. The claim that the law *ought* to be morally neutral about marriage, or anything else for that matter, is itself a moral claim. It—the claim that the law *ought* to be neutral—is not morally neutral. As Robert George points out, anyone who holds that the civil provisions governing marriage (or any other institution or practice) ought to be morally neutral does not assert that the law ought to be neutral between the view that the law ought to be neutral and competing moral views.[7] It is "obvious," he says, "that neutrality between neutrality and non-neutrality is logically impossible."[8]

A deep moral neutrality—that is, a view that is neutral between the view that the law ought to prescind from the truth of the matter about marriage and the view that the law should not prescind—is logically impossible. But this does *not* mean that a more practical form of neutrality must be rejected. It simply means that the correctness of the view in favor of a *practical* neutrality must be argued for. And sophisticated proponents of moral neutrality do argue that the *best* understanding of political morality for our society requires that the law be morally neutral with respect to marriage. They argue, George claims, that "alternative understandings of political morality, insofar as they fail to recognize the principle of moral neutrality, are . . . mistaken and ought, as such, to be rejected."[9]

What then might this (revised) argument in favor of neutrality say? Stephen Macedo has made probably the best (revised) argument for moral neutrality.[10] He defends the proposition that even if the inherited definition of marriage as a union of one man and one woman is true, the state cannot justly recognize it as such. For if disagreements about the nature of marriage "lie in . . . difficult philosophical quarrels, about which reasonable people have long disagreed, then our differences lie in precisely the territory that John Rawls rightly marks off as inappropriate to the fashioning of our basic rights and liberties."[11] And from this it follows that government must remain neutral between those conceptions of marriage that argue for its intrinsic heterosexuality (and monogamy), and those conceptions according to which "marriages" may be contracted not only between a man and a woman, but also between two men or two women (and, presumably, a man or a woman and multiple male and/or female "spouses"). Otherwise, according to Macedo, the state would "inappropriately" be "deny[ing] people fundamental aspects of equality based on reasons and arguments whose force can only be appreciated by those who accept difficult to assess [metaphysical and moral] claims."[12]

As Professor George notes, however, the meaning and significance of marriage are only available, in an effective and widespread way, where the host culture, including its positive law, embodies and encourages a sound understanding of marriage.

> [Where] ideologies and practices which are hostile to a sound understanding and practice of marriage in a culture tend to undermine the institution of marriage in that culture, thus making it difficult for large numbers of people to grasp the true meaning, value, and significance of marriage, it is extremely important that government eschew attempts to be "neutral" with regard to competing conceptions of marriage and try hard to embody in its law and policy the soundest, most nearly correct conception.[13]

The positive law, even in societies like ours where people often profess "neutrality," is still a potent teacher. The law will inevitably teach *some* lesson about what marriage is, and what parties to marriage can or should expect from it. It may *seem* that the law is innocent of such aspirations, and bereft of such presuppositions. It may *seem* that marriage, viewed legally, is all form without substance. It may *seem* that the law teaches only the lesson that marriage is tailor-made to suit the parties to it, and that the function and purpose of marriage law is to facilitate the choices of the individuals who are getting married. It may *seem* that Justice Brennan captured our notions in the *Michael H* case: "Even if we can agree, therefore, that 'family' and 'parenthood' are part of the good life, it is absurd to assume that we can agree on the content of those terms and destructive to pretend that we do. In a community such as ours, 'liberty' must include the freedom not to conform."[14] These expressions *seem* to suggest that the state can, and should, recognize and endorse marriage—if only by bestowing some three hundred or so incidental benefits upon it—without *any* specific definition of the relationship, and evidently without using evaluative criteria of what truly (and substantively) constitutes marriage.

It is impossible, however, to imagine an institution with as many legal benefits as marriage having (or proponents of the institution, and of its concomitant benefits, having) no self-understanding, no parameters, no extra-legal presuppositions or commitments. It would be bizarre, and very likely unjust, to impose the costs of such benefits and protections upon society's members without an answer to the questions: Why? How is the cost justified? What is marriage, and why is it so special? No answer to these questions is possible without *some* definition of marriage, and without *some* theory of the relationship of the parties within a marriage, and of the relationship of marriage to political society.

We find, unsurprisingly, that legal stories about marriage always contain *some* specification of marriage's value. This is especially true of those stories that embrace some form of neutrality. For example, some would argue that the most significant function of marriage today is that it furnishes emotional satisfactions to be found in no other relationships and that it provides refuge from what is perceived as the barrenness of contemporary existence. This might be true (or it might not). But "neutral" it most certainly is not. Upon what basis is *this* particular property of marriage (i.e., its ability to impart emotional satisfaction) chosen from among all its properties, held up as especially salient to deliberation by public authority, and deemed sufficient to justify the regime of special treatment we accord marriage? The argument seems to be that the state has a responsibility to recognize the intensely personal bonds between committed homosexuals. Again, why should "intensely personal bonds" be the *sine qua non* of marriage, and upon what basis does the state have a "responsibility" to endorse them? Why not the "intensely personal bonds" between siblings? Between close, but not sexually involved, friends?

Even though he does not take a negative view of same-sex marriage, Joseph Raz nevertheless correctly states the necessary relation between the positive law as it touches upon marriage and the real-world possibilities for participation in the good of marriage: "[M]onogamy, assuming that it is the only valuable form of marriage, cannot be practiced by an individual. Its success as a guiding norm requires a culture that recognizes, supports, and reinforces it publicly and through its formal institutions."[15] Raz should not be misunderstood here. Robert George contends that Raz "does not suppose that, in a culture whose law and public morality do not support monogamy, someone who happens to believe in it will somehow be unable to restrict himself to having one wife or will be required to take additional wives."[16] Raz's point, according to George, is that

> even if monogamy is a key element of a sound understanding of marriage, large numbers of people will fail to understand that or why that is the case—and will therefore fail to grasp the value of monogamy and the intelligible point of practicing it—unless they are assisted by a culture which supports, formally and informally, monogamous marriage. . . . Marriage is the type of good which can be participated in, or fully participated in, only by people who properly understand it and choose it with a proper understanding in mind; yet people's ability properly to understand it, and thus to choose it, depends upon institutions and cultural understandings that transcend individual choice.[17]

The "neutral" approach to the civil law about marriage renders that law a riddle. For one should not—indeed, one cannot—imagine that the law attaches certain benefits to the status of "marriage" without *first* determining that there is a specific relationship that *deserves* such beneficial treatment. One cannot imagine that lawmakers ever decided to create an entitlement program and called it (for some reason) "marriage," with the idea of making eligibility (to be "married") functionally related to the benefits. *If* you can enjoy the benefits, you can get married. On this view, "marriage" is an empty placeholder in a social welfare scheme.

There can be no doubt that the legal regime—of benefits, protections, and duties—which has surrounded marriage since our founding got it precisely the other way around. Marriage has regularly been said to be subject to legal regulation. But the central thrust of the many political, especially judicial, testimonies to the value of marriage has been the salutary effects this pre-political (and thus natural) institution has upon the fortunes of political society, and upon the happiness of people. For these reasons marriage has been thought worthy of extensive social and legal support.

Two examples of judicial testimony in this matter will have to suffice. In *Maynard* v. *Hill* the U.S. Supreme Court said that marriage creates "the most important relation in life" and has "more to do with the morals and civilization of a people than any other institution."[18] In addition, the Court stated that marriage "is the foundation of the family and of society, without which there would be neither civilization or progress."[19]

Why? In 1961, Justice Harlan explained, though in a summary way, *why* marriage—the union of one man and one woman—occupies this central role:

> [T]he very inclusion of the category of morality among state concerns indicates that society is not limited in its objects only to the physical well-being of the community, but has traditionally concerned it self with the moral soundness of its people as well . . . . The laws regarding marriage which provide both when the sexual powers may be used and the legal and societal context in which children are born and brought up, as well as laws forbidding adultery, fornication and homosexual practices which express the negative of the proposition, confining sexuality to lawful marriage, form a pattern so deeply pressed into the substance of our social life that any Constitutional doctrine in this area must build upon that basis."[20]

Here are the two features of marriage which lawmakers from time out of mind have picked out of that complex open-ended relationship as *critically* important to the political common good: marriage as the principle of sexual morality, and marriage as the only legitimate setting in which children should come to be, and be raised. It has surely been the undoing of marriage that, as a society, we have so detached both sex and marriage from reproduction and the rearing of children.

Common sense, as well as our legal and moral traditions, points us to the existence of some decisive relation among marriage, children, and how children come to be.[21] The practical insight that marriage has its own intelligible purpose (i.e., that it is a one-flesh communion of persons consummated and actualized in the reproductive-type acts of spouses) cannot be attained by someone who has no idea of what these terms mean. Nor can it be attained, except with strenuous efforts of imagination, by people who, due to personal or cultural circumstances, have little acquaintance with actual marriages thus understood. For this reason, whatever undermines the sound understanding and practice of marriage in a culture—including ideologies that are hostile to that understanding and practice—makes it difficult for people to grasp the intrinsic value of marriage and marital intercourse. And, as Canavan would argue, the intrinsic value of marriage is especially undermined in a society where, under the rubric of "moral neutrality," marriage is fundamentally rede-

fined in such a manner as to comport with the requirements of philosophical liberalism.

On this and other important social questions, society must give some
answer to the question of what constitutes "marriage," and this must be
reflected in the positive civil law on the subject. The responsible position
of Roman Catholic traditionalists in the matter is to recognize the inherently moral nature of positive law, and to call our nation back to that self-
understanding that undergirded our culture and legal tradition for centuries. By extending the arguments advanced in Francis Canavan's pioneering work, we can more clearly see this important fact, and the "Catholic
moment" in which we find ourselves.

Can Liberalism Cast Out Liberalism?

GEORGE MCKENNA

In a celebrated article in the *New York Times Magazine* a few years ago, editor and columnist Andrew Sullivan excoriated America's "right-wing intelligentsia" for their "scolding, moralizing conservatism." The new conservatism, he claimed, is different from the old kind, which only wanted less government and more economic freedom. It is "much less liberal, far less economic and only nominally skeptical of government power. . . . As much European as American in its forebears, this conservatism is not afraid of the state or its power to set a moral tone or coerce a moral atmosphere."[1]

Andrew Sullivan is a complex man: an observant Catholic and an observant homosexual. His Catholicism pulls him one way and his active homosexuality the other. He seems to waver between institutional conservatism (the Catholic influence) and a strange kind of antinomianism that accompanies his efforts to legitimize gay "lifestyles."[2] In this article the antinomianism seems to have won out, and it impairs his normally keen perceptions of what is going on in America. For in characterizing the new conservatism as "European" he seems not to have noticed that it is American *liberalism* that is constantly facing toward Europe. Why can't we have a health system like Sweden's? Why can't we adopt French attitudes toward sex? Why can't we help people kill themselves the way they do in the Netherlands? It is the new liberals—the liberals of academia, Hollywood, and the mainstream media—who keep hectoring us with these questions.

But perhaps this misses his point. In referring to the "forebears" of contemporary conservatism, what Sullivan seems to be invoking is not contemporary European laws and mores but the "forebears" of European conservative thought, people like Joseph DeMaistre and Louis Bonald, who spent their careers trying to roll back the French Revolution. As I will argue here, nothing could be further from what American "conservatism" is all about. But the real irony in Sullivan's mischaracterization is its inability or unwillingness to see how much contemporary liberalism owes to the thought of Europe, especially to European thought during the so-called "Enlightenment" period of the eighteenth century.

Feminist leader Gloria Steinem, who said in 1973, "[B]y the year 2000 we will, I hope, raise our children to believe in human potential, not God," has recently updated her hopes. Now she wants to "live to see the day that St. Patrick's Cathedral is a child-care center. . . ."[3] Steinem's vision has a precedent. During the French Revolution, Paris's Notre Dame Cathedral was turned into a Temple of Reason,[4] seemingly actualizing one of the great dreams of the European Enlightenment. "The time will therefore come," Condorcet wrote, "when the sun will shine only on free men who know no other master but their reason, when tyrants and slaves, priests and their stupid or hypocritical instruments, will exist only in works of history and on the stage."[5]

So Andrew Sullivan has it exactly backwards: it is contemporary American liberalism that has its "forebears" in Europe. Steinem's malicious atheism, which would have been found in the leftist backwaters a generation ago, now sails easily in the liberal mainstream. Even Condorcet's statement would shock no one at any liberal dinner party today. Maybe somebody would say, "it's a little strong" or, "Father Greeley is O.K.," but the thrust of it would not be resisted. In liberal circles, Christianity, at least orthodox Christianity, is assumed to be the natural enemy of rationality, freedom, and progress. "Faith is belief without reason," writes *Time* magazine's Roger Rosenblatt. "Fundamentally, religion opposes rational processes," and, though it builds beautiful cathedrals and paints fine Madonnas, it also "promotes ignorance, inflames bigotry, encourages superstition, erases history, invades nations and slaughters the opposition."[6] Many of the attacks on the "Religious Right" run along these lines. The *New Republic*'s John Judis does it with a syllogism. The Religious Right, he notes, opposed the Supreme Court's abortion decision of 1973. But the decision opened up a "new realm of personal freedom" and "became the basis for new kinds of consumer products, as well as sexual experimentation and novel social arrangements." By opposing it, therefore, religious conservatives have shown that they are enemies of both progress and freedom. Their ultimate motivation? Probably "a repressed discomfort with any kind of sexuality."[7] Here, then, is European-style liberalism. It promotes "novel social arrangements" and demonizes its opponents as reactionaries, enemies of freedom, tools of repression and priestcraft (or preachercraft). When fully unpacked, this liberalism is not acceptable to a majority of Americans, which is one reason why contemporary liberals no longer care to be called liberals.

There was a time within the lifetime of many when liberals did like to be called liberals. The 1945 autobiography of Republican Senator George Norris was called *Fighting Liberal*.[8] But that was because liberalism had a different meaning in 1945 than it has today. What it meant then was that the federal government should do more to fight poverty, to elevate the quality of American life, and to keep big business from harming people.[9] One of George Norris's accomplishments during the 1930s was his authorship of the bill establishing the Tennessee Valley Authority (TVA), a system of dams and reservoirs that brought flood relief, irrigation, and cheap electrical power to millions of people over a six-state area. The older strain of liberalism also had international dimensions. It wanted America to use its power for helping other people achieve economic growth, to seek reciprocal disarmament with Communist powers while keeping our own guard up, and to make greater use of the United Nations.

It was called New Deal liberalism and the label stuck, though it was somewhat misleading; there were liberal Republicans as well as liberal Democrats. It was a kind of vernacular liberalism, popular with Americans in both parties, and it had wide appeal across regional, ethnic, and religious lines. There was nothing in it that a pope would not endorse. In 1960, after delivering a powerful speech nominating Adlai Stevenson for president at the Democratic National Convention, Senator Eugene McCarthy boasted that he himself was "more Catholic than Kennedy and more liberal than Stevenson." In more recent times, this was the liberalism of the late Pennsylvania governor Robert Casey, twice elected by large majorities. A sign of the times, and of the changes wrought in liberalism, is the fact that Casey was barred from speaking at the 1992 Democratic convention because of his unabashedly pro-life views.

Today's liberalism is a strange mix of permissiveness and coercive moralism. On the one side is an easygoing tolerance based upon moral relativism. As far back as 1966, Supreme Court justice William O. Douglas, dissenting in the only case during the 1960s in which the Court actually upheld an obscenity conviction, asserted that First Amendment protection should be accorded to publications "of value to the masochistic community or to others of the deviant community."[10] Today, ironically, Douglas would get in trouble for using the term "deviant," a term that has been defined down to the vanishing point. Former NBC commentator Laura Ingraham recalls that when she was a student at Dartmouth College in the early 1980s, she and fellow pranksters at the conservative *Dartmouth Review*, using the same language that appeared in the funding application for the Gay Students Association, came within two votes of getting funding for the Dartmouth Bestiality Society.[11] And it goes beyond what traditional liberals used to call "self-regarding actions." People can now decide whether or not to kill human infants at the point of delivery, and some of the more progressive liberal thinkers (such as Steven Pinker at M.I.T., Jeffrey Reiman at American University, and Peter Singer at Princeton) see nothing monstrous or unnatural about killing infants *after* delivery.[12] It sounds like moral anarchy but it is not. It is the permissive side of the liberal ledger; but there is also an authoritarian side.

Reacting to Andrew Sullivan's claim in the *New York Times Magazine* article that conservatism is "not afraid of the state or its power to set a moral tone or coerce a moral atmosphere," one exasperated reader wrote, "[F]or the last 40 years I have been unable to turn around without being hectored by pious scolds from the sanctimonious left: don't smoke, don't litter, don't own guns, use condoms, save whales, conserve wetlands, protect moms, help moms protect abortion, conserve energy, wear ribbons (pink, yellow, red—I lose track)."[13] The correspondent complains of liberal scolding and hectoring, but it goes beyond scolding. Increasingly, the new liberalism is turning to coercion and compulsory "re-education." Examples are not hard to find, especially in the centers of liberal culture. During a classroom discussion at the University of Michigan, a student who ventured the opinion that homosexuality was a disease treatable by psychotherapy was forced to attend a formal disciplinary hearing. At the University of New Hampshire, a professor who compared writing to sex ("You and the subject become one") was suspended, forced to apologize, and ordered to undergo special counseling. The same happened to a law lecturer at the University of Pennsylvania who said, "We have ex-slaves here who should know about the Thirteenth Amendment."[14] At City College of New York, where I teach, department chairs and chairs of search committees are forced to fill out Nuremburg-like forms listing the races of the members of their departments and committees, as well as the races of job applicants. Directives, orders, and sanctions are readily used to enforce the new liberalism. From speech codes to "hate crimes," from using RICO laws (laws that were supposed to be used against gangsters!) to bankrupt pro-life organizations, to prosecuting the Boy Scouts for not accepting gay scoutmasters, and, when that fails, to expelling the Scouts from public places and cutting off their funds—the message is the same: don't trifle with us, we mean business.

This is a feature of modern liberalism that Father Francis Canavan has been pointing out for the last twenty years: despite its claims, liberalism is not remotely interested in individual "moral autonomy." What it is interested in is creating a new set of social norms to reshape the institutions of society.[15] What would the new society look like? Wisely, Canavan has not attempted to draw a comprehensive picture of a liberal utopia. He confines himself to the observation that it would be governed by a social ethic combining "humanitarianism and utilitarianism" and would regard "suffering as the absolute evil."[16] Somewhere in that utopia, I imagine, there is a place for Gloria Steinem's refurbished St. Patrick's Cathedral, with clotheslines strung across the nave.

We need to keep reminding ourselves that liberalism did not always entertain these ambitions. New Deal liberalism was a popular reform program based on the assumption that we live in communities with common interests that government can usefully serve. *Usefully serve*—nothing more than that. New Deal liberalism had no desire to reshape our values, or modify our religious beliefs, or teach us lessons in political correctness.

What *is* New Deal liberalism? What went into it, and where did it come from? It was not in any direct sense a product of European philosophy. It was, instead, a home-grown American product, an intermingling of two American political traditions, and it can only be understood in the context of this nation's history. The two traditions that produced New Deal liberalism in the 1930s were whiggery and populism.

There were, in the past, political parties with those names (though lower-case whiggery and populism were around before the parties existed and stayed around after their demise). The Whig Party, which formally began in 1836 and lasted until the end of the 1850s, has been called "the ghost of Puritanism."[17] Its intellectual roots were in New England and the "New England diaspora" of the Upper Midwest, and it echoed many strains of New England puritanism: moralism, stewardship, and the belief that America was embarked on a providential mission. The party stood for "internal improvements," a term with a double meaning. Whig leaders pushed for nationally sponsored programs of economic improvement—roads, canals, rail lines, lending institutions—but also for improvements in the "internal" regions of the human soul. They inaugurated programs of temperance, public education, prison reform, rehabilitation of the poor, and humane treatment of the insane. (And, finally, abolitionism: in the 1850s, the Northern "conscience" Whigs, reacting to the Compromise of 1850, began a concerted drive to ban slavery in the new territories, creating the split that destroyed the party.) The Whigs' moral and economic agendas were mutually reinforcing. Their economic nationalism was a harbinger of the New Deal programs a century later, except that in the Whig view, self-control was just as essential as economic progress for a well-ordered society.[18] The purpose of public schooling, said Whig educator Horace Mann, was not just to impart knowledge or useful skills but to teach children to control their "appetites and passions."[19]

Whiggery, if not the Whig Party, got a new lease on life with the election of Abraham Lincoln. A zealous Whig since he entered politics in the 1830s,[20] Lincoln held to his Whig principles in the White House. In the midst of the war he pushed for whiggish national projects such as canals, a transcontinental railroad, and the revival of a national banking system.[21] But more important was his cultural whiggery. He fought the Civil War to save "the nation" (a term he eventually preferred over "union"), an association based not simply on self-interest but on the moral propositions spelled out in the Declaration of Independence.[22]

Lincoln's communalism became the template for future Republican reformers. During the Gilded Age, when the party seemed to lose its soul to Mammon and Herbert Spencer, reformers like Herbert Croly and Theodore Roosevelt summoned it back to Lincoln's standards. To Croly, Lincoln showed "that democracy meant to him more than anything else the spirit and principle of brotherhood."[23] Roosevelt's "New National-ism" was informed by a similar idealism. Lincoln, in Roosevelt's view, adopted a Hamiltonian system of economic nationalism but grafted on it "a profound belief that the great heart of the nation beat for truth, honor, and liberty."[24]

Despite the failure of Roosevelt's Progressive candidacy in 1912, Republican Progressives like Wisconsin senator Robert LaFollette kept its spirit alive in the 1920s; and in the 1930s many Progressive Republi-cans, like Henry Wallace and Harold Ickes, ended up in the Roosevelt administration, and one, Fiorello LaGuardia, became the mayor of America's largest city. In attenuated form, whiggish Republicanism sur-vived into the 1950s. "Modern Republicanism," the watchword of the 1956 Eisenhower campaign, at least gestured toward the principle of na-tional leadership, and its strongholds generally coincided with the his-toric Whig areas of New York, New England, and the Upper Midwest.

The populist strain in New Deal liberalism was something else again. Whigs were often characterized as "conservative" because of their empha-sis on lawful government and individual self-constraint (though they were hardly conservative in their belief in the positive role of the federal government). The "People's Party," the official name for the Populists, had a more radical flavor. During its heyday, from 1892 to 1900, it denounced Wall Street, the railroads, Eastern bankers and businessmen, and allied itself with "the plain people"—ordinary Americans without a lot of money or fancy manners. While Whigs tended to be educated middle-class townsfolk from the Northeast or Upper Middle West, Populists typically came from farms or small towns in the South or trans-Mississippi West and were largely self-educated. Whigs were genteel; populists were brawlers. Kansas populist Mary Lease famously urged farmers to "raise less corn and more hell." Where the Whig relationship to banks and businesses was more or less friendly—Whigs started with the assumption that the private and public sector could work together harmoniously—the Populists took a confrontational stance. Populist orators were more likely to invoke Andrew Jackson than Abraham Lincoln.[25] Jackson was a Populist hero because of his famous rants against "the great moneyed corporations." His rhetoric bristled with warnings of "designs," "specious and deceitful plans" by a "secret conclave" of "money interests."[26] Populists often resorted to this same kind of conspiracy-talk; their 1892 platform even hinted at a worldwide plot: "A vast conspiracy against mankind has been organized on two continents, and is rapidly taking possession of the world."[27]

In one respect, though, the Populists had more in common with Lincoln than with Jackson. Jacksonianism, as Richard Hofstadter has observed, "was essentially a movement of laissez-faire";[28] it favored lower taxes, championed states' rights, and condemned the Whig program of "internal improvements" as a deceitful scheme for driving tariffs higher. The Populists, on the other hand, called not for lowering taxes but for a graduated income tax, and they even proposed federal ownership of some utilities (railroads, telephone, and telegraph).[29] But the more usual Populist solution to the monopoly problem was not government takeovers or government regulation but trustbusting: splitting big businesses into smaller, independent businesses so that competition could do its work.

Despite differences in income and culture, Populists and Whigs came from the same tradition of evangelical Christianity. Whiggery emerged from the soil of the Second Great Awakening, a series of religious revivals that erupted in New England in the early 1800s, spilled out into upstate New York and Ohio, and set off successive revivals in the Appalachians and the upper South. The Second Great Awakening (unlike the First, which occurred in the eighteenth century) entertained vast social ambitions. As historian Daniel Walker Howe notes, it "demanded the moral regeneration of society, not simply of the individuals within it." [30] Not all the Whigs were evangelicals, but virtually all of them couched their political rhetoric in the language of biblical Christianity and welcomed the public expression of religion. Lincoln demonstrated these traits not only in his speeches but in his policies, from his expansion of chaplaincy services in the army to his revival of the Puritan practice of designating special days for "public humiliation, prayer, and thanksgiving." Unsurprisingly, the same spirit was infused into Populism during its heyday in the 1890s. Writing a generation later, the historian John Hicks compared the 1892 Populist convention to a Baptist camp meeting and noted that the platform acquired "a sort of religious sanction"; it became "a sacred creed."[31] William Jennings Bryan, the Populist-Democratic candidate for President in 1896, brought the Democratic Convention to its feet by telling supporters of the gold standard that they would not be allowed to repeat the crime of Pontius Pilate: "You shall not press upon the brow of labor this crown of thorns, you shall not crucify mankind upon a cross of gold."[32]

Populism (with a small "p") did not die with the Populist Party in 1900 but worked its way into the rhetoric of Woodrow Wilson and other Democratic reformers. [33] In the 1920s its critique of unbridled capitalism helped the Democrats build a coalition with room for organized labor and big-city ethnic groups. Then came the Depression, the Republican defeat in the 1932 election, and twenty years of the New Deal.

In partisan terms, the New Deal was a Democratic phenomenon but programmatically it was a mixture of populism and whiggery. The old Whig idea of federally sponsored "internal improvements" reappeared as New Deal "public works" projects: dams, bridges, roads, tunnels, rural electrification, sponsored in whole or in part by the federal government. Some of these, indeed, had first been advanced by whiggish Republicans in the 1920s. The Tennessee Valley Authority (TVA) was largely the work of Senator George Norris, the Republican "fighting liberal." In approaching the private business sector Roosevelt tried both whiggish and populist approaches. His National Recovery Act (NRA) of 1933 used an historic Whig strategy of government-business cooperation, allowing business leaders to draw up "codes of fair competition," then enforcing them by federal law. But after the Supreme Court (then, as now, practicing judicial activism) struck down the NRA, Roosevelt turned to populism, securing the passage of bills establishing sharply graduated corporate taxes and other measures directly challenging big business—all the while excoriating business leaders as "the privileged princes of these new economic dynasties" and "the resolute enemy within our gates." [34] Roosevelt's enemies on the Right called him a socialist, but this was the rhetoric of Andrew Jackson, not Karl Marx. To the despair of Marxists and other socialists who encouraged class struggle, Roosevelt thought not in terms of class but of broad-based coalitions of reform. Norman Thomas, the perennial Socialist candidate, complained that Roosevelt's chief slogan was not, "Workers of the world, unite," but "Workers and small shareholders unite, clean up Wall Street."[35]

Just as whiggery outlasted the Whigs and populism outlasted the Populists, New Deal liberalism outlasted the New Deal era. In the 1950s, there were liberals like Hubert Humphrey and Estes Kefauver who fought to preserve the legacy of the New Deal, and, in the case of Humphrey, to extend it by taking up the cause of civil rights. In general, the populist elements of the New Deal found support among Southern and border-state Democrats, while whiggery was supported by Northern Democrats and some Northeastern Republicans. The civil rights revolution split the two regional Democratic components of the New Deal. But by the end of the 1960s they had largely reattached themselves, with the newly enfranchised black Democrats in the South putting an end to the segregationist wing of their party and encouraging "new Democrats" such as Jimmy Carter to enter the political arena. In the late 1960s there were New Deal majorities in both houses of Congress, and state and local governments were also swept into the new liberal majority.

But by the end of the 1960s, liberalism was confronted with a new challenge, this one from the Left. A bewildering variety of groups, collectively called "the New Left," accused New Dealers of selling out to the "establishment." Except for their youth, education, and affluence, the one element these groups shared was their declared hostility to the traditions of the West. Whether it was Christianity (Inquisitions, persecutions), the market economy (brutalization of the poor, destruction of the planet), Judeo-Christian social mores (uptight, repressive, hypocritical), or, indeed, the whole white race ("the cancer of human history"), the tendency was to despise everything about Western culture and champion everything that seemed opposed to it. By 1972 the more extreme elements of the New Left had burned themselves out, but now there emerged a more respectable movement: "the new politics." While avoiding the violent tactics and general scruffiness of the New Left, the new politics retained the Left's core beliefs. Gravitating toward the Democrats, its youthful leaders took over key leadership positions in the party during the 1970s, displacing or co-opting older party leaders. Their politics hasn't changed substantially since then, though they have learned how to appropriate the style and symbolism of the people they call "the family values crowd."

Liberalism has changed, then, from a traditional reform movement to a movement hostile to tradition, a movement that seeks to create new norms and reshape the institutions of society. How did that happen? What caused common-sense liberalism to turn into social radicalism? The catalyst, Canavan suggests, was the collapse of the moral consensus that once held Americans together. In 1965 Canavan made this remarkably prescient observation: "One need not be excessively pessimistic to predict that euthanasia and homosexual relations will become the subject of acrimonious public debate within the lifetime of most of those who read this article."[36] In 1965 liberals were talking about Vietnam, civil rights, and poverty; gay rights and euthanasia were clouds smaller than a child's hand. Canavan saw the tempest coming and knew that it would play havoc with the old consensus.

This was no tempest in a teapot. It wrought enormous changes in American life. In sexual mores, for example, it all but destroyed the traditional taboo against premarital sex. But did it reach the deeper regions of American morality? Did it shatter the core beliefs of most Americans? That seems doubtful. Americans may now tolerate premarital sex, but there is no evidence that their views on adultery have changed. During the Monica Lewinisky scandal, a majority of Americans expressed a very low opinion of President Clinton's morality, even as they gave him high marks for job performance. It was America's liberal elites, not ordinary Americans, who were most inclined to wink at Clinton's behavior. Their reaction was epitomized by the remark of *Time* magazine's Nina Burleigh that she would gladly perform sexual favors for the President "just to thank him for keeping abortion legal." It is in these circles, in the arts and journalistic communities and in the American academy, that the real breakdown of America's moral consensus has occurred. Queer Studies, crucifixes in urine, dung-spattered portraits of the Virgin Mary—here, finally, are the ultimate expressions of the new liberal ethos. Insulated from general elections, accountable only to like-minded people, liberals can let it all hang out.

But this is also what makes radical liberalism vulnerable to challenge. The reason liberal activists rely so much on nonelected judges to get their agenda enacted, and the reason they hide so much of it behind euphemisms, is that they know that their agenda does not appeal to the majority of Americans. Mainstreaming homosexuality, banning prayer in public places, substituting racial preferences for merit, establishing abortion on demand as a basic right and funding it with taxpayers' money—these projects have been consistent losers in public opinion surveys.[37] As long as America remains a democracy, effective resistance to these and other liberal projects is possible. But resistance has to take the form of something more than nay-saying. There has to be an alternative public philosophy, one that makes sense to the majority of Americans.

Let me first suggest what is *not* a good alternative: "fiscal conservatism" or "libertarianism." Predictably, that is just the kind of conservatism Andrew Sullivan likes. It does not oppose liberalism on social issues but fights instead, Sullivan writes, for "economic freedom, smaller government and personal choice."[38] He associates it with the 1980s and expresses regret that in today's conservative circles libertarians "are clearly on the defensive."

But libertarianism is a close ally of social radicalism. Consider Sullivan's use of the term "personal choice" in his description of libertarianism. "Personal choice" is a term much prized by abortion advocates because it obscures the moral seriousness of abortion. If abortion is a "personal" choice, then it can't be judged by any "outside," objective moral standards. It is very much like personal taste. If you don't like abortions, don't buy one. But if Canavan's diagnosis of our predicament is correct, then leaving moral decisions to the marketplace can only deepen the moral crisis. In itself, the marketplace has no morality. Its values are strictly quantitative. A conservatism based on the market-place would be no better than modern-day liberalism; it might even be worse. Commentator Jim Sleeper recently observed that "the Calvin Klein-cum-kiddie porn ads that showed up a few years ago on New York City buses were put there by private investors in the free market, not by liberals."[39] Free-market conservatism can only deepen the wounds in our moral consensus.

What could heal them? What public philosophy could bring people together in a broad-based coalition for reform and renewal of the goals of our Constitution: forming a "more perfect union," establishing justice, providing for the common defense, promoting the general welfare, and protecting vital freedoms? It would have to be a public philosophy unashamedly patriotic but never mean-spirited or chauvinistic. It would have to be guided by firm moral principles, yet possess enough flexibility to translate them into workable policies. It would promote the positive role of government, especially in funding new community initiatives— but would also insist on the primacy of families, churches, and other private groups in delivering public services. It would seek change by con-sensus and it would recognize that ordinary people—"the plain people," as the Populists used to call them—are not stupid but are quite capable of making wise decisions for themselves and their families.

What else could I be describing but New Deal liberalism? The New Deal was not, as it has often been depicted, a program of state paternal-ism, but a pragmatic response to a national crisis. It was not intended to make people dependent on government but to get them on their feet. It was not a program for doling out money to idle people but for helping people to find work. "[C]ontinued dependence upon relief induces a spiri-tual and moral disintegration fundamentally destructive to the national fibre. To dole out relief in this way is to administer a narcotic, a subtle destroyer of the human spirit."[40] The author of these words was not Ronald Reagan in 1980 but Franklin Roosevelt in 1935. The New Deal sometimes used the state vigorously, as it did by putting people to work in federally sponsored "works projects," but it was all in the context of providing the means of economic independence. In the 1930s the private economy had nearly collapsed. Today things are different, and different times call for different strategies. "Prudence," Thomas Aquinas said, "deals with matters of counsel when there are several ways of achieving a purpose." There is no theoretical formula for how to select the best way. "One may envisage a theoretical art, but scarcely a theoretical prudence."[41] Firm about ends, New Deal philosophy is flexible about means. Modern liberalism seems to have gotten it backwards: it combines moral flexibility with a rigid commitment to social programs that don't work.

Still, can New Deal–style liberalism ever displace the present form of it? Today, many New Deal Democrats have been pushed into the background or intimidated into signing on with the new liberals. Perhaps the two kinds of liberalism really are joined at the hip. Isn't it better, then, to fight liberalism with some brand of "conservatism"? The argument can be put theoretically in the form of a "house divided" metaphor (the original, not Lincoln's): how can you fight liberalism with liberalism? Though Canavan never makes this objection, his discussion of liberal "rot" suggests that it is impossible. Canavan is convinced that all forms of liberalism are rooted in hedonistic individualism, which he sees as emanating from the philosophy of John Locke.[42] Therefore, no matter what kind of liberal "flowers" emerge, they will all suffer the same blight: radical subjectivity, the inability to make rationally defensible moral judgments. Liberalism produces a mindless politics that "has no theory of what is a good life for human beings as such."[43]

It is hard to resist the logic behind Canavan's description of liberalism, but does it fit New Deal liberalism? Were the flowers of the New Deal—Social Security, unemployment insurance, the W.P.A., the G.I. Bill, housing loans, the Marshall Plan—blighted by hedonistic individualism? Can they not be defended by a morally coherent theory of the good life? "On coming into the world, man is not equipped with everything he needs for developing his bodily and spiritual life. He needs others." "Excessive economic and social disparity between individuals and peoples of one human race is a source of scandal and militates against social justice, equity, human dignity, as well as social and international peace." These philosophical premises could easily be used to justify the programs sponsored by the New Deal. Indeed, they seem to fit them much better than do the tenets of Lockeanism. Yet they are taken from the *Catechism of the Catholic Church.*[44]

Well then, maybe New Deal liberalism isn't really liberal. Maybe it would be better to see it as a kind of conservatism. This is a tempting suggestion, since New Deal philosophy does seem to run along lines different from libertarianism and cultural radicalism, the two "flowers" that Canavan sees sprouting from Lockean liberalism. Still, the temptation has to be resisted, and for two reasons. First, political labels should take some account of popular usage. We might be able to come up with a more precise term than New Deal liberalism—I would be satisfied with "whig populism"—but politics goes on in the real world. For a generation or more, New Dealers were calling themselves liberals, and being called liberals, and everyone knew what they were talking about. It seems pointless to coin some new term if the old one was meaningful to the people involved. Second, liberalism may not be such an imprecise term after all. Liberalism's original meaning—"favourable to constitutional changes and legal or administrative reforms tending in the direction of freedom or democracy"—does not seem a bad way of describing New Deal liberalism, nor does *New York Times* columnist William Safire's more recent definition of a liberal as "one who believes in more government action to meet individual needs."[45]

But how did we get from "freedom" to "government action"? Safire calls it an "about-face," which implies that the two terms are opposites. But this is not necessarily the case. The New Deal argument was, and still is, that the freedom of individuals and communities sometimes requires action by the government for protection against forces hostile to freedom—forces ranging from poverty and ignorance to the acts of unconscionable individuals and corporations. Safire seems to be aware of this argument, because he traces it back to the 1920s. But its actual historical roots, as we have seen, go much deeper: the Whigs were arguing for the liberating effects of positive government as early as the 1830s. We can push the argument back even further, to Alexander Hamilton's claim in *Federalist No. 1* that "the vigor of government is essential to the security of liberty." Hamilton's position, in fact, was adopted by Herbert Croly, Theodore Roosevelt, and other "Progressive" Republicans in the early years of the twentieth century, though they were careful to place it on a democratic foundation.

It may seem odd to associate Alexander Hamilton with the New Deal. Hamilton was an elitist and a conservative. But it is no less odd than associating Andrew Jackson with the New Deal, as Democrats are wont to do. Jackson was a *laissez-faire* and states' rights advocate, while the New Deal increased the power of the national government. In actual fact, the New Deal did not neatly fit *either* Jacksonian Democracy or Hamiltonian Federalism. Shortly before George Norris introduced his TVA bill into the new Democratic Congress in 1933, Roosevelt invited Norris to dinner at the White House. When Roosevelt lavished praise on the project, Norris teasingly asked, "What are you going to say when they ask you the political philosophy behind the TVA?" Laughing, Roosevelt replied, "I'll tell them it's neither fish nor fowl, but whatever it is, it will taste awfully good to the people of the Tennessee Valley."[46] Whether to use the government or the private sphere, whether to bring in the federal government or the states—or whether to use some mix of them all—are questions of means, not of ends. The New Deal kept ends clearly in sight, but never locked itself into a single theory for reaching those ends. It was a prudential project, and, as Aquinas noted, one can scarcely imagine a "theoretical prudence."

Has the time come for a renascence of that kind of thinking? One can anticipate this response: the New Deal was the product of a different era, a time when a basic moral consensus existed among Americans of different religious outlooks. That era is over, and whatever our nostalgia for it, we might as well face up to reality. The new liberalism, radical as it is, simply expresses the radical cleavages that divide Americans today.

The argument is based on the assumption that the majority of Americans *are* radically divided on basic core values. The assumption, I have tried to suggest, is false. There are serious divisions in America on moral questions but those divisions have not extended much beyond the higher reaches of academia and the media. As I have already noted, public opinion polls show a broad agreement of ordinary Americans on a variety of moral issues: abortion, homosexuality, public prayer, the purpose and limits of welfare spending, affirmative action, and capital punishment.[47] If they were translated into law, or given some kind of official validation, they could become the basis for a new centrist settlement. Such a settlement would not please the activists at the far ends of the spectrum—and it shouldn't. "Prophetic minorities" have often played a vital role in deepening our moral sensitivities, and for this they deserve a respectful hearing. In a free country they must be at liberty to keep the pressure on; and they have the right to push the settlement closer to their respective positions. The only requirement is that they do it by constitutional and democratic means—not by violence and not by judicial intrusion into the legislative process, which is also a form of violence.

The philosophy I have been adumbrating is not a relic of an earlier time but an approach to politics entertained by many working politicians and citizens today. The New Deal era is not dead; it is not even past. They are out there, those New Dealers, often wedged between radical liberals and fiscal conservatives, blending at times with one side and at other times with the other. Some are Democrats, some are Republicans, and increasing numbers have no reflexive loyalty to either party. But there they are, in Congress, in state and local governments, and certainly among the public at large. (An oddball few can be found in the media and the academy.) Whatever they're called—"Reagan Democrats," "bread and butter liberals," "social populists"—their viewpoint is clear enough: they want the state and the larger society to support, not usurp, the responsibilities of individuals and small communities; to protect basic freedoms but not to create a whole new array of "rights"; to regulate business when necessary but to deregulate it when it is not necessary. And they want government to respect traditional social values, not to foist brand new ones on the public. Prudent statesmen would do well to listen.

XII

The Triumph of Will:
Rights Mania, the Culture of Death,
and the Crisis of Enlightenment Liberalism

Kenneth L. Grasso

It is no secret that over the past several decades America has witnessed the emergence of what William Donohue has described as a "rights mania."[1] Not only has our public discourse come to be dominated by a seemingly endless proliferation of rights claims, but our political debates have increasingly come to be framed as clashes of rights. Indeed, our public life has been transformed both by the acceptance of a wide array of new rights claims and by a view of rights as "trumps" that take precedence over all other goods, including order, public morality, and the commonweal. Indeed, under the impact of this rights mania, as Mary Ann Glendon observes, our "catalogue" of rights has expanded "without much consideration of the ends to which they are oriented, their relationship to one another, to corresponding responsibilities, or to the general welfare."[2]

Yet, as Pope John Paul II has pointed out, this newfound emphasis on individual rights and the assertion of their priority over other claims has been paralleled by the rise of "a new cultural climate" in which violations of "the right to life" of unborn children through abortion are justified "in the name . . . of individual freedom" and sanctioned by "the state."[3] We thus confront the "remarkable contradiction" of the "right to life" of unborn children "being denied or trampled upon" in "an age when the inviolable rights of the person are solemnly proclaimed" and in a "society which makes the affirmation and protection of human rights its primary objective and its boast."[4] Ironically, moreover, the leading proponents of the rights revolution have often been among the most vocal proponents of the denial of legal protection to the unborn. Indeed, they view the right to abortion-on-demand as one of the defining attributes of a rightly ordered body politic, and the enshrinement of this right in our public law as one of the most important accomplishments of the revolution they celebrate.

My purpose here is not to criticize these disturbing developments. Nor is it to underscore the irony of the fact that our increasingly rights-obsessed society, while displaying an ever more exquisite sensitivity to hitherto unrecognized rights claims by individuals and groups, has simultaneously withdrawn the legal protection it traditionally offered its weakest and most vulnerable members. Rather, my goal is to explore the genesis of this paradoxical state of affairs. Its genesis, I will argue, is found in a particular intellectual tradition—Enlightenment liberalism. More specifically, I will contend that its genesis is found in the crisis into which Enlightenment liberalism has plunged as the implications of its constitutive, core ideas have unfolded over the past several centuries. My debt to Francis Canavan will be obvious throughout. Indeed, although I alone am responsible for the views expressed here, the account of the nature and history of liberalism offered in this essay is intended as a systematization and development of the account contained in his work. By proceeding in this way, I hope to show how Father Canavan's work helps illuminate the liberal tradition, its historical development, and contemporary America's discontents.

Before proceeding further, it is first necessary to clarify what is meant by "Enlightenment liberalism." By Enlightenment liberalism I mean something more than a practical political orientation characterized by a commitment to government that is limited in its scope, subject in its operations to the rule of law, and responsible to those it governs. These principles and practices can and have been justified in terms of a wide array of competing intellectual traditions. On the contrary, I use the term

Enlightenment liberalism to designate a particular intellectual tradition that originated in the seventeenth century and has since come to dominate modern Western political thought. For its "true nature" to be understood, as Roberto Mangabeira Unger observes, this tradition "must be seen all of a piece, not just as a set of doctrines about the disposition of power and wealth, but as a metaphysical conception of mind and society."[5] In fact, the thinkers who "laid the foundations" of liberal political theory (e.g., Hobbes, Locke, Kant, etc.) "saw those foundations as elements of a speculative account of the place of mind and society in the world," or as elements of a "metaphysical system." The "conceptions of freedom and public order commonly identified with liberalism" have been shaped in important respects by liberalism's deeper philosophical commitments.[6]

While it is true that Enlightenment liberalism and the cause of constitutional and limited government have been intimately associated over the past several centuries, these two "liberalisms" are distinct and must not be confused. Neither necessarily entails the other. As Hobbes's thought shows, for example, one can embrace Enlightenment liberalism without embracing the institutions, practices, and commitments constitutive of constitutional and limited government. Likewise, as the work of Jacques Maritain illustrates, one can steadfastly reject Enlightenment liberalism while embracing the institutions, practices, and commitments of constitutional democracy in a principled fashion.

As Alasdair MacIntyre points out, in contemporary American public life Enlightenment liberalism appears in many "guises." In fact, inasmuch as "so-called conservatism and so-called radicalism are in general mere stalking-horses for liberalism," our public argument takes place "almost exclusively between conservative liberals, liberal liberals, and radical liberals." Thus, although our public discourse may put "in question this or that particular set of attitudes or policies," it does not put into question "the fundamental tenets of liberalism" itself.[7] Indeed, Enlightenment liberalism today supplies both the conceptual framework within which we think about politics and the idiom in which our civil conversation is conducted.

The obvious question here concerns the nature of Enlightenment liberalism, the core commitments constitutive of it as a distinctive intellectual tradition. The most striking aspect of Enlightenment liberalism's model of man and society is its individualism, its insistence, as two recent writers have noted, that "politics is justifiable only by appeal to the well being, rights, or claims of individuals."[8] To grasp what is distinctive about liberalism's individualism, however, it is necessary, as Glendon remarks, to grasp "its view of what the individual is."[9] To do this, it is in turn necessary to appreciate the implications for the understanding of the human person of the nominalism and rationalism that lie at liberalism's metaphysical core. Among other things, these metaphysical commitments ultimately entail what Douglass and Mara term the "rejection of teleology," of "the claim that there is a discoverable excellence or optimal condition . . . which characterizes human beings" as such.[10]

To suggest that liberalism's identity as a distinctive intellectual tradition derives from certain core intellectual commitments is not to ignore the heterogeneity that has historically characterized liberal thought. No one familiar with the history of liberalism can fail to be aware of the disagreements exhibited by liberalism's major theoreticians. But, as Unger notes, "we should . . . not be misled by differences among liberal thinkers." It is true that the core premises that are the source of liberalism's unity are "few" in number and do not entail a single position on all political and philosophical issues. Nevertheless, ideas do have consequences, and "the number" of "philosophical positions," and "the sorts of political and economic organization" consistent with these premises, are "limited." These premises thus "determine and limit the possibilities" of liberal thought.[11]

In this context, it is particularly important to recognize that liberalism's "metaphysical postulates" do indeed "have consequences" for our understanding of the proper "organization" of political life, and, in particular, for "the determination of the proper place of the individual in social life."[12] The metaphysical commitments that lie at the heart of liberalism not only circumscribe the range of options available to thinkers operating within its horizon, but push liberal thought relentlessly in certain directions. As Canavan points out, for example, the rejection of teleology entailed by liberalism's metaphysical premises pushes it toward the view that because "what is good for human beings is not an object open to the intellect, . . . the political order must be structured to accommodate itself to subjective and conflicting notions of the good."[13]

To suggest that Enlightenment liberalism's core premises have implications for the understanding and ordering of social life is not to imply that all of these implications were immediately apparent. "There is always," as Canavan notes, "a time lag between the first introduction of a new idea and the full appreciation of its consequences."[14] Not surprisingly, therefore, the implications of liberalism's core commitments—in particular, its metaphysical postulates—"were worked out only gradually over the period of several centuries." In fact, "it is only today that we begin fully to understand what liberal individualism really implies."[15] To appreciate liberalism's role in both today's rights revolution and the embrace by this revolution of what John Paul II has aptly termed the culture of death, it is thus necessary to grasp the historical evolution of liberal theory and the crisis into which the gradual unfolding of the implications of its metaphysical premises has plunged it.

Although a systematic history of liberalism is obviously impossible here, an appreciation of the historical trajectory of liberal thought is essential. Michael Walzer has described liberalism as a "strange" and "self-subverting doctrine." Liberalism, he writes,

> seems continually to undercut itself . . . and to produce in each generation renewed hopes for a more absolute freedom from history and society alike. Much of liberal political theory, from Locke to Rawls, is an effort to fix and stabilize the doctrine in order to end the endlessness of liberal liberation. But beyond every current version of liberalism, there is always a super liberalism, which, as Roberto Unger says of his own doctrine, "pushes the liberal premises about state and society, about freedom from dependence and governance of social relations by the will, to the point at which they merge into a large ambition: the building of a social world less alien to a self that can always violate the generative rules of its own mental or social constructs."[16]

Walzer's characterization of liberalism's historical trajectory can be illustrated by contrasting the variety of liberalism that dominated early liberal thought, what John H. Hallowell called "integral liberalism," with the variety of liberalism that dominates contemporary liberal theory. At the heart of integral liberalism was an affirmation of "the absolute value and dignity of human personality" and a concomitant affirmation of the "spiritual equality of each individual" as "an end in himself" possessing "a God-given soul." Insisting that "any subjection to the will of another, to the will of any personal capricious authority" is "incompatible" with the dignity of the human person, liberalism "demanded freedom for each individual from other individuals, from the state, from every arbitrary will."[17]

Integral liberalism's commitment to individual autonomy, however, was tempered by a simultaneous belief (inherited from the Christian tradition) in the existence of an objective moral law discoverable by reason. Affirming the existence of a substantive order of obligations—toward God, others, and ourselves—that bind us prior to, and independently of, our free consent to accept them, integral liberalism believed that the "impersonal, rational and objective" truths of the natural law provided an authority to which individuals could submit without sacrificing their human dignity. It thus concluded that legitimate government was government in accordance with "the eternal truths and values" of the natural law and that binding positive laws embodied its dictates.[18]

Thus, although committed to individual autonomy, integral liberalism did "not espouse freedom . . . from all restraint," but freedom "only within the limits set by . . . natural law."[19] Precisely because of its confidence in reason's "ability to rise above will and appetite" and to perceive "a natural moral law based on our common human nature," as Canavan writes, integral liberalism was "able to regard moral judgments and civil laws as an exercise of reason and not merely as the imposition of the will of some people on others."[20]

As the work of Thomas Hobbes, on the one hand, and the subsequent history of liberal thought, on the other, attest, integral liberalism was neither the only nor the last effort to construct a theory of politics on the foundations of liberalism's metaphysics of the person. Indeed, our intellectual landscape is today dominated by a new variety of liberalism, the political theory of which differs in some significant respects from that of integral liberalism.

At the heart of this new liberalism, as Canavan notes, is the claim that "human life has no natural or God-given purposes, but only those which the self chooses for itself."[21] The result is an understanding of human beings as, in Michael Sandel's words, "free and independent" selves "unbound by moral ties antecedent to choice," sovereign wills "unencumbered by ends" not of "their own choosing." The self is thus "installed as sovereign, cast as the author of the only obligations that constrain"—save for a small number of "natural duties" which "we owe persons qua persons," such as doing "justice" and avoiding "cruelty."[22]

Beginning from this conception of human nature, the proponents of this liberalism move toward what might be called a wholly voluntarist conception of social relations. As Canavan notes, its rejection of teleology makes it difficult for liberalism "to entertain the notion of relations" as "consequences of the nature of things." The liberalism of the sovereign self thus understands social relations as "external," "accidental," "adventitious," and "contractual," rather than as consequences of man's dynamic orientation toward the fulfillment of his nature, toward the realization of his natural ends. The "individual human being" is thus seen as "an atom, motivated by self-interest, to whom violence is done if he is subjected to a relationship with other humans which he has not chosen" (121).

This voluntarist conception of social relations, in turn, "dissolves the natural and given character of institutions, particularly of that basic institution, the family." Insofar as liberalism's rejection of teleology leads to the denial of "given natural norms by which institutions can be more or less in harmony with the needs of mankind's common nature," it effectively "makes all institutions arbitrary."[23] Thus, one must speak of families, rather than "the family," for example, because as the purely conventional creation of naturally sovereign individuals, the family as such has no nature, no determinate structure.

Likewise, liberalism reduces all communities to what Carl Schneider describes as mere aggregations "of individuals united temporarily for their mutual convenience and armed with rights against each other."[24] Precluding what Elshtain terms "nonutilitarian" forms of community,[25] this understanding of social life forces us to view all human relationships through the prism of market models. It thus imprisons our thinking about social life within the horizon of what Glendon terms the "individual-state-market grid,"[26] and, as Canavan points out, effectively reduces "the basic questions of political theory" to "the proper relationship between the state and the individual" (98).

This anthropology, in turn, has profound implications for liberalism's understanding of the human good. It issues in the denial of the existence of an order of human ends that obligates us prior to, and independently of, our free consent to pursue those ends. By doing so, it leads to what Stanley C. Brubaker describes as a "dogmatic doubt"[27] about the existence of a substantive human good.

Its rejection of the very idea of a knowable and substantive human good, in turn, pushes the liberalism of the sovereign self toward what Charles Taylor has dubbed "subjectivism." As far as questions about substantive human goods are concerned, this doctrine promotes the "idea that our 'values' are our creations," ultimately resting on nothing more than "a radical choice" on our part,[28] on a choice which is not "in any way grounded in reason or the nature of things."[29] In Hobbes's classic formulation, "whatsoever is the object of any man's appetite or desire, that is it which he for his part calleth *good*: and the object of his hate and aversion, *evil*. . . . For these words of good, evil and contemptible are ever used with relation to the person that useth them: there being nothing simply and absolutely so; nor any common rule of good an evil, to be taken from the nature of the objects themselves. . . ."[30] Choice thus constitutes the good rather than being governed by it. As a result, liberalism affirms what George F. Will has aptly described as "the moral equality of appetites."[31]

This is not to suggest, however, that liberalism lacks any theory of the human good. On the contrary, as MacIntyre suggests, liberalism "does indeed have its own broad conception of the good, which it is engaged in imposing politically, legally, socially and economically wherever it has the power to do so."[32] Its rejection of any substantive conception of the good leads to what Canavan terms "an unrelenting subordination of all allegedly objective goods to the subjective good of individual choice" (76), to what Elshtain describes as "the absolutizing of choice."[33] It leads, in other words, either implicitly or explicitly to the elevation of choice to the status of the highest human good. Freedom—choice—becomes the "chief" and "central value" (84), the "basic human good."[34]

If the liberal tradition's voluntarist anthropology causes it to elevate choice to the status of the highest good, it simultaneously causes liberal-

ism to embrace a particular understanding of the nature of human freedom. From the perspective of the dominant preliberal understanding of
human freedom, as Kenneth L. Schmitz has written, freedom is "rooted
in being" and "because it is relative to the structure within which we
have received that freedom, it is a relative and not an absolute freedom." Thus, human freedom has a "directional" character. Freedom finds
"its fulfillment not in itself" but in "the good" received through it; freedom realizes itself in and through the goods perfective of the human
person, in and through the fulfillment of man's distinctively human "potentialities." The limits that flow from freedom's orientation toward
truth, goodness, and love "do not fore-shorten liberty and constrain it by
compulsion from without." Rather, they flow from "within" the very
structure of human freedom and direct it "towards its . . . fulfillment."
They are thus "for the good of that very freedom" and "nourish" it.[35]

For liberalism, on the other hand, freedom is grounded "in the simple
act of will enacting its own prerogative." Lacking an "orientation to an
inscribed good," liberal freedom is a "freedom without a given, determinate content," "an absolutely undetermined and untrammeled freedom," a
"freedom accountable only to itself."[36] As Schmitz points out, however,
"if at the surface level, liberal freedom is understood as the freedom to
choose," in reality "there is something deeper at work in liberal liberty."
Rather than nourishing itself through "the ontological good that it seeks
to attain or hopes to receive, liberal liberty nourishes itself by vindicat-
ing itself, by reconfirming its liberty in and through choices." For this
reason, inherent in liberalism's affirmation of "the primacy of free choice"
is "the right *to unchoose*." Liberal liberty "must vindicate itself in and
through its capacity to reject its past choices." Viewing them as inconsistent with freedom, liberal liberty thus precludes binding commitments.[37]
Freedom thus means what Newman termed "the right of self-will"[38]—
the right to do as we choose, to obey only ourselves.

From these conceptions of the human person, social relations, the
human good, and freedom, the proponents of today's liberalism of the
sovereign self derive a distinctive political morality whose central values
are liberty and equality. Precisely because it affirms, in Canavan's words,
the priority of "individual freedom over any other human or social good

that conflicts with it," contemporary liberalism insists that "the ideal situation is one in which each individual freely . . . sets norms for himself" (76). It affirms "the sovereignty of the individual and his indefeasible right" to "decide for himself what norms he will obey" (134), to pursue his own distinctive conception of the good life. Because "persons are equal," moreover, "their appetites are equally worthy of society's moral respect and the law's protection. Some like chocolate, some like vanilla. Some like Mozart, others prefer heavy metal. Some like girls, some like boys. Some love God, others hate him." Ultimately, "it is all the same because man is a bundle of desires and each man strives to satisfy the desires he has" (127).

Liberalism's understanding of freedom and equality leads to the conclusion that each individual is entitled to the freedom "to act on his preferences so long as they are compatible with the equal right of others to do the same" (133). From this perspective, any attempt by society or the state to decide for men the use they should make of their liberty—to decide for them the goals they should pursue—must be rejected as an "immoral" effort by some citizens to "impose their morality" on others.[39] "Whatever restrictions on individual freedom are necessary," therefore, can only be justified by their contribution to "the individual's freedom to shape his life as he will" (76). Even when it embraces the welfare state, with its activist conception of the proper role of government, the liberalism of the sovereign self "does so in order to equalize everyone's chance to live the lifestyle of his choice" (132).

The transition from integral liberalism to today's liberalism of the sovereign self is indicative of the historical trajectory of liberal thought. Indeed, the history of liberalism is largely the story of the triumph of the will: the triumph of the subjective will of the individual over the objective moral good, of "the individualism" which, in Canavan's words "is the essence of liberalism," (84) over those elements in the thought of earlier generations of liberals that had acted to restrain it.

To appreciate why liberalism moves toward an ever deeper, ever more thoroughgoing individualism, it is necessary to explore several aspects of its metaphysical foundations. The first of these is the nominalism that pervades liberal thought. Insisting that "only individual things are real,"[40] nominalism asserts that "terms like human being, cat, dog, rosebush, pine tree, iron, or gold are just names that we attach to clusters of sense impressions that resemble each other. We group them under such names for convenience in thinking and talking about them, but the names we give them are only names, and do not stand for what they really and substantially are."[41] Universal terms, therefore, are simply "concepts in our minds." They do "not refer to real common natures outside the mind," but are simply "logical terms by which the human mind groups" the individual things it encounters in reality.[42] Universal terms are fictions—mere fabrications of the human mind, mere "mental constructs that we impose" on reality for reasons of "convenience in dealing with the world" (118).

Nominalism thus denies that "the human mind sees real natures and real patterns of order in the beings perceived by the senses." Instead, it holds "that the mind recognizes only individual and particular things, and groups them under class names on the basis of similarities in the way they appear to the senses, without knowing what their real substance and nature is."[43]

Thomas A. Spragens has shown how this nominalism was intertwined with a particular understanding of the nature of reason.[44] Crystallizing at the dawn of the Enlightenment, liberalism's founders partook fully of that era's passion for mathematics. For these thinkers, reason was equivalent to logic, and mathematics in general and geometry in particular were viewed as its highest and purest manifestation. This commitment to the *esprit geometrique* had far-reaching implications for their understanding of human knowledge. It meant that authentic knowledge, like the truths of geometry, "was absolutely luminous and indubitable," "unequivocally and explicitly true, demonstrable, verifiable and proven," incontrovertible. The unrivalled "precision, clarity and certainty" of mathematics became "the formal norm for all areas of knowledge," and mathematical precision and certainty, in short, became "the ideal to which all sciences" should aspire. One of the many consequences of this "was the denigration of all aspects of the human intellect and all products of the human mind that resisted assimilation to quasi-mathematical form."[45]

This mathematizing conception of reason was joined with the *esprit simpliste*, the belief that the foundations of human knowledge consist in "simple, unambiguous ideas or perceptions."[46] Indeed, "the spirit that unifies the liberal theory of knowledge," as Unger writes, "is confidence in the primacy of the simple. The world is made of simple things. Our ability to understand it depends on our success in going from the simple to the more complex and then returning again from the latter to the former." A "whole" is thus nothing more than "the sum of its parts."[47]

This metaphysics and epistemology have profound implications. For our purposes here, the most important concern the nature and scope of human knowledge. As Spragens suggests, some sense of these implications can be gleaned by contrasting Aristotelian "empiricism" with the liberal "empiricism" that takes shape under the influence of the complex of ideas just outlined. For Aristotelian empiricism, the senses convey "to the mind images of whole existences, such as trees, dogs and people." By stripping these images of their "accidental" attributes, the intellect was able to arrive at "the substantial forms," or the "essences," of the realities being perceived. Thus, "knowledge was made possible by the capacity of the senses to receive the impression of universal forms resident within the particulars."[48]

For liberal empiricism, on the other hand, "what the senses conveyed" . . . were "impressions of 'primary qualities'" such as "extension, location and motion."[49] Thus, as Canavan notes, for liberal empiricism, reason lacks the "abstracting" capacity necessary to "grasp a common concept in the data of sense," and human knowledge begins "not with substances or wholes existing in the real world, but with the isolated, disconnected data of the senses."[50] In this view, "all we know is the impressions made on our senses by the objects in the world outside us. All we know, therefore, is what things look (sound, feel, taste and smell) like, but not what they *are*." Thus, "we do not know what a human being is, but only how he impinges on our senses."[51] Knowledge thus involves the "building up" of "the objects" encountered by the senses and "the connection among them" from this data.[52]

This understanding of human knowledge struck at the very foundation of what, prior to the rise of liberalism, had been the dominant intellectual traditions in the Western world. The foundation of these traditions was what Unger terms "the doctrine of intelligible essences." "Something has an intelligible essence," writes Unger, "if it has a feature, capable of being apprehended, by virtue of which it belongs to one category of things rather than another category."[53] Insofar as liberalism's nominalism and rationalism push it inexorably toward the conclusion that, in Canavan's words, "we cannot know the substance and nature of anything"[54] they entail the rejection of the doctrine of objective essences. This rejection, moreover, precludes a teleological conception of reality, a conception of reality that understands things in terms of "intrinsic purposes," which sees the nature of something as a "principle of development" toward a predetermined "end" or goal.[55]

This rejection of teleology initially issues in a mechanistic vision of the universe, concludes Canavan, "the world of mechanistic, atomic physics, in which atoms impinging on one another form masses and interact in relations that can be precisely measured and stated as physical laws."[56] It issues in a vision of the universe as matter in motion in accordance with mathematically expressible relations of efficient causality.

Beginning with Hume's critique of causality, however, even this vision of the universe gradually succumbed to the skepticism that issued from liberalism's metaphysics. Liberalism's rejection of the doctrine of intelligible essences, as Unger writes, means that the mind cannot "understand what the world is really like." Indeed, this rejection leads to the conclusion "that there are numberless ways in which objects and events in the world might be classified" and that "there is no basis for saying" that one classification "portrays reality more accurately than another for the only measure of the 'truth'" of a classification "is its power to advance the ends of the communities of men" who employ it.[57]

As Canavan points out, liberalism's metaphysics points to the conclusion that we "live in a world of our definitions," definitions "about which we reason in accordance with the laws of logic."[58] Insofar as these definitions can be "nothing more than mental constructs which we impose" on reality, "the world as we perceive it" becomes a "mental construct." The metaphysics of liberalism thus leads to the type of corrosive skepticism characteristic of what is sometimes called postmodernism, that is, to the denial of the very possibility of objective knowledge. In this intellectual universe, "freedom establishes the truth rather than being governed by it."[59] Truth thus ultimately becomes nothing more than "what the individual thinks is true" (133) and "the choosing self" comes to believe "that it can create reality" itself. Things are "what the choosing self wills them to be."[60]

Obviously, all of this has profound implications for our understanding of the epistemological status of moral knowledge. The dominant premodern moral traditions had taken their bearing from the idea of a teleological understanding of human nature grounded in reason's capacity to discern an intelligible human essence. These traditions, as MacIntyre notes, distinguish between "man-as-he-happens-to-be and man-as-he-could-be-if-he-realized-his-essential-nature." Ethics was "the science" that enabled "men to understand how they make the transition from the former to the latter state." Its "precepts . . . instruct us . . . how to realize our true nature and to reach our true end."[61] Man's moral good was thus rooted in his natural good, in the ends or goals inherent in his nature.

By rejecting the idea of a knowable human nature with natural needs and tendencies—with a "natural good," an "ontological good" proper to our nature—liberal metaphysics deprives moral judgments of their ontological grounding, their foundation in the very structure of human nature. But it is "this good that makes moral judgments by and about human beings possible" (121). If contemporary liberal theory is committed to "the equality of all individual desires," as Canavan notes, this is because its metaphysics ultimately deprived it of any "standard higher than individual preference . . . to appeal to."[62]

Its metaphysics thus drives liberalism relentlessly toward what MacIntyre calls moral emotivism, the view that moral judgments are ultimately expressions of "arbitrary will and desire," and that such "judgments are *nothing but* expressions of preference, expressions of attitude or feeling."[63] In this way, liberalism's metaphysics provides what Canavan describes as the "inner dynamism" pushing liberalism relentlessly toward the idea of "the subjectivity of all values" (118), or the view that "good is only what the individual personally prefers" (133). The resultant moral nihilism finds frank expression in Bruce Ackerman's confession that "the hard truth is this: There is no moral meaning hidden in the bowels of the universe. All there is is you and I struggling in a world that neither we, nor any other thing, created."[64]

I do not wish to suggest that most early liberal theorists embraced either value non-cognitivism or nihilism. On the contrary, as Spragens notes, they believed that their metaphysics and epistemology would make it possible to "place the truths of the moral order on secure foundations once and for all." "Epistemological revolutions," however, "like their political counterparts, sometimes devour their children." Rather than providing "luminous and secure foundations" for the moral principles affirmed by integral liberalism, liberalism's understanding of reason and its capacities acted to render "the whole notion of moral knowledge anomalous" and to push "moral claims beyond the pale of reason into the realm of pseudo-propositions." In a universe from which "final causes and substances had been purged," in a universe of "primary qualities," the "'is' and the 'ought' simply fell apart." Lacking a "teleological order," such a universe lacked "a normative order" to ground moral truths.[65]

Against this backdrop, it becomes clear that liberalism's movement toward a progressively deeper and more radical individualism is no accident, but rather a working out of the inner logic of the premises that lie at its metaphysical core. By issuing in the denial of an order of human ends that obligates the individual prior to, and independently of, his free consent to pursue them, liberalism's metaphysics propels it relentlessly toward the liberation of the individual will from any norm higher than its own subjective imperatives, toward a vision of the human person as nothing less (or more) than "a sovereign will free to make of itself and the world what it pleases."[66]

Admittedly, as Canavan observes, the implications of this logic were initially "held in check" by a "belief in divine revelation and natural moral law." But over time these beliefs "dissolved" in the corrosive acids of the skepticism unleashed by liberalism's metaphysics. And, as "faith in divine revelation and in the ability of reason to perceive a natural moral order" was "lost," the "autonomous individual" of liberal theory "became an independent self, a subject of rights rather than obligations, and a sovereign will bound by no law to which he himself had not consented."[67]

To grasp the crisis that besets liberalism today, it is necessary to recognize that the same inner dynamism that has pushed liberal theory toward an ever-deeper individualism renders even today's liberalism of the sovereign self inherently unstable. As radically individualistic as this liberalism is, it does acknowledge that, strictly speaking, the self is not "the author of the only obligations that constrain." Over and against obligations originating in consent, as Sandel notes, this liberalism acknowledges the existence of "natural duties," of, duties that "we owe persons *qua* persons," such as the obligation "to do justice, to avoid cruelty, and so on."[68] Thus, the proponents of this liberalism are hardly complete relativists. In fact, as Gertrude Himmelfarb has pointed out, they do affirm a number of moral absolutes.[69] One thinks here of toleration, nonjudgmentalism, etc.

The difficulty that contemporary liberalism confronts consists in reconciling its affirmation of these natural duties and absolutes with the epistemological status of moral knowledge that inexorably issues from its metaphysics. To retain their belief in their political values, as Albert W. Alschuler puts it, liberal theorists must try to "brake" their "ethical skepticism halfway down."[70] Doing so, however, proves to be impossible, because the corrosive skepticism radiating from liberalism's metaphysics dissolves all natural duties and absolutes, including those posited by the theoreticians of the sovereign self. How can the intrinsic value and dignity of the person and the rights that flow from this fact be reconciled with the denial of the very possibility of moral knowledge? How can the binding character of the moral values championed by the liberalism of the sovereign self be reconciled with the conclusion that values are arbitrary, idiosyncratic, and subjective?

As Alschuler points out, the core values championed by liberals prove to be "vulnerable to the same . . . skepticism that leads them to reject the creeds of others." Ironically, the value non-cognitivism issuing from liberalism's metaphysics renders liberal theorists "unable to justify even the minimal values they [wish to] retain."[71] Today's liberalism of the sovereign self is inherently unstable because even the minimal restraints it places on the subjective will of the individual—restraints stemming from natural duties binding individuals prior to, and independently, of consent—cannot ultimately be sustained in the face of the corrosive skepticism spawned by liberalism's very own metaphysics and epistemology.

Of course, contemporary liberal theorists do not eschew moral judgments. On the contrary, insofar as their work has as its objective the articulation of a political morality in accordance with which they believe a rightly ordered society should be organized, it abounds in moral judgments. The problem is that value non-cognitivism makes it impossible for liberal theorists to ground their own moral and political judgments in ultimates consistent with their own thinking. The reduction of moral judgments to nothing more than subjective preferences, after all, deprives liberalism's own moral judgments of any foundation other than the subjective preferences of liberals. Recall Bertrand Russell's frank admission in private conversation that, contrary to his public claims, he found himself incapable of "squaring" his desire to condemn "the Nazi policy of genocide" as "wrong in itself" with "his professed ethical theory."[72]

Furthermore, the moral skepticism that results from liberal metaphysics lays the groundwork for an ethic that differs dramatically from that championed by contemporary liberalism. "Taken by itself," as William A. Galston has written,

> relativism . . . does not entail tolerance. B seeks to impose his way of life on A; A protests that B has no rational justification for his action; B replies, "What do I care about rational justification?" or (more moderately) "My way of life requires as a necessary condition a society in which others think and behave as I do." A can continue the argument only by appealing to some principle beyond ignorance of the good. Full skepticism about the good leads not to tolerance . . . but to an unconstrained struggle among different ways of life, a struggle in which force, not reason, is the final arbiter.[73]

By generating precisely "the full skepticism about the good" of which Galston speaks, liberal metaphysics reduces politics to "an unconstrained struggle" for power. Contemporary liberalism is thus on a collision course with itself.

Against this backdrop, the crisis that has today overtaken Enlightenment liberalism begins to come into view. As we have seen, liberalism's own metaphysics results in the rejection of an order of human and political ends that bind the conscience as obligatory, independently of, and prior to, our consent to those ends. Without such an order of ends, however, politics is necessarily reduced to a matter of sheer power and will.

The central political question, therefore, becomes whose will is to be absolutized—that of the individual or that of the group? In the latter case, the result is some form of what might be called tribalism, or what Robert Bellah terms "romantic cultural particularism."[74]

As Bellah suggests, however, if liberalism's truncated conception of reason can help lay the groundwork for romantic cultural particularism, with its exaltation of the group and its "unique truth," liberalism's metaphysics of the person ultimately acts to undermine "every collective commitment whether universal or particular."[75] Its better instincts and moralistic character to the contrary notwithstanding, liberalism slides inexorably toward the view that, in Canavan's phrase, the "good is only what the individual personally prefers" (133), or an intellectual universe in which "the individual's own will is his highest law" and in which each individual creates "his own moral universe."[76]

Here we arrive at the crisis that today besets liberalism. On the one hand, the corrosive skepticism that is its offspring moves liberalism inexorably toward an individualism that is, in principle, illimitable. From the perspective of a teleological understanding of human nature, as Canavan notes, man's rights and obligations have their foundation in "the goods that are the goals of human nature." Precisely because these goals are the foundations of human rights, they "furnish criteria for judging that asserted 'rights' are valid ones,"[77] and for distinguishing valid rights claims from "spurious ones" (135). "The purposes" a right is intended to serve "define [both] its nature and its limits."[78]

By rejecting the idea of a morally binding order of human ends that obligates us independently of our consent, liberalism deprives itself of a basis for making this distinction. Because it rejects "any rational standard" (96) for determining "the relative worth of different goals" (117-18), liberalism must end up affirming "the equality of all individual desires." Insofar as it leaves us with "no standard higher than individual preference . . . to appeal to," liberalism's skepticism precludes the positing of an *ordo juris* in whose light particular rights claims could be evaluated.[79]

The result is what Elshtain describes as an ethos of "radical antinomianism," in which "all constraints on the self tend to give rise to cries of oppression,"[80] and in which the desires and wants of individuals tend to be transformed into rights that trump the claims of the common good, the demands of social and moral ecology, and even the rights of others. The inner logic of liberalism's philosophical vision thus drives it relentlessly toward an intellectual universe in which the only moral norm—if it can be called that—is something akin to the Hobbesian right of nature, an intellectual universe in which "every man has a right to every thing; even to one another's body."[81]

On the other hand, the moral skepticism in which liberalism's metaphysics ultimately descends precludes in principle the affirmation of an order of human rights antecedent to positive law. An intellectual universe in which the "good" is nothing more than what a particular individual happens to prefer has no room for an order of human rights—an order of immunities and entitlements—issuing from the very nature and dignity of the person. In such a universe, human rights can be no more than convenient fictions.

Ironically, therefore, liberalism finds it impossible to ground in ultimates or its own understanding of the nature and destiny of the human person either the rights with which it has been so closely associated historically or those which its contemporary theoreticians urge us so strenuously to take seriously. Its commitment to the dignity and rights of the human person thus hangs suspended over a moral and intellectual abyss.

This state of affairs puts liberal theorists in a difficult position. In *Taking Rights Seriously*, for example, Ronald Dworkin finds himself in the awkward position of having (a) to concede that the existence of the rights he champions cannot be demonstrated and (b) to justify his demand that we continue to take them seriously by asserting that the fact that something cannot be demonstrated doesn't mean that it isn't "true."[82] ("Which is true," as MacIntyre remarks, "but could equally be used to defend claims about unicorns and witches.")[83] It is precisely the incompatibility of the moral values contemporary liberal theorists champion with liberalism's core metaphysical premises that explains contemporary liberalism's movement toward antifoundationalism, the myriad efforts to try to ground liberal political morality in some mixture of pragmatism, appeals to solidarity, historical particularity, and the exigencies of modern democratic politics or intellectual pluralism.

It also creates serious difficulties for liberal politics. "Once we real-ize," as Leo Strauss remarks, "that the principles of our actions have no other support than our blind choice, we really do not believe in them any more. We cannot wholeheartedly act upon them any more."[84] By reduc-ing the idea of human rights to the status of a convenient fiction, liberalism's value non-cognitivism makes it difficult for us to take these rights seriously. (One cannot but think here of a recent article in the *Chronicle of Higher Education* reporting that increasing numbers of col-lege students, while they deplore the Holocaust, are reluctant to con-demn it morally.)[85] Given liberalism's premises, it is difficult, in short, to explain to ourselves why we should respect these rights in our deal-ings with others when doing so would be inconvenient or contrary to the dictates of our self-interest. It also makes it difficult to justify to ourselves the compulsion of others to respect these rights. What right have we, after all, to impose what are merely our subjective prefer-ences on others?

Likewise, liberalism's value non-cognitivism deprives us of any rea-son for believing in the superiority of a politics predicated on the exist-ence of an order of human rights, and an ethic of respect for this order, to a politics based on the theoretical denial and practical disregard of an order of human rights. Indeed, a case could well be made that an ethic of radical and fearless self-assertion represents a more logical response to the meaningless universe that issues from liberal metaphysics than the ethic of respect for rights championed by contemporary liberal theorists. By creating a situation where, in Canavan's words, "the individual self, being prior to the obligations it chooses to assume, can have no motive for choosing other than self-interest,"[86] liberalism threatens to remove all moral constraints from political life and thus to reduce politics to nothing more than an amoral struggle for power.

Indeed, as Strauss notes, "if our principles have no other support than our blind preferences, everything a man is willing to dare will be per-mitted."[87] Assuming they can do so with impunity, why shouldn't the strong prey upon the weak? Given what history teaches us about human nature and political life, this question cannot be dismissed as unwarranted. Sooner or later, all societies must be prepared to face what Irving Kristol calls "the ultimate subversive question: 'Why not?'"[88] When all is said and done, liberalism simply lacks the resources to provide a convincing answer to this question.

In any case, in the crisis into which its metaphysics plunges the liberal tradition we discern one of the principal causes of the paradoxical situation that confronts us today: namely, a rights-obsessed culture that embraces an ever-expanding catalog of rights claims yet removes from its public law the protections it traditionally afforded the unborn. It is no coincidence that contemporary America's rights revolution has occurred simultaneously with the ascendancy of both a radically individualistic ethos that views human beings as sovereign choosers, and what Alan Wolfe terms the idea of moral freedom, namely, the idea that a just society "is one that allows each individual maximum scope for making his or her moral choices."[89] Nor is it a coincidence that the rights revolution has been paralleled by what Canavan describes as a "steady relativization of the ideas of truth and moral good" (133). Through its simultaneous exaltation of the individual will and affirmation of the moral equality of desires, liberalism has played an important role in unleashing the "rights mania" we witness today.

Likewise, in a variety of ways, the crisis of liberalism has helped lay the cultural groundwork for abortion-on-demand. To begin with, as Canavan points out, liberalism's metaphysics makes it hard for it to recognize the humanity of the unborn child. It pushes liberalism relentlessly toward the view that "there is no such thing as a human nature, the possession of which makes a being human whatever its stage of development." This being the case, what makes a being human can only be its "capacities" (e.g., rationality, self-consciousness, communication, self-ownership, etc.)[90] or "appearance."[91] Since "in its embryonic state" an unborn child neither looks human nor exercises capacities constitutive of humanity it follows that it isn't human. (In the same way, this metaphysic acts to obscure the personhood of the unborn child.)

Simultaneously, liberalism's exaltation of individual autonomy finds expression in what John Paul describes as "a completely individualistic concept of freedom" that "exalts the isolated individual in an absolute way."[92] Liberalism, as Canavan observes, views a human being "as essen-

tially an individual proprietor" who "owns his body, the actions he performs with it, and the goods he acquires by those actions" (130). By
doing so, it creates a situation in which the good of individual autonomy
takes precedence over the good of human life. Thus, even when its metaphysics does not obscure the humanity of the unborn child, liberalism's
commitment to autonomy creates a situation in which a woman's right
to control her own body trumps an unborn child's right to life, a situation in which although a fetus may have a right to life "this right . . . does
not entitle" it "to use a woman's body against her will."[93]

Finally, and most radically, the utter nihilism in which liberalism
ultimately issues strikes at the very notion of the intrinsic value, the
sanctity, of human life. In the meaningless universe that arises from liberal metaphysics, "there is no natural or transcendent standard . . . to
which we can appeal to determine the worth of humanity." Thus, "human beings have only such worth and such rights as other human beings
choose to assign them." In a universe in which human life possesses no
inherent value and in which the ideas of the dignity and rights of the
human person are no more than social constructs, abortion—like the
taking of innocent human life more generally—cannot be said to be
intrinsically problematic. Thus, writes Canavan, not only "may we make
such distinctions as we choose to make among the born and unborn, the
deformed and the normal, the mentally healthy and the insane," but
"who or what dies in an abortion" becomes irrelevant: "person or not,
you [may] kill it, when it gets in the way."[94]

Against this background, it is impossible to agree with Galston's
contention that "it is Dostoevskian characters, not liberals, who argue for
the freedom to commit murder."[95] It is impossible not only because the
nihilism so brilliantly portrayed in Dostoevsky's work is (as he himself
was well aware) an inevitable outgrowth of the unfolding of the inner
dynamism of Enlightenment liberalism, but because the arguments put
forward by liberal theoreticians in favor of legalized abortion—arguments centering on the priority of individual autonomy over other goods
or the denial of the sanctity of human life—are increasingly difficult to
distinguish from arguments for "the freedom to commit murder."

Its deep complicity in America's culture of death and the character of the justifications it has come to offer for this culture, reveal the moral bankruptcy of Enlightenment liberalism and the brutal consequences of the nihilism it unleashes. Under the impact of this nihilism, liberalism's commitment to freedom and equality inexorably collapses into what John Paul describes as "the freedom of the strong against the weak,"[96] and into a regime in which individuals and groups are understood to possess only those rights that they have the power to vindicate against others.

The conclusion regarding Enlightenment liberalism that follows from all this will depend on what one thinks of the rights revolution and abortion. If one views these developments as representing social progress, as representing the liberation of America from outdated beliefs and oppressive power relations, one might well commend liberalism for its role in bringing them about. If, on the other hand, one views America's rights revolution as a political disorder, abortion as a moral abomination, and the two together as symptomatic of a broader cultural crisis signifying nothing less than the erosion of the intangible prerequisites of free government, then one may well question the ideology that has done so much to lay their intellectual groundwork. In this case, one might well join with Canavan in concluding that however much "we may applaud" its historical contribution to the rise of "limited constitutional government," liberalism "is now a menace rather than a support of constitutional democracy" (133). And one may go on to conclude that the future of ordered liberty depends on the establishment of a new and better public philosophy rooted in a richer metaphysics of the person and society than that which informs Enlightenment liberalism.[97]

XIII

The False Prophets of American Conservatism

HARRY V. JAFFA

"If we could first know where we are, and whither we are tending,
we could better judge what to do, and how to do it."—Abraham Lincoln

In the 1850s, Stephen Douglas's notion of popular sovereignty seemed to offer a painless way out of our great national crisis over slavery. It did so by having the people in each of the territories—rather than the Congress—decide for itself the slavery question. Lincoln, however, rejected this solution, insisting instead that slavery was wrong and that America must necessarily become all slave or all free. Indeed, he sought national legislation excluding slavery from the territories. It was this moral condemnation of slavery, combined with its promise of slavery's "ultimate extinction" in the slave states themselves, that the South could not accept, and that made secession and war inevitable. The compromise position championed by Douglas was exceedingly tempting to the eastern leadership of the Republican Party in 1858, and would almost certainly have been accepted, had not Abraham Lincoln stood in the way.[1]

While the crisis of today does not have the immediacy of the crisis over slavery, its underlying character is the same. It is commonplace today to compare the issue of abortion to that of slavery, and especially to compare *Roe v. Wade* to *Dred Scott*. And, indeed, the parallels are many and striking. More profound than the details of these comparisons is the one cause underlying the many resemblances. When Douglas declared that he didn't care whether slavery was voted up or voted down, that he cared only for the right of the people to decide, he gave expression to a concept of democracy that identified majority rule with indifference to the morality of the outcome of majority rule.

Such moral relativism dominates political thought in our time far more profoundly than when Douglas and Lincoln had their debates. And this moral relativism, now even more than then, takes the form of a rejection of the principles of the Declaration of Independence. This is not because it is the Declaration alone that embodies moral realism and moral rationalism. Indeed, the principles of the Declaration are expressed in many other places, in the Revolution, and in the Founding generally. The "laws of nature and of nature's God" in the Declaration represent, however, a distillation of the wisdom of a tradition of more than two thousand years. They—and the American Founding generally—represent the culmination of the attempt by Socrates, described by Cicero, to bring philosophy down from the heavens. They also represent the agreement of reason and revelation—of Athens and Jerusalem—on the moral ground of human government.

At this point, it should be noted that what Leo Strauss called the crisis of the West has deepened greatly since the end of the Cold War. The struggle against Nazis and communists produced alliances within American politics that did not need to plumb the depths of conviction to justify common action. In the last half century, the necessity to fight communism abroad and socialism at home was sufficient to bind together the various and discordant elements that made up what has been called "conservatism." Those battles having been substantially (although not permanently) won, the issues that divide conservatives have now taken precedence over the expediency of their alliance.

The end of the Cold War has also brought an end to the remission of the disease of moral relativism that is corroding the life of Western civilization. It would certainly seem that the salvation of the West must come, if it is to come, from the United States. The salvation of the United

States, if it is to come, must come from the Republican Party. The salvation of the Republican Party, if it is to come, must come from the conservative movement within it. And the salvation of the conservative movement, if it is to come, must come from the renewal and reaffirmation of the principles of the American Founding, embodied above all in the Declaration of Independence, a reaffirmation of the type that occurred in the events that led to the election of Abraham Lincoln. Such a renewal and reaffirmation, however, will require the rejection of many of the ideas that have dominated American conservatism in the last half-century.

This call for a renewal and reaffirmation of our Founding principles has recently been made in the following way by an unusual authority:

> The United States carries a weighty and far reaching responsibility, not only for the well being of its own people, but for the development and destiny of people throughout the world.... The Founding Fathers of the United States asserted their claim to freedom and independence on the basis of certain "self-evident" truths about the human person: truths which could be discerned in human nature, built into it by "nature's God."
>
> Thus, they meant to bring into being, not just an independent territory, but an experiment in what George Washington called "ordered liberty": an experiment in which men and women would enjoy equality of rights and opportunities in pursuit of happiness and in service to the common good.
>
> Reading the founding documents of the United States, one has to be impressed by the concept of freedom they enshrine: a freedom designed to enable people to fulfill their duties and responsibilities toward the family and toward the common good the community. Their authors clearly understood that there could be no happiness without respect and support for the natural groupings through which people exist, develop, and seek the higher purposes of life in concert with others.
>
> The American democratic experiment has been successful in many ways. Millions of people around the world look to the United States as a model, in their search for freedom, dignity, and prosperity. But the continuing success of American democracy depends on the degree to which each new generation, native born and immigrant, makes its own the moral truths on which the Founding Fathers staked the future of your Republic.
>
> Their commitment to build a free society with liberty and justice for all must be constantly renewed if the United States is to fulfill the destiny to which the Founders pledged their "lives...fortunes...and sacred honor."

The speaker concluded with a prayer, a prayer that our country "will experience a new birth of freedom, freedom grounded in truth and ordered to goodness." The speaker was Pope John Paul II, welcoming the new United States Ambassador to the Holy See, Lindy Boggs.[2]

There are many things that are noteworthy in this remarkable statement. What is particularly striking are the ways in which it embodies ideas that have either been ignored or denounced by many established representatives of conservative thought. For John Paul, like Jefferson and Lincoln, the rights mentioned in the Declaration of Independence, being rights with which we are endowed by our Creator, are not to be understood blindly to emancipate the passions, but rather to direct them towards the ends approved by that same Creator, ends which are in the service of the common good no less than private pleasures.

Contrary to what some prominent theoreticians of contemporary American conservatism suggest, John Paul, like Abraham Lincoln, recognizes that the truths of the Founding do not depend solely upon tradition or divine revelation, but are "discerned in human nature" by human reason grounded in "self-evident truths." It is also quite remarkable that John Paul does not speak here of "traditional values," "family values," or any other kind of values, which by definition are subjective. In the accents of Abraham Lincoln he calls for renewal in each new generation of the "moral truths" (not values) upon which the nation was founded. Contemporary America should take to heart John Paul's call for "a new birth of freedom."

We are obliged to recognize, however, that the greatest obstacles to the moral renewal called for by the Pope may be found in the elites— conservative no less than liberal—who dominate our public life. Mr. Justice Scalia, for example, has recently expounded a vision of democracy that bears a striking resemblance to Douglas's "popular sovereignty." "It just seems to me," he observes, "incompatible with democratic theory that it's good and right for the state to do something that the majority of the people do not want done. Once you adopt democratic theory, it seems to me, you accept that proposition. If the people, for example, want abortion the state should permit abortion. If the people do not want it, the state should be able to prohibit it." Indeed, he insists that "the whole theory of democracy . . . is that the majority rules; that is the whole theory of it. You protect minorities only because the majority determines that there are certain minority positions that deserve protection." Thus, he concludes that "you cannot have democratic theory and then say, but what about the minority? The minority loses except to the extent that the majority, in its document of government, has agreed to accord the minority rights." Scalia says that if the people want abortion, the law should permit it. By the same reasoning, if the people want slavery, or any other form of plunder, there is no principled ground to oppose them.[3]

In the course of the joint debates with Lincoln, Douglas said, "We in Illinois . . . tried slavery, kept it up for twelve years, and finding that it was not profitable we abolished it for that reason."[4] To this Lincoln famously replied, that Judge Douglas "says he 'don't care' whether [slavery] is voted up or voted down the Territories. . . . Any man can say that who does not see anything wrong in slavery, but no man can logically say it who does see a wrong in it; because no man can logically say he don't care whether a wrong is voted up or voted down." For Lincoln as for Jefferson— and, I need hardly add, for Pope John Paul—the great principles of right and wrong must govern the people, if the people are to be able to govern themselves. No majority, however great, can authorize what is intrinsically immoral. No nation, as George Washington reminded us, can prosper that "disregards the eternal rules of order and right which Heaven itself has ordained."[5] These rules bind the majority no less than the minority.

Someone may object that Scalia, in common with other conservative jurists is merely objecting to "unelected judges" usurping legislative powers. Of course, the usurpation of authority is always wrong. However, that the judges are unelected has nothing to do with their alleged usurpations. They are no less unelected when they decide rightly as when they decide wrongly. The manner of their appointment and their tenure are provided by the Constitution, and is authorized by the rights with which the people have been endowed by their Creator.

The independence of the judiciary was believed by those who framed and those who ratified the Constitution to be in the service of the rule of law. No one in 1787 believed that majority rule was the source of constitutional rights. They understood, as Scalia does not, that the prior recognition of the equal rights of all human persons is a necessary condition for the legitimacy of majority rule.

In his essay titled "Sovereignty," James Madison made clear that unanimous consent—that is, unanimous agreement as to the rights of minorities—underlies and logically precedes majority rule. This follows from the conviction, recognized by the Pope, but not by Justice Scalia, that the rights with which we are endowed by our Creator are the basis of the political process, and are not negotiable within the political process. In 1786, in a letter to James Monroe, Madison denounced the very idea of uncontrolled majority rule. There is "no maxim," he wrote, "which is more liable to be misapplied, and which therefore needs elucidation, than the current one that the interest of the majority is the political standard of right and wrong. Taking the word 'interest' as synonymous with 'ultimate happiness,' in which sense it is qualified with every necessary moral ingredient, the proposition is no doubt true." But, he continued, "taking it in its popular sense, as referring to the immediate augmentation of property and wealth, nothing can be more false. In the latter sense it would be in the interest of the majority in every community to despoil and enslave the minority of individuals. . . . In fact, it is only establishing, under another name and a more specious form, force as the measure of right. . . ."[6]

What is most striking here is Madison's absolute opposition to Scalia's view of the ethics of majority rule. Madison, it is true, distinguishes the popular or vulgar from the philosophic understanding of what constitutes the "interest" of the majority. This distinction, too, is unrecognized by Scalia. For Madison, the despotism of the majority is no less despotic because it is perpetrated by the majority.

Madison's condemnation of majority rule is virtually identical with Aristotle's in the third book of the *Politics*. There, Aristotle denounces the very idea that the poor, by the mere force of numbers, may take away the property of the rich. Only within the framework of natural rights—among which are the equal rights of all human persons to life, liberty, and property—can majority rule function rightly and legitimately. Madison also speaks of "ultimate happiness" as the true "political standard of right and wrong." In this sense, he says, it is "qualified with every necessary moral ingredient." Madison tacitly assumes Aristotle's definition of happiness as an "activity of virtue." Likewise, George Washington, in his first inaugural, declared that "the foundations of our national policy will be laid in the pure and immutable principles of private morality."[7] To this he added that "there is no truth more thoroughly established than that there exists in the economy and course of nature, an indissoluble union of virtue and happiness."[8]

It is clear that, for the Founding Fathers, individual rights—including the right to the pursuit of happiness—always possess that "moral ingredient" that directs them, as John Paul says, towards the common good. This is in contrast to that large body of conservative opinion today that regards natural rights as merely idiosyncratic and self-regarding.

How profoundly alienated present-day conservative thought is from the Founding principles is illustrated by the following passages from the celebrated essay titled "The Notion of a Living Constitution," written by our present Chief Justice. In it, Chief Justice Rehnquist replies to liberal judicial activists who would empower the courts to discover constitutional rights for any wrongs that, in the justices' opinion, need remedies. This would, he rightly contends, turn the Constitution into a blank paper on which the Supreme Court might write at its pleasure.

In repelling liberal judicial activism, Rehnquist admonishes those who, he says, "ignore totally the nature of political value judgments in a democratic society. If such a society adopts a constitution and incorporates in that constitution safeguards for individual liberty, these safeguards do indeed take on a generalized moral rightness or goodness. They assume a general acceptance neither because of any intrinsic worth nor because of any unique origins in someone's idea of natural justice, but instead, simply because they have been incorporated in a constitution by a people."[9] It is difficult for anyone, encountering this statement for the first time, to appreciate its absolute opposition to everything Abraham Lincoln believed, as well as to the convictions of those who framed, and those who ratified, the Constitution. It is the negation as well of Pope John Paul's message. It is not only damaging in itself but, as we shall see, it supplies the rationale for that boundless judicial activism it purports to resist. To say that safeguards for individual liberty do not have any intrinsic worth is to say that individual liberty does not have any intrinsic worth. To say that individual liberty does not have any intrinsic worth is to say that the individual human person does not have any intrinsic worth. To deny that is to deny that we are endowed with rights by our Creator. To deny that is, in effect, to deny that there is a Creator. This is atheism and nihilism no less than moral relativism.

According to Rehnquist and Scalia the only rights the people have are the rights the people themselves have decreed. The people have become their own God. A people thus conceived may choose to express their rights by any form of government whatever. The legitimacy of Hitler and of Stalin was ratified by plebiscite. The moral relativism that denies any intrinsic worth to human freedom, or human life, can justify any form of government, however criminal or brutal. Thus, Rehnquist and his followers are mistaken in supposing that it justifies majority rule more than any other form of government. The triumph of will admits no boundaries established by reason. This is unadorned positivism, relativism, and nihilism. This is the crisis at the heart of present-day conservatism. This is the crisis of the West.

Rehnquist says that safeguards for individual liberty "take on" generalized moral rightness or goodness only "because they have been incorporated in a constitution by a people." If, however, one "value judgment" has zero intrinsic worth, multiplying this zero by a million or a billion adds nothing to its intrinsic worth. The aforesaid "moral rightness or goodness" is therefore only an illusion arising from the fact that it is "generalized." On Rehnquist's premises, there is no such thing as intrinsic moral rightness, no such thing as moral truth. Morality as an intrinsic good is an illusion.

Concerning the original Constitution, let us consider that, besides its safeguards for individual liberty, it had notable and powerful safeguards for slavery. These safeguards were adopted by the same people, and at the same time, as the safeguards for individual liberty. On Rehnquist's premises, the safeguards for slavery take on the same generalized moral rightness and goodness as the safeguards for liberty. The moral equality of the safeguards for slavery and liberty in the Constitution was the heart of the argument of John C. Calhoun in 1848, and constituted the heart of the argument for secession in 1860 and 1861.

The heart of the argument for liberal judicial activism is that the antebellum Constitution gave a moral sanction to slavery, and that the original Constitution was therefore racist. The liberal argument is superior to Rehnquist's, at least to the extent that it assumes that slavery is something intrinsically immoral. The liberal argument implies that, because of its acceptance of slavery, the original intent of that Constitution has no moral authority—hence, the case for a "living constitution," in which the intent of enlightened justices replaces that of the racist framers and ratifiers.

The late Justice Thurgood Marshall, on the bicentennial of the Constitution in 1987, said we had no just cause for celebrating that racist document. Under it, he said, Negroes "had no rights which the white man was bound to respect."[10] These words, however, were not his own. They came from Chief Justice Taney's opinion for the Court in the case of Dred Scott. Taney had reached this conclusion, in part, by asserting that the proposition that "all men are created equal" in the Declaration of Independence was never understood to include black human beings, that they were regarded by those who framed and ratified the Constitution as so far inferior, and that they might be justly enslaved for their own benefit.

Taney's assertion, uncritically accepted by Marshall, is as great a falsehood as has ever been perpetrated in a public forum. Yet this falsehood, damaging to every cause supposedly held dear by Mr. Justice Marshall in his long career, has not only been given credence by him, but has been disseminated as truth. It has also been propagated by Professor John Hope Franklin, the noted historian who was appointed by President Clinton to head a commission on race relations. This lie—which may be compared to the Protocols of the Elders of Zion—has become canonical for what once was the civil rights movement. Its acceptance has transformed that movement into a movement for black power.

Taney's assertion that blacks had been excluded from the benefit of the rights asserted for "all men" in the Declaration of Independence was refuted at the time in Justice Curtis's dissenting opinion, and shortly thereafter, in one of his greatest speeches, by Abraham Lincoln. In fact, Taney's opinion concerning black inferiority had no more standing in reason than Hitler's assertions about the Jews. What is astonishing, however, is not only that Thurgood Marshall and John Hope Franklin continue to echo Taney, but that they continue to ignore the refutation of Taney by Abraham Lincoln. What is even more astonishing is that Rehnquist and his supporters on the Right are as persistent in ignoring Lincoln as are Marshall and Franklin. What unites Marshall and Franklin and their followers with Rehnquist and his followers is their common refusal to grant constitutional standing to the doctrine of natural rights enunciated in the Declaration of Independence and expounded by Lincoln.[11]

According to Lincoln, the original Constitution had recognized slavery only as a matter of necessity, not of right. Without the guarantees to slavery, the Constitution would not have been ratified. No alternative form of government—certainly not the government under the Articles of Confederation—would have been strong enough to contain slavery. Only the government of the Constitution could limit the extension of slavery, and place it "in course of ultimate extinction."

Paradoxical as it may seem, Lincoln said, it was in the interest of the slaves themselves that the concessions to slavery were made in 1787. The documentary record of the Founding is filled with recognition of the incompatibility of slavery and the principles of the Declaration of Independence. Slavery had, however, been planted in the colonies when they were dependent upon Great Britain and had no power of their own to control it. During that time, slavery had become deeply rooted and entwined in all their social institutions, their property relations, and economy. Against the charge of racism in the Founding, it can be said that it was hardly wonderful that a nation of slaveholders, on becoming independent, did not abolish slavery. What was wonderful—nay, miraculous—was that a nation of slaveholders, on becoming independent, declared that all men are created equal, and thereby made it a moral and political necessity that slavery be abolished. The American Founding, in its principles, was anti-racist to the core. But the anti-racism of the original Constitution—and its original intent—can only be understood if one distinguishes the principles of the Constitution from the compromises of that Constitution. This is what Rehnquist and his followers refuse to do. The distinction between principles and compromises is not made in the text of the Constitution, and therefore is denied any place in constitutional jurisprudence by these legal positivists. Yet without it, the charge of racism is plausible, and so is the liberal judicial activism based on it.

The conflict today between liberals and conservatives centers largely upon the interpretation of the equal protection clause of the Fourteenth Amendment. In that dispute, Taney's assertion that Negroes were never included in the proposition of human equality is the foundation of the liberal insistence that the Constitution is not, and never has been, color-blind. In a color-coded Constitution, the purpose of the Fourteenth Amendment is to remedy the grievances of blacks. There can therefore be no objections to color- or race-based remedies.

To this, Rehnquist, Bork, and their followers have no answer. They could find one only if they insisted that Taney was wrong about the original Constitution, and that the principles of the Constitution were those of the Declaration of Independence, rightly understood. From this it is apparent that conservatives and liberals alike reject the genuine principles of the Declaration of Independence.

If we widen our vision to the broader field of political philosophy, we see the conservatism of the last-half century compounded largely of paleoconservatives and neoconservatives. The many subgroups, such as economic conservatives and social conservatives, of libertarians and traditionalists, are, for present purposes, sufficiently comprehended within these two larger categories.

At the head and front of the paleoconservatives is the late Russell Kirk, whose *Conservative Mind*, published in the early 1950s, is widely credited as the defining work of contemporary conservatism. Kirk's counterpart in the world of neoconservatism is Irving Kristol. Kirk's traditionalism embodied an allegiance not merely to eighteenth-century British constitutionalism, as understood (allegedly) by Edmund Burke, but to surviving elements of the class-structured *ancien régime* within it. Kirk was a proponent of Christian civilization who rejected the French Revolution and viewed the Enlightenment as the source of virtually all evil in the modern world. Kristol, on the other hand, is someone whose very existence as a modern, nonorthodox albeit loyal Jew, was rendered possible by the Enlightenment. Kristol celebrates all those elements of upward mobility in capitalism that undermine inherited status, so dear to

Kirk, whether based on birth, old wealth, or religious conformity.

Notwithstanding the great gulf between them, Kirk and Kristol have been as one in their opposition to the doctrines embodied in the Declaration of Independence. Like Carl Becker, they held that "to ask whether the natural rights philosophy of the Declaration of Independence is true or false, is essentially a meaningless question."[12] This has been their received and unexamined premise. They are undisturbed by the fact that it renders meaningless the American political tradition itself.

Yet all their influence has been exerted to ignore or ridicule anyone who—like Jefferson, Lincoln, and Pope John Paul—believes that the truths held to be self-evident really are so, and can be proved to be so. Kirk's trivialization of the Declaration of Independence is evident in remarks he makes in an introduction to a reprinting of Albert Jay Nock's *Mr. Jefferson.* "Nock's book," he writes,

> has very little to say about the Declaration of Independence. That is as it should be, for the Declaration is not conspicuously American in its ideas or phrases, and not even characteristically Jeffersonian. As Carl Becker sufficiently explains, the Declaration was meant to persuade the court of France, and the philosophes of Paris, that the Americans were sufficiently un-English to deserve military assistance. Jefferson's Declaration is a successful instrument of diplomacy; it is not a work of political philosophy or an instrument of government, and Jefferson himself said little about it after 1776.[13]

It is doubtful whether more errors could be compressed into fewer words. It should be noted, to begin with, that authorship of the Declaration was the first of the three things by which Jefferson wished most to be remembered, and which he caused to be inscribed on his tombstone. In his celebrated letter to Henry Lee, furthermore, Jefferson said of the Declaration that, "neither aiming at originality of principle or sentiment, nor yet copied from any particular and previous writing, it was intended to be an expression of the American mind, and to give that expression the proper tone and spirit called for by the occasion."[14] Not a word about the court of France!

What Carl Becker actually said, moreover, was the exact opposite of what Kirk attributed to him. "Democratic imprudence," Becker insisted, "could not well go farther than to ask the descendant of Louis XIV to approve a rebellion based upon the theory that 'governments derive their just powers from the consent of the governed.' If the French government received the Declaration, it did so in spite of its political philosophy because it could not forego the opportunity in disrupting the British empire."[15] Contra Kirk, Becker never doubted that the Declaration of Independence was a work of political philosophy. Like Kirk, but unlike Pope John Paul II, he did not regard the Declaration as a repository of philosophic truth.

As far as the Declaration's status on not being an "instrument of government," it need only be observed that it remains, as it has always been, the first of the Organic Laws of the United States in the United States Code. All acts and deeds of the United States since 1776, including the original Constitution, have been dated from its signing. According to a joint statement of Madison and Jefferson in 1825, the Declaration is not only the act of separation of the thirteen colonies from Great Britain but "the act of Union" by which the thirteen became one.[16]

Kristol's posture toward what John Paul describes as the Declaration's "moral truths" is equally dismissive. "To perceive the true purposes of the American Revolution," he writes, "it is wise to ignore some of the more grandiloquent declamations of the moment."[17] That "all men are created equal" is of course the most grandiloquent of the aforesaid declamations. In the same essay Kristol refers to Tom Paine as "an English radical who never really understood America [and] is especially worth ignoring."[18]

In fact, Tom Paine gave the decisive impetus to independence in the winter and spring of 1776. Early in the year, General Washington toasted the king's health in his officers' mess, until he encountered the "sound doctrine and unanswerable reasoning" of *Common Sense*.[19] What finally turned George Washington to independence is what Kristol asks us to ignore. It is also worth mentioning that this man, who is said never to have understood America, carried a musket in the battle of Trenton.

In 1976, however, Tom Paine became Kristol's surrogate for Thomas Jefferson. More recently, however, Kristol has criticized not only Jefferson himself, but the entire founding. The authors of the Constitution, he now says, "were for the most part not particularly interested in religion. I am not aware that any of them wrote anything worth reading on religion, especially Jefferson, who wrote nothing worth reading on religion or

almost anything else."[20] I cannot recall a more comprehensive deprecia-
tion of the writing in which Pope John Paul discovered moral wisdom.
Nor is there a greater measure of the alienation of present-day conservatism from that wisdom. (What kind of education is possible, when
young people are told, by an ancient of the tribe, that the author of the
two greatest documents of civil and religious liberty in the history of
the world is not worth reading?)

Jefferson, being in Paris in 1787, was not, of course, one of the authors of the Constitution. Nevertheless, nothing dominated the consciousness of all the Founders, including Jefferson, more than abhorrence of the
wars of religion, and religious persecution, which had weighed down
European politics for more than two hundred years. The Constitution of
1787 heralded the *novus ordo seclorum*, the new order of the ages, when
it declared that there should never be a religious test for office.

There was no precedent for this in human history. The subsequent
provision in the First Amendment, against an establishment of religion,
and against any prohibition of its free exercise, applied—at least before
the Fourteenth Amendment—only to the federal government. But the
pure doctrine, as it applied to all free government, was enunciated the
year before the constitutional convention in the statute of Virginia for
religious liberty.

That statute, drafted by Thomas Jefferson, was the outcome of a long
and intense struggle for disestablishment of the Episcopal Church, a struggle
led by James Madison and supported by George Washington. Madison's
1785 "Memorial and Remonstrance" against religious establishment is
unsurpassed in the acuteness of its reflections on the relationship between
religious freedom, true religion, and free government. Jefferson put these
thoughts into final form in the statute, which declared that "our civil
rights have no dependence on our religious opinions, any more than our
opinions in physics or geometry."[21]

While the Virginia law of 1786 applied only to Virginia, its argument
became in time the basis not only of federal law, but that of all fifty states.
It was clear to the Founders, if not to Kristol (or to Justices Scalia and
Rehnquist), that a system of majority rule was impossible if the majority
had the power to decide in what way its citizens must worship God. No

Catholic could be compelled by majority rule to become a Protestant, or vice-versa. No Jew could be compelled by majority rule to become a Christian, or vice versa.

Only by removing all such questions of religious belief from the political process was government by majority rule possible. Nor was this designed only to provide for civil peace. Removing both penalties against nonconformity and rewards for conformity contributed greatly to the purity of religion. A man's relationship to his Maker ought to be exempt equally from the fears and temptations of politics. As Pope John Paul declares, "the fundamental right to religious freedom is the guarantee of every other human right."[22] Indeed, it is the very foundation of free government. If there is a sanctuary of conscience inside every human person where no earthly power can legitimately tread, as George Weigel has observed, then the state is, by definition, a limited government.[23] The distinction between church and state has been elaborated into the distinction between state and society, the church being the first, but not the last, of the voluntary associations exempted from control by government.

It was separation of church and state that made it possible for religion to become, as Tocqueville said, "the first" of America's "political institutions."[24] What he meant was that the churches, freed from sectarian political strife, could jointly and severally inculcate and support those moral truths common to all the churches, moral truths enshrined in the "laws of nature and of nature's God." This was also the reason why, he thought, the Americans were a more religious people than those of Europe.

While Irving Kristol does not think the Founders were interested in religion or wrote much worth reading on the subject, he is not reluctant to articulate his own theory regarding the role of religion in American democracy. A commercial society like ours, he says, must have a "religious tradition . . . to correct [its] natural propensity . . . to debase itself. It provides something else that is critically necessary, namely, some absolute foundation for our moral values. . . . But . . . values are not created; values are inherited."[25] There is, he insists "no such thing as a rationalist religion which gives you an authoritative moral code. . . . There are no rationalist Ten Commandments. Morality is derived from certain fundamental dogmatic truths, and I emphasize the word dogmatic. It is the function of a religion, in a society such as ours, to provide the dogmatic basis for those truths."[26]

In claiming that reason cannot supply the opinions—dogmas—that are necessary for the moral health of society, Kristol differs from both Pope John Paul and the Founders. In this context, he takes issue with my work. "As this pertains to the American political tradition," he writes

> we enter some controversy, which will be better understood if I compare my views to those of Harry Jaffa. . . . Mr. Jaffa, quite correctly, feels that in discussing the issue of human rights one must raise the question of what human rights are based upon. . . . You have got to have a fundamental, unshakable basis for your conviction in a given set of human rights, and Harry Jaffa's is that the rights expressed in the Declaration of Independence, in the end, rely on the natural law and natural rights tradition which goes back through Thomas Aquinas to Aristotle. I think he is wrong. As I see it, our dogma in regard to such matters as human rights comes from the Protestantized version of he Judeo-Christian tradition. . . . Why do we cherish human rights? Because of something called "the dignity of man," a key phrase. That is something that emerges out of Jewish doctrine, out of Christian doctrine, and in modern form, out of Protestantism, which insists upon the dignity of the individual soul and the relation of this individual soul to the Deity.[27]

I pass over the fact that Kristol speaks of "moral values," the language of subjectivity, rather than "moral truths." In any event, Kristol says values are inherited, not created. But which inheritance is to be prized, and which rejected? Willmoore Kendall used to say that tarring and feathering the proponents of controversial views, and riding them out of town on a rail, was as much an American tradition as freedom of speech. In a certain sense, he is correct. The right to freedom of speech has not always been respected. The key question is whether one of these traditions is superior to the other. This is a judgment that must be made by reason. Chief Justice Rehnquist would remind Kristol that he has no right to fob off his preferred values as our inheritance.

Kristol rightly celebrates the idea of the dignity of man as the source of our good inheritance. He couldn't be more right. And it is precisely this idea that is enshrined in the Declaration of Independence. The Declaration, moreover, links this dignity, as Kristol himself thinks it should be linked, to man's relationship with God. The dignity and rights of man derive precisely from their divine origin.

Kristol asserts that society needs a dogmatic foundation for its moral convictions, laying great emphasis upon the word "dogmatic." But, no-where in the records of the world is there a more eloquent and confident expression of moral conviction than the passage beginning, "We hold these truths to be self-evident . . . " Pope John Paul looks to these words for a renewal of the moral truths to which the Founders pledged their lives, fortunes, and sacred honor. But how can this be, if we are persuaded that this is mere grandiloquence, and can be conveniently ignored?

Kristol looks to the authority of the "Protestantized" version of the Judeo-Christian tradition to ground America's affirmation of the dignity of the human person. Yet, as the political sermons of the Revolutionary era collected by Ellis Sandoz show, the Protestants of that era exhibited considerably more confidence than does Kristol in the capacity of human reason to grasp the dignity of the human person and the rights that follow from it. Indeed, they are devotees of the very "natural law and rights tradition" that he believes is incapable of providing an adequate ground-ing for our commitment to human dignity.

Nowhere is this Protestant devotion better illustrated than in Rev. Samuel Cooper's sermon delivered before the Governor (John Hancock) and the legislature of Massachusetts, on the occasion of the inauguration of the government under the 1780 state constitution. "We want not indeed a special revelation from heaven," Rev. Cooper insists,

> to teach us that men are equal and free; that no man has a natural claim of dominion over his neighbors, nor any one nation any such claim upon another; and that as government is only the administration of the affairs of a number of men combined for their own security and happiness, such a society has a right freely to determine by whom and in what manner their own affairs shall be administered. These are the plain dictates of that reason and common sense with which the common parent of men has informed the human bosom. It is, however, a satisfaction to observe such everlasting maxims of equity confirmed, and impressed upon the consciences of men, by the instructions, precepts, and examples given us in the sacred oracles; one internal mark of their divine original, and that they come from him "who hath made of one blood all nations to dwell upon the face of the earth," whose authority sanctifies only those governments that instead of oppressing any part of his family, vindicate the oppressed, and restrain and punish the oppressor.[28]

What does not require a special revelation here is nothing less than the doctrines of the Declaration of Independence, which happen also to be incorporated in the Massachusetts Constitution. The truth of these doctrines is attested by right reason, which is the voice of God no less than the "sacred oracles."

That God has informed the human bosom with the plain dictates of reason and common sense has been a vital element of the Judeo-Christian tradition, at least since Aristotelian philosophy was infused into Judaism by Maimonides, and into Christianity by Thomas Aquinas. It is precisely this confidence in the capacity of reason to discern moral truth that informs the political theory of the American founding. Reason, as both American Protestantism of the Founding era and the Founders themselves realized, was nonsectarian. This truth is recognized by the Pope, but not by Kirk or Kristol.

It seems appropriate to conclude with a word or two regarding Kristol's posture toward Lincoln. If Lincoln was so benighted as to believe that "the principles of Jefferson are the definitions and axioms of free society," it would seem to follow that he, like Jefferson, never wrote anything worth reading. This would seem to be borne out by Kristol's claim that "if one were to write an American history textbook with the chapter on the Civil War dropped out, to be replaced by a single sentence to the effect that slavery was abolished by constitutional amendment in 1865, very little in subsequent chapters as now written would need revision."[29] Indeed, "a textbook on American intellectual history could safely ignore the Civil War, were it not for the fact that so much suffering should be so barren of consequence. The Civil War was and is a most memorable event—but not any kind of turning point in American history."[30]

If one could safely ignore everything Irving Kristol says it is safe to ignore, we could certainly shorten our history curricula, and begin to make some economies in college tuition. But how can anyone seriously suggest that the Civil War was barren of consequence, and that it was not a turning point of any kind in American history? The Civil War was a great rebellion against the principle that all men are created equal. In the antebellum period, the contest between those who affirmed and those who denied the truth of that proposition was conducted with the utmost intensity. It was also conducted—on both sides—with perhaps greater skill and intellectual resourcefulness than any political contest, ancient or modern.

In his "House Divided" speech, and in the ensuing debates with Douglas, Lincoln transformed the Founding itself from an event in time into an eternal idea. By doing so, he compelled the American people to understand that no one deserved freedom for himself who would deny it to another. That was the message that the American people made good with their blood. As John Paul II says, this sacrifice was not just for themselves alone, but for all mankind. It would not be safe, or wise, to think that our schoolchildren—our posterity—should ignore the Gettysburg Address. Nor is it safe for the American people in general, or American conservatives in particular, to ignore or denigrate the self-evident moral truths affirmed by the American founders and reaffirmed so eloquently by both Abraham Lincoln and John Paul II. These truths, as the Founders, Lincoln, and John Paul alike have recognized, constitute nothing less than the essential intellectual foundation of a polity dedicated to the protection and promotion of authentic liberty.

XIV

Democracy, Ethics, Religion: An Intrinsic Connection

W. NORRIS CLARKE, S.J.

During his many years of professional life as a political philosopher, Francis Canavan has worked consistently to articulate and pass on the great tradition of humanistic political philosophy, grounded in a solid philosophical anthropology, but critically rethought and adapted to our American culture and democratic way of life—a political philosophy that tries to work out a harmonious balance between individual and community, individual rights and the exigencies of the common good. I would like to add my support to his impressive work by this modest reflection on the role played by two important pieces in this synthesis, which seem to me to have an intrinsic, but often overlooked, connection with the long-term viability of our democratic way of life. By this I mean the intrinsic connection between democracy and a normative code of ethics, the latter supported by some religious belief system.

The dominant political thinking in America today is strongly, almost obsessively, committed to the ideal of separation of church and state. I think the ideal is a good one in itself, and has served us well in this country for a long time. But there is more to it than that. On the one hand, it is certainly wise for the church not to control the state and for the state not to control the church or favor one church over another. On the

other hand, it may well be that there is some intrinsic connection between the political health of a democracy and the vital functioning in it
of some code of normative ethics and some form or forms of religious
belief supporting that code and lending it its normative authority. This
connection would have both civic and transcendent dimensions. First, at
the civic level, there would be a connection between democracy and
some normative ethical code held and practiced by the majority of its
citizens. Second, this civic creed or code would be grounded in, and
supported by, some transcendent form of religious belief, and would be
subscribed to by a significant majority of the society's citizens. This does
not have to be any one form of religion, just *some* form, or a plurality of
forms, which support some similar code of normative ethical conduct. I
also wish to stress that the connection mentioned above is not based on
some religious belief or postulate, but is the result simply of an analysis
of the nature of the democratic political order as such, combined with
thoughtful reflection on the actual history of political societies—democracies in particular—in the West. I am much influenced in coming
to this conclusion by the writings of Pierre Manent and his school of
French Catholic political philosophers.[1] I am really presenting here what
are to me some especially significant conclusions inspired by their work.

Democracy and Normative Ethics

My thesis first requires me to connect the long-term healthy exercise of the
democratic way of life with the need for a normative code of ethics. The
point is this: In order for a democracy to work in practice in a sustainable
way, a significant majority of its citizens must accept and follow in practice
some normative code of ethics. Otherwise there will result a chaos of
conflicting individual or group self-interests without respect for the rights
of others; and to protect these rights there will have to be a very large
police force, perhaps one for every few citizens—in other words, the
equivalent of a police state. A police state can indeed survive in a
totalitarian or authoritarian state for a time at least, but not in an authentic
working democracy, governed by the publicly expressed will of the
majority. There is no use replying that the majority of sensible, clear-
thinking people will realize that it serves their own good to compromise

on individual desires in order to achieve certain essential common goods. If they follow no normative ethical code, they will not have enough self-discipline to display practical wisdom and act according to the virtue of prudence. Only if a significant majority of the citizens conform most of their actions to some common moral code will a viable democratic society be able to maintain itself for any appreciable length of time. Those who do happen to threaten the rights of others will be a manageable minority who can be taken care of by laws and a modest number of law enforcement officials. Lastly, the common code of ethics—common in terms of some shared core—will have to be *normative*, something that people feel they *ought* to follow, not just something they might or might not follow, according to their own whims. This code must also be perceived as something more than a product of immediate desire or a contract that persons are free to opt out of when it no longer serves their individual self-interests.

The force of this connection emerges inevitably, I think, if one reflects on certain realistic possibilities. If only five or ten percent of the population, for example, disobeys the laws laid down by the democratic government, a modest police force will be adequate to enforce the laws. But suppose some 90 percent of a society's businessmen practice serious fraud in their business operations. It would then take a very large police force to enforce the laws, probably even a police state. And if the police officials themselves are equally infected with this lack of moral probity, why cannot the fraudulent businessmen corrupt the policemen too by bribery? Such a state of affairs cannot long last in a democracy. A viable democracy, therefore, must count on the observance, for the most part, of a normative moral code of conduct by a significant majority of its citizens; a democracy of free citizens will not put up for long with a police state.

Democracy Itself Cannot Mandate a Normative Code of Ethics

The first connection has now been made: the dependence of a viable democracy on the acceptance of a normative code of ethics held and practiced for the most part by a significant majority of its citizens. A second implication now follows. It is impossible in principle for a democratic political regime to mandate that all its citizens accept any particular code of ethics, given its fundamental commitment to the equal rights of all to free speech and free personal beliefs. Nor will it do any good anyway to mandate adherence to such a code if a significant majority of its citizens are not disposed on their own to accept and practice it. If the regime tries to force some such mandate on its people against the will of a large number of persons, this will not be effective unless the regime moves toward some variant of an authoritarian or police state, as we argued above.

Now we have a problem. On the one had, a viable democratic regime requires the acceptance of some normative moral code on the part of the majority of its citizens; yet, on the other hand, it seems to be incapable of ensuring on its own that such a necessary condition be fulfilled, leaving it in a precarious state. How is this to be resolved? Is it merely a matter of chance, or the good luck of happening to have a basically well-intentioned, enlightened population? This brings us to the third item in our title: the role of religion.

Religious Belief as the Only Secure Support
for a Normative Code of Ethics

To support the argument that religious belief is the only secure foundation for a normative code of ethics, we need to turn, not primarily to some theoretical argument, but to the existential experience of mankind, i.e., to history. Now, it does seem that if we examine human history, as far as we know it, every culture has imposed on itself some normative moral code of conduct that the majority of its citizens have, for the most part, accepted and practiced; furthermore, this normative moral code is supported by the authority of some religious belief system that grounds its normative or obligatory character. That is, the code is mandated by some transcendent source. This is obvious in Judaism, Christianity, Islam, Hinduism, and seems implied in Confucianism and most other major religions. (It may be argued that Buddhism is an exception to this, since the Buddha refused to talk about any God or gods: "You must save yourself, by following the Eightfold Path of morality and meditation." This seems to have been the case in the original more simple Buddhist message, still evident in Theravada Buddhism as practiced in Southeast Asia. Still, very quickly the Buddha himself became a great transcendent figure, "greater than all gods, demons, or powers of the universe." And in the higher or Mahayana tradition, the Buddha was divinized into an eternal transcendent being with innumerable reincarnations in human form. So in practice the Buddha himself soon became by the awesome example of his own life and teaching a kind of transcendent authority figure for his way of life and its moral code. As a result, Buddhism is now classified, with good reason, as a religion, one of the great world religions, though of a special, apparently non-theistic kind.) In short, in all the durable human societies with which we are familiar, the common codes of moral conduct structuring the lives of citizens have derived their normative authority not just from the individual free choice of any individual or group of individuals, but because they were mandated by some superhuman, transcendent authority to which religious respect and obedience are due. Nothing short of this transcendent authority is adjudged really strong enough to keep under control the willfulness of our flawed human nature, with its passions and tendency towards self-centeredness and disregard of the rights of others.

It is true that small groups within a culture can maintain among themselves a moral code of conduct with no apparent religious origin or backing—that is, codes that claim to embody a purely secular morality. We see this in our Western culture with groups like the Ethical Culture Society, the secular humanist movement, and so on. But their perdurance for any length of time presupposes a high degree of intelligence, education, and self-discipline that cannot practically be extended to a whole society of ordinary people, e.g., to a democracy, where all are considered equal in their participation in self-government. In other words, the normative character of a moral code of conduct cannot be adequately grounded in the abstract formulation of the code, considered simply in itself. It needs some authoritative lawgiver, one with moral authority over those bound by the law, to confer normative moral authority on the law itself. No democracy, by its own principles, has of itself such moral authority over its free citizens.

It seems, then, that, by reflecting on both the nature of the democratic political regime and the practical experience of human nature through history, we are led to discern a structural connection in the practical political order between an effective, stable democratic regime, some common mandatory code of ethics accepted and practiced by at least a significant majority of its citizens, and some higher religious authority either mandating or supporting such a code. This trio—democracy, mandatory code of ethics, religious grounding—has now emerged as the practically necessary supporting framework or foundation for any democratic system of government.

Note that this intrinsic connection between democracy, a mandatory code of ethics, and religion is not derived from some religious belief or doctrine, or some a priori metaphysical theory, but from an objective analysis of the nature of democracy as a political regime and the experience of human history. Whether or not one is happy with this state of affairs is not really relevant; this is the way our human nature in the concrete seems to be structured—that's all. It may be objected, however, that even though past human history provides no examples of human societies whose ethical codes have not been supported by some religion-based authority, we live now, especially in the West, in a new world of secularist societies that profess no dependence on any religion as a support for their codes of law. This new political state of affairs has not yet been sufficiently tested to tell whether it can work effectively over the long run. But it seems to be working well enough at present, at least in some places, as far as can be publicly observed. America, with its separation of church and state, is given as one example of a secular society, as are also the now heavily secularized Western European democracies. The example of China is also sometimes mentioned, although China is not a democracy in any proper sense.

This seems, at first, a serious objection indeed. But let us look more closely. First of all, when we argued earlier for the need for some religious authority to ground the ethical code of a viable society, we did not mean any particular church or institutional form of religion, but only some pervasive religious belief in some higher ultimate reality, some transcendent order on which humanity depends. The United States is supposed to be a political regime independent of any public religious commitment. Yet, in fact, some 90 percent or more of the American people are reported to believe in God and our dependence on him in some way, whether this always manifests itself in public church-going, some institutional commitment, or not. The intense religious commitments, principally Christian, of the vast majority of our original settlers have sunk deep roots into the American psyche and are still operative today, as becomes evident when certain (not all) basic moral issues come up for public discussion. The moral consensus is not as broad today as it once was, granted; but it is still quite strong.

Something similar can be said, I think, about the other increasingly secularized European democracies of our time. There is still a deep residue of basic religiosity and age-old Christian moral sensibility at work in them, although now floating free of any particular church or institutional commitment within a publicly secular social framework. What about the experience of the Soviet Union, with its explicit rejection of any religious foundation for its way of life, public morality, etc.? With the collapse of the Soviet political regime, its official Marxist profession of atheism, and the heavy pressure of a totalitarian state to enforce its laws and public morality, it is clear that a serious erosion of public morality has taken place, as shown by the rampant corruption and contempt for the common good manifested now at many levels of Russian society.[2] Still, there seems to have remained a profound residue of the deeply religious spirit in the Russian soul, as has been shown by the return in large numbers of ordinary people to the practice of their traditional Orthodox Christianity. It remains to be seen what the long-range effect on the former Soviet Union will be, particularly among the young. The situation in China also remains an open question. There may well be a substantial remnant of traditional Confucian morality embedded in the consciousness of the masses. History has not yet recorded its judgment on this remarkable sociopolitical experiment, evolving unpredictably before our eyes.

But suppose now that we were to witness the radical erosion or total eradication of any religious belief in the large majority of people in some democratic society. What then would be the result, in the long run, for such a society? Since we have no experience of any such society, we have no sure way of knowing; we can only speculate, based partly on our experience of the past, partly on our practical knowledge of our flawed human nature, and partly on our analysis of the intrinsic connections between the democratic way of life and a normative code of ethics. The experience of the past seems clear enough. The French Revolution was the first attempt to dispense entirely with religious support or grounding for the viability of a society's political life. The experiment, as we well know, turned out to be a disastrous and short-lived failure, for many reasons, but not least because its explicit rejection of any religiously grounded normative code of ethics produced a situation in which there were no effective restraints on the appetite and thirst for power on the part of the revolution's organizers.

Conclusion

Let us recapitulate now our central claim, and then point out some important implications. Our central claim is that democracy is not a form of government that can maintain itself effectively over the long term through its political resources alone. It needs rather to be inserted in a larger supporting web of human culture within which a normative code of ethics is accepted and practiced (for the most part) by a significant majority of its citizens, and within which some form of religious belief that transcends the human order supports this normative code with its own ultimate moral authority. Democracy, when defined solely as a set of institutional relationships or formal structures, cannot provide this normative authority.

Democracy cannot be rendered viable when it is viewed in purely political terms. Its amalgam of political resources is analogous to the keystone of an arch. Like that keystone, it needs other supporting stones (i.e., a larger cultural framework) to support it. It is a matter not only of honesty but also of basic political wisdom to recognize this, rather than acting as if democracy's cultural framework were somehow dispensable. Democracy as a political way of life makes good sense—perhaps the best sense, all things considered. But it requires a larger human cultural fabric to transcend and support it.

The special merit of Pierre Manent and his school of French Catholic political philosophers is to have presented the careful scholarly evidence, both historical and philosophical (but especially historical) for the conclusions I have reached here—so much so as to win the respect of a wide circle of European scholars, even those outside the Catholic or Christian orbit. They maintain that the evidence for the structural connection I have outlined above is not a matter of any special religious belief or metaphysical postulate, but accessible to any unbiased student of Western political history as being the rule throughout the whole of Western history, for all types of political regimes, but more urgently in the case of democracies.

If what I have argued is indeed the case, then to encourage policies that tend to weaken the strength of a shared normative code of ethics and/or a supporting shared religious belief is not politically wise. Rather, it automatically tends to weaken the vitality of the democratic way of life. Thus, to interpret the separation of church and state in such a way as to reduce religion to a purely private matter, with no influence on public life or conduct, and to prohibit the teaching in our public education system either of a commonly shared normative code of ethics, or of respect for the latter's religious grounding—all of which we face increasingly today—is to erode the foundations of a healthy democratic way of life. It also by that very fact tends to foster a deeply flawed, unrealistic political philosophy.

XV

And Now for Something Different:
A Good Word on Behalf of the Legal Positivists

HADLEY ARKES

But then again . . . let me say a word on behalf of legal positivism. I say "then again," because, as my friends know, I have expended most of my slender arts as a writer, over the last thirty years, in making the case for natural rights and natural law. That is, I have been part of a project, joined by some gifted writers in the academy, to restore the tradition of natural law and work against the current of our times. That current has been defined, of course, by moral relativism in forms now so familiar that most people are hardly even aware of them. Historians seem barely conscious of any vice of "historicism," serenely assuming that we all know, for example, that the American Founders were merely men of their own age. The sentiments of the Declaration of Independence had stirred the souls of that age, and there is no gainsaying their deep political effect; and yet the historians understand, with a knowing wink, that the "self-evident" truths of the Declaration were merely the sentiments that summoned credence at the time. Almost no historian admits to believing, as Lincoln did, that the proposition "all men are created equal" is in fact, as the Founders thought, a self-evident or necessary truth, "applicable to all men and all times."

Conservatives in our politics may decorously turn aside from a vulgar relativism, but they too have absorbed the currents of the age. In their case, that absorption takes the form of a polite diffidence, a certain backing away from the claim to know of "moral truths." That posture nicely coincides with a legal "positivism" that may be borne now of prudence. The conservative is even more keenly aware than liberals that the country is divided, not merely on matters of taste, but on matters of consequence that run to the moral root. Under these conditions, the conservative is even more likely than the liberal to retreat to some modest set of "neutral" rules that might provide the ground of the law. It would not be a law that truly reaches the highest questions, or takes on moral questions in a serious way. It may be a law reduced to the sparest set of "house rules," the rules that would merely permit us to live together in a peaceful and tolerable way. But as the conservative backs into this position, he may also betray a certain want of confidence that marks his acceptance of a species of "soft" relativism. He may persuade himself that all moral perspectives are bound up with religious convictions or matters of belief, and that there is something irreducibly "sectarian" about any set of moral convictions. He is more likely then to complain, as one celebrated conservative jurist did many years ago, that we have no "theory" of natural rights.

But when we speak of natural rights or natural law as a "theory," we already mark a decisive step away from the conviction that there are moral truths, anchored as axioms, in the very "laws of reason." One might as aptly ask, "Do I use syntax when I order coffee?" The person who says anything like that would indicate that he is quite unaware of the logic, or the structure of understandings, that must be in place before his question can make sense.

In a similar way, I would suggest, the person who seeks a "theory" of natural law or natural rights might not be aware of the structure he is putting in place as the ground for his question. To speak of a "theory" of natural rights is to suggest that we may detach ourselves, in a posture of judgment, to weigh a series of contending theories put before us for our credence. The question makes sense only on the assumption that we have access to standards of judgment that would allow us to compare the different theories for their persuasiveness, their soundness—in short, for their truth. But once we have access, in that way, to the grounds for making reasoned judgments about competing theories of law and justice, we would have discovered (perhaps by accident, perhaps by grace) nothing less than the principles of natural law. To put it another way, we cannot seriously talk about the legal judgments that are justified or unjustified without using "the laws of reason"; and when we back into the laws of reason, we are "doing" natural law.

Some of our leading conservative jurists have also registered their moral skepticism by pronouncing their dubiety about a jurisprudence of natural rights. And yet, the same accomplished men soon show their reliance on propositions, or principles, that could not find their source in the positive law. Alexander Hamilton pointed out the problems regarding the grounding of the positive law, and with his typical grace reached beyond the understanding of most lawyers. For example, in *Federalist 78*, he noted the rule that guided the courts in dealing with statutes in conflict: The statute passed later is presumed to have superseded the law enacted earlier. The same rule does not come into play, of course, with the Constitution, for a Constitution framed earlier would have to be given logical precedence over the statute that came later. Were that not the case, the Constitution would lose its function, or its logic, as a restraint on legislative power. But these rules for the interpretation of statutes are nowhere mentioned in the Constitution. As Hamilton remarked, they were "not derived from any positive law, but from the nature and reason of the thing."[1] Somewhat later, in *Federalist 81*, he went on to point out that the notion of "parliamentary supremacy" in Britain had never been taken to mean that the legislature was empowered to overturn a verdict rendered in court. The understanding seemed to be settled that the legislature might act instead to "prescribe a new rule for future cases." But here, too, this understanding was not expressed anywhere in the positive law of the Constitution. And so what made it valid or authoritative, as an understanding bound up with the Constitution itself? As Hamilton explained, this understanding was simply anchored in "the general principles of law and reason."[2]

It might be helpful, at this point, to distinguish Hamilton's argument from that of my friend Robert Bork, a self-proclaimed positivist, who is, by all of his reflexes, a moralist of the most reliable judgment. In an exchange in the pages of *First Things* (the journal, as opposed to the distinguished book of the same title), I noted that Bork had taken, as the anchoring principle of his jurisprudence, the proposition that, in a conflict between the natural law and the positive law, the positive law must be given precedence.[3] I noted that this was a tenable principle of construction (for reasons I shall dilate upon in just a moment) but it must be noticed also that this anchoring proposition, held by Bork and others, is nowhere to be found in the positive law. Certainly it is not part of the positive law of the Constitution. Therefore, what is the ground on which Bork treats it, not only as a truth, but as one of those *primary* truths that has the function of ordering a host of lesser judgments in the law? Apparently, for Bork, this proposition seems to reveal its validity in itself, as something that could be grasped by any creature of reason who would only reflect for a moment on the problem in a serious way. But that is to say, it is one of those propositions that may stand as an axiom or a first principle. And if we can grasp at least one proposition of this kind, we must open ourselves to the possibilities of grasping more than one.[4]

And at the same time, the truth somehow passed by in the sweep of this argument—the truth that dare not speak its name—is that there is a ground in natural law for this operating rule, this disposition to give primacy to the positive law. In his dissenting opinion in the Dred Scott case, Justice Benjamin Curtis drew on cases from the American South and the border states to recall the ancient maxim that slavery was so contrary to the natural law that it could be sustained only by positive law.[5] Blackstone stated the settled understanding when he taught that where the positive law was silent, the natural law would come back into force.[6] The natural law, we might say, was the residual law; and that sense of natural justice would be controlling on those occasions, certain to arise, where the positive law could not possibly fill in all the details or anticipate every contingency that might arise.

In all strictness of course—if the matter were considered, that is, according to a more stringent logic, abstracted from political life—the truth of the matter would be just the reverse. Justice Joseph Story touched the heart of the matter when he insisted that the natural law was really the matrix or foundation of the positive law, and any propositions that were at odds with those deep axioms could not really have a coherent claim to be regarded as law. And so, for example, a primate of the species of undergraduates, trying to be provocative, may cast up the sentiment that "I have a right to believe I don't exist." Playful it may be, but it is, in all strictness, an incoherent rights claim. Its incoherence is revealed as soon as the question is posed, "Who is the bearer of that right—the one who does not exist?" Even if a pixilated legislature were willing to enact such a "right" in the positive law, it would not cease to be incoherent. And that, I think, is the sense that Story brought to the matter when he argued, in the case of *La Jeune Eugenie*, that slavery was contrary to the natural law, and therefore that the slave trade could not be enforced by courts of law, even if the positive law made its accommodation and respected that branch of "commerce."[7]

And yet Story managed to function as a worldly judge in a system of law in which he knew full well that a decision had been made at the highest level to cast the protections of the positive law around the institution of slavery. Lincoln would later remark that the commitment to return fugitive slaves—the commitment registered in Article IV of the Constitution—had been "nominated in the bond." It was part of the prudential compromise with slavery made at several points in the Constitution, and it was utterly necessary, he knew, to the agreement that preserved the Union and brought forth the Constitution. The Constitution would also bar any attempt to restrict the importation of certain persons until 1808—meaning, of course, the import of slaves as part of the international traffic in slavery. It was another instance, as Lincoln said, in which "covert language" was used—language that would make an accommodation with slavery without mentioning the hateful practice by name and incorporating, in the text of the Constitution, a moral endorsement of the institution. That was indeed the formula: a prudential compromise with an existing evil, which was at root incompatible with a polity founded on the proposition that "all men are created equal." Without that accommodation, the trade in slaves would continue and expand, unrestricted, unabated; and on the other hand, fugitives from slavery, making their way North, would never be returned. There was of course seepage in enforcement. As Lincoln remarked, "the great body of the people abide by the dry legal obligation in both cases," but the laws were "each as well enforced, perhaps, as any law can ever be in a community where the moral sense of the people imperfectly supports the law itself."[8] But it was, again, a prudential compromise, and that kind of compromise could be justified only when "prudence" was governed by a sense of rightful ends. What justified the arrangement to Lincoln, and to the Founding generation, was that it was the only practicable way of bringing forth a Union that was committed, in its constituting premises, to "natural equality" and the natural liberty of human beings.

Slavery would be tolerated within a regime that would cast up barriers in principle to the expansion of slavery within the territories of the United States. At the same time, the supply of slaves from abroad would be cut off, at its earliest moment under the Constitution, by the administration of President Jefferson, himself the owner of slaves. In other words the positive law would become an instrument of prudence and statesmanship: The positive law could deal with circumstances on the ground, with the shape that evils took in the peculiar landscape of America. It could become, that is, an instrument used by practical men of affairs as they confronted the things that impaired perfect justice. And it could be used for the highest purposes of prudence—to plant the rightful lessons in the law and seek to bring about, over time, a better congruence between the principles of justice and the character of life in the country as it was actually lived. Aquinas caught this melancholy sense of the problem when he famously observed that the purpose of the law was to lead people to virtue, not suddenly, but gradually.

It may be an unsettling recognition for some of my friends among the positivists, but some of us find common ground with them precisely because we understand that there is a ground in natural law to justify the positive law. That is especially the case when the positive law becomes the vehicle of statesmen, applying the arts of prudence and judgment, in trying to honor the rightful ends of political life. But it still seems to come as a surprise to some of these practical men of the law when we point out that there is no necessary tension between the natural law and the positive law: Any system of natural law would actually require a supporting system of positive law, and at the same time, the positive law, even on the most prosaic matters, would find its justification in the natural law. We may all have, for example, a sense of why certain speeds in a car, on a winding, narrow lane, may be the cause of serious hazards, both to the driver and to others. We may also grasp, quite readily, why the law would be justified in restraining people from driving in a manner that poses dangers to innocent members of the public. We roughly grasp, in other words, a principle engaged here, and yet it would be a matter of art and experience to convert that principle into a regulation that says, for example, "45 miles per hour, on *this* branch of the road, rather than the 50 miles per hour that prevails elsewhere on the same road." We know that, in nature, there is no such "principle," prescribing 45 rather than 50 or 55 miles per hour. But with this move, we contrive a regulation of the positive law, which can translate the deeper principle into terms that have a bearing on the landscape before us, or the peculiar circumstances of our lives. And yet, we may not be alert in the same way to the fact that the law becomes comprehensible and justifiable precisely because there is, behind it, that deeper principle that tells us that to protect innocent lives by restraining recklessness would be justified.

There is, then, a sustaining, necessary relation between the positive law and the natural law, and if we could linger with the problem, we might make the further case that the obligation to respect even a bad positive law is a commitment that finds its ground in the natural law. I will leave that problem for another day, but I would sketch the outline of the account in this way: The insistence on respecting the law is bound up with the importance of giving reasons or justifications before laws are made—or unmade. To move outside the law always carries the risk of a spirit lawless in temper and substance, of being the act of people so persuaded of their own views that they are drawn into the temptation of refusing to recognize a law beyond themselves. And so concerned might they be with their own integrity that they do not pay sufficient regard to the dangers posed to many innocent, unreflective people when the laws break down, and many things are put at hazard.

But that, as I say, will be left to elaborate on another occasion. My main object here has been to recall the critical points in which natural law and positivism are not at all at odds, but tend to be joined in principle in a common discipline of the law. And for the sake of reinforcing that point, I would like to recall a case from our recent past that seems to have sustained some enduring caricatures in our law and politics. That case draws a special, mordant interest because it was persistently muddled in the arguments put before the Supreme Court, and it has been muddled in the same measure in the understandings that have continued to envelop the case. The case in point was that notable controversy known as *Bob Jones University v. U.S.*, decided in 1983.[9] The case was extraordinarily controversial for the same reason that makes the very mention of the university a continuing source of acrimony and political labeling in our own day.

For one thing, Bob Jones University, as a fundamentalist school, preserved some attitudes toward Catholicism that were less than flattering. But needless to say, that was not the offense that drew the anger and condemnation of the liberal members of the political class. The real ground of contention came over race. Bob Jones University was a Christian, fundamentalist school, and among the tenets held firmly by the founders of the school was the conviction that, in the design of the Creator, revealed in the Bible, the races should be distinguished and separated in the economy of nature. In accordance with that belief, the university had initially held itself apart racially, by opening itself only to whites and refusing admission to blacks. But under opposition from the government, and the overhanging threat of litigation, the university backed away from those policies in the 1970s. By the time the case was brought against the school, black students were admitted along with whites, but the original tenets of the university were preserved at one, primal level: The university barred dating and marriage across racial lines. The university was open, that is, to black students who were unmarried, but a strict disciplinary rule barred students who would date and marry across racial lines. This form of discrimination became, of course, a source of lingering controversy and continually led to charges of racism. But as one looks more closely into the policy, it becomes evident very quickly that there were complications that made this case quite unlike those other, leading cases on racial discrimination that have been so thoroughly contested and litigated over the past forty years.

Still, the clichés that surround the discussion of this case have not been altered, even minutely, since the case was argued in the 1970s and early 1980s. And yet, the remarkable haze that surrounded this case should have been dispelled by Justice William Rehnquist, in his dissenting opinion in the case. What Rehnquist brought to the case was a mind-clearing dose of positivism. Rehnquist asked the simplest, most elementary questions. But as simple as they were, those questions would have allowed people on all sides to have seen through the haze—to have seen clearly, without affectation, what was before them.

There was actually a brace of cases here, involving two fundamentalist schools in the South. The "companion" case came in an action against the Goldsboro Christian Schools in Goldsboro, North Carolina. Like Bob Jones University, the Goldsboro schools regarded themselves as Christian fundamentalist in character. The Goldsboro Schools encompassed the grades ranging from kindergarten through high school. The complex of Bob Jones ran far more comprehensively, from kindergarten through college and even graduate school. But apart from those gross differences in structure, there were some notable differences in the schools' policies bearing on race, and those differences should have had a bearing, in turn, on the way these cases were resolved. The ruling elders of the Goldsboro School held that the races had sprung from the three sons of Noah—Ham, Shem, and Japheth. Orientals and blacks were Hamitic in this view; the Hebrews were Shemitic, and whites were Japhethitic. Once again, the teaching of the Bible was thought to prescribe a separation of the races. And until 1963, in accord with that understanding, the school had followed a fairly consistent policy of admitting only white students, with one class of exceptions: children of mixed races, where one of the parents had been white. In holding to this policy, the ruling elders of the school were showing a certain obduracy, even in the face of a formidable body of federal laws that were turning decidedly against them in the 1970s.

The most notable change, bearing on private schools, came with *Runyon v. McCrary*[10] in the 1970s. When that case was finally decided by the Supreme Court in 1976, it became part of a revival of the Thirteenth Amendment. The Fourteenth Amendment had been directed to the action of states—that is, to the discriminations that were imposed with the force of law by officers of state and local governments. The Thirteenth Amendment was not addressed distinctly to the states, but in sweeping away slavery, or "involuntary servitude," its principal legal mission was to sweep away the laws that sustained slavery at every point in the states and local communities. Still, the Amendment had not spoken of states, and that reticence opened the way to a novel and extravagant reading in the surge of civil rights activism in the 1960s: The "new" Thirteenth Amendment would be taken as a powerful ground of authority for the federal government to reach individuals and private entities directly, striking at the lingering "badges and incidents" of slavery. Intimidations by private thugs, or discrimination by private corporations, could now come within the purview of the Civil Rights Acts of the 1860s. In *Runyon v. McCrary*, the Supreme Court would accept the argument that the Civil Rights Act of 1866 could plausibly reach a private, secondary school that discriminated on the basis of race in its admissions to the school.

But while *Runyon v. McCrary* was making its way through the federal courts in the early 1970s, the new doctrines were being sounded in the rulings in the lower courts, and it was becoming clear to the directors of Bob Jones University that the times, and the laws, were a-changing. That new reading of the old Civil Rights Act had a breakthrough in the federal court of appeals in 1975.[11] The directors of Bob Jones University were hardly witless, and so in 1975 they took the critical step of revising their policies on admissions when they provided for the admission of black students. Still the change was calibrated: The school would admit black students who were unmarried and who posed no problem about dating across racial lines.

These simple but telling shifts made a striking difference in the position of these two fundamentalist schools in relation to the federal law. What seems surprising in retrospect was that these differences should have gone so thoroughly unnoticed, and that the judges and commentators had not been alerted to these differences by the very form of the case, or the way in which the case would be presented to a court of law. In both instances, with Bob Jones University and the Goldsboro Schools, the action came in response to a move by the Internal Revenue Service to strip them of their status as educational institutions exempt from taxation. We would hardly suppose that the IRS simply scanned the landscape looking for private schools to unsettle or challenge. The move in the IRS apparently came as complaints were registered about schools that were receiving a benefit conferred by the government even while they were engaging in striking forms of racial discrimination.

But that very way of bringing the case, or posing the challenge, already sent up signals that should have meant something to people who were practiced in the reading of law: The form of the case revealed that there was no complainant claiming to be injured by the policies of racial discrimination in these schools. Nothing taking place in these private schools was alleged to have violated anything in that formidable body of federal law that barred racial discrimination even in private businesses or private schools. Again, the form of the case had to be regarded as quite telling: Who would have chosen merely to contest the tax exemption given to these schools if he could have contested a case of racial discrimination covered in the federal laws? After all, if the people offended by the schools succeeded in their complaints to the IRS, no ruling of the IRS would have dislodged those policies on racial discrimination. The result of the holding would have been—as indeed it was—that Bob Jones University, as a private, religious school, could continue to honor its biblical understanding, but it would simply have to pay more for its freedom to respect its own doctrines. The exemption from taxes would be withdrawn, and Bob Jones University would have to pay back taxes of about $160,000.[12]

In contrast, something far more astounding and decisive would have taken place if the school had been sued, or indicted, under federal law. A judgment of guilt, pronounced by a judge or jury, would have had a pronounced moral resonance. And if the case had been litigated under the same statute involved in *Runyon v. McCrary*, the school might have been subject, in a civil suit, to compensatory and punitive damages.[13] The directors of the school then would have come under the most pressing incentive to divest themselves of the policies that had brought down on the school the terrible swift sword of the federal authorities.

Plainly, for anyone who was truly offended by Bob Jones University, and determined to see the school punished, the path of choice was to register a complaint and launch a suit under the Civil Rights Acts. Since that path was not taken, the implication is plain: Apparently the groups that litigate over civil rights could not find a person who was turned away from the school on account of race.

But if this were true, it would have altered the very premises on which the case was argued, and the scheme under which the case was placed and understood. For in the absence of any violation of federal law, the argument was made in the courts that Bob Jones University was an unworthy recipient of benefits under the tax code because the policies of the school, on the matter of race, ran counter to "the public policy" of the United States. And yet the school was not charged with breaking any federal laws. What would it mean, then, to say that the school was running counter to the "public policy" of the federal government? Which "public policy," expressed where, if not in the statutes of the United States? Would that explanation be found in the tax code itself? Could Bob Jones University be at odds with the "public policy" of the United States, even though it was not violating any statute or executive order of the federal government?

Whether or not the question was framed exactly in these terms, there was a problem to be explained, and the puzzle led the judges back into the momentous question of the disjunctive or conjunctive "or." The "or" in question found its place in marking, in the statutes, the categories of institutions that could claim an exemption from taxes. A list of exemptions had always attended the income tax, running back to the Act of 1894, which had been struck down by the Court. Every subsequent act made provisions to exempt certain institutions whose flourishing seemed to be desirable for the public good. Section 501(c)(3) has become rather famous by now as the section covering all kinds of organizations connected with the academy or education or literary enterprises. By the language of Section 501(c)(3), exemptions are provided to "[c]orporations

. . . organized and operated exclusively for religious, charitable . . . *or* educational purposes" [emphasis added]. The question raised by Chief Justice Burger, in his opinion for the majority, was whether that "or" was "disjunctive." Did the statute not mark off "educational" institutions," along with "charitable" and "religious" organizations, as separate, distinct categories of groups? The categories would seem to be separate, and organizations falling into any one of them could claim an exemption.

The attack on Bob Jones University, however, required the IRS and the courts to diagram the sentence by insisting that the "or" was not "disjunctive" but conjunctive or appositional. It was more like the "or" in: "We will put the accent, in these lectures, on points that are foundational, primary, or elementary." "Elementary," in this sense, does not stand in contradistinction to "primary" and "fundamental." It is but another way of explaining what all of the other terms in the series are seeking in part to describe. And this is how the IRS, and the critics of Bob Jones University, now proposed to read the tax laws. And so when the laws conferred exemptions on corporations "organized and operated exclusively for religious, charitable . . . or educational purposes," it could now be taken to mean that all of these organizations had to be charitable in some way. (Curiously, the same reasoning did not require that they all be "religious" in some way.) Chief Justice Burger was willing to follow here the line of argument, welling up from the bureaucracy and the lower courts, that the notion of "charitable" was somehow implicit in the understanding that attached to all groups thought worthy enough to merit an exemption from taxes. As Burger put it, a study of the tax code "reveals unmistakable evidence that, underlying all relevant parts of the Code, is the intent that entitlement to tax exemption depends on meeting certain common-law standards of charity—namely, that an institution seeking tax-exempt status must serve a public purpose and not be contrary to established public policy."[14]

But if there really was, over the years, an understanding, settled but unspoken, that all of these organizations had to be charities, it is rather odd that Congress had never bothered to make that point more explicit, since it was not instantly evident that any literary or educational institution had to be "charitable." A simpler and more plausible construction, it seems to me, is that the list of exemptions assumed, of course, that the institutions under these categories were benign, wholesome, *legitimate*. It seemed to go without saying that the exemption for "educational" institutions would not go to Mr. Fagin's school of Pickpocketry, or to a school of film that specialized in the making of pornographic movies. The point is so fundamental or axiomatic that it hardly needs saying, and yet it is unmistakable. The tax code would not cover a school for thieves.

The same argument found expression in the lower federal courts, and one of the judges invoked the example of Fagin's School of Pickpocketry.[15] That argument was recalled by Chief Justice Burger, in his opinion for the Court, along with this further example: that if anything with the appearance of a "school" could qualify for an exemption, then "a band of former military personnel might well set up a school for intensive training of subversives for guerrilla warfare and terrorism in other countries." But Justice Rehnquist, in dissent, found the analogy unpersuasive. And yet, regrettably, his explanation was rather less than luminous. "I have little doubt," he wrote, "that neither the 'Fagin School for Pickpockets' nor a school training students for guerrilla warfare and terrorism in other countries would meet the definitions contained in the regulations."[16] Rehnquist seemed to think that the standards of judgment for why this would be so would become suitably manifest if one simply considered the understandings spelled out by the IRS as it sought to explain what was meant by organizations or institutions dedicated to an "educational" purpose:

> The instruction or training of the individual for the purpose of improving or developing his capabilities. . . . The instruction of the public on subjects useful to the individual and beneficial to the community. . . . An organization whose activities consist of presenting public discussion groups, forums, panels, lectures, or other similar programs. Such programs may be on radio or television. . . . An organization which presents a course of instruction by means of correspondence or through the utilization of television or radio . . . . Museums, zoos, planetariums, symphony orchestras, and other similar organizations.

A student I knew twenty years ago at Amherst performed as a magician, and he would later stage his performances at meetings of corporate boards. As part of his training in the arts of illusion, he had studied the art of pickpocketry. And, as he intimated to me, the masters who could impart the subtleties of that craft had not always used those arts simply to entertain. It was quite conceivable that there could be an academy to instruct in magic, and that the school would incorporate pickpocketry in the curriculum. What guaranteed that the instruction offered in that school would never be used for corrupt ends? How would one be sure that the art of picking pockets would not be used to steal rather than entertain? Any activity we could name, from driving a car to using a pen, could be directed to a harmful and wrongful end. A school of driving could instruct students in the art of driving getaway cars, much as the CIA would instruct some of its people in the art of defensive and evasive driving. Pens could be used for the ends of forgery and fraud. For Rehnquist and his colleagues, it seemed to go without saying that the inventory of groups marked off in the tax code would be decent, respectable organizations, not enterprises directed to illegitimate ends.

But how did one understand or define "illegitimate" ends? If we take the matter to the root, we would mark off the illegitimate by understanding the things that were in principle right or wrong. For Rehnquist the problem was serenely free of puzzles, because the answer to the question was rather direct and simple. In the understanding of a legal positivist, the question here was "What was illegitimate in the eyes of the law?" and the question posed in that way was answered unequivocally: What was illegitimate were the things that were made unlawful; the things that were against the law. And by that, one did not mean things that were roughly thought to be unrespectable or shady, but things that were quite precisely defined in the attributes and boundaries of their wrongness by statutes, executive orders, and the rulings of courts. They were marked off, that is, as wrongs by the precision that typically attended the instruments of the positive law.

The difference in the two answers pointed to notably different grounds of judgment. For in the tradition of law that encompassed the natural law not everything that was wrong or immoral would be made illegal. The difference was marked by prudence, or perhaps even by the want of imagination, in recognizing the wrongs that deserved to be reached and condemned by the law. The test of legality was a modest, scaled-down test, which would have made the problem in cases like *Bob Jones* far more tractable. Nevertheless, as I have argued, the positive law finds its ground and justification in principles that are antecedent to the positive law, and not always set down, or posited, in the laws. And if the problem in the Bob Jones case had been informed by that larger, or more comprehensive, understanding, the problem would have been dramatically altered.

Consider, for a moment, how the differences would have played out. Let us suppose that the argument had been cast seriously as a question of principle. The argument might be made, in strenuous terms, that racial discrimination is categorically wrong, wrong in principle; and if that were the case an enterprise that incorporated in its charter a commitment to racial discrimination would be as illegitimate as a school that incorporated in its charter a commitment to theft. To say that racial discrimination is wrong in principle is, of course, to do more than utter a piety. An insistence of that kind puts one at odds with the whole ensemble of policies and rationales that have been built up, over thirty years, to support "affirmative action," understood as "racial preferences," or the assignment of compensating benefits based on race.

Lincoln famously remarked that, "as I would not be a *slave*, so I would not be a *master*."[17] Since he rejected the institution of slavery in principle, his rejection was utterly independent of the question of whether he happened to be on the *advantaged* or *disadvantaged* end of that relation. In a similar way, some of us have argued that the question in racial discrimination must be whether there is indeed something not merely contingently wrong, but wrong in principle, about the notion of assigning benefits and disabilities on the basis of race. If that question had been posed in *Brown v. Board of Education*, it might have sounded something like this: Was it in principle wrong to separate children in schools on the basis of race; or was it only contingently wrong—was it wrong only as it impaired or improved the performance of black children in the schools? If students were separated on the basis of race, and the performance of the students improved, would the segregation have ceased to be wrong? In my own experience, most people wish to say that the segregation would still be wrong, but they seem at sea in making the argument, or rendering the explanation.

Yet by this point in the seasons of our experience there have been ample arguments brought forth to make that case. In my own construction, offered at proper length in the past, the wrong of racial discrimination is rooted in the very logic of law and moral judgment.[18] By that construction, racial discrimination would be wrong of necessity, wrong categorically, in any system that dares call itself a system of "law." In one way or another, the inclination to discriminate on the basis of race involves a willingness to draw adverse moral inferences about people on the basis solely of their race. And so the assumption seems to be that if we knew a person's race we would have a ground for inferring that his presence, as a neighbor, would degrade or improve the neighborhood; that his presence as a colleague would worsen or enhance the character of the enterprise. In either case, there is a certain backing into a theory of "racial determinism," as though race essentially controlled, or "determined," the moral conduct of any person.

But of course we may all be identified with a certain race, and so the implication would be that none of us, really, is in control of his own acts. When the matter is reduced to those terms, or taken to the root, it should be clear that the willingness to discriminate on the basis of race denies that moral autonomy, or freedom, that is the very premise of our standing as "moral agents." If none of us is in control of his own acts, then none of us is responsible for anything he does. We may not then be held responsible by the law—and neither, of course, may we be the object of praise or comdemnation. But one of the first implications that arises from the logic of morals itself is that we do not hold people blameworthy or responsible for acts they were powerless to affect. Thomas Reid, the Scottish philosopher put the same point in another way when he stated, as a necessary "first principle" in morals, that "what is done from unavoidable necessity . . . cannot be the object of blame or moral approbation."[19]

If this argument is correct, then it could truly be said that the wrong of racial discrimination is anchored in the very logic of law itself. A decision to reject racial discrimination in point of principle must mark a willingness to break decisively from schemes of racial determinism, even when they are advanced as "benign." If a political candidate is favored solely on account of his blackness, then another candidate must be disfavored solely on account, say, of his whiteness. And it is clearly just as wrong to assume, on the basis of race, that any white candidate comes from a rich and advantaged background as it is to assume, solely on the basis of race, that a black candidate comes from a poor family that has suffered the injuries of discrimination. If we would break away from that scheme in principle, we would presumably commit ourselves to the notion of judging innocence or guilt, merit or demerit, on the strength of what the individual himself has done, not on the things we know in general about that racial group of which he happens, willy-nilly, to be a member. And so we would say then that it is wrong in principle to assign benefits and disabilities on the basis of race. If we think that is a "wrong," then it would be a matter of moral indifference as to whether the persons suffering the disabilities, or the costs, happened to be black or white.

But to return to the Bob Jones case, let us assume for a moment that the Court had staked out this position in principle as the ground of its judgment. What difference would it have made? In the first place, it would go without saying that no institution that forms its character around racial discrimination could possibly be reconciled with a system of law. Therefore, it could not count as a "legitimate" institution claiming the exemptions that are offered under the law to legitimate schools or educational enterprises. But if this is so, the rejection of that school, as a legitimate school, would have *nothing at all to do with the pattern of public policy*: Even if there were no laws or executive orders on racial discrimination—even if all of those laws were swept from the books—this school would still be constituted on a "wrongful" basis. It still could not be a legitimate school and receive an exemption.

That would indeed be the statement of the most stringent argument in terms of moral principle. And yet to state it in that way, with its full force, is to note that it is radically at odds with the opinion that the majority actually rendered in the Bob Jones case. In fact, neither side on the Court—neither the majority nor the dissenters—thought that there was a categorical proposition engaged here. Neither side rejected racial discrimination at the level of moral principle.

There is a notable contrast between the argument in principle and the argument actually advanced by the majority in this case. On this point, the evidence was telltale. Witness Chief Justice Burger's opinion. Within the space of three pages, the Chief Justice gave this account of the wrong of the case five times over:

– "But there can no longer be any doubt that *racial discrimination in education* violates deeply and widely accepted views of elementary justice." [592; my italics]

– "An unbroken line of cases following *Brown v. Board of Education* establishes beyond doubt this Court's view that *racial discrimination in education* [my emphasis–HA] violates a most fundamental national public policy, as well as rights of individuals."[593]

– "Congress, in Titles IV and VI of the Civil Rights Act of 1964, Pub. L. 88-352, 78 Stat. 241, 42 U. S. C. §§ 2000c, 2000c-6, 2000d, clearly expressed its agreement that *racial discrimination in education* violates a fundamental public policy." [593; my italics]

– "Few social or political issues in our history have been more vigorously debated and more extensively ventilated than the issue of racial discrimination, particularly in education."[595]

– "Whatever may be the rationale for such private schools' policies, and however sincere the rationale may be, *racial discrimination in education* is contrary to public policy." [595]

"Racial discrimination in education": The wrong was narrowed by the majority to a "contingent" wrong—a wrong that was contingent upon its effects in certain settings. As in the famously miscast opinion in *Brown v. Board*, the wrong was apparently not a wrong in principle. The wrong inhered, rather, in some injury that was inflicted on black students distinctly *in schools*.

However, the embarrassment in *Brown v. Board* was that there was no evidence of any injury of that kind.[20] The Court had cast its decision in that narrow, empirical way as a device for avoiding a deeper argument cast in terms of principle. But even though the argument was miscast, the Court did confront, in *Brown,* some genuine cases of racial segregation. And yet, the point, strangely passed over in this sweep of rhetoric, was that there was, in the case of Bob Jones University, no instance of racial discrimination that the law had ever condemned or reached. Strictly speaking, there had been no "racial discrimination" in education because no one had been barred from the school on the basis of race. To put it another way, no racial barrier had come into play to restrict admission to the school, and therefore to any educational program within the school. Chief Justice Burger sought neatly to glide around that item of embarrassment by elaborating his case: The executive branch, he said, had consistently placed the weight of its authority "behind eradication of racial discrimination," and he cited here, most notably, the orders of President Truman barring racial discrimination in federal employment and the orders of President Kennedy in prohibiting racial discrimination in housing supported by federal funds.[21] True enough, but like "the flowers that bloom in the spring," they had nothing to do with the case. There was no allegation of racial discrimination in employment or housing—or even in access to the school. If any of these laws or executive orders had been violated, there would have been plaintiffs alleging injuries and seeking remedies far more devastating than the removal of tax exemptions.

In the full panoply of federal laws, statutes, and executive orders that touched on the matter of race, nothing had been violated. That there was, in the policies of the school, a posture of racial discrimination, could hardly be gainsaid. But the sovereign point, curiously and serenely ignored, was that the kind of discrimination involved in this case had never been addressed by the federal laws, and they were not likely to be addressed by the laws at any time in the foreseeable future. There was a policy of discrimination regarding dating and marriage across racial lines, but the meaning of that practice was dramatically altered as soon as one recognized that there had been *no racial tests of admission* to this *private* school. The school was a private association composed of students of different races, but these students shared the fundamentalist persuasion of Bob Jones University. Black or white, they apparently accepted the tenets of the school—otherwise they would not have sought admission. It was apparently no strain for them to conform to the policy of confining their dating and marriage within racial lines. Since it was a private school, no one was compelled by law to attend. That elementary point, curiously passed over, meant also that the policy of discrimination in the choice of a spouse was never a policy imposed by law. It was a matter wholly of private choice, reflecting the code that was shared in this private enclave by the students who had attached themselves, willingly, to Bob Jones University.

Let us take another example. We might imagine, for example, one of those computer dating services where "singles" look for partners. The service is private; no one who does not wish to join is compelled to be a member and come under its rules. But let us suppose, further, that the members are asked for their preferences in partners, and that in the range of preferences, it is considered legitimate for them to record a preference for people of their own race. Evidently, a preference of that kind is regarded as legitimate, even on the part of people who regard themselves as the most cosmopolitan of liberals. Even black people quite committed to civil rights have expressed a certain resentment at times toward men who could have married a black woman, but married instead outside their race. But it was mainly in the journals of Left-liberal opinion—periodicals like the *New York Review of Books*—that one was first likely to encounter ads in the "personals columns" reading thus: "SWM seeks SWF." Translation: Single *white* male seeks single *white* female. The *NYRB* would never have run an ad saying, "White landlord seeking white tenants." That kind of ad was against the law (namely, the Fair Housing Act of 1968), for one thing, but the *NYRB* would not have run an ad of that kind even before it was against the law. If there was a genuine principle engaged here on the wrong of racial discrimination, that principle should be quite indifferent to the nature of the "good" or service that is being advertised. The comparisons could not help but yield a moral lesson patently clear: Apparently, even the most liberal wings of the political class—and the most fervent supporters of civil rights—did not believe that the principle that barred racial discrimination applied in a sweeping, categorical way to every instance of racial discrimination. The principle on racial discrimination might reach to private businesses, and even to owners of single-family dwellings who were renting space in their private homes. But evidently the editors did not think that this "principle" carried over to the *private choice of a partner for sex and marriage*.

Or to refine the matter yet further, the understanding of the editors might have mirrored the understanding of the political class who formed the government and shaped the laws: They might have understood that the principle regarding racial discrimination did indeed cover, in its sweep, all instances of racial discrimination, public and private; but in the most ancient traditions of the law, they might also have understood that, on grounds of prudence, the legislators did not choose to cover, with the laws, this particularly private and intimate domain.

In all strictness, of course, the principle did indeed cover even these cases of discrimination: The principle held that it was it was wrong to draw adverse moral inferences on the basis of race—to assume that, if we knew a person's race, we would know whether he was a good or bad person, to be welcomed or shunned. Precisely the same logic came into play here: On the basis of race one could not infer that a potential partner was more or less worthy of that affection or that enduring respect that would justify an enduring attachment. My own students, confronting the case, have been inclined to argue that there might, after all, be "aesthetic" reasons for preferring people of a certain color or complexion. But that kind of argument rather backs into the moral case. Imagine a man who informed us that he had chosen his wife of many years wholly on "aesthetic" grounds. He had been drawn to her complexion and blonde coloring—a coloring that beautifully matched the drapes and furnishings in his apartment. But then, he tells us, he decided to do his apartment over in Art Deco—and she no longer "went with the drapes."

That hypothetical reliably delivers a laugh because one realizes, instantly, that this kind of consideration, in the choice of a spouse, is laughably disproportionate. It trivializes utterly the character of the choice, and to grasp that it trivializes is to grasp, at the same time, that there is an inescapable moral dimension to love and marriage among creatures who are constituted as moral beings. To speak of an attachment lasting through time is to speak of the things that make a partner enduringly worthy of one's love and respect, even as looks wither with age. But to speak in those accents is, of course, to speak of nothing less than the moral ingredients that must ever be woven into love and marriage between human beings, or "moral agents."

Even in the case of ordinary businesses, it was presumably open also to owners of restaurants to claim that they too had certain "aesthetic" considerations uppermost in their minds when they made a decision, say, to confine their restaurants or nightclubs to white persons in formalwear. But a claim of that kind would not have stood against the laws that barred racial discrimination in businesses open to transactions with the public.

And no more would it become a plausible ground of evasion if the federal laws on civil rights had ever reached these intimate decisions in the choice of a partner for sex or marriage.

In any event, it was clear beyond caviling that nothing of this kind came within the reach of any laws or executive orders of the United States. No federal law sought to reach cases of racial discrimination in the decisions made by private persons in the choice of a partner for sex or marriage. There is a danger of getting carried away here by slogans just a bit too quick or glib, and so there is probably a need to remind ourselves that the very notion of "laws of marriage" implies the most emphatic restriction on the kinds of decisions that private persons make in the choice of partners for sex and marriage. That is exactly what laws of marriage do. They typically impose those restrictions when they bar men and women from marrying their natural children, when they bar people from marrying more than one person they love, and when they confine marriage to a couple composed of one man and one woman. To cite but one example, Congress took a keen interest in the suppression of polygamy in Utah in the nineteenth century.

The point, then, is not that the laws may not interfere with the preferences of private persons in their choice of marriage partners. Nor is it that the federal government may not seek to address the question of marriage with laws that restrict private persons' decisions. The more precise point is that neither federal nor state law had sought to reach those private decisions in which people turned away from potential partners on the basis of race. Justice Rehnquist, as a positivist, simply read the laws before him, and it was apparent to him that the laws had no such reach. And as a positivist, too, it did not seem to be his business to fret over the question of whether there was, behind the positive laws regarding racial discrimination, any principle of categorical sweep. But it was equally plain that no judge on the liberal side saw a principle of that kind engaged in the case either. More than that, even people outside the Court, including people on the Left, were emphatically unwilling to embrace such a principle. They held to the view apparently held by all members of the Court and most liberals in the country: namely, that it was legitimate to make discriminations based on race in choosing a partner in sex and marriage. But if that were so, what ground of complaint was left regarding those gentle people at Bob Jones University? The only vice of the people at Bob Jones is that they shared the moral perspective that prevailed at the *New York Review of Books*.

Or, at least, they shared the moral perspective that the *NYRB* had about the kind of racial discrimination that stood beyond the reach of the law. But that brings us back to Justice Rehnquist and his simple, persisting positivism. Justice Rehnquist manages to embrace many refinements and subtle arts of argument in law and politics, but he finds a certain advantage in refracting these rich shades of law and argument through the prism of his positivism. When faced with a complaint of the kind that arose in the Bob Jones case, his first question (as a positivist) was: Was there in fact a law that reached this matter? When the Court insisted that the policies of Bob Jones University ran "counter to the public policy of the United States," the positivist raised the simple, but necessary challenge: Where, in the statutes or executive orders of the United States, was there anything that bore on the wrong alleged at Bob Jones University? Is there any instrument, in federal law, by which to judge the preferences of race that are indulged by private persons in the choice of their own partner in sex and marriage?

The positivist Rehnquist, who insisted on measuring the law precisely, was the one who focused a light that had the precision of a laser. People may have had the sense that there was something wrong with the policies of Bob Jones University, but there are many things regarded as wrong or sinful that the law does not reach. By asking in the first place whether the law has reached the matter at hand, the positivist implicitly puts the challenge to the complainant: What account would he give of the wrong he sees engaged in the case? Is it something that is wrong only because it is forbidden in statutes (like missing the deadline on the filing of taxes)? Or is the wrong really a wrong in principle, something we are supposed to know even if it weren't written down—e.g., that the laws on theft would cover computers and cars, even though those objects are mentioned nowhere in the law? If the claim is that there is a principle of that kind in the case, it should be stated. It was apparent that no one, on the Left or Right, was willing to assert such a principle here, which could have covered both Bob Jones University and the *New York Review of Books*.

In fact, it should have been plain from the very cast of the argument offered by the Court that the majority was light years away from even recognizing the properties of an argument in principle. For what the Chief Justice proceeded to do was to mark off the inventory of statutes and executive orders touching on racial discrimination, especially, as he said, "in education." Consider, in contrast, the teacher of physics who seeks to explain to his students the principle that comes into play when a ball rolls down an inclined plane. He wants to explain to them that the rate of acceleration is directly related to the angle of inclination: that as the angle becomes steeper, the ball rolls faster. Would he seek to give an account of that principle by giving us an inventory of all the results that came about when the experiments were tried with blue planes or wooden planes, with balls made of plastic or aluminum? Would he recite a long inventory of the speeds clocked by the balls as the angle of inclination was altered in each trial? Or would he rather show the students an example, draw on their common sense understanding of what happens as angles of hills and roads become steeper—and then simply draw from the example the principle?

If the Court thought that there was a wrong here that ran to the deepest principles of the law, then Chief Justice Burger and his colleagues should have given an account of that principle. They should not have been distracting themselves and their readers by listing the inventory of statutes and executive orders—all of them beside the point—and citing them as though they somehow formed, in their mass, a principle that no one had yet bothered to explain.

In this posture, the majority revealed its own disarray, but in a strange twist that adds another dimension to the story, the Chief Justice, in the last paragraph of his opinion, let on that he and his colleagues were quite aware of that disarray. It must stand as the most telling of signs that only at the very end—and with the briefest of paragraphs—did the Court bother to consider the defense that went to the core: namely, the contention of the university that nothing in its arrangements violated any policy on racial discrimination found in the laws of the United States. To this contention the Chief Justice thought it sufficient to reply in one sentence: "[D]ecisions of this Court firmly establish that discrimination on the basis of racial affiliation and association is a form of racial discrimination, see, e.g., *Loving* v. *Virginia*, 388 U.S. 1 (1967); *McLaughlin* v. *Florida*, 379 U.S. 184 (1964); *Tillman* v. *Wheaton-Haven Recreation Assn.*, 410 U.S. 431 (1973)." To that, Burger saw fit to add not one word explaining the relevancy of the three cases he was citing. But anyone who knew anything of those cases would have seen at once why there was no willingness to linger with an explanation: The cases were radically inapt. *Loving* v. *Virginia* involved a *statute* that barred marriage across racial lines. *McLaughlin* v. *Florida* involved *laws* that barred mixed racial couples from cohabiting outside of marriage. *Tillman* v. *Wheaton-Haven Recreation Assn.* involved a private association formed around a swimming pool in Silver Spring, Maryland. The association barred black people as members, and in this case refused to admit a black woman as the guest of a member. The association was nominally private, but for all intents and purposes, it was open to all white persons in the community without any principle of restriction apart from race. The pool functioned then, in effect, as a facility open to the public. The Court, at the time, was reviving the Thirteenth Amendment and expanding the reach of the old Civil Rights Acts to private schools and housing. And so, in the third case, a private business open to the public had actually barred people on the basis of race and run afoul of the Civil Rights Acts.

Nothing in these cases offered the remotest precedent for a policy of condemning the *private* choices made by private persons on matters of sex and marriage that were not regulated by the law. The fact that the Chief Justice introduced this issue so late, and dealt with it in such a cursory way, with no explanation, was a telling sign that he recognized the utter inaptness of what he was saying. From another angle, Burger's opinion might have been read as a kind of "wink from the bench": It was the Chief Justice saying, in effect, "I know that this is inapt, that these cases cannot provide any precedent for what we are doing or any explanation of this judgment. But everyone expects us to do *something*. All of the respectable people, in the media and the law schools, expect us to come down against racial discrimination, and not on the side of what they see as a bunch of dim-witted bigots. You know, and we know, that we cannot quite supply a rationale here, but we will have said enough to get through the day, and at times that is as much as one can do. If we are lucky, people will see in the case a principle that we never quite explained, and for the rest, the details may fade from memory."

Anyone who followed the work of the Court at the time was quite aware of the political predicament in which the Court had found itself. The Reagan administration had initially come out in favor of its allies among the religious conservatives. The administration inclined toward what would later be Rehnquist's position, and so it tended to support the university. But then the political heat seemed to build; respectable people on all sides were condemning the policies of the university. Suddenly, the administration found itself in an awkward position, which would have required in turn explanations too complicated for the public to bear. It fell to the Court then to dispose of what had become a political problem. The Reagan administration could not find the words to make the political case for its allies among the fundamentalists, and so it sought a quiet way of avoiding embarrassment.

But Rehnquist, with his positivism, would have provided both a political and legal argument. That argument, spare as it was, would have left the conservatives on a higher moral ground, looking down on the critics of Bob Jones University. Rehnquist the positivist would have pointed out that many people across the landscape are seized with an awareness of wrongs that are not necessarily embodied in statutes and condemned with the force of positive law. To have a sense that something is wrong is one thing, but it is quite another matter to state the principle that explains the wrongness and justifies the reach of the law. Fagin's School of Pickpocketry would not receive a tax exemption because theft is against the law.

In applying principles to cases, the administrators at the IRS would find a need to flex their imaginations even in prosaic cases; but the law has been cast in the form of a statute precisely so that administrators would be spared the need every day to be inventive and inspired. It may indeed be that the principle that condemns discrimination on the basis of race would cover, in its sweep, even people who draw away from lovers and potential spouses on account of their race. That may be the case, and yet, strictly speaking, the law has not incorporated that judgment anywhere in its statutes, or in the orders of agencies and courts. By that reckoning, then, Bob Jones University did not run afoul of anything in the laws or public policy of the United States. And for that sovereign reason, Bob Jones University could not be regarded as anything other than a "legitimate" institution. If the institution passes all of the tests of accreditation that are required of schools, it stands as a legitimate educational enterprise, and it properly claims then, as a matter of right, any tax exemption that would flow to an educational enterprise. The strong burden would have to be placed on anyone who claims otherwise. End of story.

But not of the overtones. As I have suggested, this spare application of positivism could have illuminated the fog in this case by bringing out, more vividly, the properties and requirements of a principled argument, thereby revealing quite dramatically how far most people were from satisfying those requirements. But in bringing those matters out more fully, Justice Rehnquist the positivist would have offered more than a narrow, legal defense, the equivalent of arguing over the question of what the meaning of "is" is. The argument cast by the positivist would have exposed the moral posturing in the case as just that—posturing without substance. The positivist would have compelled jurists to become more fastidious in paying attention to the precise meaning of the statutes and executive orders. He might also have made lawyers even more aware of how high the bar of principle was placed—just how demanding was the argument they had to make if they were pretending to claim for themselves the mantle of a moral principle here.

In sum, the positivist, asking spare, focused questions, would have been the carrier of a genuine discipline of legal and moral judgment. He would not only have reminded his colleagues and readers of the properties of a principle, but he would have recalled to them also that the law is a blending of prudence and statecraft, as well as being the craft of reason. That wondrous blending may account for why I have been able to say over the years, without too much irony, that some of my best friends are positivists. For it becomes ever clearer that the best positivists have been speaking sense all their lives. With their attachment to the conventions of lawfulness, they become the agents of an insistent rationality. They appeal at every turn to the "laws of reason" without being aware at all times that they are doing anything remotely "philosophic." They are constantly bringing into view the natural law, even while they earnestly profess that they are not practicing it. They remain then the best of company, for when we are with them, we can never be far from the natural law.

XVI

Judicial Activism and Regime Change

George W. Carey

I begin with the proposition that the fundamental character of our constitutional order has been altered by the emergence of a judicial activism whose origins are to be found in the decisions of the Warren Court. For this reason, the contemporary concerns expressed about the role of the Court are of a different and far more critical order than those of earlier eras when the Court found itself at the center of controversy. Put otherwise, the issues surrounding the Court today are what we commonly call "regime questions," the most significant of which relate to whether modern judicial activism is compatible with the separation of powers and republican self-government, arguably the two most basic principles of our Constitution. By contrast, the controversies of earlier eras were largely "tactical" in nature; intramural disputes within the confines of the constitutional framework and principles inherited from our Founding Fathers. These propositions and contentions, I hasten to add, will be examined more fully in due course.

My principal concerns, however, go beyond elaborating on this unprecedented reach of judicial power. They relate instead to the lack of serious public debate over this development and the failure of those who seek to justify it to come to grips with the fundamental "regime" questions. The consequences of this, as I will endeavor to show, is that theories justifying judicial activism are narrow, cramped, and truncated; totally inadequate for the purposes of justifying judicial supremacy.

The Contention of Equivalence

The foregoing is self-evident to many, principally the critics of the modern Court and the powers it has assumed in recent times. But as noted above, many, if not most, advocates of judicial activism either ignore it or gloss it over, as if it were merely a reformulation of the more traditional objections to judicial review or an expression of discontent with specific decisions.

To be perfectly clear about this charge requires some elaboration. We can profitably begin by observing that the "avoidance" of these issues by activists takes many forms. One of the most popular, familiar to most critics of judicial activism, is to deny the unprecedented nature of the present controversy, to argue that the charges of judicial abuse of power today are very similar to those of the middle 1930s, when a "conservative" Court invalidated major elements of Roosevelt's New Deal program. Maintaining that the New Dealers were quite justified in their attacks, whereas today's critics are wrongheaded, these activists counter that it all comes down to "whose ox is being gored." In other words, what motivates modern critics is portrayed as no different from that which motivated the critics of the New Deal era, namely, disagreement with the substance of the Court's decisions.

While I have not seen any surveys on this matter, I know from personal experience that this argument is persuasive with students, graduate and undergraduate, even those who have emerged from constitutional law courses. By all evidences, it is widely accepted in our most prestigious law schools. It is, we might say, the argument of equivalence; that is, the controversies surrounding the Court since the 1950s are essentially no different from those of the New Deal era or, for that matter, from others of lesser intensity that have arisen in the course of our history. We find this equivalence reflected in the treatment that the mass media give to the contemporary controversies surrounding the Court's power and role in our system, namely, in their insinuation that this is a "political" issue on a par with, say, whether tax rates should be raised or lowered.

Now, as serious students well know, to picture the modern controversy in these or like terms is misleading, if not intellectually dishonest. To do so simply ignores or skirts the distinctions that are raised by contemporary critics and the resulting questions that ultimately must be faced if the Court is not eventually to lose all semblance of legitimacy.[1] The equivalence argument, quite simply, fails to acknowledge a critical difference between the Court's behavior since the Warren era and the earlier periods of our history when it was also the center of controversy. As Charles S. Hyneman put the matter nearly four decades ago, prior to the Court's desegregation opinion in *Brown v. Board of Education* (1954),[2] the Court's decisions "had the effect of reinstating the regime of law that existed prior to the particular enactment; or, if some of the previous law had been repealed because of the new statute, Congress and the president were notified to patch up the now-incomplete coverage of the law." But in *Brown*, the Court mandated that states with segregated schools had "to fashion legislation of a kind they had never had on their statute books and to institute some social relationships that had never prevailed in those places."[3] To put this in other terms, the Court in effect legislated; it moved beyond the "nullification" of laws by imposing a remedy.[4]

The full extent of the Court's newly asserted power is often overlooked. Richard E. Morgan puts the current state of affairs in its proper perspective by noting that after the desegregation rulings "progressive reformers" came to look upon the courts "as a source of governmental power that could force unpopular changes that could not be secured through representative institutions." "If judges," Morgan continues, "could sidestep the electoral and legislative processes, bypassing the very forms of the Constitution, in order to serve the higher good of ending Jim Crow, then judges could do many things about which the country was deeply divided."[5] The *Brown* decision, in short, raised the Court to what Hyneman termed a "new plateau" of power; a plateau never envisioned by the Framers or those who ratified the Constitution. Moreover, the Court's newfound power to promote the "good" served to fundamentally alter the functions, powers, and roles of the major departments created by the Constitution.

Now the Court not only can "trump" any legislative act—that is, exercise its traditional power of judicial review—it can also, in effect, legislate without regard for the separation of powers principle embodied in our Constitution. And when it uses the Constitution as the basis for its legislation, barring a change of mind on its part, its decisions and policies can be reversed only by amending the Constitution.

To portray this development in other terms, no longer is it accurate to think of judicial powers being employed within the constitutional morality set forth in *Marbury v. Madison*, the case commonly regarded as providing the theoretical foundations for judicial review. Nor does the reasoning set forth by Marshall in *Marbury* support the most significant and controversial decisions of the modern Court. Rather, to comprehend the scope of powers claimed by the modern Courts, one must begin with the *Brown* decision. The "logic" of this decision forms the foundations for a new regime, one marked by a degree and kind of judicial supremacy never envisioned by the staunchest critics of judicial power at the time of our founding.[6]

The Lack of Genuine Dialogue

While these observations are, as I have remarked, commonplace for those who have looked with virtually any degree of skepticism at the powers asserted or exercised by the Court during the past fifty years, they prompt puzzling questions: Why is it that the proponents of judicial activism dodge the real issues involved in the controversy? Why do they throw up smoke screens to avoid the central questions? Or why do they attempt to maintain the fiction that the modern Court is operating within the traditional limits set forth by Marshall in *Marbury*? Why, in sum, haven't we experienced an open, intellectually honest, and civil debate, one in which the role and function of the modern Court is explained and justified, if possible, in terms of the basic values and precepts of republican government?[7]

There would seem to be no single or simple answer to these questions. Certainly an important factor in stifling open discussion is what Richard Morgan has called the "Brown card." In this connection he writes: "The scenario is familiar: after arguing that some particular judicial initiative or other is without foundation in text, or original understanding, or history, and is therefore *illegitimate*, the critic of judicial activism is faced with the question, 'Well then, you must be opposed to *Brown v. Board of Education*.'"[8] Intimidation, the fear of being branded a racist, has beyond any question muted discussion of the central issues in the manner Morgan suggests. And, as his comments intimate, this intimidation— which stemmed from the high moral ground taken by the Court in its *Brown* decision—created both an opening and a "cover" for the Court to use its authority for the advancement of a political agenda, the goals of which could not be achieved through the political processes specified in the Constitution. Politically speaking, moreover, the political and ideological sectors of society that benefit the most from this state of affairs have every reason to oppose genuine dialogue over the Court's legitimate authority.

The impact of *Brown*, however, goes well beyond strictly partisan considerations. The decision would appear to constitute a turning point in the field of constitutional interpretation. In retrospect, it is as if a new universe opened up that sanctioned entirely new rules of interpretation while simultaneously providing new avenues for speculation and theorizing about the underlying principles and purposes of the Constitution. The decision certainly marked the end of the traditionalist understanding of the legitimate rules of interpretation and the proper functions of the Court. From this perspective, what seems clear is that *Brown* provided the opening for the forces of progressivism to use the Court as a vehicle to reinterpret the Constitution and our tradition in a manner congenial to their basic tenets. With *Brown*, this is to say, the field was wide open for new modes of imaginative interpretation whereby the goals long sought by progressives could not only be attained, but could also be wrapped in the mantle of newly discovered constitutional mandates.

Given the opportunities that *Brown* created, it is quite understandable why the activists never wanted to fight a rearguard action with the traditionalists. To do so would be analogous to the winner of a close election asking for a recount. Besides which, their attention naturally focused on the exploration of this new realm and on what modes of interpretation would best serve their ends. Perhaps, too, they regarded confrontation over what had transpired as unnecessary, even meaningless, because the genie was out of the bottle, so to speak, and there could be no turning back. They may well have thought the "forces" of history on their side, that it was inevitable that the Court would reach this new plateau of power, and that the only question now was in what ways this newfound power could be utilized.

Whatever the reasons, judicial activism clearly seems to have won the day—not, as we have stressed, through the processes of rational persuasion, deliberation, or debate, but rather by obscuring the enormity of the change in the regime produced by activism and by ignoring, deliberately or not, the fundamental questions raised by this change. Turning back the clock is possible, but highly unlikely.[9] This is not to say that judicial activism is the product of grassroots democracy or that it enjoys widespread popular acceptance, but rather to acknowledge that it has the intense support of the intellectual and cultural elite who, operating against the backdrop of an ignorant and apathetic public, would strenuously and successfully resist any retrenchment of judicial power.[10]

Judicial Activism and New Horizons

This situation, to say the least, does not bode well either for the future of constitutionalism or republicanism. It is also exacerbated by the fact that activists are busily engaged in marking out new frontiers of judicial power. To see this, one need only sample the theories of constitutional interpretation and judicial power that have been spawned as a result of the desegregation decisions. They teach us that there is greater need than ever to confront the problems raised by judicial activism.

The theories of constitutional interpretation I have in mind are those that are commonplace in law and graduate school courses; they are part of the intellectual landscape, accepted as legitimate approaches to an understanding of our constitutional order or, if not that, as providing the rationale for greatly expanded judicial authority. They constitute a large portion of readings one finds in edited works designed to introduce students to the various schools of constitutional interpretation and their understanding of the role of the judiciary. The schools represented in these readings range from those "narrow" in scope, formulations that place some bounds on judicial power, to those that are "broad," offering vague and indeterminate boundaries. But all of them, in one fashion or another, expand judicial power far beyond what was contemplated by the Framers, and most would allow the Court enormous latitude to set forth policy in key social, economic, and political areas. A brief examination of the relevant readings in one of the better, but typical, collections, *Modern Constitutional Theory* (hereafter, *MCT*), should suffice to illustrate my point.[11]

We can profitably begin this brief survey by building upon an observation made by Sanford Levinson. In the course of denying that there are or can be any objective standards for determining what is a correct or incorrect constitutional interpretation, he remarks that theories that identify these objective standards are built upon the premise "that there is something 'in' the Constitution that can be extracted if only we can figure out the best method to mine its meaning." In this enterprise, the theorist seeks to find the "essential meaning" of the Constitution by cracking its "code," that is, finding "the secret of the text."[12] In other words, the theorist looks for the fundamental principles or values that best explain the why's and wherefore's of both the structure and processes set forth in the Constitution with the goal of identifying the Founders' intentions. The theorist, in this process, is obliged to extrapolate from the constitutional provisions to find and order these principles and values, but once discovered they form the precepts by which the Court is to interpret the Constitution. Equally important, they also serve to define the limits of legitimate judicial power.

Levinson rightly regards John Hart Ely's approach as one that presumes to have unlocked a constitutional code. In an important sense, Levinson is correct in this assessment: Ely's theory, the essence of which is reproduced in *MCT,* looks at the Constitution as designed to "preserve liberty" by setting forth an "extensive set of procedural protections, and by a still more elaborate scheme designed to ensure that in the making of substantive choices the decision process will be open to all on something approaching an equal basis, with the decision-makers held to a duty to take into account the interests of all those their decisions affect." Ely is intent upon showing that the "code" is not to be found in "substantive rights entitled to permanent protection," or, for that matter, in an ideol-

ogy built around substantive ends. He quotes with approbation the conclusion of Judge Linde that "as a charter of government a constitution
must prescribe legitimate processes, not legitimate outcomes."[13]

Ely's theory, as will be evident in short order, is "narrow"; that is, he
holds that the Court's legitimate functions relate to securing the democratic processes and guaranteeing "fairness" in these processes, principally
for "discrete and insular minorities" that are disadvantaged and thus susceptible to abuse by majorities.[14] His "construct" stands somewhere between a textually based originalism and the more extreme and "wider"
activist formulations. While he is highly sympathetic to the charge that
substantively based activist theories undermine the republican principle,
he still manages to find a significant role for the Court in providing
"virtual representation" for minorities disadvantaged in the political processes, a role which, when examined closely, would allow the Court to
exercise a wide range of significant powers.[15]

More importantly, theories such a Ely's—i.e., those aimed at restricting the Court principally to "process" concerns—can be seen as opening wide avenues for theories of constitutional interpretation that would
appear to accord the Court virtually unlimited powers. Along these lines,
MCT includes a short selection by Laurence Tribe which argues, in effect,
that there can be no such thing as a pure "process" theory of constitutional
interpretation. With Ely's formulation expressly in mind, Tribe asks "which
groups are to count as 'discrete and insular minorities'? What are instead
to be deemed appropriate losers in the ongoing struggle for political acceptance and ascendancy?" The essential distinguishing test, he maintains, must be whether "the law is part of a pattern that denies to those
subject to it a meaningful opportunity to realize their humanity." Making such a determination, he concludes, requires that we "look beyond
process to identify and proclaim fundamental substantive human rights."[16]
This formula could easily give the Court considerable latitude for both
invalidating legislation and actively seeking resolution. Why shouldn't
the Court take positive steps when the opportunity presents itself, if
this means helping people to realize the "meaningful opportunity" to which
Tribe refers?

Yet Tribe's position also seems relatively restrictive when compared with others of activist persuasion who also take exception with Ely's views. In another selection, much is made of the fact that Ely and other process-oriented theorists take no account of "potential majorities," i.e., "the mass of people who are not now politically active and whose interests can be most routinely blocked by more effective interests." These inequalities, the author argues, are not due to apathy or contentment with the system, but rather "inequalities of power, wealth, status, and education." Relying primarily on the works of the political scientist Robert A. Dahl, the author details the ways in which these inequalities operate to permanently disadvantage these potential majorities in the decision-making processes. Inequalities of information and education, for instance, make it difficult for the members of potential majorities "to recognize and articulate their own interests." Additionally, the dominant and organized interests have the resources to condition the attitudes and outlook of the members of the potential majorities, thereby blinding them to their true interests. To the extent that process-oriented theories buy into this perception of American politics, the Court would seem to have wide discretionary authority to institute any number of "reforms" designed to remove the inequalities that prevent equal concern and respect for any groups or individuals, not simply racial and ethnic minorities. For instance, this theory would justify the Court imposing campaign finance "reform" of its own making. Indeed, the Court would be justified in advancing whatever it could to promote political equality, broadly conceived.[17]

The same indeterminacy is found in other formulations. Another selection advances the argument that Ely and other proceduralists are plainly wrong to found their schemes on the presumption that the Framers sought a system that would respond to the will of the majority: "At every turn, they [the Framers] buffered majority will, insulated representatives from direct influence of majority factions, and provided checks on majority decision making."[18] The Framers' goal, according to this line of reasoning, was to protect liberty, understood in terms of individual rights. For this writer, then, the protection of liberty so understood is the key for breaking the constitutional "code"; it accounts for the "constitutional architecture" such as the "separation of powers, checks and balances, and federalism—all of which are more comfortably accepted as devices for protecting individual rights."[19] In this scheme, the Court's role is clear. It bears "the primary responsibility for guarding the value [liberty] that underlay the entire constitutional structure."[20] The conclusion of this analysis is that "Ely had it exactly backwards. A better understanding of the system we have is that *majoritarian government exists to support the Bill of Rights.*"[21]

Whatever limits to judicial authority this understanding would appear to provide vanish once we come to realize just how these rights can be manipulated to provide for new, unenumerated, rights.[22] Certainly such an understanding is an invitation to regard the Ninth Amendment as an almost infinite source of rights that the judiciary could legitimately mine to advance its visions of the good society. On this matter, we need only consider the position of Thomas Grey, who asks whether there is an "unwritten Constitution." He answers in the affirmative, contending that the Founders recognized that "written constitutions could not completely codify the higher law." "Thus," as he would have it, "in the framing of the original American constitutions it was widely accepted that there remained unwritten but still binding principles of higher law. The Ninth Amendment is the textual expression of this idea in the federal Constitution."[23] Given this view, it is not at all difficult to see how the Court would be free to act in a totally arbitrary and capricious fashion, the more so as there is, and has been for some years, an active and powerful "rights industry" in the United States.[24]

A View from the Bench

This survey, though brief, is sufficient, I believe, to indicate the parameters and character of the intellectual universe that prevails within the academic circles of the legal profession. To be sure, we find a variety of theories and many highly imaginative interpretations of key provisions of the Constitution—e.g., due process, equal protection, the Ninth Amendment. But all these endeavors are similar in their thrust. Either they seek to find justifications for the Court's assumption of powers or they advance theories that would support an even more expansive judicial role. Taken as a whole, they provide rationales for the exercise of raw judicial power.

Consider the judicial "pragmatism" of Judge Richard Posner. As he puts it, "a pragmatist judge always tries to do the best he can do for the present and the future, unchecked by any felt *duty* to secure consistency in principle with what other officials have done in the past." He amplifies upon the differences between the pragmatic judge and one that holds "that the law is a system of rules laid down by the legislatures and merely applied by judges." The pragmatic jurist, he writes, "is concerned with securing consistency with the past only to the extent that such consistency may happen to conduce to producing the best results for the future."[25] The means, *inter alia*, that he must be concerned with whether his decision will have "bad results" by departing "too abruptly from precedent." "There is," he observes, "often a trade-off between rendering substantive justice in the case under consideration and maintaining the law's certainty and predictability."[26]

Posner acknowledges that "precedent, statutes, and constitutions" can be "sources of potentially valuable information," but the pragmatist judge should regard them only in this light.[27] Indeed, the pragmatic approach requires that judges seek out reliable knowledge and information that would bear upon the case at hand—even, when appropriate, consulting the laws and practices of other nations and "world public opinion"—rather than relying upon dogma or some vision of the natural law.[28] He contends that pragmatism also encourages inquiry and questions: "The conventional judge," he argues, "is apt not to question his premises." He may feel, for instance, "that 'hate speech' is deeply harmful, or that banning it would endanger political liberty," but "he is not likely to take the next step," namely, to "seek through investigation" to determine whether he is right or wrong.[29] Yet, Posner realizes that often full and reliable knowledge is not available for judges who must make decisions. In these cases, the pragmatic judge should draw upon his "extrajudicial experience for guidance."[30]

Interestingly, Posner does not see much danger in judges, at least judges "of the higher American courts," drawing upon their "extrajudicial experience": They are "generally picked from the upper tail of the population distribution in terms of age, education, intelligence, disinterest, and sobriety" and are "schooled . . . on listening to both sides, . . . on sifting truth from falsehood, and on exercising detached judgment." In this regard, he goes so far as to contend that "at their best, American appellate courts are councils of wise elders and it is not completely insane to entrust them with responsibility for deciding cases in a way that will produce the best results in the circumstances rather than just deciding in accordance with rules created by other organs of government or in accordance with their own previous decisions."[31]

A Middle with No Beginning

I have focused on Posner's approach to illustrate the degree to which it is now commonplace to advance activist views without having to face difficult questions. Whereas sixty years ago Posner's pragmatism would have been regarded as truly radical, the more so coming from a sitting federal judge at the appellate level, today it can be viewed as just another (albeit interesting) approach that seeks to justify expansive judicial authority. No doubt, the rationales that now abound to justify various kinds of judicial activism, most of them advanced by the law school professoriat, serve to "shield" or "protect" him from the withering attacks that might otherwise have come his way. As matters stand, his approach is relatively "tame," no more radical than the countless others that have been forthcoming and accorded legitimacy by the reigning authorities in the contemporary legal community. His views, thus, are not at all shocking, but rather quite in keeping with those that are regularly voiced in the faculty lounges of our more prestigious universities.

At the same time, his approach also illustrates the salient shortcomings of the prevailing views concerning the role of the judiciary in our constitutional system. First, as noted above, we find little appreciation of just how far his pragmatism elevates the courts to a position that is inconsistent or incompatible with the basic principles of our constitutional design. Second, and very much related, there is no effort to distinguish the role of the courts from that of the legislature. Posner's pragmatism highlights this point perhaps better than other theories of judicial power: The things that pragmatic judges should ideally do before rendering decisions (e.g., anticipating reactions, gathering relevant information, asking the right questions, taking public opinion into account) are precisely those that responsible legislators have traditionally done as a matter of course. Posner's judge, in short, can be seen as an unaccountable legislator. And third, there is little if any concern about the abuse of judicial power, little attention devoted to demarcating the boundaries of judicial discretion.

My concerns with the expansion of judicial power and the theories that seek to justify this growth or its extension can be cast in other terms. From the vantage point of the traditional theory that has been displaced in recent decades, the union of the judicial and legislative powers was deemed tyranny. In *Federalist 47*, Publius quoted approvingly from Montesquieu about the dangers of such a union: "'Were the power of judging joined with the legislative, the life and liberty of the subject would be exposed to arbitrary control, for the *judge* would then be *the legislator*."[32] This view was founded on both a theory and practice of long standing that were well understood at the time the Constitution was framed and ratified. But the same cannot be said about any of the formulations that would allow for judicial activism. That is, the proponents of judicial activism, by all evidences, seem to feel that this union of powers, far from leading to tyranny, might well serve noble and higher ends of one kind or another. And they are implicitly asking for a drastic alteration of the Framers' Constitution to empower the judiciary to advance these ends.

What is lacking, however, is the articulation of the theoretical grounds that would lead one to conclude that such a union is harmless. To articulate these theoretical grounds would necessarily involve stepping outside of the narrow intellectual universe of the judicial activists. It would involve having to answer in a systematic fashion "prior questions"—e.g., What are the ingredients of political liberty? What institutional arrangements are best suited for its maximization? Are there distinct functions of government that warrant a division of authority? What role should the people play in the decision making process? What are appropriate means to ensure accountability of the decision makers? By what means can abuses of power by the decision makers, in whatever capacity, be controlled?

My point can be put succinctly. All the efforts to advance judicial activism presuppose a political philosophy that is never articulated. Such efforts are at best volume two of a three-volume collection. They start in the middle, so to speak, leaving the reader to concoct the beginning as best he can.

Judicial Activism: A Rudderless Boat

This is not to say that we are without some understanding of what shape a fully developed theory of judicial activism would take. Most proponents of judicial activism clearly display a lack of confidence in, or even a distrust of, the legislative branch. This branch, we are informed, either does not recognize "problems," or it is undemocratic in its composition, structure, or processes, or it is frequently deficient in according a "fair" hearing to minority concerns. Moreover, legislatures are often pictured as hostile to "progressive" measures that would improve the lot of the politically "disadvantaged" sectors of society. So we have every reason to believe that a full-blown activist theory would significantly reduce the role and power of legislatures. Indirect confirmation of this suspicion is to be found in the activists' lack of concern about the problems associated with legislative delegation of powers.

Likewise, activist theory demands a very high degree of centralization. Aside from the fact that the ends associated with most versions of activism are universal in nature, requiring for their realization centralized decision making, the states are viewed by most activists as even less enlightened than the national government: They are generally pictured as more prone to bow to special interests, to exhibit an insensitivity to the "rights" of minorities, to cater to provincial interests. While some states are far better than others, most activists expressly point to the need for central control over all states.[33]

To go no further, the underlying theory of judicial activism, while far from being articulated, appears to conform with the central tenets of progressivism. It certainly is one with progressivism in holding that certain ends and principles are axiomatic, beyond debate, and thus beyond rejection or modification by representative institutions accountable to the people. There would seem to be a "moral science," analogous in character to the physical sciences, consisting of a coherent body of mutually consistent axioms and principles which, when properly applied, reveal goals and policies whose fairness and justness is self-evident, needing no affirmation from the likes of legislative bodies.

But, once again, judicial activists leave it to us to speculate about the nature of the underpinnings of their conception of such a moral science. What are its sources? What are its assumptions about the nature of man and his place in the order of being? What are the rules for applying its principles to the "real" world? Do its axioms and principles keep house with one another? If not, which take priority? Why are the people and their representatives less able than, say, judges to see the imperatives of this moral theory? Indeed, are the moral foundations and imperatives of judicial activism compatible with republican self-government?

To conclude, judicial activism is far more than simply another school of constitutional interpretation. The more we examine it, the more we find that it bears the earmarks of an ideology hostile to the basic principles of the Founders' Constitution. Its critical voids, instrumental to its successes, render it a highly dangerous heresy; that is, it possesses enormous destructive potential, but unlike a heresy, it provides no principled guidance for the construction of a new, much less better, political order.

XVII

On Merely Being Intelligent: Canavan's Views and Reviews

JAMES V. SCHALL, S.J

"*In this our day, one can get a reputation for being conservative merely by being intelligent.*"—Francis Canavan, review of *Statecraft as Soulcraft*, by George Will[1]

"*Unger's communitarianism, it must be said, approaches the Utopian in that his ideal of community would seem to be realizable only in a religious order—and how imperfectly it is realized even there only the members of a religious order know.*"
—Francis Canavan, review of *Knowledge and Politics*,
by Roberto Mangabeira Unger[2]

What is the "work" of an academic? Not with total injustice do we measure it in terms of books published, articles in "refereed" journals—a practice not easily distinguished from censorship even by academics themselves—the number of students taught, theses directed, faculty meetings attended. But most underrated in the academic measuring process are a professor's book reviews and pieces in journals of opinion, wherein ideas are more sharply presented and fought about. This neglect is unfortunate in that in the occasional essay, column, or book review we can often discover something "unscientific" about a professor-person that we might easily have missed in his or her more academic writings, for example, his wit and sharp opinion—something, in the case of Francis Canavan, that is often most memorably displayed to his friends and associates at the many academic conferences of greater or lesser fame in which he has participated. Without a tape recorder or video camera on the spot, these latter interchanges have, alas, often passed into the oblivion of post-conference forgetfulness, unless, hopefully, they made their way into the recollections and memories of those who heard Canavan in person.

I recall a meeting of exalted academic standing at which Canavan was present in the audience as a spectator. As usual, the panel consisted of five members, of which I was one. The panel chairman informed us in the beginning that we each had ten minutes to "summarize" our profound findings, after which there would be about half an hour of discussion. As is routine in these scholarly affairs, the first couple of speakers took about twenty minutes apiece, then the other three hurried through their presentations. This arrangement left about five minutes for what is piously called "discussion." During the presentation, one of the longer papers was delivered by a professor who earnestly informed us, as he would show us more clearly in his forthcoming book, that St. Augustine and St. Thomas were the major causes of intolerance and absolutism in the modern world. It was one of those amazing feats of silliness that can only happen at an academic conference.

In any case, when it finally came to the few minutes of "discussion," the chairman asked if any of the panelists had any remarks. Knowing that Father Canavan could not resist such a temptation, I immediately suggested that we skip comments from the panel and go immediately to questions from the floor. The first question, of course, was from Canavan and was directed to the astonishingly wrongheaded idea that our young professor developed in his paper about St. Augustine and St. Thomas. I am sure that the young man did not know who Father Canavan was, but he is not soon going to forget the danger of offering this ludicrous thesis before attentive academics with clipped New York accents dressed in clerical garb.

The next best thing to hearing Father Canavan in action is to read his shorter pieces. For many years, he did a regular column of about a thousand words every month, maybe every quarter, in an obscure pro-life publication called *The Catholic Eye,* whose mailing address was suspiciously identical to that of *National Review.* Later most of these columns were published in book form with the unfortunate, but, so to speak, pointed title of *Pins in the Liberal Balloon*.[3] The essays in this book are indeed polemical, but they display a clarity of reason that reduces each question taken up to its basic principle. The essays are more than just "pins" or pricks in an ideological balloon. Each in a serious yet witty way establishes a principle, the deviation from which has caused the problem at hand.

How did he proceed? Canavan began his review of Robert George's *Making Men Moral*, a book that displays the same clear, incisive reasoning that Canavan himself possesses, in this way: "Aristotle says somewhere that the ability to think largely consists in the ability to make distinctions. Then in another place, he says that most people are not good at making distinctions."[4] We should be especially attentive when someone manages to make Aristotle amusing. The late Henry Veatch was good at this, as is Canavan. It was, after all, Aristotle himself who pointed out the intimate relationship between wit and humor, intelligence and metaphysics—all are questions of seeing the relations existing among things.

The value of Canavan's shorter "views and reviews," as I call them, is that he makes and spells out the distinctions that "most people" are not able to make themselves. These same ordinary people, however, can grasp a distinction when a Canavan makes it explicit. I do not think, nor I suspect does Canavan think, that most people fall into error because they think wrongly. Usually, they think wrongly because they have already fallen into some moral disorder that they try to justify by argument. What is most useful for the ordinary person, subject to so much media and academic sophistry, is to see laid out clearly and briefly the arguments that are said to justify a given moral disorder. In good Aristotelian fashion, Canavan does not think it takes a genius to see what's right. Anyone can usually grasp the truth—unless they don't want to.

Let me, by way of example, cite a typical Canavan column. I would note that when, as in this case, the erroneous principle is articulated by a cleric, Canavan is especially pert. His subject is the Pope's teaching on the illicity of contraception, a teaching Canavan believes was in fact quite correct and which he has defended with especial acuity. Canavan broaches this issue in a piece in *Pins in the Liberal Balloon* titled "The Logic of Contraception." Canavan begins by recalling an article by a fellow priest, John Giles Milhaven, who at the time was a Jesuit moral theologian. The article appeared in the March-April 1970 issue of *The Critic*. Canavan quotes the following passage:

> The dissent [among theologians against the teaching of the Church], which was motivated by the practical needs of married people, was justified ethically by the principle that deliberately willed sexual activity need not always be open to procreation. The principle is a direct contradiction of the classic natural law principle that not only excluded any use of contraception in marriage but was also the key principle prohibiting say deliberate sex outside of marriage. So far as I know, the theologians who rejected the natural law principle in order to permit contraception have found no convincing one to replace it to prohibit all extramarital sexual behavior.

The first thing that Canavan notes about this intriguing paragraph is that its author "not long afterwards left the priesthood, married a wife, and took upon himself the burdens of married people." "It cannot be said, therefore," he adds with some relish, "that he was unsympathetic to their practical needs."

What interests Canavan is the last sentence of the passage, a sentence which he finds himself in full agreement with. In fact, he adds, "very few [theologians] have even tried to find an argument that allows contraception in marriage but prohibits all sexual activity outside of marriage." The key word here is "argument." Canavan then zeroes in on the principle involved. He remarks that those theologians, like Charles Curran, who reject the papal position, still try, however illogically, to insist that some "reason" must be given for employing contraceptives in marriage. Why should they bother? Since these theological liberals hold that "the [sexual] act has no natural and morally obliging structure and purpose," any restrictions placed upon the act can only be a function of "intention" or "circumstances." "Intention" and "circumstances," of course, are either external to the act or outside its central essence. We should "intend" to do good in the right time and right circumstances, but the "good" is not simply the intention to do it. It is what is done. As Aristotle says, "good" intentions cannot justify murder or adultery because these acts themselves are already not good.

The next step in this argument, Canavan continues, is to realize that it is not just a question of acts inside marriage. "The logic of contraception calls into question the idea that any particular kind of sexual act is the uniquely normal and permissible one." To clarify his argument Canavan proposes a question "seldom confronted by pious liberals." At this point, in parentheses, Canavan remarks of the "pious liberals" that "they are the worst kind [of liberals], because they piously refuse to admit unwelcome facts or to face what they regard as shocking and alarmist questions." The "unwelcome facts" and the "shocking questions" that are not faced, no doubt, emphasize the ease and rapidity with which we have passed from worrying about acts within marriage to the position that any sort of sexual act is permissible, no matter with whom or by whom or for whom. The early liberals said this latter consequence would not follow. Today, everyone sees that this is what happened. So the question comes down to this: "why, if it is permissible to sterilize the sexual act while performing it (what contraception does), it is nonetheless necessary to perform it with the organs of procreation, and with them alone."[5] The link between the act and its abiding purpose is broken with contraceptive use. Once broken, anything goes. This logic is what is at stake in the papal argument. The popes recognize that a slight error in principle would lead to vast destructive consequences. If sex can have no relation to the generation of offspring, then any sort of sex in any condition is quite reasonable in principle. But if the relation between act and purpose exists, then only that sex related to openness to children is permissible.

The argument has vast political and practical consequences. Take, for example, "the issue [of] whether homosexual relations are wrong in themselves and deserving of no protection by society or are merely the object of popular but irrational disgust." Needless to say, some quarter century after Canavan wrote these words, the popular, and even legally sanctioned position, is that there is nothing wrong with homosexual acts or any other kind of sexual acts as such. It is all a question of personal taste. All types of consensual sexual acts are permissible, and it is increasingly considered intolerant and intolerable to publicly challenge the legitimacy and "normalcy" of any form of sexual activity. A university in England recently prohibited the use in speech of the phrase "normal sex" on

campus as discriminatory because there is no such thing as "normal sex"!
That would imply a purpose, a principle.

Canavan has a certain sympathy for what he calls "hardnosed" liberals in these matters—at least they are consistent. "Hardnosed liberals," he observes, "say flatly that there is nothing wrong with homosexual relations per se because no sexual relations of any kind are or can be wrong in themselves. Pious liberals confine themselves to deploring homosexual promiscuity while pleading for understanding for homosexuals. As between the two of them, we must prefer the hardnosed liberals, because they at least know what they mean and say it." Thus, if there is no principle involved, if the sexual act has no natural structure, then sexual activity with anyone, of any gender, of any marital or nonmarital status—including sexual activity involving children and even animals—is legitimate. "Whether it is a morally good thing to do depends entirely on one's intention and the circumstances, not on the nature of the act."

Canavan concludes this short essay by pointing out that this question first came up in the Church of England in the 1920s, even before the Lambeth Conference's approval of contraception in 1930. At that time, some Anglican thinkers argued that the consequences of accepting contraception would lead to the approval of any sort of sexual activity. The pious liberals refused to recognize this. But it has come about as those theologians predicted. The reason is that "to accept contraception as legitimate, even within marriage and for serious reasons, is to pull out the linchpin that holds the whole structure of Christian sexual morality together." The Church of England has the dubious honor of leading the way here. What is surprising, perhaps, is the degree to which dissenting Catholics have followed its lead.

Returning to the debates in the Catholic world concerning the Church's teaching on contraception, Canavan invokes Paul VI's insistence that "each and every marriage act must remain open to the transmission of life." Granted that not every act actually produces life, it is nevertheless true that in an uncanny way this "openness" remains the key. "Take it out," he insists, "and the structure of Christian sexual morality falls apart." Canavan finishes his essay by recalling that the very dissent of the theologians who initially approved contraception gradually led them to approve everything else. Whatever one chooses to make of this record, Canavan implies, there is a logic to it, both a logic that saves what marriage and begetting are about and a logic that justifies almost anything.[6] It all depends, as Aristotle said, on a "slight error" in the beginning. The error in question being the belief that what counts is not the act but the intention.

As a kind of commentary or afterthought on this essay, it is amusing to note Canavan's review of Jill and Leon Uris's book, *Ireland: A Terrible Beauty*.[7] I mention his assessment of this book because of its prophetic insight. Its authors, he writes, seem to believe that "the root of Ireland's troubles is sexual repression." In the authors' view, Ireland was plagued by "a reactionary hierarchy, trained in a Maynooth Seminary, staffed by Jansenists [that] foisted an inhuman morality on a downtrodden and obedient people. The same hierarchy now stands in the way of 'desperately needed progressive reforms.' The essential reforms are these: contraception, abortion, and divorce. Given these, the Urises are confident that Ireland will produce a generation of vigorous, self-confident men and women who will create a new nation of unsurpassed vitality." Dripping with irony, this marvelous summary of the authors' prescription to cure Ireland's ills clearly shows the "Irish" in Canavan. Impartial observers of Ireland today might legitimately wonder if the country and its bishops have not indeed preferred the Urises to the old Maynooth Seminary—now no longer Jansenist but subsumed into the Irish university system. Canavan himself thought that the effect of the Urises' formula would be to make the once distinct Ireland "just like Europe." If this is progress, we certainly have it.

Not unexpectedly, given his extensive writings on the thought of Edmund Burke and his stature in the field of Burke scholarship, a good portion of Canavan's book reviewing concerns books on Burke. To give some idea of the flavor of Canavan's often pungent reviews of these books, let me begin with a volume with which Canavan was sympathetic, namely Harvey Mansfield's *Selected Letters of Edmund Burke*, which Canavan reviewed in *Interpretation*.[8] Canavan was favorably impressed with this volume. But the reason why I want to begin with this particular review is that in it Canavan reveals both his clear perception of the issues at stake and his own enjoyment of what we might call "making distinctions," or the unexpected delight of the academic vocation. "One might . . . question," Canavan wrote,

> Mansfield's opinion that in Burke's thought the authority of the past and the claims of the future "substitute for divine providence to ensure that present government governs with a sense of shame." Burke's appeals to divine law were too explicit and too frequent to admit of that interpretation.
>
> These may only be the nits that scholars love to pick and which are half the fun of academic life. They do not, in any case, seriously detract from the value of this well-edited selection of Burke's letters.[9]

What is to be admired in this brief comment is not merely its humor but, at the same time, the delicacy with which Canavan deals with the frequently encountered view that Burke was not serious about his references to divine law. Neither the past, nor the future, nor both put together provide, for Burke, a substitute for divine providence.

Canavan's attention to detail can be seen in another way in his review of Michael Freeman's *Edmund Burke and the Critique of Political Radicalism*, which appeared in the *American Political Science Review*.[10] "The book's title is a bit misleading," he remarks, "since it is more a critique of Burke's conservatism than a presentation of his critique of political radicalism. It is a curious lacuna in the work that Freeman does not bother to tell us what was the radical political ideology that Burke attacked." Canavan's ironic phrase, "a curious lacuna," serves to alert the reader that the agenda of the author is other than it appears from his title.

Canavan has waged a constant battle with those interpreters of Burke who refuse to see in him anything more than an advocate of English empiricism or radical historicism. Thus, regarding Stephen Browne's *Edmund Burke and the Discourse of Virtue*, Canavan writes, "Browne's weakness is in his understanding of the foundations of Burke's political thought."[11] This is, of course, a pretty basic weakness. What were those foundations? "They were, at the deepest level, theological, particularly the doctrine of the divine creation of the universe and its governance by divine providence, and philosophical, the doctrine of natural law. Browne's limited understanding of natural law appears in the following paragraph, in which every proposition is simply wrong." (The passage in question is then quoted.) Two weaknesses are cited, one theological in nature and concerning creation, one philosophical and concerning natural law. The book's author seems to have understood neither. Such astute comments, I think, alert the attentive reader to serious problems in the work cited.

Evidently, English scholars in particular have a difficult time understanding the metaphysical side of Burke. They continually want to make Burke into something like Bentham, into a chronicler of facts. This unfortunate propensity finds expression even in the writings of some English scholars whose work Canavan otherwise admires, such as F. P. Lock. Canavan's manner of pointing out this problem is again entertaining and crisp.

> One of Great Britain's more unfortunate exports to her far-flung dominions [Lock was then at the University of Queensland in Australia] has been the empiricist tradition in philosophy. It leaves a scholar, even one empowered with a good mind [as Canavan believes to be the case with Lock] incapable of perceiving any intellectually respectable ground for choice between the simple-minded rationalism of Thomas Paine and what appears as the mysticism and irrationalism of Burke's approach to the transcendent order. Neither of these is acceptable to the empiricist mind. But then, the empiricist mind also has its limitations.[12]

Frequently, in his reviews of books on Burke, Canavan comes across passages in which he himself is mentioned; often there is a paraphrase of his position in the book. An example of this is found in Paul Hindson and Tim Gray's *Burke's Dramatic Theory of Politics.* In this book, the following description of typical natural law thinkers, Canavan included, is presented: "[The] natural law thesis [is that] a single set of moral principles or natural law informs Burke's political philosophy and . . . he simply applies these fixed principles to all political issues." Canavan is pleasingly brusque about this understanding of his thesis: "I must say I cannot imagine a more complete misunderstanding than the words quoted above of what those of us who situated Burke within the tradition of natural law are saying."[13]

One last, and most egregious, misunderstanding of Burke needs to be mentioned, namely, that of Isaac Kramnick's *The Rage of Edmund Burke.* Kramnick, who teaches at Cornell University, has as his evident purpose to show, on the basis of his psychoanalytic reading of Burke, that those scholars, of which Canavan is cited as one, who use Burke as a thinker to "defend Western Civilization" had in mind mainly "the threat of world communism." To counteract this group of conservative thinkers, Kramnick tries to show that Burke himself had an "inner ambivalence" and feeling of doubt about aristocracy. Burke had no objective purpose. He had two warring sides of his personality, which confused sexual roles and political roles.

Canavan has little patience with this sort of analysis, of course. "As one of the persons named in that passage (of Kramnick), I may claim the right to comment on it. I am, as it happens, the world's leading authority on the subject of what I think, and I can testify that in anything I have written on Burke, communism was about the last thing on my mind. I do not recall so much as mentioning it." Canavan, no doubt "the world's leading authority" on what he himself thinks, finally points out that he could use the same dubious methodology on Kramnick as Kramnick used on Burke.

> Thus, one could ask what there is in Kramnick's ethnic, social, cultural and religious heritage that makes him read Burke the way he does. Does his urge to psychoanalyze Burke betray a culturally induced inability to understand what Burke was talking about? Does his own personal ambition explain the kind of scholarship he engages in? What are the sexual hangups that dispose him to find sexual problems lurking everywhere beneath the words and deeds of a public figure?

Canavan acknowledges that this sort of approach to Kramnick's work is probably unfair, but it is difficult to see on what grounds Kramnick could object to it. "After all," Canavan adds, "a mind that can read the writings of Burke from end to end and find little in them beyond 'the revelation of Burke's own tortured self' is the kind of mind that invites speculation about itself."[14] Indeed.

Another side of Canavan's mind is revealed in certain longer reviews that enable him to consider the whole scope of Western history. I am thinking here of his review of the three volumes of Ernest Fortin's *Collected Essays,* of James Hitchcock's *The Decline and Fall of Radical Catholicism*, of Hans Blumenberg's *The Legitimacy of the Modern Age,* and of John Lukacs's

The Passing of the Modern Age. In his sympathetic review of Fortin, Canavan remarks,

> As Fortin himself says, "a number of interlocking themes, all of them controversial, form the warp and woof of these collected essays." He is not a man to shun controversy and will not be surprised when he encounters it. I will conclude by mentioning a few bones that I have to pick with him.
>
> I have never agreed with his insistence that modern papal teaching on natural or, as we now say, human rights is a significant departure from traditional natural-law doctrine, which emphasized duties over rights. He attributes to Aquinas the view that "even without divine grace [human] nature is complete in itself and possesses its own intrinsic perfection in that it has within itself that by means of which it is capable of attaining its end." But this is an understanding of Aquinas that is no longer commonly held. Finally, Fortin acknowledges that Dante wrote as a Christian, but says that whether he also thought as a Christian is open to question. [15]

Each of these issues—the primacy of duties to rights, Aquinas's views on the relationship between divine grace and the *telos* of human nature, and the question of whether Dante was an Averroist who hid his real non-Christian teachings—deserve a booklength treatment. But Canavan at least identifies the key issues.

In his review of the Blumenberg book, a book designed to nullify any classical or medieval critique of modernity, Canavan again shows his familiarity with the relevant theological and philosophical principles at stake:

> Most fundamental to Blumenberg's thesis is his acceptance of the theory, which was current in certain quarters of the late middle ages, that if an omnipotent God creates, he must create everything possible. . . . That is to say that God cannot create unless he creates another God. That may be where a rigorous thinker ends up if he starts with the premises of nominalist metaphysics and epistemology, but Blumenberg pays insufficient attention to the question of whether one must start there. [16]

This comment of Canavan is mindful of something that Etienne Gilson once remarked, that although we are free to choose our first principles, once we choose them, we can no longer think as we want but as we must. The notion that God must create everything possible or that He must create Himself are among the consequences of nominalist first principles. In fact, not only does God not need to create anything, but the one thing He cannot do is "re-create" Himself.

Looking back after thirty years, Canavan's reading of Hitchcock's thesis regarding radical Catholicism still makes very good sense. Writing on the causes of the failure of the *aggiornamento* hoped for after Vatican II, Canavan cites Hitchcock's central thesis: "[T]he radicals have chiefly themselves to blame for the failure. . . . 'The official progressive myth,' he [Hitchcock] says, continues to argue that it was 'not the reformers discovering the inadequacy of their own ideas and programs which brought disillusionment but rather the institutional Church, which refused calls for meaningful reforms.'" "But," adds Canavan, "the myth is false." The real problem was in the minds of the reformers, in their inability to see themselves or their own presuppositions.

At the end of this lengthy review, Canavan adds a comment of his own that puts in a broader context Hitchcock's more narrowly confined discussion. "The most massive and obvious religious phenomenon in modern society," Canavan observes, "is the dechristianization of Western culture. It is not a total dechristianization but it is a profound one, affecting all aspects of social life, and it has been going on for at least three hundred years. It seems to me that any adequate explanation of the situation of the Church in the modern world must account for this mass apostasy from Christianity." Canavan rightly points out that this secularization included both Catholic and Protestant societies, so it cannot be seen as unique to Catholicism. Moreover, this secularization was not carried out by those "disillusioned" with existing Church structures and seeking to reform them. The revolt of modernity was directed at Christianity itself.

Canavan offers a very realistic judgment about the nature of the problem. "To the post-Christian world," he writes,

> Christianity is not the self-revelation of the personal and transcendent God, but a mythological hangover from a more primitive age; Christian morality does not liberate men for the service of God but deforms and oppresses them by its exaggerated and misdirected demands. The post-Christian mind will not be budged from these convictions by anything short of a genuine and thorough religious conversion. No reconciliation through the medium of a progressivist Christianity is really possible.[17]

Cavavan notes that this revolt against Christianity is also a revolt against reason. And he calls attention to the character of Western atheism, which replaces God with man and rejects divine or rationally grounded norms.

Published six months before the Hitchcock review, Canavan's review of John Lukacs's *The Passing of the Modern Age* is titled "The New Dark Ages." He begins the review by citing an unnamed "cynical Jesuit" who remarked that "we have . . . a genius for anticipating the past." This kind of "genius," Canavan playfully remarks, is not a monopoly of Jesuits but is "a common property of liberal Catholic intellectuals today." What is it that this genius proposes? It is that "the Church's only hope for the future . . . is to adapt herself as rapidly as possible to the modern world." But to do this, Canavan thinks, is to adapt oneself not to the future but to the past.[18]

The crisis of culture that Lukacs deals with is "chiefly an interior one." Canavan sympathizes with Lukacs's description of this crisis as it manifests itself in the contemporary world's attitude toward democracy, the state, morality, art, and the Church itself. Elsewhere he notes other manifestations of this same "interior" crisis. "It takes a remarkably unphilosophical mind," he writes in his review of a book by Bernard Nathanson, "to think that being human consists in looking human. But unphilosophical minds are what many Americans have, especially among the opinion making elites." In this review, Canavan in particular noted what happens when we insist in deceiving ourselves about what we are doing. "Prove to the hilt that the unborn child is a fully human being, and the answer of a substantial number of influential people will be, 'so what?' These people have moved beyond denying the humanity of the fetus to questioning the value of human life at any stage if it suffers the misfortune of being 'unwanted' or 'not meaningful.'"[19] In short, even if it's made clear that unborn children are in fact human beings, those committed to abortion will find some other "justification" for their position. Philosophy yields to will.

In an article published in the *Wall Street Journal,* Paul Cassell noted that "Colleen Reed, among many others, deserves to be remembered in any discussion of our error rates (i.e., the number of executions that were in error of facts)." "She was," he continued,

kidnapped, raped, tortured and finally murdered by Kenneth McDuff during the Christmas holidays in 1991. She would be alive today if McDuff had not narrowly escaped

execution three times for two 1966 murders. His life was spared when the Supreme
Court set aside death penalties in 1972, and he was paroled in 1989 because of prison
overcrowding in Texas. After McDuff's release, Reed and at least eight other women
died at his hands. Gov. George W. Bush approved McDuff's execution in 1998.[20]

Many believe that modern states can simply keep types like McDuff in
prison all their lives. But this incident shows that fashionable theories
about the prison's purpose and the nature of the criminal, combined with
concerns about the growing costs of prisons, often cause such murderers
to be released. Surely some civil officials are responsible, along with
McDuff, for these murders.

I bring this matter up here because of Canavan's 1979 review of
Walter Berns's *For Capital Punishment*. Berns remarked that, today, prisons are used to keep criminals "off the streets while they corrupt one
another behind bars." Berns had argued that the purpose of punishment is
not reeducation or reform, nor is it solely the protection of others. It is
also educative, both for the prisoner and for the public. To punish is to
announce what things are seriously wrong and at the same time give the
prisoner personal knowledge of the consequences of his actions.

In this review, however, Canavan recalled a personal incident that
affected his outlook on the matter. "My cousin the cop told me some years
ago of an armed robber who was shot and wounded while fleeing from
the scene of the crime," Canavan recollected in the review.

> Later, lying in his hospital bed, he said to the policeman guarding him: "You know that
> cop that shot me—he's crazy!—man, crazy! You don't shoot people anymore. You used
> to do that, but now you don't shoot people. That cop's crazy!" Having gone on in this
> vein for some time, he then said: "You know, I've done a lot of things and I've got away
> with a lot of things, but I don't think I'll try that any more. I might meet this crazy cop
> again and he might just blow me right out of here."

Reflecting on his cop cousin's narrative, Canavan observes, "I remain
persuaded that we shall always have with us a certain number of people
who need to be convinced that they might just get blown right out of here!"

Canavan then offered the following general reflection on the need and
nature of punishment:

> But we must come to believe again that punishment, regularly and predictably in-
> flicted, will in fact deter, and, moreover, that crime deserves to be punished. Retribu-

tion is not a barbaric reason for punishing; it is the right reason. For only so can the community affirm the moral order in which it is based and can citizens be satisfied that justice is being done. By punishing criminals retributively, the law performs the educative function of blaming their deeds and of approving those who do not commit such deeds. Take that away and you erode society's faith in itself as a moral community where men are trained to obey the laws, and, if they disobey, are punished as moral agents responsible for their own actions.[21]

This is as good a statement of the classical position on the subject that one could find. It is a combination of Canavan's cop cousin's practical wisdom, Walter Berns's logic, Plato's theory of justice, and Aquinas's theory of law.

In conclusion, I think that we see in his reviews and columns the wide range of Canavan's interests and the acuity of his mind. He catches the little, annoying things. He explains the broad truths. Of annoying things, he writes, in a review of *The Crisis of Liberal Democracy*, that although he thought it a very good book, "it is a pity the book crawls with typographical errors to such an extent that one is forced to wonder if anyone proofread it." But he kindly adds, "I have been assured that the errors have been corrected in a second printing."[22] Of broad truths, he observes in the context of a review of Ellis Sandoz's excellent *A Government of Laws*, that "the American founders wrought their handiwork within an understanding of the world shaped by Biblical, classical, and Christian thought, and their work is intelligible only as having been done in no other view of the world. It was ultimately the divine moral order that subordinated government itself to law and denied arbitrary power to any human authority: hence a government of laws, not of men."[23] This statement is both a succinct statement of Professor Sandoz's position and an insightful summary of the principles involved in any theory of government.

Canavan's exasperation at dubious thinking is everywhere evident. Regarding Robert Nozick's famous book, *Anarchy, State, and Utopia*, Canavan asked, "why should one want to defend the inviolable right of the individual to do, not what is good in itself or will make him a better human being or will help him to save his soul, but simply what it pleases him to do?"[24] Yes, why would anyone want this right? I suspect that the real reason is that it is the only way to avoid the implications for the nature and scope of freedom of the three alternative foundations for it that Canavan identifies—what is good in itself, what will make us better human beings, and what we need to do to save our souls.

To conclude this review of Canavan reviews with an unexpected turn, in 1987 the Louisiana State University Press published a book of mine titled *Reason, Revelation, and the Foundations of Political Philosophy*. In looking through Canavan's work I came across a review of this very book. Somehow, I didn't recall that he had reviewed it at the time. So, in the light of what I knew about Canavan's keen wit, it was with some trepidation that I read this review while preparing this essay. The title of the review is "Politics is Only Politics," which is a very accurate summation of what I was trying to argue. Canavan rightly pointed out that the book was not about current political elections. "Ten years from now," he asked rhetorically, "who will remember anything about the 1988 campaign, except that the man who got elected ran against what's-his-name?" Dukakis is not particularly memorable for sure. Canavan understood the audience and the scope of the book. Although the concern that it addresses "may seem speculative and remote from actual political life," it "is in fact a real one in our world. It is to make politics be only politics and nothing more, and to keep political thought from turning itself into a metaphysics—an 'explanation of *all that is*'—or pretending to be a divine revelation."[25] That indeed exactly summarizes my point. Canavan too understood the place of revelation in the argument, as a response to the inability of even the best philosophy to answer all of its own questions. Needless to say, there is at least one author who thinks Canavan is a dandy reviewer!

Thus, the views and reviews of Francis Canavan are well worth remembering and rereading. Canavan writes both for those who believe in God and for those who believe that this is the best possible world. In a column called, "Nearer to the Heart's Desire," Canavan wrote the following lines, mindful of what he had said of the Blumenberg book about modernity, addressed to those who think that God somehow "muffed it" in creation:

> Particularly in recent centuries, God has had a bad press for not making a better job of
> the world that He created. Much of modern atheism is less the result of rigorous

intellectual argument than of emotional refusal to believe in the Creator of a world like this one. People cannot forgive Him for not creating the best of all possible worlds, when He could have done so. If we reflect upon the matter, however, it becomes clear that, if there is no God, this *is* the best of all possible worlds, because it is the only possible world.[26]

The essence of Canavan's mind is found in that passage.

We find a certain soberness in Canavan when he reaches the essence of the modern mind that *will not*—the words remind one of Genesis—accept the possibility of God creating a free creature who must also seek his own destiny freely, even when it is offered to him freely. "Men do not stop believing in God," Canavan writes, "because they have discovered that the world is meaningless. Rather, they conclude that the world is meaningless because they have stopped believing in God. Their reasons for disbelief, no doubt, are many and various. But one of the more powerful ones is a sentimentality that will not accept the world that is as God's world."[27] This "sentimentality that will not accept" is the modern political metaphysics that seeks in every way possible to prove that this is, indeed, the best possible world because it "knows" that God did not create it and therefore men are not responsible for what they do.

The last word belongs to Canavan. He did indeed earn a reputation "merely by being intelligent." And as "a member of a religious order," he knew that utopia, the perfect society, cannot exist in this world, even in—perhaps especially in—religious orders. As far as I can see, this last truth left him with a certain capacity for delight that enabled him to enjoy this less than perfect world in which he lived and, at the same time, enabled him to avoid blaming God if things did not go right. But if Canavan is deserving of any punishment for his worldly and literary deeds, I think it best to call on his cousin, the cop, to administer it.

APPENDIX

Published Writings of Francis Canavan, 1947–2001*

BOOKS:

The Political Reason of Edmund Burke. Durham, N.C.: Duke University Press, 1960.

Freedom of Expression: Purpose as Limit. Durham, N.C.: Carolina Academic Press, 1984.

Edmund Burke: Prescription and Providence. Durham, N.C.: Carolina Academic Press, 1987.

Pins in the Liberal Balloon. New York: National Committee of Catholic Laymen, 1990.

The Political Economy of Edmund Burke: The Role of Property in His Thought. New York: Fordham University Press, 1995.

The Pluralist Game: Pluralism, Liberalism, and the Moral Conscience. Lanham, Md.: Rowman & Littlefield, 1995.

EDITED BOOKS:

The Ethical Dimension of Political Life. Durham, N.C.: Duke University Press, 1983.

Miscellaneous Writings. Vol. 4, *Select Works of Edmund Burke*, a new imprint of the

---

* Book reviews are not included.

Payne Edition, with a new fourth volume. Indianapolis: Liberty Fund, 1999.

ARTICLES, BOOK CHAPTERS, AND PAMPHLETS:

"Evolution of the First Amendment." *America*, 22 November 1947.

"The State as Educator." *Thought* XXV (September 1950).

"Subordination of the State to the Church according to Suarez." *Theological Studies* XII (September 1951).

"The Finality of Sex." *CatholicWorld*, January 1954.

"Fourth Republic: Ideology vs. Politics." *America*, 8 May 1954.

"Northern Ireland: A People Divided." *America*, 6 August 1955.

"Edmund Burke's College Study of Philosophy." *Notes and Queries* (December 1957).

"Civil Rights." *CatholicWorld* (June 1958).

"Edmund Burke's Conception of the Role of Reason in Politics." *Journal of Politics* XXI (February 1959). Reprinted in *Essays in the History of Political Thought*, ed. Isaac Kramnick. Englewood Cliffs, N.J.: Prentice-Hall, 1969. Also in *Perspectives in Political Philosophy*, ed. James V. Downton and David K. Hart. New York: Holt, Rinehart & Winston, 1971.

"Politics and Geography." *America*, 25 July 1959.

"Public Power and Private Rights." *America*, 12 September 1959.

"Politics and Catholicism." *Social Order* (December 1959).

"The Catholic and the Community." *Saint Peter's College Alumni Bulletin*, November 1960.

"The Kissing Has to Stop." *America*, 26 November 1960.

"Obscenity and the Law." *America*, 10 December 1960.

"Christian Ethics and Nuclear Warfare: a Catholic Summary." In *Christian Ethics and NuclearWarfare*, ed. Ulrich S. Allers and William V. O'Brien. Washington, D.C.: Georgetown University,1961.

"Politics and Constitutional Law." *America*, 25 March 1961.

"The Revolution That Failed." *America*, 1 July 1961.

"The Levels of Consensus." *Modern Age* V (Summer 1961).

"The Mood in Britain." *America*, 25 November 1961.

"The Will to Live." *America*, 18 November 1961.

"The Human Touch in Politics." *America*, 23-30 December 1961.

"Reports from France." *America*, 10 February 1962.

"The French Army vs. the OAS." *America*, 7 April 1962.

"Spain and the Common Market." *America*, 7 July 1962.

"Imagination in Politics." *America*, 18 August 1962.

"The Wearing of the Orange." *America*, 23 September 1962.

"After de Gaulle." *America*, 20 October 1962.

"Thomas Paine." In *History of Political Philosophy*, ed. Leo Strauss and Joseph Cropsey. Chicago: Rand McNally, 1963.

"Edmund Burke." In *History of Political Philosophy*, ed. Leo Strauss and Joseph Cropsey. Chicago: Rand McNally, 1963.

"Britain Faces the Future." *America*, 12 January 1963.

"Le Probleme scolaire aux Etats-Unis." *Etudes* (Paris), January 1963.

"The Forbidden Prayer." *Catholic Herald* (London), 8 March 1963.

"The Politics of Religious Equality." *America*, 11 May 1963.

"Peace on Earth." *America*, 22 June 1963.

"New Pluralism or Old Monism." *America*, 9 November 1963.

"Burke as a Reformer." In *The Relevance of Edmund Burke*, ed. Peter J. Stanlis. New York: P. J. Kennedy, 1964.

"Church, State and Council." In *Ecumenism and Vatican II*, ed. Charles O'Neill, S.J. Milwaukee: Bruce, 1964 .

"Man and Space." *Queen's Work*, January 1964.

"Freedom to Die." *America*, 11 January 1964.

"Cigarettes and Brimstone." *America*, 1 February 1964.

"Gentle Thoughts on Murder." *America*, 11 April 1964.

"Conscience and Pluralism." *America*, 18 April 1964.

"Whose Constitution Is It?" *America*, 27 June 1964.

"The Disenchantment of General de Gaulle." *America*, 8 August 1964.

"The School: Whose Is It?" *America*, 15 August 1964. Reprinted as "Qu'est-ce donc aue l'ecole?" *Pedagogie* (Paris), December 1964; and "A qui appartient l'ecole?" *Orientations* (Paris), n.d. [1965].

Politics, Pluralism and Schools. New York: America Press, 1965.

"The New Education Bill." *America*, 23 January 1965.

"Changing Jewish Attitudes." *America*, 13 February 1965.

"Implications of the School Prayer and Bible Reading Decisions: The Welfare State," *Journal of Public Law* 2 (1964).

"Reflections on the Revolution in Sex." *America*, 6 March 1965. Reprinted in *American Catholic Horizons*, ed. E. K. Culhane, S.J. Garden City, N.Y.: Doubleday, 1966.

"Academic Revolution at St. John's." *America*, 7 August 1965.

"Papal Letter on Celibacy." *America*, 30 October 1965.

"The Declaration on Religious Liberty." *America*, 20 November 1965. "Law and Morals in a Pluralist Society." *Pax Romana Journal*, no. 5, 1965. Reprinted in *Catholic Mind*, April 1966; and *Quis Custodiet?* no. 12 (1966).

"St. John's University: The Issues." *America*, 22 January 1966.

"Reforms That Priests Want." *America*, 23 April 1966.

"The Mood of Catholic Education." *America*, 30 April 1966.

"History Repeats Itself." *America*, 21 May 1966. Reprinted in *Human Life Review* 5 (Spring 1979).

"Puerto Rico's Future." *America*, 30 July 1966.

"The Catholic Concept of Religious Freedom as a Human Right." In *Religious Liberty: An End and a Beginning*, ed. John Courtney Murray, S.J. New York: Macmillan, 1966.

The Sex Revolution. New York: America Press, 1966.

"The Church Has the Right to Speak on Public Issues." *Catholic News* (New York), 2 February 1967. Reprinted in *Catholic Mind*, April 1967; and in *Readings in Social Theology*, ed. Everett J. Morgan, S.J. Dayton, Ohio: Pflaum Press, 1969.

"Edmund Burke." *New Catholic Encyclopedia.* New York: McGraw-Hill, 1967.

"To Make a University Great." *America*, 15 July 1967.

"The Catholic Enlightenment." *Triumph*, February 1968.

"Abortion Laws—In Defense Thereof." *Women Lawyers Journal* LIV (Summer 1968).

"High Road to the Gutter." *Triumph*, October 1968.

"Education in a Pluralist Society." In *The Divine Synthesis*. Raleigh, N.C.: Diocese of Raleigh, 1968.

"Student Unrest in Universities." *Bulletin of the Society of Professional Investiga-*

tors, June 1969.

"Rumors of Disbelief." *Triumph*, February 1970.

"The Logic of Contraception." *Triumph*, June 1970.

"Constitutional Casuistry: Cases of Conscience." In *Law and Justice*, ed. Carl Beck. Durham, N.C.: Duke University Press, 1970.

"'University Governance' For What Purpose?" *Point* I (May 1971).

"Freedom of Speech and Press: For What Purpose?" *American Journal of Jurisprudence* XVI (1971). Reprinted in *Readings in American Democracy*, ed. Paul Peterson. Dubuque, Iowa: Kendall/Hunt, 1979.

"An End to Tenure." *Point* II (May 1972).

"What Possible Future?" *Fordham* (Fall 1972).

"The Process That is Due." *Journal of Higher Education* XLIV (February 1973).

"Burke on Prescription of Government." *Review of Politics* 35 (October 1973).

"Individualism and the Malaise of Modernity." *Triumph*, 8 October 1973.

"The Impact of Recent Supreme Court Decisions on Religion in the United States." *Social Studies* (Ireland) III (April 1974): 137-157. Reprinted in *Journal of Church and State* XVI (Spring 1974).

"Civil Law and Society's Conscience." *Law and Justice* 45 (Michaelmas 1974). Reprinted as "Law and Society's Conscience" in *Human Life Review* II (Winter 1976).

"A More Perfect Union: The American Government." In *Forum: Religious Faith Speaks to American Issues*, ed. William A. Norgren. New York: Friendship Series, 1975.

"The Problem of Belief in America." *Communio* II (Winter 1975).

"Knowledge and Politics." *Thought* 50 (December 1975).

"La democratie americaine face a de nouveaux defis." *Projet* (Paris) 107 (Juillet-Aout 1976).

"The Prospects for a United Ireland." In *Prospects for Constitutional Democracy*, ed. John H. Hallowell. Durham, N.C.: Duke University Press, 1976.

"The Theory of the Danforth Case." *Human Life Review* II (Fall 1976): 5-14. Reprinted in *Law & Justice* 58/59 (Trinity/Michaelmas 1978).

"The Burke-Paine Controversy." *Political Science Reviewer* 6 (1976).

"The Problem of Indoctrination." In *The Ethics of Teaching and Scientific*

Research, ed. Sidney Hook, Paul Kurtz, and Miro Todorovich. Buffalo: Prometheus Books, 1977.

"Simple-Minded Separationism." *Human Life Review* 3 (Fall 1977).

"Genetics, Politics and the Image of Man." *Proceedings of the Conference on Fabricated Man and the Law*. St. Louis: Institute for the Theological Encounter with Science and Technology, 1977. Reprinted in *Human Life Review* 4 (Spring 1978).

"ERA: the New Legal Frontier." *Human Life Review* 4 (Fall 1978).

"John Milton and Freedom of Expression." *Interpretation* 7 (1978).

"The Dilemma of Liberal Pluralism." *Human Life Review* 5 (Summer 1979).

"J. S. Mill on Freedom of Expression." *Modern Age* 23 (1979).

"The Pluralist Game." *Law and Contemporary Problems*. 44 (1981). Reprinted in *Christian Faith and Freedom*, ed. Paul L. Williams. Scranton, Pa.: Northeast Books, 1982; and *Human Life Review* 9 (Summer 1983).

"The Justice Amendment." *Human Life Review* 8 (Winter 1982).

"The Founder of Conservatism." *Modern Age* 26 (1982).

"The Girl in the Glass Box." *Human Life Review* 9 (Winter 1983).

"Our Pluralistic Society." *Communio* 9 (1982).

"Murray on Vatican II's *Declaration on Religious Freedom*." *Communio* 9 (1982).

"Liberalism in Root and Flower." In *The Ethical Dimension of Political Life*, ed. Francis Canavan S.J. Durham, N.C.: Duke University Press,1983.

"On Being Personally Opposed." *Human Life Review* 9 (Fall 1983).

"The Pluralist Church." *Human Life Review* 10 (Winter 1984).

"Time Out of Mind: Burke's Constitution." In *Natural Right and Political Right: Essays in Honor of Harry V. Jaffa*, ed. Thomas B. Silver and Peter W. Schramm. Durham, N. C.: Carolina Academic Press, 1984.

"Law and the Value of Human Life." *Human Life Review* 10 (Fall 1984).

"Pluralism and the Limits of Neutrality." In *Whose Values?*, ed. Carl Horn. Ann Arbor, Mich.: Servant Books, 1985.

"The Cuomo Thesis." *Human Life Review* 11 (Winter/Spring 1985).

"A Pearl in the Garbage." *Human Life Review* 11 (Summer 1985).

"A New Fourteenth Amendment." *Human Life Review* 12 (Winter 1986). Reprinted as "Pitfalls of Judicial Review." *Law & Justice* 58 (1987).

"Natural Law and History." *Vera Lex* 6 (1986).

"Judicial Power and the Ninth Amendment." *Intercollegiate Review* 22 (Spring 1987).

"From Tragedy to Farce." *Human Life Review* 13 (Spring 1987).

"Unity in Diversity." *World & I* 2 (September 1987).

"The Relevance of the Burke-Paine Controversy to American Political Thought." *Review of Politics* 49 (1987).

"Religious Freedom: John Courtney Murray, S.J., and Vatican II." *Faith & Reason* 13 (1987). Reprinted in *John Courtney Murray and the American Civil Conversation*, ed. Robert P. Hunt and Kenneth L. Grasso. Grand Rapids, Mich.: Eerdmans, 1992. Also reprinted as "Apostle of Religious Freedom" *Crisis*, May 1993.

"The Civil Rights Game." *Human Life Review* 15 (Winter 1989).

"Government, Individualism, and Mediating Communities." In *A Society in Peril*, ed. Perrotta and Blattner. Ann Arbor, Mich.: Servant Books 1989.

The Light of Faith. Minneapolis: Calix Society, 1989.

"A Liberty Interest." *Human Life Review* 15 (Fall 1989).

"From Frog to Prince." *Human Life Review* 16 (Spring 1990).

"The Popes and the Economy." *First Things* 16 (October 1991). Revised and expanded version published in *Notre Dame Journal of Law, Ethics & Public Policy* 11, 2 (1997).

"American Pluralism vs. American Egalitarianism." In *Church and State in America: Proceedings Fourteenth Convention: Fellowship of Catholic Scholars*, Denver, Colorado 1991, ed. George Kelly. New York: St. John's University Edition, 1992.

"The First Amendment and Pornography." In *Moral Ideas for America*, ed. Larry P. Arnn and Douglas A. Jeffrey. Claremont, Calif.: The Claremont Institute, 1992.

"Political Choice and Catholic Conscience." In *When Conscience and Politics Meet: A Catholic View*. San Francisco: Ignatius Press, 1993.

"The Sexual Revolution, Explained." *New Oxford Review* (November 1993). Reprinted as "The Sexual Revolution Is Immoral." In *Sexual Values: Opposing Viewpoints*, ed. Charles P. Cozic. San Diego: Greenhaven Press, 1994.

"Kirk and the Burke Revival." *Intercollegiate Review* 30 (Fall 1994).

"A Child Is Born." *Crisis*, February 1995.

"Ireland to the Left." *Crisis*, June 1995.

"The Choosing Self." *Human Life Review* 21 (Summer 1995).

"The Image of Man in Catholic Thought." In *Catholicism, Liberalism, and Communitarianism*, ed. Kenneth L. Grasso, Gerard V. Bradley and Robert P. Hunt. Lanham, Md.: Rowman & Littlefield, 1995.

"Debating Abortion." *National Review*, 17 June 1996.

"A Truly 'Eerie' Film?" *New Oxford Review* (September 1996).

"On Restoring the Natural Law." *Catholic Social Science Review* I (1996).

"Burke and the Problem of Constitutional Liberty," in *Liberty Under Law: American Constitutionalism Yesterday, Today, and Tomorrow*, Kenneth L. Grasso & Cecilia Rodriguez Castillo, eds. Lanham, Md.: University Press of America, 1997.

"A Horror of the Absolute." *Human Life Review* 23 (Winter 1997).

"Problems with Darwinism." *New Oxford Review* 64, 3 (April 1997).

"That Eminent Tribunal." *First Things* 85 (August-September 1998).

"Intimate Relationships." *New Oxford Review* 66, 4 (April 1999).

"Foreword" and "Biographical Note." In *Select Works of Edmund Burke*, 4 vols., a new imprint of the Payne Edition, plus a new fourth volume, *Miscellaneous Writings*. Indianapolis: Liberty Fund, 1999.

"The Empiricist Mind." *Human Life Review* 25 (Spring 1999).

"Lifestyle Trumps Morality." *Human Life Review* 25 (Fall 1999).

"The Dying of the Mind." *Human Life Review* 26 (Summer 2000).

NOTES

Introduction: The Achievement of Francis Canavan
by Kenneth L. Grasso and Robert P. Hunt

1. Bradley's remark appears on the back cover of the paperback edition of *The Pluralist Game: Pluralism, Liberalism, and the Moral Conscience* (Lanham, Md.: Rowman & Littlefield, 1995), a book that contains a number of Father Canavan's most important essays on law, religious pluralism, and public morality.
2. John Hallowell, *The Moral Foundation of Democracy* (Chicago: University of Chicago Press, Midway reprint, 1973), 89.
3. Peter J. Stanlis, review of *Edmund Burke: Prescription and Providence*, in *Review of Politics* 50 (1988): 743–47.
4. Francis Canavan, *Edmund Burke: Prescription and Providence* (Durham, N.C.: Carolina Academic Press and Claremont Institute of Statesmanship and Political Philosophy, 1989), xiii.
5. Ibid., 4, 13.
6. Francis Canavan, editor's foreword to *Select Works of Edmund Burke: A New Imprint of the Payne Edition* (Indianapolis: Liberty Fund, 1999), 1:xii.
7. Francis Canavan, *The Political Reason of Edmund Burke* (Durham, N.C.: Duke University Press, 1960), 95.
8. Francis Canavan, "The Relevance of the Burke-Paine Controversy to American Thought," *Review of Politics* 49 (1987): 175.
9. *The Political Reason of Edmund Burke,* 194.
10. "The Relevance of the Burke-Paine Controversy," 175.
11. See George Weigel, *Catholicism and the Renewal of American Democracy* (New York: Paulist Press, 1989).
12. *The Pluralist Game,* 115, 118.
13. Ibid., 132–33.
14. Ibid., 134, 133, 137.

15. Francis Canavan, "The Image of Man in Catholic Social Thought," in *Catholicism, Liberalism, and Communitarianism: The Catholic Intellectual Tradition and the Moral Foundations of Democracy*, ed. Kenneth L. Grasso, Gerard V. Bradley, and Robert P. Hunt (Lanham, Md.: Rowman & Littlefield, 1995), 20.

16. Ibid., 18.

17. Ibid., 22.

18. Francis Canavan, "The Popes and the Economy," *First Things* 16 (October 1991): 35–41.

19. Edmund Burke, "First Letter on a Regicide Peace," in *The Works of the Right Honorable Edmund Burke* (London: Rivington, 1803–1827), 8:87.

20. "Letter to Sir Hercules Langrishe," in *Works*, 6:309.

21. George's remark appears on the back cover of the paperback version of *The Pluralist Game*.

22. Francis Canavan, *Pins in the Liberal Balloon: Sixty Short Essays on the Church in the Modernist World* (New York: The National Committee of Catholic Laymen, 1990), 52.

Chapter I: Edmund Burke and British Views of the American Revolution: A Conflict over Rights of Sovereignty, by Peter J. Stanlis

1. Francis Bernard, *Select Letters on the Trade and Government of America* (London, 1774), 31–32.

2. *The Letters of Horace Walpole*, ed. Helena Paget Toynbee (Oxford, 1903), 8: 449. Walpole's pro-American views are well described by J. C. Reily, "Horace Walpole, Friend of American Liberty," in *Studies in Burke and His Time*, vol. 16, no. 1 (1974): 5–21.

3. *Letters of David Hume*, ed. John Y. Greig (Oxford, 1946), 2:237, 300–01.

4. *The Letters of James Boswell*, ed. Chancey Brewster Tinker (Oxford, 1924), 1:233.

5. See Davis Stevens, "Adam Smith and the Colonial Disturbances," in A. S. Skinner and T. Wilson, eds., *Essays on Adam Smith* (Oxford, 1975), 202–17.

6. Francis Hutcheson, *System of Moral Philosophy* (1755), vol. 2, bk. 2, 308.

7. *Gentleman's Magazine* (1775), 445, 597, and (1776), 136 respectively.

8. *Memoirs of the Life of Edward Gibbon*, ed. George Birkbeck Hill (London, 1900), 212–13.

9. *The Works of Samuel Johnson*, ed. Arthur Murphy (London, 1850), 2:612.

10. Ibid., 617.

11. Ibid., 626.

12. Edmund Burke, "Speech on American Taxation," in *Works*, 1:435.

13. Ibid., 404.

14. Ibid., 405–6.

15. Later, in his speech in support of a motion to repeal the tax on tea, Burke observed in retrospect that "at the close of the last war large additions were made unnecessarily to the English army." See *Burke's Speeches on American Taxation, on Conciliation with America and Letter to the Sheriffs of Bristol*, ed. F. G. Selby (London, 1956), introduction, xxxi. Also, in his "Speech Introducing a Motion for an Enquiry into the Causes of the Late Disorders in America" (May 9, 1770), he noted that "the Stamp Act was to go to the pay of the army; but this struck at the root of their assemblies. . . ." He added: "They deny your right to send out an army to them. They have resolved that the establishment of a standing army is an invasion of the rights of the people." *Edmund Burke on the American Revolution*, ed. Elliott R. Barkan (New York, 1966), 11, 14.

16. *Works,* 1:279.

17. Ibid., 401.

18. *Sir Henry Cavendish's Debates of the House of Commons*, ed. John Wright (London, 1841–43), 1:

398–99. See also, *Writings and Speeches*, 2:231–32.

19. *Works*, 1:434.

20. Ibid., 435.

21. Ibid., 432–33.

22. Rockingham to William Dowdeswell, September 13, 1774, in Wentworth Woodhouse MSSR-1504, Rockingham Papers, Sheffield Public Library.

23. *Works*, 2:31.

24. Edmund Burke, *On Conciliation with the Colonies and Other Papers on the American Revolution*, ed. Peter J. Stanlis (Lunenburg, 1975), 165.

25. *Works*, 1: 509. The first half of Burke's aphorism is carved on the pedestal of his statue in Washington, D.C..

26. *Works*, 5: 465.

27. Ibid., 462.

28. Ibid., 479. He added that the colonial charters "ought by no means to be altered at all but at the desire of the greater part of the people who live under them."

29. *Parliamentary History*, 19: 517.

Chapter II: Burke and Human Rights, by F. P. Lock

1. Louis Henkin, *The Age of Rights* (New York: Columbia University Press, 1990).

2. A. Owen Aldridge, "The Case for Edmund Burke," *The Eighteenth Century: Theory and Interpretation*, 36 (1995): 83–90; quotation from 85.

3. This is not to minimize the importance of different theories about the origins of rights. For Burke, "natural rights" derived from the natural law, and therefore ultimately from God. The prevailing secularism of our time prefers to regard them as "inherent" and therefore "human." Nevertheless, different opinions about the origins of rights need not impede agreement about a descriptive list of such rights, a task to which (as I suggest) Burke is relevant. Aquinas offers a suggestive parallel. As John Finnis has argued, although he uses no term translatable as "human rights," he clearly possessed the concept, and his treatment of rights may therefore be relevant to modern societies; *Aquinas: Moral, Political, and Legal Theory* (Oxford: Oxford University Press, 1998), 136–7.

4. *"Nonsense upon Stilts": Bentham, Burke and Marx on the Rights of Man*, ed. Jeremy Waldron (London: Methuen, 1987).

5. "Appeal from the New to the Old Whigs" (1791), in *Works* (London: Bohn, 1854–89), 3:11.

6. References to the *Reflections* (abbreviated as *R*) are to the edition by J. C. D. Clark (Palo Alto, Calif.: Stanford University Press, 2000).

7. In their anthology *Western Liberalism: A History in Documents from Locke to Croce* (London: Longman, 1978), E. K. Bramstead and K. J. Melhuish exclude Burke on the ground that he "repudiated the doctrine of natural rights" (157).

8. The *Déclaration* was debated during August 1789 and presented to the king for approval on October 2; a convenient text is in *French Revolution Documents*, ed. J. M. Roberts (Oxford: Blackwell, 1966), 1:171–3.

9. Keith Michael Baker, "The Idea of a Declaration of Rights," in *The French Idea of Freedom: the Old Régime and the Declaration of Rights of 1789*, ed. Dale Van Kley (Palo Alto, Calif.: Stanford University Press, 1994), 154–96.

10. Adda B. Bozeman, *The Future of Law in a Multicultural World* (Princeton, N.J.: Princeton University Press, 1971), 96–7, 24–5, 148; Chris Brown, "Universal Human Rights: A

Critique," in *Human Rights in Global Politics*, ed. Tim Dunne and Nicholas J. Wheeler (Cambridge: Cambridge University Press, 1999), 103–27.

11. Mary Ann Glendon, *Rights Talk: The Impoverishment of Political Discourse* (New York: Free Press, 1991); Charles Taylor, "Atomism," in *Philosophy and the Human Sciences: Philosophical Papers* (Cambridge: Cambridge University Press, 1985), 187–210. The quotation from Hobbes is from *Leviathan*, pt. 1, chap. 13.

12. Adamantia Pollis and Peter Schwab, "Human Rights: A Western Construct with Limited Applicability," in *Human Rights: Cultural and Ideological Perspectives*, ed. Pollis and Schwab (New York: Praeger, 1979), 1–18.

13. Waldron, *Nonsense upon Stilts*, 166–209; R. J. Vincent, *Human Rights and International Relations* (Cambridge: Cambridge University Press, 1986); Charles Taylor, "Conditions of an Unforced Consensus on Human Rights," in *The Politics of Human Rights*, ed. Obrad Savic (London: Verso, 1999), 101–19.

14. Michael Ignatieff, *The Rights Revolution* (Toronto: Anansi, 2000), 10. Johannes Morsink, *The Universal Declaration of Human Rights: Origins, Drafting, and Intent* (Philadelphia: University of Pennsylvania Press, 1999) defends the Declaration against the charge of ethnocentricism.

15. Joseph Pappin III, "Burke's Philosophy of Rights," in *The Enduring Edmund Burke: Bicentenary Essays*, ed. Ian Crowe (Wilmington, Del.: Intercollegiate Studies Institute, 1997), 115–27.

16. Quentin Skinner, "Meaning and Understanding in the History of Ideas" (1969), reprinted in *Meaning and Context: Quentin Skinner and His Critics*, ed. James Tully (Cambridge: Polity Press, 1988), 32–43.

17. Draft for Speech on the Unitarian Petition, May 11, 1792, in *Works*, 6:113–14.

18. Other examples include "these new doctors of the rights of men" (*R* 32) and "their rights, as men, to take fortresses, to murder guards, to seize on kings" (*R* 321). I count about thirty such passages.

19. *The Works of Samuel Johnson*, ed. Arthur Murphy (London, 1850), 3:11.

20. *R* 87. The passage in square brackets was an afterthought, added to the third edition. The first edition reads "But as to the share [etc.]."

21. "Thoughts and Details on Scarcity" (1795), in *Writings and Speeches*, ed. Paul Langford and others (Oxford: Clarendon Press, 1981), 9:143–4.

22. Francis Canavan, *The Political Economy of Edmund Burke: The Role of Property in His Thought* (New York: Fordham University Press, 1995), 116–46.

23. As seems to be implied by Article 23 (1) of the United Nations Universal Declaration of Human Rights.

24. F. P. Lock, *Edmund Burke* (Oxford: Clarendon Press, 1998), 1:319–23

25. "Thoughts and Details on Scarcity" (1795), in *Writings and Speeches*, 9:120–45.

26. Francis Canavan, *Edmund Burke: Prescription and Providence* (Durham: Carolina Academic Press, 1987), especially 107–12.

27. Lock, *Edmund Burke*, 1:330–3.

28. Though Burke had been increasingly hostile to the Dissenters since 1784, only in January 1790, when he learned of Price's anniversary sermon, did his enmity become public.

29. "Notes for a Speech on the Dissenters Bill," April 1779, in *Writings and Speeches*, 3:432–5.

30. Peter J. Stanlis, *Edmund Burke and the Natural Law* (Ann Arbor, Mich.: University of Michigan Press, 1958), 43–5.

31. *Writings and Speeches*, 9:436–44.

32. *Writings and Speeches*, 9:449–50.

33. *Writings and Speeches*, 9:445.

34. Conor Cruise O'Brien, *The Great Melody* (Chicago: University of Chicago Press, 1992), 40–1.

35. Burke to Sir Lawrence Parsons, March 7, 1793, in *Correspondence*, ed. Thomas W. Copeland and others (Cambridge: Cambridge University Press, 1958–78), 7:359.

36. *Writings and Speeches*, 9:476.

37. W. E. H. Lecky, *History of Ireland in the Eighteenth Century* (London: Longmans, Green, 1892), 2:212–17, 311–14.

38. *Writings and Speeches*, 9:606, 625.

39. Draft for Speech on the Unitarian Petition, May 11, 1792; Northamptonshire Record Office, Fitzwilliam (Burke) Papers, A.xxvii.102.

40. Locke, *Two Treatises*, 2:8:95; Paul Langford, *Public Life and the Propertied Englishman, 1689–1798* (Oxford: Clarendon Press, 1991).

41. Draft for Speech on the Unitarian Petition, May 11, 1792; Northamptonshire Record Office, Fitzwilliam (Burke) Papers, A.xxvii.99.

42. "Letter to Sir Hercules Langrishe" (1792), in *Writings and Speeches*, 9:625.

43. John Elster, "Majority Rule and Individual Rights," in *On Human Rights*, ed. Stephen Shute and Susan Hurley (New York: Basic Books, 1993), 176–216, 249–56. Elster refers to the debates in the Constituent Assembly, but not to Burke.

44. "Speech on the Duration of Parliaments," May 8, 1780, in *Writings and Speeches*, 3:590.

45. "Speech on the Unitarian Petition," May 11, 1792, in *Works*, 6:113–14.

46. "Speech on 3 February 1766," in *Writings and Speeches*, 2:50.

47. "Tract on the Popery Laws," in *Writings and Speeches*, 9:454–5.

48. "First Letter on a Regicide Peace" (1796), in *Writings and Speeches*, 9:249.

49. *Empire and Community: Edmund Burke's Writings and Speeches on International Relations*, ed. David P. Fidler and Jennifer M. Welsh (Boulder, Colo.: Westview Press, 1999), introduction, especially 40–2, 61.

50. "Speech on 16 February 1788," in *Writings and Speeches*, 6:346–52.

51. Lock, *Edmund Burke*, 1:488–9.

52. Abdullahi Ahmed An-Na'im, "Towards a Cross-Cultural Approach to Defining International Standards of Human Rights: A Meaning of Cruel, Inhuman, or Degrading Treatment or Punishment," in *Human Rights in Cross-Cultural Perspectives: A Quest for Consensus*, ed. An-Na'im (Philadelphia: University of Pennsylvania Press, 1992), 19–43.

53. Vincent, *Human Rights and International Relations*, 131.

54. John Rawls, "The Law of Peoples," in *On Human Rights*, ed. Shute and Hurley, 42–82, 220–30; quotations from 68, 70.

55. I am grateful to Dr. J. A. W. Gunn for reading an early version of this essay, and to Dr. J. C. D. Clark for allowing me to make pre-publication use of his new edition of *Reflections on the Revolution in France*.

Chapter III: Edmund Burke on Tradition and Human Progress: Ordered Liberty and the Politics of Change, by Joseph Pappin III

1. *Correspondence of the Right Honourable Edmund Burke*, ed. Charles Williams, Earl Fitzwilliam, and Sir Richard Bourke (London: Francis and John Rivington, 1844), 4:465.

2. Anthony Quinton, "Conservatism," in *A Companion to Contemporary Political Philosophy*, ed. Robert E. Goodin and Philip Pettit (Oxford: Blackwell Publishers, Ltd., 1995), 253.

3. Conor Cruise O'Brien, *The Great Melody: A Thematic Biography and Commented Anthology of Edmund Burke* (London: Sinclair-Stevenson, 1992). See the "Appendix: An Exchange with Sir Isaiah Berlin," 605–18, esp. 608.

4. A.N. Whitehead, *Adventures of Ideas* (New York: Macmillan, 1954), 354.

5. Edmund Burke, "Speech on Conciliation with America." *The Works of the Right Honourable Edmund Burke* (London: Bohn's British Classics, 8 vols., 1854–89), 1:501.

6. *Correspondence,* 4:465.

7. "Appeal from the New to the Old Whigs," in *Works,* 3:16.

8. *Works,* 6:113.

9. "Letter to a Member of the National Assembly," in *Works,* 2:564.

10. *Works,* 2:295.

11. "Speech on the Impeachment of Warren Hastings," February 16, 1788, in *Works,* 7:99.

12. "Tracts on the Popery Laws," in *Works,* 6:21.

13. "Speech on the Impeachment of Warren Hastings," February 15, 1788, in *Works,* 7:14, and February 16, 1788, in *Works,* 7:101.

14. *The Correspondence of Edmund Burke*, ed. Thomas W. Copeland, 10 vols. (Cambridge: Cambridge University Press; Chicago: The University of Chicago Press, 1958–78). References above found in *Correspondence,* 3:374; 4:416; 9:48; 6:266; 9:84; and 10:40.

15. "Speech on the Petition of the Unitarians," in *Works,* 6:113–14.

16. Jean Le Rond d'Alembert, *Preliminary Discourse to the Encyclopedia of Diderot*, trans. Richard N. Schwab (Indianapolis: Bobbs-Merrill, 1963), 84–85.

17. Ibid., 84.

18. Baron d'Holbach, *System of Nature*, trans. H. D. Robinson, (Boston: Mendum, 1853), 48.

19. Ibid., 44.

20. "On the Interpretation of Nature," in *Diderot's Selected Writings*, ed. Lester G. Crocker (New York: Macmillan, 1966), 86–87.

21. "Reflections," in *Works,* 2:455.

22. "Speech on Representation in Commons, 1782," in *Works,* 6:148.

23. "Philosophical Inquiry into the Sublime and the Beautiful," in *Works,* 1:127.

24. Ibid., 143.

25. Ibid., 85.

26. *Correspondence,* 6:460. Cf. Francis Canavan, S.J., *The Political Reason of Edmund Burke* (Durham, N.C.: Duke University Press, 1960), 19. In this groundbreaking study of Burke, Canavan states, "The central idea in Burke's thought was that of order," and he claims that "[d]espite [Burke's] constant denunciations of 'metaphysics,' his thought had unmistakable metaphysical foundations. . . ."

27. "Appeal from the New to the Old Whigs," in *Works,* 3:80.

28. "First Letter on a Regicide Peace," in *Works,* 5:213–14.

29. Ibid., 216.

30. "Speech on the Impeachment of Warren Hastings," June 12, 1794, in *Works,* 8:275.

31. Ibid.

32. St. Thomas Aquinas, *Summa Contra Gentiles*, trans. Anton C. Pegis (Notre Dame, Ind.: University of Notre Dame Press, 1975), bk. 1, chap. 11.

33. "Reflections," in *Works,* 2:364.

34. "Speech on the Impeachment of Warren Hastings," February 16, 1788, *Works,* 7:93–94.

35. Ibid., 16.

36. Alasdair MacIntyre, *Whose Justice? Which Rationality?* (Notre Dame, Ind.: University of Notre Dame Press, 1988), 217–19.

37. "Speech on Representation in Commons, 1782," *Works* 6:146.

38. *Reflections, Works* 2:422.

39. *Correspondence* 6:95.

40. "Speech on Representation in Commons" (1782), in *Works,* 6:146.

41. *Correspondence*, 1844, 4:460.

42. *Works,* 2:83 and 64.

43. "Reflections," in *Works,* 2:364.

44. "Speech on Conciliation with America," in *Works,* 1:464.

45. Alasdair MacIntyre, *After Virtue*, 2nd ed. (Notre Dame, Ind.: University of Notre Dame Press, 1984), 222.

46. Ibid.

47. "Reflections," in *Works,* 2:435.

48. "Appeal from the New Whigs to the Old," in *Works,* 3:80.

49. *Works,* 3:340.

50. Ibid.

51. *Correspondence*, 1:130.

52. *Works,* 5:164.

53. "Speech on the Impeachment of Warren Hastings," June 12, 1794, in *Works,* 7:274.

54. "Reflections," in *Works,* 2:308–09.

55. "Letter to a Member of the National Assembly," in *Works,* 2:555.

56. "Reflections," in *Works,* 2:307.

57. "Speech on the Impeachment of Warren Hastings," February 16, 1788, in *Works,* 7:60.

58. Ibid., June 3, 1794, 8:59.

59. Ibid.

60. "Reflections," in *Works,* 2:304.

61. "Speech on the Impeachment of Warren Hastings," February 16, 1788, in *Works,* 7:101–02.

62. "Letter to a Member of the National Assembly," in *Works,* 2:553.

63. "Letter to the Sheriffs of Bristol," in *Works,* 2:7–8.

64. Ibid., 30.

65. "Reflections," in *Works,* 2:405.

66. "Letter to the Sheriffs of Bristol," in *Works,* 2:40.

67. "Letter to a Member of the National Assembly," in *Works,* 2:555.

68. "First Letter on a Regicide Peace," in *Works,* 5:216.

69. "Reflections," in *Works,* 2:368.

70. Michael Freeman, *Edmund Burke and the Critique of Political Radicalism* (Oxford: Blackwell, 1980), 99.

71. "Letter to William Elliot," in *Works,* 5:76.

72. *Correspondence*, 7:387.

73. "Speech on the Duration of Parliaments," in *Works,* 6:132.

74. *Correspondence*, 2:150.

75. "Reflections," in *Works,* 2:307.

76. "First Letter on a Regicide Peace," in *Works,* 5:153, 154.

77. "Philosophical Inquiry into the Sublime and Beautiful," in *Works,* 1:78.

78. "Second Letter on a Regicide Peace," in *Works,* 5:236.

79. Ibid.

80. "Appeal from the New Whigs to the Old," in *Works,* 3:79.

81. "Speech on the East-India Bill," in *Works,* 2:197.

82. "Reflections," in *Works,* 2:364.

83. "Speech on Conciliation with America," in *Works,* 1:509.

84. "Reflections," in *Works,* 2:370

85. "First Letter on a Regicide Peace," in *Works,* 5:153.

86. "Reflections," *Works,* 2:353.

87. *Correspondence,* 6:439.

88. *Correspondence,* 7:17.

89. Ibid., 9:317.

90. "Speech on Conciliation with America," in *Works,* 1:486.

91. "Letter to the Sheriffs of Bristol," in *Works,* 2:33.

92. "An Abridgment of English History," in *Works,* 6:294.

93. "Letter to a Member of the National Assembly," in *Works,* 2:554.

94. "Reflections," in *Works,* 2:358.

95. "Speech on Conciliation with America," in *Works,* 1:477.

96. "Speech on the Economical Reform," in *Works,* 2:58.

97. "Reflections," in *Works,* 2:516–17.

98. *Correspondence,* 1844, 4:465.

99. "Speech on Economic Reform," in *Works,* 2:64.

100. Ibid.

101. Ibid., 64–65.

102. Ibid., 65.

103. *Correspondence,* 6:48.

104. "Letter to Sir Hercules Langrishe," in *Works,* 3:340.

105. "Appeal from the New to the Old Whigs," in *Works,* 3:16.

106. *Correspondence,* 6:48–49.

107. "Letter to Sir Hercules Langrishe," in *Works,* 3:309.

108. "Letter to a Member of the National Assembly," in *Works,* 2:535.

109. "Reflections," in *Works,* 2:368–69.

110. Ibid., 310.

Chapter IV: The Problematical Relation between Practical and Theoretical Virtue in Aristotle's *Nicomachean Ethics*, by Germaine Paulo Walsh

1. Aristotle's presentation of the relationship between the human good and happiness is rather ambiguous. Although he certainly associates the two, he does not define them in quite the same way. According to Ronna Burger, "Aristotle's 'Exclusive' Account of Happiness: Contemplative Wisdom as a Guise of the Political Philosopher," in *The Crossroads of Norm and Nature: Essays on Aristotle's* Ethics *and* Metaphysics, ed. May Sim (Lanham, Md.: Rowman & Littlefield, 1995), Aristotle does not ever identify happiness precisely with the human good, given that happiness is something final or complete, whereas the human good, Aristotle subtly suggests, is essentially the "search itself" for "the sought-for human good," 85; see also 96, note 31.

2. While there are sections of the *Nicomachean Ethics* (hereafter, *NE*) other than X.7–8 which have sparked much controversy over Aristotle's understanding of the human good, especially the two accounts of pleasure—the first in VII.11–14 and the second in X.1–5—it is X.7–8 that is believed to be Aristotle's clearest statement about the incompatibility of theoretical and practical activity, and the superiority of the former over the latter.

3. I am not claiming that all the interpretations of the *NE* can easily be reduced to two, but that with respect to the specific issue of the role of theoretical activity in human happiness, there are two general ways of understanding how it fits into Aristotle's overall theory.

4. Stephen R. L. Clark, *Aristotle's Man* (Oxford: Clarendon Press, 1975); John Cooper, *Reason*

and the Human Good in Aristotle (Indianapolis: Hackett Publishing Co., 1986); W. F. R. Hardie, *Aristotle's Ethical Theory* (Oxford: Oxford University Press, 1980); Anthony Kenny, *The Aristotelian Ethics* (Oxford: Oxford University Press, 1978); Richard Kraut, *Aristotle on the Human Good* (Princeton, N.J.: Princeton University Press, 1989); Carnes Lord, *Education and Culture in the Political Thought of Aristotle* (Ithaca, N.Y.: Cornell University Press, 1982); Leo Strauss, *The City and Man* (Chicago: University of Chicago Press, 1964); and Aristide Tessitore, *Reading Aristotle's* Ethics: *Virtue, Rhetoric, and Political Philosophy* (Albany, N.Y.: State University of New York Press, 1996).

5. There are two different versions of the "exclusive" interpretation. According to the more extreme version, referred to by scholars as the "intellectualist" version, Aristotle's arguments in X.7–8 show that happiness consists solely in theoretical contemplation, and thus that practical virtue does not play any role in happiness. See Clark, Cooper, and Kenny. According to the more widely accepted version of the exclusive interpretation, referred to by scholars sometimes as the "dominant" version, and sometimes as the "two lives" version, Aristotle argues that there are two different kinds of happiness possible for human beings, one associated primarily with theoretical activity (which these scholars identify with philosophy per se), the other with practical activity. Those who argue in favor of this position assert that the sublime pleasure of theoretical activity is so intense that it leads "philosophers" to view practical activity as a distraction. That is, although moral virtue is not necessarily inimical to intellectual virtue, it is virtually impossible for a person to devote himself to both types of activities. See Hardie, Kraut, Lord, Strauss, and Tessitore. In recent years there has been such severe criticism of the "intellectualist" version that one well-known supporter of this view has abandoned it in favor of the "dominant" or "two lives" view; see John Cooper, "Contemplation and Happiness: A Reconsideration," *Synthese* 72 (1987): 187–216.

6. J. L. Ackrill, "Aristotle on *Eudaimonia*," in *Essays on Aristotle's* Ethics, ed. Amelie Oksenberg Rorty (Berkeley: University of California Press, 1980); Ronna Burger, "Aristotle's 'Exclusive' Account of Happiness," "The Argument and Action of Aristotle's *Ethics*," Lecture in the Series "Gestalten und Werke der Antike," Siemens Stiftung, Munich, June 1994; "Wisdom, Philosophy, and Happiness: On Book X of Aristotle's *Ethics*," in *Proceedings of the Boston Area Colloquium in Ancient Philosophy*, ed. J. Cleary and D. Shartin (Lanham, Md.: University Press of America, 1992); and "Ethical Reflection and Righteous Indignation: *Nemesis* in the *Nicomachean Ethics*," in *Essays in Ancient Greek Philosophy*, vol. 4, *Aristotle's Ethics*, ed. J. Anton and A. Preus (Albany, N.Y.: State University of New York Press, 1991); Trond Berg Erikson, *Bios Theoretikos* (Oslo: The Norwegian Council for Science and the Humanities, 1976); Werner Wilhelm Jaeger, *Aristotle: The Fundamentals of the History of His Development* (Oxford: Clarendon Press, 1948); David Keyt, "Intellectualism in Aristotle," in *Essays in Ancient Greek Philosophy*, vol. 2, ed. J. Anton and A. Preus (Albany, N.Y.: State University of New York, 1983); Jon Moline, "Contemplation and the Human Good," *Nous*, March 1983: 37–53; J. D. Monan, *Moral Knowledge and Its Methodology in Aristotle* (Oxford: Clarendon Press, 1968); Mary P. Nichols, *Citizens and Statesmen: A Study of Aristotle's* Politics (Lanham, Md.: Rowman & Littlefield, 1992); "Response to Aristotle's Science of the Best Regime," *American Political Science Review* 89 (1995): 152–55; Martha C. Nussbaum, *The Fragility of Goodness: Luck and Ethics in Greek Tragedy and Philosophy* (Cambridge: Cambridge University Press, 1986); Nancy Sherman, *The Fabric of Character: Aristotle's Theory of Virtue* (Oxford: Clarendon Press, 1989); and Jennifer Whiting, "Human Nature and Intellectualism in Aristotle," *Archiv für Geschichte der Philosophie* 68 (1986): 70–95.

7. There are three distinct versions of the "inclusive" interpretation. According to one version,

which I refer to as the "Platonic remnant" view, although Aristotle does indeed understand theoretical activity to be an essential part of happiness, his arguments in X.7–8 are a "remnant" of his earlier Platonism, there due to editorial oversight, lingering confusion, or out of respect for the Platonic position. That is, given the anomalous character of Aristotle's statements in X.7–8, it is appropriate to dismiss his arguments there altogether. For arguments in favor of the "Platonic remnant" view, see Nussbaum, Monan, Erikson, and Jaeger. According to a second version of the "inclusive" interpretation, referred to by some scholars as the "superstructure" view, Aristotle does not argue that one must choose between practical and theoretical activity, but rather that the happy life is one which in some way combines aspects of both. Aristotle's statements in X.7–8 are not irreconcilable with the rest of the *NE*, but are intended to stimulate further reflection on the complexity of the human good, in light of the special place of theoretical activity within the happy life. For arguments in favor of the "superstructure" view, see Ackrill, Keyt, Sherman, and Whiting. According to a third version of the inclusive interpretation, which I refer to as the "deeds as test" view, Aristotle's statements in X.7–8 are indeed anomalous, but purposefully so, with the intent of sparking further reflection about the meaning of happiness. Aristotle calls into question his own explanation of happiness as consisting in theoretical activity immediately after making it, by raising the question of whether this theory about happiness is confirmed by "the deeds" or "facts" (*ta erga*) of life (1179a17–23). For arguments in favor of the "deeds as test" view, see Burger, "Aristotle's 'Exclusive' Account of Happiness," "The Argument and Action of Aristotle's *Ethics*," "Wisdom, Philosophy, and Happiness," and "Ethical Reflection and Righteous Indignation"; Moline, "Contemplation and the Human Good"; and Nichols, *Citizens and Statesmen*, and "Response to Aristotle's Science of the Best Regime."

8. The distinction between these two kinds of thinking is a fundamental issue throughout Aristotle's analysis of the intellectual virtues. To excel in practical thinking or prudence is to understand those things that are "variable," especially human actions or affairs, while to excel in theoretical thinking or simply "wisdom" is to understand those things that are "invariable," which Aristotle sometimes refers to as the "highest things." There are some difficulties of translation in this context of which the reader should be aware. In VI.1–2, Aristotle refers to these two kinds of thinking in a rather straightforward fashion, as *praktike dianoia*, i.e., "practical thinking," and *theoretike dianoia*, i.e., "theoretical thinking." Beginning in VI.3, however, Aristotle refers to these two types of thinking differently. There he uses the word *phronesis*, which is generally translated as "practical wisdom," or "prudence." "Prudence" is, I think, the better translation of *phronesis*; to refer to it as "practical wisdom" is somewhat misleading, since Aristotle goes on to use the word *sophia*, which means simply "wisdom," in reference to strictly theoretical activity. That is, given the way in which Aristotle defines *sophia* in VI.7, most scholars assume that he means that "real" wisdom is theoretical thinking, and thus they usually translate *sophia* as "theoretical wisdom." Adding to these somewhat confusing difficulties is Aristotle's use of *theoria* throughout Book VI, and in other parts of the *NE*. As a verb, Aristotle uses *theorein* in its more general meaning of "to study" or "to apprehend" something. That is, in using it as a verb, he does not apply it only to the study of "invariable things." Despite this fact, however, scholars often translate it as "contemplate" rather than "study" or "apprehend," when it is used in reference to the "invariable things." When used as a noun, however, Aristotle seems to use *theoria* as a synonym of *sophia*, i.e., in reference to theoretical thinking only. Given these problems of translation, I will indicate the Greek fairly frequently.

9. For a similar argument, see Moline, who argues that X.7–8 is in fact a "flirtation with

Anaxagorean intellectualism" that is "best understood as [Aristotle's] using a species of irony." That is, X.7–8 is "Aristotle's philosophical holiday," "a marvelous end-of-term jest . . . preceded by a warning in X.6 that we need amusement and diversion to restore us for work, and followed in X.9 by a precis of a massive term's work to come, the *Politics*" (Moline, "Contemplation and the Human Good," 46).

10. Translations of the *NE* are for the most part those of Hippocrates G. Apostle, *Aristotle's Nicomachean Ethics* (Grinnel, Iowa: Peripatetic Press, 1984), though in some instances I make modifications. Unless otherwise noted, all citations are to the *NE*.

11. I.2.1094a24; II.6.110632; VI.1.1138b23.

12. To give a comprehensive interpretation of Aristotle's account in the *De Anima* (hereafter, *DA*) of the "parts" or "divisibility" of the soul, and of the way in which human beings acquire knowledge, would be beyond the scope of this paper. My main point here is to show only that in the *DA* Aristotle raises some serious objections to the theory that knowledge is gained through an affinity of subject and object, which he attributes to Empedocles, among others.

13. II.7.1107a30–34; VII.2.1145b27; VII.8.1150b31–32; IX.8.1168a35–1168b2; X.8.1179a17–23.

14. According to Apostle, "no assumption is made here as to whether these parts of the soul, besides being distinguishable by definition, are separate in any manner or not" (Apostle, *Aristotle's* Nicomachean Ethics, 278, note 4).

15. Nichols makes a similar argument in her discussion of the problems inherent in Aristotle's discussion of "philosophic activity" in *Pol* VII.1–3, *Citizens and Statesmen*, 132–36.

16. In the *DA* Aristotle states that there are in fact three species of desire: appetite (*epithumia*), spirit or anger (*thumos*), and wish (*boulesis*). While wish is in the rational part of the soul, appetite and spirit are in the nonrational part, though spirit is "closer" to reason than is appetite, II.3.414b103; see also III.9, and *NE* VII.6.1149a24-b23. For an explanation of the various species of desire, see Nussbaum, 274–82. For a thoughtful account of how Aristotle's remarks about the species of desire bear on his "parts of the soul" theory, see Laurence Berns, "Spiritedness in Ethics and Politics: A Study of Aristotelian Psychology," *Interpretation* 12 (1984): 335–48. In commenting on Aristotle's presentation of the soul's parts, Berns remarks, "The different powers of the soul, then, are not to be understood as spatially separated 'parts,' but as interpenetrating powers," 337, note 10.

17. Both art (*techne*) and prudence (*phronesis*) are directed toward those objects whose principles are variable, but while art has to do with rational production (1140a1–15), prudence has to do with rational action. The difference between production and action, Aristotle remarks, is in their respective ends: "Production has an end other than itself, but action does not: good action (*eupraxia*) is itself an end" (1140b5–7).

18. With intellect (*nous*, which in other contexts Aristotle uses in a manner that is better translated as "insight," or as the strictly theoretical "part" of the intellect) one apprehends the "fundamental principles" (*archai*) that are understood, though they cannot be demonstrated or proven (1140b31–1141a9); with scientific knowledge, one exercises one's grasp of those fundamental principles and engages in demonstration, thereby acquiring further knowledge (1139b25–35); with wisdom, one has both intelligence and scientific knowledge, and thus has "the most precise form of knowledge" (1141a16–19). For an excellent account of the technical meanings of these various intellectual abilities, see Sherman, *The Fabric of Character*, 3, note 2.

19. Sherman remarks that since the end of prudence is "the whole of good living," that "inclusive end," i.e., the whole of good living, is at least a part of what the prudent person apprehends or studies (Sherman, *The Fabric of Character*, 89).

20. Similarly, Aristotle remarks in Book V that some people think that those who are just have

some type of knowledge that enables them to be as capable, if not more capable, of acting unjustly than the just are. Identifying this kind of knowledge with justice is similar to identifying prudence with cleverness. As Martin Ostwald notes in his translation of *Nicomachean Ethics* (New York: Macmillan, 1962), the argument reported in V.9 that justice is a kind of knowledge is that used by Socrates against Polemarchus in the *Republic* 333e–334b, 140, note 67. For a good discussion of the Socratic claim that virtue is knowledge, see W. W. Fortenbaugh, *Aristotle on Emotion* (New York: Harper & Row, 1975), 63–67.

21. For an excellent discussion of the way in which Aristotle uses the example of Priam to indicate the vulnerability of happiness to circumstances, see Nussbaum, *Fragility of Goodness,* 327–34.

22. According to Apostle, Aristotle's point is to show that the prudent person deliberates well in regards to achieving whatever ends are constitutive of happiness. As he states, "Happiness is an unqualified end, but part of happiness is a qualified end relative to happiness as a whole. For example, an *action*, which is an end in itself, may require good deliberation to be virtuous, but since it is not the whole happiness of a man it is a qualified end" (Apostle, *Aristotle's* Nicomachean Ethics, 289–90, note 9).

23. As D. K. W. Modrak explains, "the direction of thought" of prudence is different from that of theoretical thinking, since with prudence, the particulars, which are gained through experience, "remain at the center of cognition," whereas with theoretical thinking, "the particulars serve solely as the means to the universal," "Aristotle on Reason, Practical Reason, and Living Well," in *Essays in Ancient Greek Philosophy*, vol. 4, *Aristotle's Ethics*, ed. J. Anton and A. Preus (Albany, N.Y.: State University of New York Press, 1991), 188.

24. *Gnome* has a whole range of connotations, including equity, good judgment, and sympathetic understanding (1143a18–24).

25. *Sunesis*, according to Aristotle, deals with the same objects as does prudence (i.e., the variable things, of which doubt and deliberation are possible), but while "prudence issues commands," understanding only "passes judgment" (1143a5–8). The distinction between prudence and understanding that Aristotle makes here is a significant one, I believe, in regards to the fullness of intellectual virtue, since the continent person discussed in Book VII is described as having understanding but not prudence.

26. See note 18.

27. Clearly Aristotle believes that "natural virtue"—a sort of inborn propensity to do (or to avoid) certain kinds of actions in certain ways—has a great deal to do with character. In explaining its role in the achievement of virtue in Book VI, he builds on the argument he makes at the end of Book II. There he advises those who seek to become good to be aware of two potential problems: first, to understand what problematic inclinations human beings face generally (such as indulging in excessive pleasures of the body), and second, to understand one's own personal inclinations: "We should take into consideration also the errors which have the greatest attraction for us personally. For the natural inclinations of one person differ from those of another, and we each come to know these by our pains and pleasures" (1109b2–4).

28. Commenting on the difference between continence and virtue, Amelie Oksenberg Rorty makes a similar argument: "All sorts of habits must supplement that of reasoning well about practical matters. The virtuous man must not only have good intellectual habits of various sorts, but also sound habits of action involving habitual desires of genuinely good ends that are properly described, as well as good emotional dispositions of various sorts. One does not become moral simply by learning to reason as the moral man reasons; one must also acquire the habit of acting as the moral man acts," "Plato and Aristotle on Belief, Habits, and

Akrasia," *American Philosophical Quarterly* 7 (1970): 56–57.

29. According to David J. Depew, the key difference between Plato's and Aristotle's under-standing of moral virtue lies in their respective views of the proper relation between reason and desire. Believing that the tension between reason and desire is irresolvable, Plato identifies "the highest function of political life" as "the repression of desire." Aristotle, however, having "deep confidence" in the compatibility of reason and desire, presents a view of political life that "does not repress, deflect, or manage desire, but completes the education of desire for intrinsically good things," "Politics, Music, and Contemplation in Aristotle's Ideal State," in *A Companion to Aristotle's Politics*, ed. D. Keyt and F. Miller (Cambridge, Mass.: Blackwell, 1991), 378–80.

30. Aristotle clarifies this distinction even further in Book VII, arguing that there is a real difference between virtue and continence, and similarly, between vice and incontinence, and explains why Socrates did not see any real difference between the two.

31. Although Aristotle refers to this intellectual capacity in this chapter as simply wisdom (*sophia*), the way in which he describes it is virtually identical to what he elsewhere calls theoretical thinking (*theoretike dianoia*) and what he calls simply theory (*theoria*) in X.7–8. That is, he seems to be identifying wisdom with knowledge of the "invariable things." See note 8.

32. Solon is mentioned in X.8.1179a10–14.

33. According to Burger, in VI.7, Aristotle speaks in a "Presocratic voice," demoting the human good in a way that "overturns the starting point of the *Ethics*." As such, she claims, "political science, far from being architectonic," as Aristotle claims at the opening of the *Ethics*, "has become subordinate to astronomy, or perhaps better, astral theology" (Burger, "Wisdom, Philosophy, and Happiness," 299). For a similar argument, see Moline, "Contemplation and the Human Good," 47.

34. VII.6.1149b32.

35. For similar arguments, see Deborah Achtenberg, "The Role of the *Ergon* Argument in Aristotle's *Nicomachean Ethics*," in *Essays in Ancient Greek Philosophy*, vol. 4, *Aristotle's Ethics*, ed. J. Anton and A. Preus (Albany, N.Y.: State University of New York Press, 1991), 64–69; and Fortenbaugh, *Aristotle on Emotion*, 67–70.

36. In X.7–8, Aristotle identifies the intellect (*nous*) solely with the capacity for theoretical thinking. (See note 18.) However, in other contexts, specifically in IX.4 and IX.8, he identifies the intellect with the capacity for practical thinking as well. On this point, see Modrak, 189–90.

37. As Burger states, "To convey the reality of this merely human happiness, Aristotle has had to introduce the image of a life of happiness of 'separated mind'" (Burger, "Wisdom, Philosophy, and Happiness," 301).

38. I discuss these two arguments together because they are so closely related.

39. "Nor indeed will the 'good-as-such' be more of a good because it is everlasting: after all, whiteness which lasts for a long time is no whiter than whiteness which lasts only for a day" (1096b3–4).

40. As Modrak states, "By framing the objective in terms that rule out its achievement, Aristotle calls our attention to human limitations" (Modrak, "Aristotle on Reason, Practical Reason, and Living Well," 192, note 28).

41. See note 5.

42. Tessitore, 63.

43. Tessitore, 110–11.

44. See, for example, VIII.5, where Aristotle argues that each friend views the other as an object of affection and choice, an object which is good and pleasant without qualification; IX.7,

where Aristotle indicates the way in which friends in some sense "produce" each other, and the permanence and pleasure that results from that achievement; and IX.9, where Aristotle explains how friendship contributes to happiness, particularly in regards to the continuity that friendship provides.

45. Burger points out that Aristotle immediately calls this understanding of self-sufficiency into question, introducing it into his argument as "so-called self-sufficiency." In X.7–8, according to Burger, self-sufficiency "no longer means the capacity of an activity itself to make life complete, but only the capacity for that activity itself to be carried on independently of necessary conditions." She goes on to note the strangeness of Aristotle's claim that theoretical activity is superior because it requires less "equipment," remarking that this claim is analogous to "a professor [defending] his life as superior because he requires a fraction of the politician's salary" (Burger, "Aristotle's 'Exclusive' Account of Happiness," 89).

46. See, e.g., Larry Arnhart, "Statesmanship as Magnanimity: Classical, Christian, and Modern," *Polity* 16 (1983): 263–83; Réné Gauthier, *Magnanimité: L'Idéal de la grandeur dans la philosophie païenne et dans la théologie chrétienne* (Paris: Librairie Philosophique J. Vrin, 1951); and Harry V. Jaffa, *Thomism and Aristotelianism: A Study of the Commentary of Thomas Aquinas on the* Nicomachean Ethics (Chicago: University of Chicago Press, 1952). Arnhart argues that Aristotle shows that magnanimity is expressed both in contemplative and practical activity (265–67). Gauthier argues that in suggesting this comparison, Aristotle indicates that the magnanimous person is actually the "philosopher," who, like the Unmoved Mover, engages in theoretical thinking, rather than practical activities that bring honor (272–301). Jaffa argues that Aristotle's point is to show that the magnanimous person is the practical counterpart of the contemplator of X.7–8; the magnanimous person's failure to achieve the self-sufficiency he seeks shows that he (and practical activity in general) is inferior to the contemplator (and theoretical activity in general, chap. 6).

47. See also *Pol* II.1–5, where Aristotle refutes Plato's arguments in the *Republic*.

48. "What sorts of things could be called good for their own sake? Are they the goods that are pursued without regard to additional benefits, such as thinking, seeing, certain pleasures, and honors? For even if we pursue these also for the sake of something else, one would still classify them as things that are good for their own sake" (1096b16–19).

49. For a more comprehensive explanation of this view, see my "Virtue and Friendship in Persuasion: Jane Austen's 'Aristotelian' Understanding of Happiness," in *Nature, Woman, and the Art of Politics*, ed. Eduardo A. Velásquez (Lanham, Md.: Rowman & Littlefield, 2000).

50. For more detailed arguments on this issue, see Depew, "Politics, Music, and Contemplation," 365–70, and Nichols, *Citizens and Statesmen*, 152–63.

51. For a similar argument, see Burger, "Wisdom, Philosophy, and Happiness," 301–03, and Modrak, "Aristotle on Reason, Practical Reason, and Living Well," 189.

52. For a similar argument, see Burger, "Aristotle's 'Exclusive' Account of Happiness," 91; "The Argument and Action of Aristotle's *Ethics*," 21; "Wisdom, Philosophy, and Happiness," 304–7; and "Ethical Reflection and Righteous Indignation," 135–137; Joseph Cropsey, "Justice and Friendship in the *Nicomachean Ethics*," in *Political Philosophy and the Issues of Politics* (Chicago: University of Chicago Press, 1977), 254; Moline, "Contemplation and the Human Good," 39; and Nichols, "Response to Aristotle's Science of the Best Regime," 154.

Chapter V: The Evolution of Catholic Thought in the Last Two Centuries by Gerald A. McCool, S.J.

1. Gerald A. McCool, S.J., "Maritain's Defense of Democracy" *Thought* 29 (1979): 132–42.
2. In the course of the nineteenth century the governments of France, Spain, Portugal, Italy, and Prussia took punitive measures against Catholic religious orders and other institutions of the Church. In the 1870s, Italy occupied the papal states and Bismarck launched a fierce attack on the Catholic Church.
3. For the baroque scholastic revival see Gerald A. McCool, S.J., "Why St. Thomas Stays Alive," *International Philosophical Quarterly* 19 (1990): 275–87. An excellent overview of Bellarmine's life and work can be found in James Brodrick, S.J., *Robert Bellarmine, Saint and Scholar* (Westminster, Md.: The Newman Press, 1951). This is a shorter and updated version of Brodrick's pioneering two-volume study on Bellarmine published in 1928. The hostility of the seventeenth- and eighteenth-century absolute governments toward Bellarmine can be seen from the fact that, despite his eminent sanctity, Bellarmine was not beatified and canonized until the twentieth century, three hundred years after his cause was introduced.
4. Indirect power over secular governments is no longer claimed by the Holy See.
5. A fine summary of Suarez's political philosophy can be found in the third volume of Frederick Copleston's multi-volume *History of Philosophy* (Westminster, Md.: The Newman Press, 1953), 380–405.
6. See Thomas F. O'Meara, O.P., *Romantic Idealism and Roman Catholicism: Schelling and the Theologians* (Notre Dame, Ind: University of Notre Dame Press, 1982), 65–66.
7. For seventeenth-century Jansenism see Hubert Jedin, ed., *History of the Church: The Church in the Age of Absolutism and Enlightenment* (New York: Crossroad, 1981), 6:57–70. For eighteenth-century Jansenism, see Jedin, *History,* 6:57–70. For eighteenth-century episcopalism and Febronianism, see Jedin, *History,* 6:443–69.
8. For the coordinated effort of the European governments to bring about the papal suppression of the Society of Jesus and thereby secure their own control over the independent Jesuit network of schools, see William V. Bangert, S.J., *A History of the Society of Jesus* (St. Louis: The Institute of Jesuit Sources, 1986), 273–408.
9. Bellarmine's social theory was not revived until the nineteenth century.
10. For the gravamina of the German Imperial Church against Rome and the Congress of Ems see Jedin, *History,* 6:458–69.
11. For the extreme rationalism of the Catholic theological faculties under Bavarian state control see O'Meara, *Romantic Idealism and Roman Catholicism,* 37–41.
12. For Austrian Josephinism see Jedin, *History,* v. 6, 458–69.
13. For Joseph de Maistre and Felicite de Lamennais, see Gerald A. McCool, S.J., *Nineteenth Century Scholasticism: The Search for a Unitary Method* (New York: Fordham University Press, 1989), 37–46.
14. Many of the French bishops were returned royalist exiles who were still imbued with the ecclesiology of the *ancien régime.* Their Gallicanism increased their hostility toward Lamennais. See McCool, *Nineteenth Century Scholasticism,* 26 ff.
15. The social blindness of the early-nineteenth-century Catholic bourgeoisie is made very clear by de Lubac in his penetrating and sympathetic study of Proudhon, *Proudhon et le catholicisme.*
16. For Liberatore's philosophy and its importance for Catholic social ethics, see McCool, *Nineteenth Century Scholasticism,* 145–66.
17. For Taparelli's contribution to the revival of St. Thomas see McCool, *Nineteenth Century Scholasticism,* 83–6. Taparelli's five-volume work *Saggo teoretico di diretto naturale appoggiato sul fatto* (1840–43) made a major contribution to the revival of Catholic social theory. Taparelli has been credited with the introduction of the stress on rights into modern

Catholic social ethics. His work has been neglected and would reward further study.

18. The German Jesuit review, *Stimmen der Zeit*, was a very important channel for the dissemination of Catholic social theory. This was also true of the French Jesuit review, *Action Populaire*, whose director, Gustave Desbuquois, collaborated with the German Jesuit Gustav Gundlach, a renowed social theorist, and with the American Jesuit John LaFarge of the Jesuit review, *America*, in the preparation of Pius XI's proposed encyclical against anti-Semitism. LaFarge was one of the pioneers in the American campaign for racial justice.

19. For the continuity in papal social thinking from Leo XIII to John Paul II, see Gerald A. McCool, S.J., "From Leo XIII to John Paul II: Continuity and Development," *International Philosophical Quarterly* 40 (2000): 173–83.

20. After special studies in philosophy and economics, Gustav Gundlach, S.J., participated actively in the political life of the Weimar Republic and collaborated closely with Eugenio Pacelli, the future Pius XII, while the latter was papal nuncio. With another German Jesuit, Oswald von Nell-Breuning and the French Jesuit: Gustave Desbuquois, Gundlach played a major role in the drafting of Pius XI's *Quadragesimo Anno*. Paul VI, as is well known, was very much influenced by the social and political philosophy of Jacques Maritain. For the careers of Gundlach and Desbuquois and their extensive input into papal teaching see Georges Passelecq and Bernard Suchecky, *The Hidden Encyclical of Pius XI* (New York: Harcourt Brace, 1997), 41–56.

21. See Passelecq and Suchecky, *The Hidden Encyclical,* in which the history of the proposed encyclical is presented in detail.

22. Although they were later reconciled, the distinguished Dominican theologian Reginald Garrigou-Lagrange ended his friendship with Jacques Maritain after the publication of *The Things That Are Not Caesar's*. The equally distinguished Jesuit theologian Louis Cardinal Billot was so outspoken in his disapproval of Pius XI's condemnation of Maurras that Pius XI forced him to resign his cardinalate and go into retirement. For the sympathy of the French Jesuits associated with *Etudes* toward Maurras see Pierre Vallin, "Etudes: Histoire d'une revue," *Etudes* special issue (2000): 18–21.

23. For Maritain's social and political philosophy, see Gerald A. McCool, S.J., *From Unity to Pluralism: The Internal Evolution of Thomism* (New York: Fordham University Press, 1989), 151–55. See also Gerald A. McCool, S.J., "Maritain's Defense of Democracy," *Thought* 34 (1979): 132–47.

24. This concern was shown by John XXIII in his encyclical *Mater et Magistra* and by Paul VI in his encyclical *Populorum Progressio*. The unjust social and economic disparity between the northern and southern hemispheres has become a recurring theme in contemporary papal social teaching.

25. See Rocco A. Buttiglione, *Karol Wojtyla: The Thought of the Man Who Became John Paul II* (Grand Rapids, Mich.: Eerdmans, 1997), 179–231.

26. *Fides et Ratio* (Boston: Pauline Press, 1998), 66–9, 76–9.

27. See McCool, "From Leo XIII to John Paul II: Continuity and Development."

Chapter VI: Defending Authority in a Cynical Age, by Joseph Koterski, S.J.

1. For an analysis of the rhetoric of rights, see Mary Ann Glendon's study of contemporary political discourse in *Rights Talk: The Impoverishment of Political Discourse* (New York: Free Press, 1991).

2. Three comparatively recent scandals involving the U.S. presidency may serve as cases in

point, for they have touched both political parties: Watergate, Iran Contra, and Whitewater.

3. J. M. Bochenski, *Was ist Autorität? Einführung in die Logik der Autorität* (Freiburg-im-Breisgau: Herderbücherei, 1974), 18.

4. Chaucer, *The Canterbury Tales*, General Prologue A308.

5. Bernard of Clairvaux, *De Gradibus Humilitatis.*

6. Yves Simon, *A General Theory of Authority* (Notre Dame, Ind.: University of Notre Dame Press, 1962), 13–22.

7. Karl Jaspers, *Die Idee der Universität* (Berlin: Springer, 1946), translated by H. A. T. Reiche and H. F. Vanderschmidt as *The Idea of the University* (Boston: Beacon, 1959); see also *Die Schuldfrage, ein Beitrag zur deutschen Frage* (Heidelberg: Lambert Schneider, 1946), trans. E. B. Ashton as *The Question of German Guilt* (New York: Capricorn, 1961).

8. Romano Guardini, *Power and Responsibility: A Course of Action for the New Age*, trans. Elinor C. Briefs (Chicago: Henry Regnery, 1961).

9. Hannah Arendt, *Eight Exercises in Political Thought* (1954), esp. chap. 3, "What is Authority?"

Chapter VII: Questioning the New Natural Law Theory: The Case of Religious Liberty as Defended by Robert P. George in *Making Men Moral*, by Keith J. Pavlischek

1. This chapter is a revised version of an article that originally appeared in *Studies in Christian Ethics* 12, no. 2 (1999).

2. *The Pluralist Game: Pluralism, Liberalism and the Moral Conscience* (Lanham, Md.: Rowman & Littlefield, 1995).

3. He is also, at times, delightfully witty and sarcastic. Mocking the cant of so much American pro-choice rhetoric, in a symposium of American pro-life scholars and activists addressing the issue of "Killing Abortionists," George wrote: I am personally opposed to killing abortionists. However, inasmuch as my personal opposition to this practice is rooted in a sectarian (Catholic) religious belief in the sanctity of human life, I am unwilling to impose it on others who may, as a matter of conscience, take a different view. Of course, I am entirely in favor of policies aimed at removing the root causes of violence against abortionists. Indeed, I would go so far as to support mandatory one-week waiting periods, and even nonjudgmental counseling, for people who are contemplating the choice of killing an abortionist. I believe in policies that reduce the urgent need some people feel to kill abortionists while, at the same time, respecting the rights of conscience of my fellow citizens who believe that the killing of abortionists is sometimes a tragic necessity—not a good, but a lesser evil. In short, I am moderately pro-choice. See "Killing Abortionists: A Symposium," *First Things* 48 (December 1994): 24–31.

4. Russell Hittinger, *A Critique of the New Natural Law Theory* (Notre Dame, Ind.: University of Notre Dame Press, 1987). While not explicitly referring to Finnis, Grisez, or George, Hittinger's essay "Natural Law and Catholic Moral Theology," in *A Preserving Grace: Protestants, Catholics and Natural Law*, ed. Michael Cromartie (Grand Rapids, Mich.: Eerdmans, 1997), is an implicit critique of their position and a spirited defense of a more traditional natural law position.

5. *Making Men Moral* (Oxford: Oxford University Press, 1993).

6. See Alasdair MacIntyre, *Whose Justice? Which Rationality?* (Notre Dame, Ind.: University of Notre Dame Press, 1988), 188.

7. See John Finnis, *Natural Law and Natural Rights* (Oxford: Clarendon Press, 1980), 48–49.

8. Hittinger, *A Critique of the New Natural Law Theory*, 160–62.

9. Hittinger, *A Critique of the New Natural Law Theory*, 162.

10. Hittinger, *A Critique of the New Natural Law Theory*, 164.

11. Germain Grisez and Russell Shaw, *Beyond the New Morality* (Notre Dame, Ind.: University of Notre Dame Press, 1974; rev. ed. 1980), 78.

12. Grisez and Shaw, *Beyond the New Morality*, 79.

13. Grisez and Shaw, *Beyond the New Morality*, 82.

14. Leo XIII, encyclical letter on "The Constitution of States," *Immortale Dei*, November 1, 1885, 35, 32.

15. Leo XIII, encyclical letter on "The Nature of Human Liberty," *Libertas*, June 20, 1888, 36.

16. If one cannot appeal to theological or religious reasons to support legal intolerance, one can hardly appeal to theological or religious reasons to oppose it. Leo XIII's and St. Augustine's theological opposition to coercion would be excluded as well.

17. Hittinger, *A Critique of the New Natural Law Theory*, 171.

18. See Hittinger, *A Critique of the New Natural Law Theory*, 170, and MacIntyre, *Whose Justice? Which Rationality?* 188.

19. Hittinger, *A Critique of the New Natural Law Theory*, 166.

20. In an earlier version of this chapter, an anonymous referee asked: "Is it not the case that for something to be a participation in the basic good of religion and in that respect valuable-per-se does not imply that in the final analysis all religious practices are equally valuable?" The referee is concerned that I give the impression that George is a "religious indifferentist." First, I'm not sure that George provides a way to sort out what needs to be sorted out to answer the question. All he provides is some notion of religion as a "good," but it is undefined and rather free-floating in terms of its ontological and moral specification. I'm inclined to suggest that the distinction suggested by the referee makes sense only if one methodologically prescinds from what one knows about religion "in the final analysis," or if one has a wholly fideistic understanding of the object of religion "in the final analysis." But if one has reason not to be fideistic about the object of religion or has reason to believe that religions are not equally valuable per se, then it would be a philosophical and theological mistake (though not necessarily a political mistake) to treat them as such. Does this make George a religious "indifferentist"? Perhaps not, "in the final analysis," but George seems methodologically content proceeding with the assumption that the object of devotion is wholly irrelevant, that is, indifferent, to the "value" of religion. Were he to employ this methodological assumption in discussions of, say, sexual expressions of friendship, then he would be forced into a radically different position on homosexuality. George is particularly concerned with insisting that moral judgments concerning the good of sexual activity must be considered in relation to the object of affection. He is unwilling to say of any form of religious devotion (even what "in the final analysis" he might call idolatry) what he says of homoerotic sexual activity, namely that it is disordered. To employ the terms of the referee, if George were to approach the matter of homoerotic sexual activity in the same way he approached the matter of idolatry, he would be led, I think, to conclude that all sexual activity is equally valuable per se, even though "in the final analysis" not all sexual activity is equally valuable. The "final analysis" regarding homoerotic sexual activity impinges on the good of friendship in a way that idolatry does not impinge on the good of religion. Again, it seems to me that for George the proposition "this particular act of religious devotion (idolatry) is a sin" is epistemologically inferior to the proposition "this particular form of sexual expression (homoerotic sexuality) is a sin." This is, to say the least, highly problematic from a Christian perspective. Contrast it, for instance, with St. Paul's

discussion in Romans 1.

21. Alasdair MacIntyre, *Three Rival Versions of Moral Enquiry* (Notre Dame, Ind.: University of Notre Dame Press, 1990), 141.

22. MacIntyre, *Whose Justice?* 197.

23. MacIntyre, *Three Rival Versions*, 133–35.

24. Ibid., 142.

25. Canavan, "The Catholic Concept of Religious Freedom as a Human Right," in *Religious Liberty: An End and a Beginning,* ed. John Courtney Murray, S.J. (New York: Macmillan, 1966), 72–80.

26. Canavan, "Religious Liberty: John Courtney Murray and Vatican II," in *John Courtney Murray and the American Civil Conversation,* ed. Robert P. Hunt and Kenneth L. Grasso (Grand Rapids, Mich.: Eerdmans, 1997), 168.

27. Canavan, *The Pluralist Game,* 107.

28. Canavan, "Religious Liberty: John Courtney Murray and Vatican II," 168.

29. I want to thank Jay Budziszewski, Francis Canavan, Russell Hittinger, Timothy Samuel Shah, and James Skillen for helpful comments on earlier drafts of this article.

Chapter VIII: Catholicism, Liberalism, and Religious Liberty, by Robert P. Hunt

1. John Courtney Murray, *We Hold These Truths: Catholic Reflections on the American Proposition* (New York: Sheed and Ward, 1960), 32.

2. R. Bruce Douglass, "Introduction," *Catholicism and Liberalism: Contributions to American Public Philosophy,* ed. R. Bruce Douglass and David Hollenbach (New York: Cambridge University Press, 1994).

3. Ibid., 9.

4. Ibid., 9–10.

5. Paul E. Sigmund, "Catholicism and Liberal Democracy," in *Catholicism and Liberalism,* 235.

6. *Everson v. Bd. of Ed. of Ewing Township, N.J.,* 330 U.S., 15–16.

7. Ibid., 31–32.

8. Black, cited in David M. O'Brien, *Constitutional Law and Politics,* vol. 2: *Civil Rights and Liberties,* 3rd ed. (New York: W.W. Norton & Company, 1997), 660.

9. Murray cited in Jo Renee Formicola, "Catholic Jurisprudence on Education," in *Everson Revisited: Religion, Education, and Law at the Crossroads,* ed. Jo Renee Formicola and Hubert Morken (Lanham, Md.: Rowman & Littlefield, 1997), 86.

10. See Daniel L. Dreisbach, "*Everson* and the Command of History: The Supreme Court, Lessons in History, and the Church-State Debate in America," in *Everson Revisited,* 23–57, for an excellent bibliographical overview on the scholarly debate over the meaning of the religion clauses.

11. Stephen V. Monsma, "The Wrong Road Taken," in *Everson Revisited,* 127–28.

12. *Dignitatis Humanae,* section 6. All further references to this document will be taken from the translation supplied by John Courtney Murray in *Religious Liberty: An End and a Beginning* (New York: Macmillan, 1966), 162–189. The document will be cited parenthetically as *DH,* and the section number will be given followed by the page number in Murray's book.

13. 120 S. Ct. 2530: 2541. Interestingly, Justice O'Connor, in her separate concurrence, and Justice Souter, in his dissent, also appeal to the "neutrality" principle. O'Connor does not "quarrel with the plurality's recognition that neutrality is an important reason for upholding government-aid programs against Establishment Clause challenges" (2557). Souter contends

that in "endorsing the principle of no aid to a school's religious mission . . . government can in fact operate with neutrality in its relation to religion" (2597). The disagreements among Thomas, O'Connor, and Souter do not revolve around the question of whether government should be neutral in religious matters, but what "neutrality" in religious matters truly means.

14. Black, *Engel v. Vitale*, 370 U.S. 421 (1962), cited in *The Supreme Court on Church and State*, ed. Robert S. Alley (New York: Oxford University Press, 1988), 199.

15. *U.S. v. Seeger*, 380 U.S. 176.

16. *Welsh v. U.S.*, 398 U.S. 341–43.

17. Francis P. Canavan, *The Pluralist Game: Pluralism, Liberalism, and the Moral Conscience* (Lanham, Md.: Rowman & Littlefield, 1995), 33.

18. *Board of Education of Kiryas Joel*, 512 U.S. 687 (1994), cited in Gerard V. Bradley, "Déjà Vu, All Over Again: The Supreme Court Revisits Religious Liberty," *Crisis* 13, no. 4 (April 1995): 41.

19. *Employment Division v. Smith*, 110 S. Ct. 1595 (1990), cited in Bradley, "Déjà Vu," 41.

20. Canavan, *The Pluralist Game*, 32.

21. Bradley, "Déjà Vu," 42.

22. David A. J. Richards, *Toleration and the Constitution* (New York: Oxford University Press, 1986), 105.

23. Ibid., 108.

24. Ibid., 133.

25. Ibid., 136.

26. Ibid., 145.

27. Ibid., 134.

28. Canavan, *The Pluralist Game*, 139.

29. Kenneth L. Grasso, "Beyond Liberalism: Human Dignity, the Free Society, and the Second Vatican Council," *Catholicism, Liberalism, and Communitarianism: The Catholic Intellectual Tradition and the Moral Foundations of Democracy*, ed. Kenneth L. Grasso, Gerard V. Bradley, and Robert P. Hunt (Lanham, Md.: Rowman & Littlefield, 1995), 39 ff.

30. David Hollenbach, S.J., "A Communitarian Reconstruction of Human Rights: Contributions from Catholic Tradition," in *Catholicism and Liberalism*, 133.

31. Ernest Fortin, "The Trouble with Catholic Social Thought," *Boston College Magazine* (Summer 1988): 37–42.

32. John Courtney Murray, "The Declaration on Religious Freedom: A Moment in Its Legislative History," in *Religious Liberty: An End and a Beginning*, 15–42.

33. Ibid., 25.

34. John Courtney Murray, "Governmental Repression of Heresy," in *Proceedings of the Third Annual Meeting of the Catholic Theological Society of America* (Chicago, 1948), 56.

35. Murray, "The Declaration on Religious Freedom," 24.

36. Ibid., 29.

37. Ibid.

38. Robert P. George, *Making Men Moral: Civil Liberties and Public Morality* (New York: Oxford University Press, 1993), 221–22.

39. Francis P. Canavan, "The Catholic Concept of Religious Freedom as a Human Right," in *Religious Liberty: An End and a Beginning*, 76.

40. Murray, *We Hold These Truths*, 47.

41. Murray, "The Declaration on Religious Freedom," 28.

42. Angela C. Carmella, "*Everson* and Its Progeny: Separation and Nondiscrimination in Tension," in *Everson Revisited: Religion, Education, and Law at the Crossroads*, 117.

43. Robert P. George, *The Clash of Orthodoxies: Law, Religion, and Morality in Crisis* (Wilmington, Del.: ISI Books, 2001), 7.

Chapter IX: Church and State in Liberal America:
Locke and Tocqueville Revisited, by Thomas A. Spragens Jr.

1. John Locke, *A Letter Concerning Toleration* (Indianapolis: Bobbs-Merrill Co., 1955; originally published in 1689), 17.
2. Locke, *Letter*, 27.
3. Ibid., 46.
4. Alexis de Tocqueville, *Democracy in America*, ed. Richard Heffner (New York: Mentor Books, 1956), 47–8.
5. Ibid., 48, 150.
6. Ibid., 156.
7. See, for example, Francis Canavan, *The Pluralist Game: Pluralism, Liberalism, and the Moral Conscience* (Lanham, Md.: Rowman & Littlefield, 1995).
8. Locke, *Letter*, 46.
9. Ibid., 52.
10. Ibid., 51.
11. See Stanley Hauerwas and William H. Willimon, *Resident Aliens: Life in the Christian Colony* (Nashville: Abingdon Press, 1989). For an account of the "Christ of culture" rubric, see H. Richard Niebuhr, *Christ and Culture* (New York: Harper, 1951).
12. Tocqueville, *Democracy in America*, 156.
13. Stephen Macedo, *Liberal Virtues* (Oxford: Clarendon Press, 1990), 278. For less sanguine views of the same cultural dynamics, see Ronald Beiner, *What's the Matter with Liberalism?* (Berkeley: University of California Press, 1992) and Alasdair MacIntyre, *After Virtue* (Notre Dame, Ind.: University of Notre Dame Press, 1981), esp. chap. 3.
14. Locke, *Letter*, 43.
15. John Rawls, *Political Liberalism* (New York: Columbia University Press, 1996), 217.
16. Rawls, *Political Liberalism*, 194. As intimated elsewhere in this essay, however, the proper way to understand the concrete meaning and the practical demands of "reasonableness" and "toleration" are contestable. Believers may not find it proper or obligatory to construe these terms in precisely the manner that Rawls does, therefore.
17. T. A. Spragens, *Civic Liberalism* (Lanham, Md.: Rowman & Littlefield, 1999), chap. 8.
18. John Stuart Mill, *On Liberty* (Indianapolis: Bobbs-Merrill Co., 1956; originally published in 1859), 129.
19. Patrick Neal, *Liberalism and Its Discontents* (New York: New York University Press, 1997), chap. 3. Philosophically, Michael Sandel makes the same point in a somewhat different way when he contrasts the neo-Kantian decisionism he sees as supplying the moral metaphysic of the "procedural republic" with moral beliefs in which the believer sees himself or herself as being "claimed by religious commitments they have not chosen." *Democracy's Discontent* (Cambridge, Mass.: Harvard University Press, 1996), 65.
20. For overlapping accounts of the liberal civic virtues, see Richard Dagger, *Civic Virtues* (New York: Oxford University Press, 1997), chaps. 8, 11, and 12; William Galston, *Liberal Purposes* (Cambridge: Cambridge University Press, 1991), chap. 10; and my *Civic Liberalism*, chap. 8.
21. Galston, *Liberal Purposes*, 279.

Chapter X: Liberalism and Marriage:
The Pluralist Game Revisited, by Gerard V. Bradley

1. Francis Canavan, *The Pluralist Game: Pluralism, Liberalism, and the Moral Conscience* (Lanham, Md.: Rowman & Littlefield, 1995), 13. (All further citations in the body of the text are to this edition, a collection of articles written by Father Canavan over a period of thirty years, from 1963 to 1993.)
2. Joseph Cardinal Ratzinger, *Crises of Law* (Zenit News Agency, at http://www.zenit.org/english/archive/documents/crises-of-law.html).
3. Ibid.
4. *Poe v. Ullman,* 367 U.S. 497,546 (1961) (Harlan, J., dissenting).
5. It is important to note here that "common good" should not be understood along utilitarian lines. The common good of political society includes a decent concern for public morality and, as we shall see, maintenance of the conditions that help people to understand what marriage is and to succeed in the marriages they enter into.
6. An example of how the truth about marriage fits with the common good may be *Griswold v. Connecticut,* 381 U.S. 479 (1968). *Griswold* did not state a right to use contraceptives, even within marriage. Justices White and Goldberg came close to saying as much, but the center of gravity of the case is something quite distinct. Marital privacy, consisting of the confidentiality that marital friendship requires for its enjoyment, joined to spatial privacy in one's home, is at the core of *Griswold.* The opinion of the Court refers to the "intimate relation of husband and wife," "privacy surrounding the marriage relationship," and, finally, this understanding of marriage: "a coming together for better or worse, hopefully enduring, and intimate to the degree of being sacred." Ibid., 480–83.
7. See Robert P. George, "'Same-Sex Marriage' and 'Moral Neutrality,'" in *The Clash of Orthodoxies: Law, Religion, and Morality in Crisis* (Wilmington, Del.: ISI Books, 2001), 75–89. Much of what is contained in the next few paragraphs follows Professor George's argument.
8. Ibid., 75.
9. Ibid., 76.
10. Stephen Macedo, "Reply to Critics," *Georgetown Law Journal* 84 (1995): 329.
11. Ibid., 335.
12. Ibid.
13. George, "'Same-Sex Marriage' and 'Moral Neutrality,'" 86–87.
14. *Michael H. v. Gerald D.,* 491 U.S. 110, 141 (1989).
15. Joseph Raz, *The Morality of Freedom* (Oxford: Clarendon Press, 1986), 162.
16. See George, "'Same-Sex Marriage' and 'Moral Neutrality,'" 87.
17. Ibid., 87–88.
18. 125 U.S. 190 (1888), 211.
19. Ibid.
20. *Poe v. Ullman,* 367 U.S. 497, 545–46 (1961) (Harlan, J., dissenting).
21. Much of this part is based upon Robert P. George and Gerard V. Bradley, "Marriage and the Liberal Imagination," *Georgetown Law Journal* 84 (1995): 301.

Chapter XI: Can Liberalism Cast Out Liberalism?, by George McKenna

1. Andrew Sullivan, "Going Down Screaming," *New York Times Magazine*, October 11, 1998, 48.
2. Both sides of his personality were on display in his book on homosexuality, *Virtually Normal*

(New York: Alfred A. Knopf, 1995). On the one hand he argues that homosexual "marriage" can be justified by conservative ideology: It could "buttress the ethic of heterosexual marriage by showing how even those excluded can wish to model themselves on its shape and structure" (112). On the other hand, "there is something baleful about the attempt of some gay conservatives to educate homosexuals and lesbians into an uncritical acceptance of a stifling model of heterosexual normality" (203). In this vein he suggests that a good reason for legitimizing "gay marriage" is that it might teach heterosexual couples to loosen up a bit and maybe emulate the style of gay relationships, which usually include an "understanding of the need for extramarital outlets" (202).

3. *Saturday Review of Literature*, March 1973, 30; AP dispatch, October 8, 1995, quoted by William Donohue of the Catholic League for Religious and Civil Rights, in a letter to Democratic congressman Maurice Hinchey. It was at a rally for Hinchey that Steinem made the remark about St. Patrick's Cathedral. See *Catalyst*, a Catholic League publication, December 1996.

4. Historian Simon Schama describes the dechristianization *fete:* "A mountain made of painted linen and papier-mache was built at the end of the nave where Liberty (played by a singer from the Opera) dressed in white, wearing the Phrygian bonnet and holding a pike, bowed to the flame of Reason and seated herself on a bank of flowers and plants." Simon Schama, *Citizens: A Chronicle of the French Revolution* (New York: Alfred A. Knopf, 1989), 778.

5. Antoine-Nicolas de Condorcet, *Sketch for a Historical Picture of the Progress of the Human Mind*, trans. June Barraclough (New York: The Noonday Press, 1955; originally published in 1795), 179.

6. Roger Rosenblatt, "Defenders of the Faith," *Time*, November 12, 1984, 112.

7. John B. Judis, "Crosses to Bear," *New Republic*, September 12, 1994, 23–24.

8. George W. Norris, *Fighting Liberal: The Autobiography of George W. Norris* (New York: The Macmillan Company, 1945).

9. David Riesman and Michael Maccoby, "The American Crisis," in *The Liberal Papers,* ed. James Roosevelt (Garden City, N.Y.: Anchor Books, 1962), 47; Allen S. Whiting, "Communist China," Ibid., 283–302; Quincy Wright, "Policies for Strengthening the United Nations," Ibid., 313–40.

10. *Ginzburg v. U.S.*, 383 U.S. 463, 489 (1966). I am grateful to Father Francis Canavan for this citation, as I am to him for the point that it illustrates. See Canavan, *The Pluralist Game: Pluralism, Liberalism, and the Moral Conscience* (Lanham, Md.: Rowman & Littlefield, 1995), 101.

11. Laura Ingraham, *The Hillary Trap* (New York: Hyperion, 2000), 54.

12. Singer, the most forthright of the three, argues that "the life of a newborn baby is of less value than the life of a pig, a dog, or a chimpanzee" and that "the grounds for not killing persons do not apply to newborn infants." See his *Practical Ethics* (London; Cambridge University Press, 1979), 121, 122. Pinker and Reiman are somewhat more reticent about their views. Pinker allows that infanticide is "immoral" but insists that it is "normal" because it is an inheritance from earlier stages of humanity when survival required it. Indeed, "we are all descendants of women who made the difficult decisions that allowed them to become grandmothers in that unforgiving world, and we inherited that brain circuitry that led to those decisions." He extrapolates from this an "explanation" of why a teenage suburbanite drowned her baby in a toilet at the senior prom. Steven Pinker, "Why They Kill Their Newborns," *New York Times Magazine*, Novermbr 2, 1997, 52. Reiman, who declines "to settle the issue about the moral status of infanticide," nevertheless claims that newborns are not "persons" with a right to life. They do not "possess in their own right

a property that makes it wrong to kill them." See his *Critical Moral Liberalism: Theory and Practice* (Lanham, Md.: Rowman & Littlefield, 1997), chap. 8.

13. Letter of Don Doyle, *New York Times Magazine*, November 8, 1998, 20.

14. Jonathan Rauch, "In Defense of Prejudice," *Harper's*, May 1995, 38, 44.

15. Canavan, *The Pluralist Game,* 76, 86.

16. Ibid., 86.

17. William Lee Miller, *Arguing about Slavery: The Great Battle in the United States Congress* (New York: Alfred A. Knopf, 1996), 376.

18. J. David Greenstone, *The Lincoln Persuasion: Remaking American Liberalism* (Princeton, N.J.: Princeton University Press, 1993), 264.

19. Horace Mann, "The Necessity of Education in a Republican Government," in *Lectures on Education* (Boston: William B. Fowle, 1848), 124.

20. Allen C. Guelzo, *Abraham Lincoln: Redeemer President* (Grand Rapids, Mich.: Eerdmans, 1999), 93.

21. Ibid., 374–80.

22. Ibid., 453–54.

23. Croly, 94. Croly had undisguised contempt for the Whigs—not because of their programs but because of their political ineffectiveness and lack of energetic leadership (see 67–70). It apparently never occurred to him that Lincoln, Croly's *beau ideal*, remained a Whig at heart.

24. Quoted in William Henry Harbaugh, *Power and Responsibility: The Life and Times of Theodore Roosevelt* (New York: Farrar, Straus, and Cudahy, 1961), 56. Contrary to widespread belief, Roosevelt arrived at his "New Nationalism" more or less independently of Croly. See Charles Forcey, *The Crossroads of Liberalism: Croly, Weyl, Lippmann* (London: Oxford University Press, 1961), 127–38.

25. The other earlier figure often invoked by Populists was Thomas Jefferson, but Jefferson is more problematic. There were proto-populist elements in his speeches and writings, especially his majoritarianism, his suspicion of courts and other elite institutions, and his professed love for the "cultivators of the earth." But his debunking of biblical Christianity and his initial enthusiasm for the "atheist" French Revolution were quite out of line with the evangelical spirit of 1890s populism.

26. Andrew Jackson, "Farewell Address," in *A Compilation of Messages and Papers of the Presidents,* ed. James D. Richardson (New York: Bureau of National Literature, Inc., 1897), 4:1523–27.

27. "Populist Party Platform (1892)," in Michael B. Levy, *Political Thought in America: An Anthology*, 2nd ed. (Prospect Heights, Ill.: Waveland Press, 1992), 357.

28. Richard Hofstadter, *The American Political Tradition* (New York: Vintage Books 1976; originally published in 1948), 72.

29. "Populist Party Platform (1892)," 358–9.

30. Daniel Walker Howe, *The Political Culture of American Whigs* (Chicago: University of Chicago Press, 1979), 153. Typically, Lyman Beecher, an evangelical Whig leader (and father of Harriet Beecher Stowe) insisted that "our nation had been raised up by Providence to exert an efficient instrumentality in this moral renovation of the world." Quoted in Perry Miller, *The Life of the Mind in America: From the Revolution to the Civil War* (New York: Harcourt, Brace & World, 1965), 12.

31. John D. Hicks, *The Populist Revolt: A History of the Farmers' Alliance and the People's Party* (Lincoln, Neb.: University of Nebraska Press, 1961), 232.

32. William Jennings Bryan, "Speech Before the Democratic National Convention, Chicago, 1896," in *American Populism,* ed. George McKenna (New York: G.P. Putnam's Sons, 1974),

139.

33. In an article published a month before his inauguration, Wilson declaimed against "the big manufacturers, the bankers, and the heads of the great railroad combinations," calling them "the masters of the government of the United States." See "Freemen Need No Guardians," in Levy, *Political Thought in America*, 350.

34. James MacGregor Burns, *Roosevelt: The Lion and the Fox, 1892–1940* (New York: Harcourt, Brace & World, Inc., 1956), 274, 275. Arthur Schlesinger Jr. finds two New Deals, one from 1933 to 1935 and the second from 1935 up to the Second World War. The early one, exemplified by the National Recovery Act, "accepted the concentration of economic power as the central and irreversible trend of the American economy and . . . proposed the concentration of political power as the answer." The later one relied more on trustbusting to restore healthy competition. See Schlesinger, *The Politics of Upheaval*, vol. 3 of *The Age of Roosevelt* (Boston: Houghton Mifflin Company), 385–408. Historian David Kennedy, in a more recent account, finds the distinction to be a matter of "hair-splitting" and suggests that the Roosevelt Administration regularly mixed the two approaches, both of which "evolved organically out of the social thought of the previous two decades as well as the circumstances of the Depression." David M. Kennedy, *Freedom from Fear: The American People in Depression and War, 1929–1945* (New York: Oxford University Press, 1999), note, 248.

35. Quoted in Burns, *Roosevelt*, 242.

36. Canavan, *The Pluralist Game*, 9. Writing at the far end of what Canavan saw coming in 1965, philosopher Robert George writes: "People no longer disagree merely about the proper or most effective means of protecting public goods and combating public evils. People today disagree about what is a public good and what is a public evil. And the disagreement is not merely about what is to count as a *public*, as opposed to a purely *private*, good or evil; it is about what is *morally* good or evil in itself." Robert P. George, "Moral Pluralism, Public Reason, and Natural Law," in *Is a Culture of Life Still Possible in the United States?* (South Bend, Ind.: St. Augustine's Press, 1999), 21.

37. "Pro-choice" wins out over "pro-life" as a label people identify with, but when questioned further, most people turn out to be more pro-life than pro-choice. Most would support the right to abortion in only three cases: where a woman's life or health is impaired, in cases of fetal deformity, and in cases where the pregnancy was caused by rape or incest. In all other cases, including "when a woman or family cannot afford to raise the child" they believe it should be illegal. They also oppose second-trimester abortions, and by a substantial margin (65 percent in 1996). This puts them at odds with the *Roe v. Wade* decision of 1973 and subsequent holdings of the Supreme Court. They also support, and by even larger percentages (in the 70s and 80s) a variety of pro-life abortion regulations, such as 24-hour waiting periods, requirements that doctors inform patients about alternatives to abortion, requirements that girls under eighteen obtain parental consent, and a law requiring husbands to be notified if the woman decides to have an abortion (similar to the one struck down by the Court in the 1992 case of *Planned Parenthood v. Casey*). George Gallup Jr., *The Gallup Poll: Public Opinion 1996* (Wilmington, Del.: Scholarly Resources, Inc., 1997), 109–16.

Questions about the use of racial preferences can also be tricky. When people are asked if they support "affirmative action," a majority answer yes. But that is only because a substantial percentage mistakenly think that "affirmative action" simply means that "well-qualified minorities get access to the schools and jobs that they deserve." When asked about what "affirmative action" really means, namely, the awarding of preferential treatment to women and certain minorities, a majority opposes such programs. George Gallup Jr., *The Gallup Poll: Public Opinion 1997* (Wilmington, Del.: Scholarly Resources, 1998), 257–58.

Most people polled by Gallup (59 percent) believe that homosexual behavior is morally wrong and 52 percent do not think that it should be considered an acceptable "alternative life-style." A larger percentage (63 percent) in a 1994 poll conducted by the National Opinion Research Center at the University of Chicago thought sexual relations between two adults of the same sex was "always wrong." Susan Mitchell, *The Official Guide to American Attitudes* (Ithaca, N.Y.: New Strategist Publications, Inc., 1996), 389. In the 1997 Gallup poll a large minority (46 percent) thought network television shows "currently contain too many homosexual characters and situations" (compared to 33 percent who think they contain the "right amount" and 9 percent who think they contain "too few"). Given the stigma now attached to "homophobia," it is reasonable to suspect that the percentage who think that homosexuality is being overplayed in the media is actually higher. Some 12 percent in the poll had "no opinion" on this question and these may include many who do not approve of the media's mainstreaming of homosexuality. Gallup, 1997, *The Gallup Poll: Public Opinion 1997*, 69, 218–19, 221.

Support for school prayer also remains high. A 1995 Gallup poll showed 71 percent of respondents favor an amendment that would permit prayers to be spoken in public schools. George Gallup Jr., *The Gallup Poll: Public Opinion 1995* (Wilmington, Del.: Scholarly Resources, Inc., 1996), 106.

38. Sullivan, *Going Down Screaming*, 48.

39. Jim Sleeper, "Yankee Doodle Dandy," *Los Angeles Times Book Review*, July 2, 2000, 7.

40. Franklin D, Roosevelt, "Annual Message to Congress, January 4, 1935," in *The Public Papers and Addresses of Franklin D. Roosevelt* (New York: Random House, 1938), 4:19–20.

41. *Summa Theologiae*, 2a–2ae. lvii. 2, *ad* 3.

42. Canavan, 116–18, 132–33.

43. Ibid., 132.

44. *Catechism of the Catholic Church* (Mahwah, N.J.: Paulist Press, 1994), 470. The second of these two quotations is cited in the Catechism and is taken from *Gaudium et Spes*, one of the key documents of the Second Vatican Council.

45. *The Oxford English Dictionary* (New York: Oxford University Press, 1961), 6:238. Cf., Walter John Raymond, *Dictionary of Politics*, 7th ed. (Lawrenceville, Va.: Brunswick Publishing Corp., 1980), 283: "A political philosophy which justifies, in the traditional sense, protest against an arbitrary government that is unresponsive to the needs of the vast majority." Safire's updated version is in *Safire's Political Dictionary* (New York: Random House, 1978), 373.

46. Quoted in Eric Goldman, *Rendezvous With Destiny* (New York: Vintage Books, 1956), 263.

47. See note 37.

Chapter XII: The Triumph of Will:
Rights Mania, the Culture of Death, and the Crisis of Enlightenment Liberalism
by Kenneth L. Grasso

1. William A. Donohue, *The New Freedom: Individualism and Collectivism in the Social Lives of Americans* (New Brunswick, N.J.: 1990), 26.

2. Mary Ann Glendon, *Rights Talk: The Impoverishment of Political Discourse* (New York: The Free Press, 1991), xi.

3. John Paul II, *Evangelium Vitae* [The Gospel of Life] (Boston; Pauline Books and Media [1995]), section 3, 15.

4. Ibid., 18, 34–5.

5. Roberto Mangabeira Unger, *Knowledge and Politics* (New York: The Free Press, 1975), 6.

6. Ibid., 11–12, 10.

7. Alasdair MacIntyre, *Whose Justice? Which Rationality?* (Notre Dame, Ind.: University of Notre Dame Press, 1988), 392.

8. R. Bruce Douglass and Gerald M. Mara, "The Search for a Defensible Good: The Emerging Dilemma of Liberalism," in *Liberalism and the Good*, ed. R. Bruce Douglass, Gerald M. Mara, and Henry S. Richardson (New York: Routledge, 1990), 257.

9. Glendon, *Rights Talk*, 67.

10. Douglass and Mara, "The Search for a Defensible Good," 258.

11. Unger, *Knowledge and Politics*, 3, 8, 11, 8, 6.

12. Ibid., 11.

13. Francis Canavan, review of *Knowledge and Politics*, by Roberto Mangabeira Unger, *Thought* 50 (December 1975): 433.

14. Francis Canavan, *Pins in the Liberal Balloon: Sixty Short Essays on the Church in a Modernist World* (New York: The National Committee of Catholic Layman, 1990), 93.

15. Francis Canavan, *The Pluralist Game: Pluralism, Liberalism, and the Moral Conscience* (Lanham, Md.: Rowman & Littlefield, 1995), 69. Further citations of this work will be given parenthetically in the text.

16. Michael Walzer, "The Communitarian Critique of Liberalism," *Political Theory* 18 (February 1990): 14, 15.

17. John H. Hallowell, *The Decline of Liberalism as an Ideology* (University of California Publications in the Social Sciences, vol. 1, no. 1, 1943; reprint, New York: Howard Fertig, 1971), 5, 6, 31, 8, 33, 23.

18. Ibid, 33, 11, 36.

19. Ibid., 6–7.

20. Canavan, *Pins in the Liberal Balloon*, 110.

21. Ibid., 132.

22. Michael J. Sandel, *Democracy's Discontent: America in Search of a Public Philosophy* (Cambridge, Mass.: The Belknap Press of Harvard University Press, 1996), 12, 14.

23. Francis Canavan, "From Ockham to Blackmun: The Philosophical Roots of Liberal Jurisprudence," a lecture delivered at St. Vincent's College, Latrobe, Pennsylvania, April 20, 2001, 14. The lecture will be published in *Courts and the Culture Wars*, ed. Bradley C. S. Watson (Lanham, Md.: Lexington Books, forthcoming).

24. Carl Schneider, "Moral Discourse and the Transformation of American Family Law," *Michigan Law Review* 83 (1985): 1859.

25. Jean Bethke Elshtain, "A Pope for All Seasons" in *Ecumenical Ventures in Ethics* ed. Reihard Hutter and Theodor Dieter (Grand Rapids, Mich.: Eerdmans, 1998), 26.

26. Glendon, *Rights Talk*, 143.

27. Stanley C. Brubaker, "Tribe and the Transformation of American Constitutional Law," *Benchmark* 4 (Spring 1990): 122.

28. Charles Taylor, *Philosophical Papers I: Human Agency and Language* (Cambridge: Cambridge University Press, 1985), 29.

29. Charles Taylor, *The Ethics of Authenticity* (Cambridge, Mass.: Harvard University Press, 1991), 18.

30. Thomas Hobbes, *Leviathan*, ed. Michael Oakeshott (New York: Macmillan, 1962), chap. 6, 48.

31. George F. Will, *Statecraft As Soulcraft: What Government Does* (New York: Simon & Schuster,

1983), 158.

32. MacIntyre, *Whose Justice? Which Rationality?* 336.

33. Jean Bethke Elshtain, "Catholic Social Thought, the City and Liberal America" in *Catholicism, Liberalism and Communitarianism: The Catholic Intellectual Tradition and the Moral Foundations of Democracy* (Lanham, Md.: Rowman & Littlefield, 1995), 100.

34. Francis Canavan, "The Choosing Self," *Human Life Review* 21 (Summer 1995): 20.

35. Kenneth L. Schmitz, "Liberal Liberty and Human Freedom," *Chesterton Review* 20 (May-August 1994): 213, 124, 222, 224.

36. Ibid., 223, 224, 223, 214.

37. Ibid., 223–4.

38. John Henry Cardinal Newman, "An Address to His Grace the Duke of Norfolk," in *Newman and Gladstone: The Vatican Decrees*, with an introduction by Alvin S. Ryan (Notre Dame, Ind.: University of Notre Dame Press, 1962), 130

39. Canavan, "The Choosing Self," 21.

40. Canavan, "From Ockham to Blackmun," 4.

41. Canavan, "From Frog to Prince," *The Human Life Review* 16 (Spring 1990): 43. The nominalist understanding of the structure of reality, Canavan continues, is illustrated by "the last line in Umberto Eco's nominalist novel, *The Name of the Rose*." It reads: "'*Stat rosa pristina nomine: nomina nuda tenemus*—The archetypical rose consists in its name; we have nothing but names.' Since the data of the senses are always singular and concrete, and essences are universal within a species or class, a nominalist never knows the essence of a rose or what 'roseness' consists in, but only groups certain flowers under the name of 'rose' because they look sufficiently alike." Canavan, "The Empiricist Mind," *The Human Life Review* 25 (Spring 1999): 77.

42. Canavan, "From Ockham to Blackmun," 2.

43. Canavan, "The Empiricist Mind," *The Human Life Review* 25 (Spring 1999): 77.

44. Thomas A. Spragens Jr., *The Irony of Liberal Reason* (Chicago: University of Chicago Press, 1981).

45. Ibid., 45, 30, 31, 33, 30, 54.

46. Ibid., 23.

47. Unger, *Knowledge and Politics,* 47.

48. Spragens, *The Irony of Liberal Reason,* 40.

49. Ibid.

50. Canavan, "The Empiricist Mind," 77.

51. Canavan, "From Frog to Prince," 43.

52. Canavan, "The Empiricist Mind," 77.

53. Unger, *Knowledge and Politics,* 31–2.

54. Canavan, "From Frog to Prince," 43.

55. Canavan, "The Empiricist Mind," 78, 74.

56. Ibid., 78.

57. Unger, *Knowledge and Politics,* 32.

58. Canavan, "From Ockham to Blackmun," 4.

59. Canavan, "The Empiricist Mind," 78, 79.

60. Canavan, "The Choosing Self," 22.

61. Alasdair MacIntyre, *After Virtue*, 2nd ed. (Notre Dame, Ind.: University of Notre Dame Press, 1984), 52.

62. Canavan, *Pins in the Liberal Balloon*, 42.

63. MacIntyre, *After Virtue*, 72, 12.

64. Bruce A. Ackerman, *Social Justice in the Liberal State* (New Haven, Conn.: Yale University Press, 1980), 368.

65. Spragens, *The Irony of Liberal Reason,* 198, 200, 212–13.

66. Canavan, "The Image of Man in Catholic Thought" in *Catholicism, Liberalism and Communitarianism,* 18.

67. Canavan, *Pins in the Liberal Balloon,* 42, 93.

68. Sandel, *Democracy's Discontent,* 14.

69. Gertrude Himmelfarb, *One Nation, Two Cultures* (New York: Vintage Books, 1999), 123.

70. Albert W. Alschuler, *Law without Values: The Life, Work and Legacy of Mr. Justice Holmes* (Chicago: University of Chicago Press, 2000), 5, 6.

71. Ibid., 5.

72. Frederick Copleston, S.J., *Memoirs* (Kansas City, Mo.: Sheed & Ward, 1993), 136. Copleston says Russell "said something like this: 'I find myself in a dilemma. On the one hand I certainly want to condemn the Nazis' behavior towards the Jews as wrong in itself. On the other hand my ethical theory does not allow me to say this'" (137).

73. William A. Galston, *Liberal Purposes* (Cambridge: Cambridge University Press, 1991), 90.

74. Robert N. Bellah, "Cultural Pluralism and Religious Particularism" in *Religion in America: Historical Roots, Philosophical Concepts and Contemporary Problems,* ed. Henry B. Clark II (Los Angeles: Center for the Study of the American Experience, 1982), 40.

75. Ibid., 42.

76. Canavan, "The Choosing Self," 20.

77. Canavan, "The Image of Man in Catholic Thought," 20.

78. Canavan, *Freedom of Expression: Purpose as Limit* (Durham, N.C.: Carolina Academic Press, 1984), 152.

79. Canavan, *Pins in the Liberal Balloon,* 42.

80. Jean Bethke Elshtain, "Democratic Authority at Century's End" in *Liberty under Law: American Constitutionalism, Yesterday, Today and Tomorrow,* ed. Kenneth L. Grasso and Cecilia Rodriguez Castillo, 2nd ed. (Lanham, Md.: University Press of America, 1998), 29.

81. Hobbes, *Leviathan,* 14, 103.

82. Ronald Dworkin, *Taking Rights Seriously* (Cambridge, Mass.: Harvard University Press, 1978), 81.

83. MacIntyre, *After Virtue,* 70.

84. Leo Strauss, *Natural Right and History* (Chicago: University of Chicago Press, 1950), 6.

85. Robert L. Simon, "The Paralysis of 'Absolutophobia,'" *Chronicle of Higher Education,* June 27, 1997, B5. Other observers of the contemporary academic scene have noted a new found reluctance on the part of students to condemn ritual sacrifice (Kay Haugaard, "Students Who Won't Decry Evil—A Case of Too Much Tolerance," *Chronicle of Higher Education,* June 27, 1977, B4); female circumcision, or the cold-blooded murder of civilians by terrorists (Alison Hornstein, "The Question That We Should Be Asking," *Newsweek,* December 7, 2001, 14).

86. Canavan, "The Choosing Self," 20.

87. Strauss, *Natural Right and History,* 4.

88. Irving Kristol, *On the Democratic Idea in America* (New York: Harper & Row, 1972), 20.

89. Alan Wolfe, *Moral Freedom* (New York: W.W. Norton, 2001), 195.

90. Canavan, "The Empiricist Mind," 74

91. Canavan, "From Frog to Prince," 44.

92. *Evangelium Vitae,* 19, 36–7.

93. Canavan, *Pins in the Liberal Balloon,* 124.

94. Ibid., 83, 155.

95. William A. Galson, "Defending Liberalism," *American Political Science Review* 76 (September 1982): 627.

96. *Evangelium Vitae*, 19, 37.

97. Support for this essay comes in part from The Pew Charitable Trusts and the Earhart Foundation. The opinions expressed in this essay are those of the author and do not necessarily reflect the views of either The Pew Charitable Trusts or the Earhart Foundation.

Chapter XIII: The False Prophets of American Conservatism, by Harry V. Jaffa

1. Before World War II, Lincoln scholarship was dominated by the "unnecessary war" thesis. I believe *Crisis of the House Divided* (Chicago: University of Chicago Press, 1959) and Don Fehrenbacher's *Prelude to Greatness* (Palo Alto, Calif.: Stanford University Press, 1962) were the first serious books to take seriously the thesis of the "House Divided" speech.

2. For the text of John Paul II's remarks, see "John Paul II on the American Experiment," *First Things*, no. 82 (April 1998): 36–37.

3. Antonin Scalia, "Of Democracy, Morality and the Majority: Address at Gregorian University" (May 2, 1996), *Origins* 26 (1996): 81–90.

4. Abraham Lincoln, *The Lincoln-Douglas Debates of 1858*, ed. Robert W. Johannsen (New York: Oxford University Press, 1965), 256–57.

5. George Washington, "First Inaugural Address," in *The Inaugural Addresses of the Presidents*, ed. John Gabriel Hunt (New York: Gramercy Books, 1995), 6.

6. *The Writings of James Madison*, vol 2, ed. Gaillard Hunt (New York: G.P. Putnam's Sons, 1990), 272–73.

7. Washington, "First Inaugural Address," 5.

8. Ibid., 6.

9. William Rehnquist, "The Notion of a Living Constitution," *Texas Law Review* 54 (May 1976): 704.

10. Thurgood Marshall, "Reflections on the Bicentennial of the U.S. Constitution," *Harvard Law Review* 101 (November 1987): 4.

11. Robert Bork, in *The Tempting of America*, went to the length of denying slavery any status in the Constitution of 1787. Taney, in *Dred Scott*, he wrote, had invented a right to own slaves that is "nowhere in the Constitution." In fact, there are at least three places in the Constitution in which slavery is recognized.

12. Carl Becker, *The Declaration of Independence: A Study in the History of Political Ideas* (New York: Harcourt, Brace, 1922), 277.

13. Russell Kirk, introduction to *Mr. Jefferson,* by Albert Jay Nock (Delavan, Wisc.: Hollberg Publishing Corporation, 1983), xvi.

14. "Letter from Thomas Jefferson to Henry Lee" (May 8, 1925), in *The Political Writings of Thomas Jefferson*, ed. Edward Dumbauld (Indianapolis: Bobbs-Merrill, 1955), 88.

15. Carl Becker, *The Declaration of Independence: A Study in the History of Political Ideas* (New York: Vantage Books, 1942), 230.

16. Most of the colonial assemblies, in their resolutions calling for independence, called for union at the same time.

17. "The American Revolution as a Successful Revolution," in *The American Revolution: Three Views* (New York: American Brands Inc., 1975), 39.

18. Ibid.

19. Samuel Eliot Morison, *The Oxford History of the American People*, vol. 1 (New York: New American Library), 292.

20. Robert A. Godwin and Robert A. Licht, eds., *The Spirit of the Constitution: Five Conversations* (Washington, D.C.: AEI Press, 1990), 81. This volume consists of a transcription of a series of conversations about the Constitution in which Kristol was a participant.

21. "The Statute of Virginia for Religious Freedom," in *Documents of American History*, ed. Henry Steele Commager (New York: Appleton-Century-Croft, 1948), 125.

22. John Paul II, "John Paul II on the American Experiment," 36.

23. George Weigel, "Religious Freedom: The First Human Right," in *The Structure of Freedom*, ed. Richard John Neuhaus (Grand Rapids, Mich.: Eerdmans, 1991), 39, 50.

24. Alexis de Tocqueville, *Democracy in America*, trans. George Lawrence, ed. J. P. Mayer (New York: Harper & Row Perennial Library, 1988), 292.

25. Irving Kristol, "On the Character of the American Political Order," in *The Promise of American Politics: Principles and Practice after Two Hundred Years*, ed. Robert L. Utley Jr. (Lanham, Md.: University Press of America, 1989), 13.

26. Ibid., 13–14.

27. Ibid., 14.

28. Samuel Cooper, "A Sermon on the Day of the Commencement of the Constitution," in *Political Sermons of the Founding Era*, ed. Ellis Sandoz (Indianapolis: Liberty Press, 1991), 637.

29. Kristol, "On the Character of the American Political Order," 3.

30. Ibid., 4.

Chapter XIV: Democracy, Ethics, Religion:
An Intrinsic Connection, by W. Norris Clarke, S.J.

1. Cf. Pierre Manent, *An Intellectual History of Liberalism* (Princeton, N.J.: Princeton University Press, 1994); *The City of Man* (Princeton, N.J.: Princeton University Press, 2000); Daniel Mahoney, "Pierre Manent and the New French Thought," *Crisis,* January 1995: 38–39; Kenneth Grasso, Gerard Bradley, Robert Hunt, eds., *Catholicism, Liberalism, and Communitarianism: The Catholic Intellectual Tradition and the Moral Foundations of Democracy* (Lanham, Md.: Rowman & Littlefield, 1995).

2. Cf. the powerful and insightful article of Michael Novak, "The Godlessness that Failed," *First Things*, no. *104* (June 2000): 35–39, a chilling account of the tremendous erosion of "human capital" (psychological, moral, religious) caused by the seventy years' pressure of Soviet atheism on the citizens of the Soviet Union.

Chapter XV: And Now for Something Different:
A Good Word on Behalf of the Legal Positivists, by Hadley Arkes

1. *The Federalist Papers* (New York: Random House, n.d.), 507.

2. Ibid., 526.

3. "Natural Law and the Law: An Exchange [with Robert Bork]," *First Things* (May 1992): 45–48.

4. Ibid.

5. As Curtis wrote:

   Slavery, being contrary to natural right, is created only by municipal law. This is not only plain in itself, and agreed by all writers on the subject, but is inferable from the Constitution, and has been explicitly declared by this court. The Constitution refers to slaves as "persons held to service in one State, under the laws thereof." Nothing can more clearly describe a *status* created by municipal law. In *Prigg v. Pennsylvania,* . . . this court said: "The state of slavery is deemed to be a mere municipal regulation, founded on and limited to the range of territorial laws." In *Rankin v. Lydia,* . . . the Supreme Court of Appeals of Kentucky said: "Slavery is sanctioned by the laws of this State, and the right to hold them under our municipal regulations is unquestionable. But we view this as a right existing by positive law of a municipal character, without foundation in the law of nature or the unwritten common law." I am not acquainted with any case or writer questioning the correctness of this doctrine [emphasis added]. *Dred Scott v. Sandford,* 339 U.S. (1857), 624.

6. See Blackstone, *Commentaries on the Laws of England* (Oxford: Clarendon Press, 1765), bk. 1, 91. I am using here the edition published by the University of Chicago Press in 1979, with a copy of the original plates and preserving the same pagination.

7. Story put the matter with a stringent directness: "[The trade in slaves] is repugnant to the great principles of Christian duty, the dictates of natural religion, the obligations of good faith and morality, and the eternal maxims of social justice. When any trade can be truly said to have these ingredients, *it is impossible that it can be consistent with any system of law,* that purports to rest on the authority of reason or revelation. And it is sufficient to stamp any trade as interdicted by public law, when it can be justly affirmed, that it is repugnant to the general principles of justice and humanity [empasis added]." See Story in the case of *La Jeune Eugenie,* 2 Mason 809 (1822).

8. See "Lincoln in His First Inaugural Address," in *The Collected Works of Abraham Lincoln,* ed. Roy P. Basler (New Brunswick, N.J.: Rutgers University Press, 1953)., 4:269.

9. 461 U.S. 574.

10. 427 U.S. 160.

11. See *McCrary v. Runyon,* 515 F. 2d 1082 (CA4).

12. *Bob Jones University v. United States,* 584.

13. 42 U.S.C. Sec. 1981

14. *Bob Jones University,* 586.

15. The point was made by Judge Leventhal in *Green v. Connally,* 330 F.Supp. 1150, 1160 (DC), summarily aff'd *sub nom. Coit* v. *Green,* 404 U.S. 997 (1971). The argument by Leventhal was recalled by Chief Justice Burger in ibid., 592.

16. Ibid., 619.

17. Lincoln in *The Collected Works of Abraham Lincoln,* 532; italics in the original.

18. My fuller arguments here can be found in *First Things* (Princeton, N.J.: Princeton University Press, 1986), 85–89, and *The Philosopher in the City* (Princeton, N.J.: Princeton University Press, 1981), chap. 2, and especially 43–48.

19. Thomas Reid, *Essays on the Active Powers of the Human Mind* (Cambridge, Mass.: MIT Press, 1969; originally published in 1788), 361.

20. For a review, and a critical account, of the "evidence" presented in *Brown v. Board,* see Arkes, *The Philosopher in the City,* 233–36, 240; and see Arkes, "The Problem of Kenneth Clark," *Commentary* (November 1974): 37–46.

21. *Bob Jones University,* 594.

Chapter XVI: Judicial Activism and Regime Change, by George W. Carey

1. On this issue see my article, "The Philadelphia Constitution: Dead or Alive?" in *The End of Democracy? II: A Crisis of Legitimacy,* ed. Mitchell S. Muncy (Dallas: Spence Publishing, 1999). See also the Symposium, "The End of Democracy?" *First Things* (November 1996): 18–

42.

2. *Brown v. Board of Education*, 347 U.S. 483 (1954). This case is also referred to as *Brown I*, *Brown II* being the 1955 decision concerned with the implementation of the *Brown I* decision. References to *Brown* in the text are to *Brown I*. In *Bolling v. Sharpe* (347 U.S. 497 [1954]) the Court also outlawed segregation in the public schools of the District of Columbia by advancing the very dubious proposition that the "due process" clause of the Fifth Amendment embraced "equal protection."

3. Charles S. Hyneman, *The Supreme Court on Trial* (New York: Atherton Press, 1963), 199. Hyneman, to my knowledge, was the very first to observe that with its desegregation decisions (i.e., *Brown* and *Bolling*) the Court had reached an unprecedented "plateau of power."

4. Even a casual reading of *Federalist* 78 reveals just how far the activists' conception of judicial power is at odds with that of the Founders. In this essay, Hamilton writes: "The judiciary . . . has no influence over either the sword or the purse, no direction either of the strength or of the wealth of the society, and can take no active resolution whatever." Hamilton, Madison, and Jay, *The Federalist*, ed. with an introduction by George W. Carey and James McClellan (Dubuque: Kendall/Hunt, 1990), 402.

 Why the "no active resolution whatsoever" injunction has fallen by the wayside is an interesting question. Suffice it to say, activists can and do claim legitimacy for the Court's legislative role on the ground that the political branches, which presumably represent the people, do not seek to curb the Court. The Court's present status in their view rests upon this tacit popular consent. For an excellent work on this issue and the disparity between the Founders' views and those of the activists see William Gangi, *Saving the Constitution from the Courts* (Norman: University of Oklahoma Press, 1995).

5. Richard E. Morgan, "Coming Clean about Brown," in *City Journal* 6 (Summer 1996) 49. Morgan's fine article is a "must" for those unfamiliar with the background surrounding *Brown* and the uses to which it has been put over the decades in the debates over the proper role of the judiciary.

6. The Anti-Federalist Brutus, whose most widely read essays focus on the potential for the abuse of judicial power under the Constitution, never believed the Court would assume "positive" powers in the manner of the modern courts. On the contrary, he felt the Court would "rule" through the use of its power to nullify laws. "The legislature . . . will not go over the limits by which the courts may adjudge they are confined. And there is little room to doubt but that they will come up to those bounds, as often as occasion and opportunity may offer, and they may judge it proper to do it." Essay XII, *The Anti-Federalist*, ed. Herbert J. Storing (Chicago: University of Chicago Press, 1981), 168–9.

7. One very notable exception is Christopher Wolfe's splendid book, *Judicial Activism: Bulwark of Freedom or Precarious Security?* (Lanham, Md.: Rowman & Littlefield, 1997). This is an extremely well-balanced analysis.

8. Morgan, "Coming Clean," 50. It is interesting to note how even the severest critics of the modern Court—including Lino Graglia and Robert Bork—though critical of the way in which the Court reached its decision in *Brown*, attempt to justify the result on constitutional grounds. As Morgan notes, Mary Ann Glendon, while critical of the trend of judicial decision making set by *Brown*, nevertheless finds it to be "a great act of statesmanship." Far more refreshing is the position of Raoul Berger, a champion of originalism, expressed to me in the course of a conversation. In his view, the Court acted unconstitutionally in *Brown* and, though it should not reverse itself, it should mend its ways.

9. Morgan seems to be more optimistic than I am about the prospects of curbing the Court's

activism. Through appropriate legislation and, above all, an amendment that would bar "government at any level from making decisions that either advantage or disadvantage persons based on race," he believes, "*Brown* would lose its capacity to intimidate." He feels that this would open the way for mounting "a truly comprehensive attack on judicial activism." "Coming Clean," 51, 52. In my view, activism now has a momentum, an acceptance that has carried it well past the stage where the *Brown* decision is critical. At one point, Robert Bork appears to have thought that a theory of constitutional interpretation that "would enable us to say what is the limit of the judge's legitimate authority" might suffice to curb activism. *The Tempting of America* (New York: The Free Press, 1990), 141. In this work he argues that "originalism" would serve this purpose. Later, it would appear, he perceived need for a constitutional amendment that would provide a check on judicial activism. "There appears to be only one means by which the federal courts, including the Supreme Court, can be brought back to constitutional legitimacy. That would be a constitutional amendment making any federal or state court decision subject to being overruled by a majority vote of each House of Congress." *Slouching towards Gomorrah* (New York: Harper Collins, 1996), 117. Bork's solution, I need hardly add, is hardly realistic—testimony to the extent activism has found support in politically critical sectors of society.

10. In fact, if the past is any guide, those proposing to confine the Court to its traditional role would be stigmatized as "reactionaries," out to decimate the Founders' Constitution for purely partisan purposes.

11. *Modern Constitutional Theory: A Reader*, ed. John H. Garvey and T. Alexander Aleinikoff, 4th ed. (St. Paul: West Publishing, 1999). This, being one of the more comprehensive collections, is well suited to indicate the range of activist thinking. I do not mean to suggest that this work does not contain articles that take exception to activism. These articles, however, are in the main concerned with issues and contentions that do not deal with the "regime issues" raised by activism. (See text below.)

12. Sanford Levinson, "Law as Literature," in *Modern Constitutional Theory*, 128–29. Levinson borrows a good deal from the deconstructionism of Richard Rorty and Stanley Fish for his analysis. At one point he comments: "For some years I have organized my own courses in constitutional interpretation around the central question, 'But did the Court get it right?,' as if one could grade any given opinion by whether or not it measured up to the genuine command of the Constitution. Answering such a question, of course, requires the development of a full set of 'principles and methods of correct interpretation,' and my courses have involved a search for such principles and methods." He goes on to say, "I still spend a great deal of time examining various approaches . . . but I have less and less confidence this is a sensible enterprise." While he finds it "disconcerting" to allow "the Nietzschean interpreter into the house of constitutional analysts," he "increasingly find[s] it impossible to imagine any other way of making sense of our own constitutional universe" (131).

13. John Hart Ely, "Policing the Process of Representation: The Court as Referee," in *Modern Constitutional Theory*, 18.

14. *Modern Constitutional Theory*, 5. These terms are taken from the famous footnote in *U.S. v. Carolene Products Co.* (1938), one of the first assertions by the Court that it might move beyond its traditional role. Ely interprets this footnote as a call for the Court to virtually represent minorities by protecting them "from denial of equal concern and respect" in the decision-making processes (11).

15. *Modern Constitutional Theory*, 13. For an extensive critique of Ely's approach see Christopher Wolfe's *The Rise of Modern Judicial Review* (New York: Basic Books, 1986).

16. Laurence H. Tribe, "The Puzzling Persistence of Process-Based Constitutional Theories," in

Modern Constitutional Theory, 20.

17. Richard Davies Parker, "The Past of Constitutional Theory—and Its Future," in *Modern Constitutional Theories,* 69. Parker makes much of the fact that he is of the 1960s generation. In his view, at the time he wrote the article, his generation of legal scholars had not developed an "orthodoxy" of their own, nor were they under the spell of the established orthodoxy. Thus, they were capable of looking at "doing constitutional law" from a fresh perspective.

18. Rebecca L. Brown, "Accountability, Liberty, and the Constitution" in *Modern Constitutional Theory,* 240.

19. Ibid., 237.

20. Ibid., 243.

21. Ibid., 246.

22. This, of course, is precisely what happened in *Roe v. Wade,* in which the Court "discovered" the "right of privacy."

23. Thomas C. Grey, "Do We Have an Unwritten Constitution?" in *Modern Constitutional Theory,* 111.

24. As a general rule, those who see the Ninth Amendment as a rich source of rights do not take into account the reasons why this amendment was considered necessary in the first place. On this issue, see Raoul Berger, "The Ninth Amendment," *Selected Writings on the Constitution* (Cumberland, Va.: James River Press, 1987). Berger concludes after looking at the historical record that the Ninth Amendment "added no unspecified rights to the Bill of Rights; instead it demarked an area in which the 'General Government' has no power whatsoever" (202).

    Given the ascendancy of judicial activism, the potentialities for using the Ninth Amendment in a manner that would enormously expand the scope of judicial legislation are virtually limitless. Such interpretations would also expand the powers of the national government. Most interesting on this score is Robert E. Morgan, *Disabling America: The "Rights Industry" in Our Times* (New York: Basic Books, 1984).

25. Richard A. Posner, "Pragmatic Adjudication," in *Modern Constitutional Theory,* 194.

26. Ibid., 195.

27. Ibid., 195.

28. Ibid., 199. Writing with regard to the issue of proportional sentencing for the crime of marijuana possession and use, he writes: "If a law could be said to be contrary to world public opinion I would consider this a reason, not compelling but not negligible either, for regarding a state law as unconstitutional even if the Constitution's text had to be stretched a bit to cover it. The study of other law, or of world public opinion as crystallized in foreign law and practices, is a more profitable inquiry than trying to find some bit of eighteenth-century evidence that maybe the framers of the Constitution wanted courts to make sure punishments prescribed by statute were proportional to the gravity, or difficulty of apprehension or profitability or some other relevant characteristic of the crime" (199).

29. Ibid., 200.

30. Ibid., 197.

31. Ibid., 197–8.

32. *The Federalist,* 251.

33. While virtually all serious students of the circumstances surrounding the adoption of the Fourteenth Amendment recognize that the process of "incorporation" has no constitutional basis, the activists are obliged to defend this process in order to keep the states under judicial control. Their need may well account for their tortured interpretations of this amendment,

as well as for their deep-seated hostility to "originalism."

Chapter XVII: On Merely Being Intelligent: Canavan's Views and Reviews by James V. Schall, S.J.

1. Francis Canavan, review of *Statecraft as Soulcraft*, by George Will, in *America* 149 (July 16, 1983): 34.

2. Francis Canavan, review of *Knowledge and Politics* by Roberto Mangabeira Unger, in *America* 132 (May 3, 1975): 343.

3. Francis Canavan, *Pins in the Liberal Balloon: Sixty Short Essays on the Church in a Modernist World* (New York: National Committee of Catholic Laymen, 1990).

4. Francis Canavan, review of *Making Men Moral*, by Robert George, in *International Philosophical Quarterly* 34 (December 1994): 512. See Robert Sokolowski, "The Method of Philosophy: Making Distinctions," *Review of Metaphysics* 51 (March 1998): 515–32, where this Aristotelian point made by Canavan is further drawn out.

5. *Pins in the Liberal Balloon*, 76–78.

6. Ibid.

7. Francis Canavan, review of *Ireland: A Terrible Beauty*, by Jill and Leon Uris, in *America* 134 (January 31, 1976): 76.

8. Francis Canavan, review of *Selected Letters of Edmund Burke*, edited by Harvey Mansfield, in *Interpretation* 13 (September 1985): 434–35.

9. It might be noted that the present writer, on the basis of this review, was tempted to title this reflection on Canavan's work, "Half the Fun of Academic Life." "On merely being intelligent," from the chosen title, may in fact, point to the other half of the fun.

10. Francis Canavan, review of *Edmund Burke and the Critique of Political Radicalism*, by Michael Freeman, in *American Political Science Review* 75 (September 1981): 741–42.

11. Francis Canavan, review of *Edmund Burke and the Discourse of Virtue*, by Stephen Browne, in *Review of Politics* 57 (Winter 1995): 162–64.

12. Francis Canavan, review of *Burke's Reflections on the Revolution in France* by F. P. Lock, in *Review of Politics* 48 (Fall 1986): 431.

13. Francis Canavan, review of *Burke's Dramatic Theory of Politics*, by Paul Hindson and Tim Gray, in *Theological Studies* 50 (September 1989): 617.

14. Francis Canavan, review of *The Rage of Edmund Burke*, by Isaac Kramnick, in *America* 136 (January 21, 1978).

15. Francis Canavan, review of *Collected Essays*, by Ernest Fortin, in *Interpretation* 25 (Winter 1998): 262–263.

16. Francis Canavan, review of *The Legitimacy of the Modern Age*, by Hans Blumenberg, in *Teaching Political Science* 14 (Winter 1987): 257–263.

17. Francis Canavan, review of *The Decline and Fall of Radical Catholicism*, in *Triumph* 6 (May 1971): 32–36.

18. Francis Canavan, review of *The Passing of the Modern Age*, by John Lukacs, in *Triumph* 6 (May 1971): 14–16.

19. Francis Canavan, review of *The American Papers: Inside the Abortion Mentality*, by Bernard Nathanson, in *New Oxford Review* 51 (December 1984): 25.

20. Paul Cassell, "We're Not Executing the Innocent," *Wall Street Journal* (June 16, 2000): 14.

21. Francis Canavan, review of *For Capital Punishment*, by Walter Berns, in *National Review* 31 (August 17, 1979): 1042–1044.

22. Francis Canavan, review of *The Crisis of Liberal Democracy*, in *International Philosophical Quarterly* 28 (1988): 112.

23. Francis Canavan, review of *A Government of Laws*, by Ellis Sandoz, in *Thought* 51 (December 1991): 428.

24. Francis Canavan, review of *Anarchy, State, and Utopia*, by Robert Nozick, in *America* 133 (July 19, 1975): 37

25. Francis Canavan, review of *Reason, Revelation, and the Foundations of Political Philosophy*, by James V. Schall, in *Homiletic and Pastoral Review* 89 (January 1989): 69.

26. Francis Canavan, *Pins in the Liberal Balloon*, 25.

27. Ibid., 27.

ABOUT THE CONTRIBUTORS

Hadley Arkes is Edward Ney Professor of Jurisprudence and American Institutions at Amherst College. He is the author of numerous books and essays, including *First Things, Beyond the Constitution, The Return of George Sutherland,* and the forthcoming *Natural Rights and the Right to Choose.*

Gerard V. Bradley is professor of law at the Notre Dame Law School. He has published extensively in the areas of constitutional law, religion, and public life. His books include *Church-State Relationships in America,* and he is the co-editor of *Catholicism, Liberalism, and Communitarianism: The Catholic Intellectual Tradition and the Moral Foundations of Democracy.*

George W. Carey is professor of government at Georgetown University, where he teaches courses in American political theory. The founder and editor of the *Political Science Reviewer,* he is the author of *In Defense of the Constitution* and *The Federalist: Design for a Constitutional Republic.*

W. Norris Clarke, S.J., is professor emeritus of philosophy at Fordham University. From 1961 to 1985, he was the editor-in-chief of the *International Philosophical Quarterly,* which he co-founded. He is also the former president of both the American Catholic Philosophical Association and the Metaphysical Society of America. The author of some seventy articles, his books include *Person and Being, Explorations in Metaphysics,* and *The One and the Many: A Contemporary Thomistic Metaphysics.*

Kenneth L. Grasso is professor of political science at Southwest Texas State University. He has co-edited several books, including *John Courtney Murray and the American Civil Conversation* and *Catholicism, Liberalism and Communitarianism: The Catholic Intellectual Tradition and the Moral Foundations of Democracy.*

Robert P. Hunt is professor of political science at Kean University. His articles have appeared in journals such as *First Things,* the *Review of Politics,* and the *Catholic Social Science Review,* and he is the co-editor of *John Courtney Murray and the American Civil Conversation* and *Catholicism, Liberalism, and Communitarianism: The Catholic Intellectual Tradition and the Moral Foundations of Democracy.*

Harry V. Jaffa is a Distinguished Fellow of the Claremont Institute. He is also professor emeritus of government at Claremont McKenna College and the Claremont Graduate School. Among his many books are *Crisis of the House Divided: An Interpretation of the Issues in the Lincoln-Douglas Debates* and the first volume of its sequel, *A New Birth of Freedom: Abraham Lincoln and the American Civil War.*

Joseph W. Koterski, S.J., is the chair of the Philosophy Department at Fordham University. At Fordham he serves as chaplain and tutor at Queens Court Residential College for Freshmen and as the editor-in-chief of the *International Philosophical Quarterly.* He has published many articles on the history of medieval philosophy and on ethics, and he recently edited *Prophecy and Diplomacy: The Thought of Pope John Paul II.*

F. P. Lock is professor of English at Queen's University in Kingston, Ontario. His *Edmund Burke: Volume 1, 1730–1784,* appeared in 1999. He is currently working on the second volume.

Gerald A. McCool, S.J., professor emeritus of philosophy at Fordham University, has written extensively on the relationship between the philosophy of St. Thomas and Catholic theology and social teaching in the sixteenth- and seventeenth-century scholastic revival, as well as on the Thomistic movement of the last two centuries. His books include *Nineteenth Century Scholasticism: The Search for a Unitary Method, From Unity to Pluralism: The Internal Evolution of Thomism,* and *The Neo-Thomists.*

George McKenna, professor of political science at City College of the City University of New York, is the author of *The Drama of Democracy* and co-editor of the forthcoming, thirteenth edition of *Taking Sides: Clashing Views on Controversial Political Issues.* His articles have appeared in the U.S. and abroad in such periodicals as *Atlantic Monthly, Yale Review, History of Political Thought,* and *First Things.*

Joseph Pappin III is professor of philosophy in the Division of Continuing Education Academic Programs at the University of South Carolina, Columbia. He is the author of *The Metaphysics of Edmund Burke,* and has published articles on Augustine, Aquinas, Burke, Sartre, Maritain, Yves Simon, Kierkegaard, Karl Rahner, and Karol Cardinal Wojtyla in such journals as *Philosophy Today,* the *Thomist, Modern Age,* and the *American Catholic Philosophical Quarterly.* He is currently President of The Edmund Burke Society of America.

Keith Pavlischek is program director of the Pew Civitas Program in Faith and Public Affairs, a program of leadership development and civic education for doctoral scholars, and a Fellow at the Center for Public Justice. He is the author of *John Courtney Murray and the Dilemma of Religious Toleration.*

James V. Schall, S.J., is professor of government at Georgetown University. His books include *At the Limits of Political Philosophy, On the Unseriousness of Human Affairs,* and *Another Sort of Learning.*

Thomas A. Spragens Jr. is professor of political science at Duke University. His publications include *The Irony of Liberal Reason, Reason and Democracy,* and *The Politics of Motion: The World of Thomas Hobbes.* His most recent book, *Civic Liberalism: Reflections on Our Democratic Ideals,* was awarded the Elaine and David Spitz Book Prize for 2001.

Peter J. Stanlis is Distinguished Professor of Humanities, Emeritus, at Rockford College. For thirteen years he served as the editor of the *Burke Newsletter* and *Studies in Burke and His Time*. His books include *Edmund Burke and the Natural Law* and *Edmund Burke: The Enlightenment and Revolution*.

Germaine Paulo Walsh is associate professor of political science at Texas Lutheran University. She has published articles on Aristotle's understanding of friendship and on Jane Austen's political philosophy.

INDEX

F

G

H